D0411856

CLOAK OF ENEMIES

CLOAK OF ENEMIES

CHURCHILL'S SOE, ENEMIES AT HOME AND THE 'COCKLESHELL HEROES'

TOM KEENE

Cover images. *Front*: © Peeter Viisimaa/iStockphoto. *Back*: At Southsea, a Cockle Mark II follows canoes of another unit. *Author photograph*: © Peter Kersey.

All efforts have been made to identify the sources of the images in this book and any further information regarding their origin is welcome.

First published 2012

by Spellmount, an imprint of
The History Press
The Mill, Brimscombe Port
Stroud, Gloucestershire, GL5 2QG
www.thehistorypress.co.uk

© Tom Keene, 2012

British Library Cataloguing in Publication Data.
A catalogue record for this book is available from the British Library.

ISBN 978 0 7524 7975 0

Typesetting and origination by The History Press
Printed in Great Britain

CONTENTS

Cloak of Enemies is dedicated, with my love, to my wife Marguerite and to my daughters Emily, Anna and Isabelle.
It is also dedicated to the imperishable memory of those Royal Marines whose names appear below:

Major 'Blondie' Hasler
Marine Bill Sparks
Lieutenant Jack MacKinnon
Marine James Conway
Sergeant Sam Wallace
Marine Bobby Ewart
Corporal Bert Laver
Marine Bill Mills
Corporal George Sheard
Marine David Moffatt

ACKNOWLEDGEMENTS

My thanks are due to my friend David Balment, who lit the fuse; to Simon Willis who had the courage to back an early idea and to Dr Mike Barry who supported it; to Dr Harry Bennett and Professor Kevin Jefferys at the University of Plymouth; to the late Peter Siddall, nephew of 'Cockleshell Hero' Royal Marines Corporal George Sheard and to Dr Peter Kersey and Mike Leck. In addition, I wish to place on record my gratitude to earlier historians, all of whom have been unfailingly generous with their advice, time and support, and upon whose works I have come to lean heavily: to that doyen of SOE historians, the late Professor Michael Foot, former wartime SAS Brigade intelligence officer, and Professor David Stafford whose efforts others struggle to emulate; to Mark Seaman, Lynne Olson, Gill Bennett, Neville Wylie, Roderick Bailey, Robert Lyman, Nigel West and Stuart Allan. The staff at the following prestigious institutions have also been unfailingly professional, patient and helpful: The National Archives, Kew; the Imperial War Museum, Lambeth and Duxford; the Bodleian Library, Oxford; the Churchill Archives Centre, Churchill College, Cambridge; the London School of Economics and Political Science, Holborn; the Liddell Hart Centre for Military Archives at King's College, London; and the Broadlands Archive, Hartley Library, University of Southampton. I owe a particular debt of gratitude to Mark Bentinck, Royal Marines historian in the Naval Historical Branch, to David Harrison, Dr Ian Herrington, Jonathan Wyatt, the singer Jane Birkin (daughter of David Birkin DSC), Ursula Townsend (wife of Richard Townsend DSC) and to François Boisnier MBE whose tireless efforts in France over many years have led to the creation of 'The Frankton Trail'. I am also particularly grateful to Lord Paddy Ashdown, inspirational former leader of Britain's Liberal Democrat Party and member of Britain's elite SBS, to whom I have been privileged to offer advice on his own book about brave men and murky waters near Bordeaux seventy years ago.

LIST OF ABBREVIATIONS

ACNS(H)	Assistant Chief of the Naval Staff (H)
BCRA(M)	*Bureau Central de Renseignement et d'Action (Militaire)*
BEF	British Expeditionary Force
Bren	British magazine-fed light machine gun (.303 cal.)
BPB	Boom patrol boat
CAS	Chief of Air Staff
CCO	Chief of Combined Operations
CCS	Combined Chiefs of Staff
CD	Symbol for head of SOE
CEO	Chief Executive Officer
CIGS	Chief of the Imperial General Staff
Clams	Small explosive devices
CND	*Confrérie de Notre-Dame*
CO	Combined Operations
CODC	Combined Operations Development Centre
COHQ	Combined Operations Headquarters
COS	Chiefs of Staff
D	Section D of the Secret Intelligence Service (SIS)
DCO	Director of Combined Operations
D/CD(O)	Deputy CD (Operations)
DDOD(I)	Deputy Director Operations Division (Irregular)
DF	SOE Escape Line Section
DMI	Director of Military Intelligence
DMO	Director of Military Operations
DNI	Director of Naval Intelligence
DRC	Defence Requirements Sub-committee
DZ	Drop zone
EH	Electra House. Early precursor of the Political Warfare Executive
F	British Independent French Section, SOE

FFI	*Forces Françaises de l'Intérieur*
FOPS	Future Operational Planning Section
FTP(F)	*Francs-Tireurs et Partisans (Français)*
Gestapo	*Geheime Staatspolizei*
IO	Intelligence officer
ISTDC	Inter-services Training and Development Centre
ISRB	Inter-services Research Bureau (early cover name for SOE)
JIC	Joint Intelligence Committee
JPS	Joint Planning Staff
MEW	Ministry of Economic Warfare
MOI	Ministry of Information
MGB	Motor gun boat
MTB	Motor torpedo boat
MI5	Domestic UK Security Service
MI6	Synonym for SIS
MI(R)	Military Intelligence (Research)
NID(C)	Naval Intelligence Division (Clandestine)
OCM	*Organisation Civile et Militaire*
OT	Organisation TODT
PCO	Passport Control Office
PE	Plastic explosive
PWE	Political Warfare Executive
RV	Rendezvous
RF	Gaullist 'Free French' Section, SOE
RMBPD	Royal Marines Boom Patrol Detachment
RNVR	Royal Naval Volunteer Reserve
SAS	Special Air Service Regiment
SD	*Sicherheitsdienst.* Intelligence agency of the SS
SIGINT	Signals Intelligence
SIS	Secret Intelligence Service
SMG	Sub-machine gun
S01	Early re-naming of Electra House (EH) operations
S02	Early re-naming of Section D operations
SOE	Special Operations Executive
STEN	Magazine-fed, mass-produced light sub-machine gun (9mm cal.)
SSRF	Small Scale Raiding Force
SS	*Schutzstaffel.* Hitler's personal bodyguard
STS	Special training schools
W/T	Wireless telegraphy
ZNO	*Zone Non-occupée*
ZO	*Zone Occupée*

FOREWORD

BY LORD PADDY ASHDOWN GCMG KBE PC

For any serious student of the Second World War, and especially of the role played in it by Britain's secret and clandestine organisations, *Cloak of Enemies* is, quite simply, required reading.

It is difficult to read this book without feeling anger, even disgust, at the lost opportunities – and the lost lives – which were the product of the climate of secrecy, rivalry and suspicion which infected even the highest level of those engaged in Britain's secret war.

Cloak of Enemies reveals in depth for the first time the stifling cloak of secrecy and suspicion even from other departments in Whitehall that was the true hallmark of the early days of the Special Operations Executive. It catalogues in fascinating detail the enmity which existed between the first Chairman of SOE – the driving and egotistical Hugh Dalton – and an early Director of Combined Operations, the septuagenarian hero of Zeebrugge, Admiral Sir Roger Keyes.

It reveals for the first time the true depth of willful obstruction and discord between SOE and SIS – and especially its effective chief, Claude Dansey – in relation to clandestine cross-Channel sea operations and even to the running of agents on the European mainland.

It chooses a particular operation, Operation *Frankton*, to illustrate the impact of this rivalry and duplication on relations between SOE and Combined Operations. In the course of this Dr Keene reveals startling evidence that proper co-operation between the two organisations might have made that iconic raid unnecessary, or at the very least would have made it more effective and less costly in the lives of brave young men. Dr Keene's book unveils for the first time that, at the very time when Combined Operations was sending ten Royal Marines to attack German blockade runners in Bordeaux harbour believing this was 'the only way' to hit this national strategic target, SOE had a team of six British officers based in a café 100m from the quay where the blockade runners were moored, who were equipped with explosives, enjoyed direct and regular radio communication with London, were supported by an extensive network of French agents and had their own dedicated escape network.

This work makes a major contribution to our understanding of how Whitehall's secret organisations worked, especially in the desperate, amateur-ish early days of the Second World War. But it is fascinating, not just for what it reveals of the past, but also I suspect, for the lessons it provides, some of which Whitehall still needs to learn today.

Lord Paddy Ashdown GCMG KBE PC
2012

PRELUDE

The Special Operations Executive (SOE) was conceived as a desperate solution to desperate times. Cloaked in a confusion of competing origins, it did not evolve slowly from within the matrix of established British security organisations but was born abruptly on to a battlefield of national survival.

The SOE owed its existence and much of the bitter controversy that surrounded its six-year life to a series of political and strategic negatives. First among these was the British government's determination not to repeat the static trench slaughter of the First World War. Instead, they would rely upon other methods of defeating Germany. Second, the early control of SOE was successfully lobbied for by a minister not best suited to its command: an abrasive, left-wing politician, whose heavy-handed, overbearing behaviour and empty boasts served merely to confirm the initial suspicion and hostility of those agencies whose support and co-operation would be critical to its success. A third strategic negative was the War Cabinet's belief that the way to Allied victory lay through economic blockade, propaganda and 'war from within'. This proved to be a flawed doctrine. It was one that evolved from wishful thinking, a misplaced faith in First World War successes and a failure to grasp strategic truths. That same British government placed early, unrealistic and unachievable expectations upon a new creation – subversion – that had been swiftly and erroneously dubbed the 'fourth arm' of modern warfare by its ambitious new minister. Above all, however, SOE owed its existence to expediency and to the climate of the times in which it was conceived; times in which a revolutionary and uncomfortable new concept gained reluctant leg-room because that which had been relied upon from the past had not worked.

In that hot, endless summer of 1940, Britain was fighting for survival and reeling from the realisation that many of the strategic and moral assumptions that had bolstered the last days of peace and 'Phoney War' had been smashed beneath the grinding tank tracks of Hitler's May *Blitzkrieg*. Among these was a belief that Britain's war would be fought primarily on the sea and in the air, that

France would remain a fighting partner in the struggle to defeat Germany and that the Channel coast would remain in Allied hands. Instead, the Norwegian campaign had turned into a costly and bloody fiasco, the French Second Army had crumbled and German tanks had rolled to the Channel coast. That same month the French government asked for an armistice and the hastily formed British Expeditionary Force was evacuated home through Dunkirk to an England braced to meet invasion. It is against this background that SOE took fragile root.

Cloak of Enemies examines the political and military environment in which SOE was conceived and created, and in which it struggled to assert itself between 1940 and 1942. Its aim is to chart for the first time the collective impact of the hostility, rivalry and obstruction SOE encountered from those organisations and officials charged with its support. It will suggest that, as a direct result of such hostility, SOE developed an ethos of excessive secrecy which, together with a sense of beleaguered political encirclement, led directly to the squandering of British servicemen's lives. It will trace those links of internal betrayal from Whitehall in 1940 to the front line of operations in enemy-occupied France in December 1942.

In scrutinising the political and military environment in which SOE was created, this book will examine the consequences that flowed from that pre-invasion climate in which hasty and urgent decisions had to be taken. It will explain why it was that SOE was wished into an existence in which the deliberate undermining of its development by many of the government agencies pledged to its support appears to have been almost inevitable. It will examine and identify the signal moments of failure and omission where a lack of strategic clarity ensured the early frustration of SOE's development and operational effectiveness.

Many books have been written about SOE which have made reference to SOE's troubled relationship with the Foreign Office, the Chiefs of Staff (COS), the Secret Intelligence Service (SIS), the Ministry of Information (MOI) and the Admiralty. Yet all have done so within a context which has positioned those difficulties as stepping stones on the broader path of SOE's development and questionable strategic vindication as part of the invasion of Normandy's Order of Battle. None has devoted itself solely to the detailed evolution and tactical implications of those collective rivalries, nor to the shifting political loyalties endemic to 'high politics' in wartime Whitehall. Published works have not concentrated upon the cumulative effects of those disagreements, nor upon that sense of beleaguered encirclement endured by SOE as a result. Most importantly, they have not examined in depth the consequences, duplications and confusions that flowed from such a climate. *Cloak of Enemies* charts the evolution of those embittered relationships, the distrust and hostility that was their hallmark and the direct impact those relationships had upon operations in the field.

It will do so by examining in detail SOE's relationship with one particular military mission, Operation *Frankton*. It will show how, had early warnings been heeded, a more open relationship would have made unnecessary an operation that later became famous as the 'Cockleshell Heroes'. In this, Royal Marine canoeists paddled 70 miles up the Gironde River to place 'limpet' mines on Axis shipping in Bordeaux docks. Eight of the ten raiders failed to return. Operation *Frankton* has been chosen because SOE files, previously undiscovered, reveal the true cost of that inter-service rivalry and distrust. It has been chosen also because the attack described by one German officer as 'the outstanding Commando raid of the war'[1] has attracted an iconic status which has led to the promulgation of myths, obscuring the truth regarding both Operation *Frankton*'s planning and its achievements. These too will be examined and, where necessary, corrected.

Notes
1 Lucas Phillips, C.E., *Cockleshell Heroes* (Heinemann, London, 1956), p.4.

CHAPTER ONE

TWILIGHT THINKING: THE ROAD TO 1940

The concept that lay at the mainspring of the Special Operations Executive – subversion, 'war from within' – was light years removed from the cosy, Anglo-centric world of politics, appeasement and positive disarmament that occupied Westminster a few short years before the outbreak of the Second World War. Winston Churchill, the premier who was to galvanise Britain's war efforts in 1940 and instruct Dr Hugh Dalton, the Minister of Economic Warfare, to 'set Europe ablaze', was perceived by many in the mid-1930s to be dangerous parliamentary company: 'a brilliant man, but rash, hot-headed, impulsive',[1] a shining diamond of unstable, mercurial gifts with a penchant for self-damage.

'The strange dress, ridiculous hats, heavy drinking and pronounced speech impediment did little to encourage the Tory old guard to respect him for much more than having been proved right about the German threat',[2] records one historian, while one lord wrote on the eve of war: 'There are, I believe, a fair number of people who think and say that in these times Winston ought to be in the government, but why? Look at his past history … could anybody have a worse record? But we are a forgetful and forgiving people.'[3] Churchill was perceived to have undermined his own brilliance by vehement opposition to Indian independence. He had also damaged a burgeoning reappraisal as the voice of national warning of the growing Nazi menace by his purblind, unswerving loyalty to his monarch over the King's determination to marry the divorced American Wallis Simpson.

Those few MPs who had opposed their government's policy of appeasement as Mussolini invaded Abyssinia in 1935 and Hitler ordered German troops to occupy the demilitarised Rhineland in 1936, found themselves isolated and at risk. They were in a Parliament dominated by those who supported Prime Minister Stanley Baldwin's rosy-cheeked view of a cosy, comfortable Europe that only a small minority saw was heading for catastrophe. Baldwin, aged 68 when he came to power for the third time in 1935, attracted around him those with similar views. Men described by Canadian diplomat Charles Richie as:

'Methodical, respectable, immovable men, with no understanding of this age – of its despair, its violence and its gropings – blinkered in solid comfort, shut off from poverty and risk.'[4] It was a description that might have been written for the prime minister himself. Disinterested in foreign policy, out of touch with the nation he led, steeped in a bucolic past which no longer existed, irritated and alarmed by Churchill's growing insistence upon air parity with a rearming Germany, Stanley Baldwin, the prime minister whose temper was 'unrelievedly pacifist',[5] shared with his Cabinet colleagues a reluctance to be told 'uncomfortable things'[6] about the scale of German rearmament. In this, he was in many ways in tune with the nation he served. Like Chamberlain, the leader who would soon replace him, Baldwin was a highly sophisticated political animal whose powerful Commons majority and canny reading of Westminster ensured personal survival. His 'parity' pledge to Parliament of November 1934 that 'the British government are determined on no condition to accept any position of inferiority with regard to what air force may be raised in Germany in the future'[7] was followed by an admission six months later that he had indeed misled Parliament. Yet Baldwin's admission was readily accepted by the House, causing Churchill to telegraph his son Randolph the next day: 'Government escaped as usual.'[8] When Baldwin eventually stepped down in May 1937 he did so with the goodwill of the nation still riding behind him: 'No man has ever left in such a blaze of affection', recorded MP Harold Nicolson in his diary.[9] It was a fondness perhaps, a public yearning, not just for the man but for the age that was also passing.

Baldwin was replaced by Chancellor Neville Chamberlain, who would keep Churchill out of government until the outbreak of war. Working with Churchill, complained Chamberlain, was like arguing with a brass band.[10] *Time* magazine observed: 'There is perhaps no man in Parliament whom Mr Chamberlain likes less than Mr Churchill.'[11] Neville Chamberlain himself would be vilified by history as the morning-suited champion of appeasement, a former lord mayor of Birmingham whose lacklustre performance at the despatch box at a time of national crisis was described by one MP as resembling 'the secretary of a firm of undertakers reading the minutes of the last meeting'.[12] Yet that is an image perhaps shaped too conveniently by hindsight, for Neville Chamberlain, before his eclipse, was seen to be a powerful, tough and vindictive politician and consummate administrator, who carried the Commons (with a 220-seat Conservative majority) and the press with him between the outbreak of war and the Norway debate in May 1940.

Appeasement may have become deeply unpopular, but it was not always thus: pre-war, not a single local association registered public protest against such a policy.[13] Chamberlain's post-war legacy, however, would be an arrogant and misplaced belief in his own powers of diplomacy, the betrayal of Czechoslovakia at Munich and the wilful neglect of Britain's defences; a premier who would lead

Britain first to shame and then to war and about whom Churchill would confide: 'There is a total lack of drive and Chamberlain does not know a tithe of the
neglects for which he is responsible.'[14] Yet Chamberlain, like Baldwin before him,
was a politician whose refusal to contemplate the nightmare of another conflict
closely mirrored that of the people he served. That nation, however, was one
largely uninformed about the growing menace facing Europe; a nation denied
the facts of European rearmament by a broadsheet press who saw it as their duty
to mirror government policy. Geoffrey Dawson, editor of *The Times*, a newspaper widely regarded as the government's mouthpiece, wrote: 'I do my utmost,
night after night, to keep out of the paper anything that might hurt Nazi suscep-
tibilities.'[15] The Air Ministry had stated that Britain needed fifty fully equipped
front-line squadrons to offer a credible air defence, yet, despite politicians'
promises and constant goading from a Churchill armed with leaked Air Ministry
estimates and top-secret Foreign Office memoranda, only twenty-seven squadrons were operational. Britain had, in total, 1,600 front-line aircraft; Germany
had in excess of 3,000. Yet, eighteen months before the outbreak of war, the
prime minister would still claim that the RAF would be 'an effective instrument
for our purpose'.[16] On land, Britain's regular army numbered 180,000, with a further 406,000 hastily induced and under-trained Territorial part-time soldiers[17]
to measure against Germany's 500,000 regulars and a further 500,000 in reserve.
Only the Royal Navy enjoyed a numerical and qualitative ascendancy over the
rapidly rebuilding German fleet. Yet if Britain went to war, warned Lord Gort,
the newly appointed Chief of the Imperial General Staff (CIGS), she would do so
'seriously deficient in modern equipment', and he added: 'In the circumstances it
would be murder to send our forces overseas to fight against a first-class power.'[18]
Fighting, evidently, was something the army should strive to avoid. Kingsley
Martin, editor of the *New Statesman*, caught the mood of the times: 'By 1938
there was a feeling that things had gone so far that to plan armed resistance to the
Dictators was now useless. We should, therefore, seek the most peaceful way of
letting them gradually get all they wanted.'[19] By February 1939, however, whilst
'His Majesty's Government deeply deplores the need for expenditure of these
vast sums on armaments', defence spending across all three services had finally
begun to rise: from £262 million in 1937 to £580 million by 1939.[20]

If Britain's uniformed armed services were under-equipped, under-manned
and ill-prepared for the conflict that lay ahead, then so too were her secret
services, the clandestine agencies with whom SOE would soon be required to
become rival bed-fellows. Britain's Secret Intelligence Service came into existence in 1909 as the Secret Service Bureau and, in the inter-war years, existed on
a shoestring.[21] Its primary task was to acquire intelligence by clandestine means.
It was also created to act as a screen between services and foreign spies, to act
as intermediary between service departments and British agents abroad and

to organise counter-espionage. The Secret Service Bureau had two sections: a Home Section (later to become MI5) and a Foreign Section (to become SIS and MI6) controlled by the end of the First World War by the Foreign Office, an agreement regularised by the Secret Service Committee of 1921 who stipulated that SIS should not only be made exclusively responsible for espionage on behalf of all three services, but should henceforward be funded by the Foreign Office secret vote. This was a stipulation that was to have significant consequences twenty years later. SIS had ended the war with more than 500 officers and staff. By January 1920 that figure had dropped to just five, including the head of the service itself, Commander Mansfield Smith Cumming RN. The official chronicler of British intelligence in the Second World War, Professor F.H. Hinsley, wrote: 'Whilst the resources deployed on military intelligence are bound to be run down in peacetime, they were reduced after 1918 for a longer period and to a greater extent than was wise.'[22]

In the inter-war years, SIS budgets were cut and cut again: from £240,000 to £125,000 in 1919 and then, at the urging of its own paymaster, the Foreign Office, to just £65,000 a year before rising to £90,000 after objections from the then Secretary of State for War, Winston Churchill.[23] Improvements were slow in coming. As late as 1935 the head of SIS complained that the total budget of SIS had been so reduced that it now equalled the cost of maintaining just one Royal Navy destroyer in home waters.[24] Part of the reason for such drastic cutbacks lay in the Secret Service's inability to identify threat with sufficient force and clarity as to make unanswerable their own case for the funds that were needed. Whilst MI5 concentrated on the threat of Communist subversion at home and SIS concerned itself with the Bolshevist threat abroad, the growing threat nearer home posed by fascist Nazi Germany remained dangerously out of focus. Not only was SIS at this time staffed mainly by passed-over, rigid-thinking, former Royal Naval officers, recruited in his own image by Admiral Hugh Sinclair, the new head of SIS, but even when SIS agents were sending back their warnings from the field there was:

> ... a total lack of co-ordination of the reports of their own agents in many cases, a lack of co-operation between MI6 and NID [Naval Intelligence Department] and a failure on the part of the Secret Service to give coherent guidance to the Government. A stronger government would have asked more questions; this particular government just did not wish to know.[25]

Small wonder then that, when reviewing SIS budgets in 1936, the Defence Requirements Sub-committee (DRC) of the Committee of Imperial Defence warned: 'If [its] allowance is not augmented, and very largely augmented, the organisation cannot be expected to fulfil its functions, and this country will be most dangerously handicapped … nothing less than £500,000 will be really adequate.'[26] DRC's recommendations were accepted in principle by the Defence Policy and Requirements Committee at the end of January 1936. The Chief of the Secret Service still regarded the sum, however, as wholly inadequate.

If the financial needs of those who gathered intelligence were poorly served by those who controlled the purse strings, then perhaps it was because of two separate but interlocking reasons: how intelligence-gathering was viewed by the establishment itself and how it was viewed by its own paymaster, the Foreign Office. This was the same body that, under pressure from the Treasury, had pressed for a SIS budget reduction in 1920. The one-time head of SIS, Commander Mansfield Smith Cumming RN, may once have described espionage as 'capital sport',[27] but it was a sport that found itself offside with the mores of an establishment that viewed intelligence-gathering as both underhand and unsporting. In one of the first textbooks on military intelligence, Colonel G.A. Furse had written:

> The very term 'spy' conveys to our mind something dishonourable and disloyal. A spy, in the general acceptance of the term, is a low sneak who, from unworthy motives, dodges the actions of his fellow beings to turn the knowledge he acquires to his personal account. His underhand dealings inspire us with such horror that we would blush at the very idea of having to avail ourselves of any information obtained through such an agency.[28]

Although written at the turn of the century, it was a view that found an echo in the official history of British intelligence eighty years later: 'The higher ranks of the armed forces showed some antipathy to the intelligence authorities, or at least a lack of interest in their work. Whatever their origin – resentment against the influence which the intelligence branches had wielded; dislike of the officer class for the less gentlemanly aspects of intelligence work; anti-intellectualism on the part of fighting men – such prejudices certainly existed and produced a vicious circle.'[29] Intelligence work, wrote Professor Hinsley, was viewed as a professional backwater suitable only for those officers with a penchant for foreign languages and an inability to command men in the field.

The Foreign Office, soon to regard the Special Operations Executive 'first of all as a joke and then as a menace',[30] brought its own particular attitude to those same corridors of power the SOE must soon hope to penetrate if it was to survive. Since time immemorial the business of the Foreign Office had been to advise government on foreign policy, its advice and insights garnered from the reports, papers and messages sent in and delivered to its embassies abroad. Crucially, the Foreign Office saw its business not as espionage but as the furtherance of diplomacy. The reports it received were considered to be 'information' rather than intelligence, despite whatever risks might have been taken to obtain them. To that end, the Foreign Office distributed the information it received from its worldwide network of embassies as and when it felt fit. It had no intelligence branch of its own and recognised no need to consult those who had, even though an increasing number of those reports they did circulate were found to be alarmist and inaccurate.[31] Thus, although the Foreign Office was nominally in charge of SIS, 'it hardly concerned itself with guiding their activities or smoothing their day-to-day difficulties'.[32] It was an attitude that did not ease with the passage of time. Jack Beevor, the assistant to Sir Charles Hambro, the head of SOE between June 1941 and July 1943, wrote after the war:

> The whole concept of secret warfare, embracing espionage, counter-espionage, guerrilla warfare, secret para-military and para-naval operations, was an anathema to some. Such secret activities involved varying degrees of illegal and unethical methods which would violate normal peacetime morality and would not only be improper but often criminal.[33]

Spying, sabotage, blackmail, underhand methods of intelligence-gathering – all were abhorrent to a Foreign Office that saw itself as both the originator of all important information and the final arbiter of its interpretation, worth and distribution. Long before the creation of SOE, the Foreign Office and those who practised the polished manners of diplomacy believed that subversion on the soil of another nation was not only illegal, and therefore morally unjustifiable, but dangerous, unpredictable folly that worked counter to the Foreign Office's often delicate best interests: it could set up unintended chain reactions, cause diplomatic embarrassment, upset friendly neutrals, even provoke unwanted foreign intervention. The gathering of intelligence was seen to threaten the very diplomacy that had assumed centre stage since the appointment of Neville Chamberlain as prime minister in 1937.

Understandable though the Foreign Office's preferences might be, that aloof detachment and reluctance to offer Foreign Office-sourced information for the detached analysis of others, that unwillingness to pool best-thinking about the state of German rearmament and Nazi intentions with the three services, was to have profound consequences. With it came a reluctance to attend meetings of the newly formed Joint Intelligence Committee (JIC).

The JIC was set up in June 1936 to replace the stillborn Inter-Service Intelligence Committee (ISIC) described as 'the first determined attempt to set up an organisation in which the three services could jointly undertake the administration and assessment of intelligence'.[34] Created at a time when the value of intelligence was under-played and all defence departments were still chronically short of funds, the ISIC simply disappeared. The JIC was a second attempt to meet a need that now, in the urgent, accelerated passage of just a few months, was seen with greater intellectual clarity; a committee set up in the belief that intelligence or 'information' stored but not assessed, shared or utilised was intelligence wasted. The JIC was set up to ensure that intelligence that might be of potential inter-service interest could be assessed and swiftly disseminated to the appropriate fighting service. Yet the Foreign Office did not attend a meeting of the JIC until November 1938 and thereafter, for some while, only attended spasmodically. It would take the outbreak of war before a system was put in place that effectively co-ordinated the evaluation and dissemination of intelligence across both services and government departments. Despite this, vital intelligence about German mobilisation and her growing military strength was passed to those in Parliament best placed to act upon it. Indeed, it was these detailed, persistent and largely unpopular warnings from the floor of the House of Commons that defined the climate of the times in which SOE was to have its origins.

Britain was alerted to the growing threat posed by a rearming Germany, not because of the measures put in place to ensure the central, co-ordinated analysis of foreign intelligence, but despite the existence of such clouded, imperfect mechanisms. Vital documents were leaked without the authorisation of Foreign Secretary Lord Halifax by civil servants within the Foreign Office, who risked dismissal and even civil action for stepping beyond permitted protocols. Those papers were leaked primarily to Winston Churchill, a privy councillor without government office. They were intended not for Churchill but for the top-secret deliberation of the Air Ministry, the Industrial Intelligence Centre, Industrial Intelligence in Foreign Countries Sub-committee and, ultimately, the Committee of Imperial Defence itself. They were fed to Churchill by Desmond Morton, formerly of SIS and now head of the government's Industrial Intelligence Centre, who lived within walking distance of Chartwell, Churchill's 'great keep' and country retreat in Westerham, Kent. They came too from Sir Robert Vansittart, the dynamic and privately wealthy Permanent Under-secretary of State at the Foreign Office, whose leaks and thinly disguised reports from inside Germany led to Whitehall's irritated accusation that he was running his own 'private detective agency'.[35] Churchill also received information from Vansittart's Foreign Office junior, Ralph Wigram, the highly strung, doom-seeing head of the Central Department. Meanwhile, papers about specific RAF deficiencies were leaked by Wing Commander Torr Anderson, Director of the Royal Air Force Training School. Significantly, many of those reports that informed Churchill and his colleagues of the state of covert German rearmament and the developing network of secret factories, airfields and carefully disguised aircraft assembly plants that were springing up across Germany came not from paid agents of the SIS but from unpaid, amateur patriots: businessmen, journalists, travellers and foreign nationals inside Germany, principal amongst whom was a Mr Roy

Fedden of the Bristol Aeroplane Company. Servicemen, too, played a critical role: Wing Commander M.G. Christie, Britain's Air Attaché in Berlin, used his own aeroplane to observe German factories and aerodromes.[36] The reason for this reliance upon the unpaid amateur is not hard to find: the SIS budget had been slashed to the bone.

Those few who did work for SIS reported to Claude Dansey, a former regular army officer recruited by Admiral Sir Hugh 'Quex' Sinclair, who had replaced Mansfield Smith Cumming as head of SIS – also known as 'C'– in 1923. Dansey had served with Winston Churchill in the South African Light Horse in the Boer War. He was to become the nemesis of SOE in its early days. The historian Hugh Trevor-Roper remembered Dansey as 'an utter shit: corrupt, incompetent, but with a certain low cunning'.[37] Lieutenant Colonel James Langley, one of the officers who later ran MI9, the escape and evasion organisation which also felt the lash of Dansey's tongue, remembered him differently:

Dansey was, in fact, one of those powerful people who prefer to keep their power hidden: an *éminence grise* rather than a ruling monarch but a highly influential personage for all that. What Dansey wanted done was done and what he wanted undone was undone.[38]

Dansey became second-in-command, but effectively he was head of SIS in the years immediately prior to the outbreak of the Second World War. He remained in his post throughout SOE's formative, vulnerable years, retiring into civilian obscurity in 1944. That he was to hate SOE from the moment of its inception is beyond doubt. An examination of Dansey's covert role within SIS explains why:

From the very beginning Dansey was doubtful about both the wisdom and the value of such an organisation and he was at all times extremely aware of the dangers it presented to his networks in the field.[39]

Dansey's first job was in charge of the Passport Control Office (PCO) in Italy. This effectively made him head of Rome Station for SIS. In 1936 the story was put about that Dansey had been involved in financial malpractice. 'Disgraced', he was recalled to London. In fact, it is claimed his dismissal and temporary retire-ment to Switzerland was simply a front. After discovering that Britain's peacetime network of European agents had been exposed and that the over-worn cover story of Passport Control Office was known to every taxi driver in Europe, he had, with the approval of the head of SIS, set about creating his own ghost 'Z' network of more than 200 amateur intelligence agents scattered across Europe. These were there not simply to supplement those already known to work for SIS but to replace the entire 'blown' network in time of war or occupation. Dansey's agents were given 'Z' numbers. Dansey himself was known as Z1 or 'Colonel Z'. Obsessed with the need for secrecy, with working in the shadows, Dansey considered the use of sabotage to be 'rude and noisy'.[40] His post-war biographers were to conclude: 'Dansey maintained to the end that SOE was filled with undisciplined amateurs who were more dangerous to his agents than they were to the enemy and were therefore to be avoided and frustrated at every opportunity'. Dansey was thus to share with the Foreign Office, which kept his own organisation on short rations, an abhorrence of all that SOE was to stand for.

Notes

1 Gardner, Brian, *Churchill in His Time: A Study in a Reputation 1939–1945* (Methuen, London, 1968), p.1.

2 Roberts, Andrew, *The Holy Fox* (Phoenix, London, 1991), p.187.

3 Roberts, *The Holy Fox*, p.187. Lord Hardinge, ex-Permanent Under-secretary at the Foreign Office to Lord Erskine, 18 August 1939.

4 Olson, Lynne, *Troublesome Young Men* (Farra, Straus and Giroux, New York, 2007), p.71.

5 Cowling, Maurice, *The Impact of Hitler* (Cambridge University Press, London, 1975), p.147.

6 Gilbert, Martin, *Winston Churchill: The Wilderness Years* (Macmillan, London, 1981), p.120.

7 Oral Answers, House of Commons Debates, 22 February 1934. Volume 295, Cols 857–983.

8 Gilbert, Martin, *Winston S. Churchill*, Volume V (Heinemann, London, 1976), p.651.

9 Nicolson, Harold, *Diaries and Letters: The War Years 1939–45* (Collins, London, 1968), p.175.

10 Stewart, Graham, *Burying Caesar* (Weidenfeld & Nicolson, London, 1999), p.270.

11 Olson, *Troublesome Young Men*, p.198.

12 Nicolson, *Diaries and Letters: The War Years 1939–45*, p.35.

13 Jefferys, Kevin, *May 1940: The Downfall of Neville Chamberlain* (The Parliamentary History Yearbook Trust, London, 1991). Parliamentary History, Volume 10, Pt 2, p.365.

14 CHAR 2/371 at Churchill Archives Centre, Churchill College, Cambridge. Letter dated 8 January 1939 from Winston Churchill to his wife Clementine from the Chateau de L'Horizon, Cannes.

15 Olson, *Troublesome Young Men*, p.122.

16 *The Times*, Tuesday 22 March 1938, p.16.

17 *The Times*, 15 June 1939, p.11. On 10 June, the eve of a nationwide recruitment drive, the figure had been 288,579.

18 Olson, *Troublesome Young Men*, p.127.

19 Manchester, William, *The Caged Lion* (Cardinal, London, 1989), p.311.

20 CHAR 2/371 at Churchill Archives Centre, Churchill College, Cambridge. Chamberlain statement to the Commons relating to defence, 15 February 1939.

21 Jeffery, Keith, *MI6: The Secret History of the Secret Intelligence Service 1909–1949* (Bloomsbury, London, 2010), p.248 and chapter heading.

22 Hinsley, F.H., *British Intelligence in the Second World War*, Volume 1 (HMSO, London, 1979), p.10.

23 Hinsley, *British Intelligence in the Second World War*, Volume 1, p.50.

24 Jeffery, *MI6: The Secret History of the Secret Intelligence Service*, p.246.

25 Deacon, Richard, *A History of the British Secret Service* (Granada, London, 1980), p.314.

26 Hinsley, *British Intelligence in the Second World War*, Volume 1, p.50.

27 Read, A. and Fisher, D., *Colonel Z* (Hodder & Stoughton, London, 1984), p.69.

28 Read and Fisher, *Colonel Z*, p.13.

29 Hinsley, *British Intelligence in the Second World War*, Volume 1, p.10.

30 Lord Gladwyn, *The Memoirs of Lord Gladwyn* (Weidenfeld & Nicolson, London, 1972), p.103.

31 Hinsley, *British Intelligence in the Second World War*, Volume 1, p.42.

32 Hinsley, *British Intelligence in the Second World War*, Volume 1, p.5.

33 West, Nigel, *Secret War* (Hodder and Stoughton, London, 1992), p.7.

34 Hinsley, *British Intelligence in the Second World War*, Volume 1, p.35.

35 Hinsley, *British Intelligence in the Second World War*, Volume 1, p.48.

36 Hinsley, *British Intelligence in the Second World War*, Volume 1, p.61.

37 Read and Fisher, *Colonel Z*, p.11.

38 Read and Fisher, *Colonel Z*, p.12.

39 Read and Fisher, *Colonel Z*, p.269.

40 Read and Fisher, *Colonel Z*, p.255.

CHAPTER TWO

MOVING PYRAMIDS WITH A PIN

In 1938, a year before the outbreak of war, other moves were afoot within both SIS and the War Office that were to thrust aside the outdated thinking of a gentler age. Already the new form of warfare that was soon to transform Europe had been glimpsed beyond the southern horizon: in Spain. As the Spanish nationalist commander General Emilio Mola had approached Madrid during the opening stages of the Spanish Civil War in 1936, he had broadcast on the radio that the four columns of his advancing troops would be assisted by a 'fifth column' of nationalist supporters waiting inside that beleaguered city. Although Madrid held out against the general for a further three years, it was a phrase that caught Europe's nervous imagination. It did so as both Italy and Germany moved beyond their frontiers to dominate a quiescent, alarmed Europe and eastern Africa by a combination of fear and the threat of overwhelming military force.

More in form than in substance, the somewhat mythical powers of this new form of subversive almost-warfare which crumbled national resolve and corrupted enemy forces from within worked its way into the European psyche. Talk of the 'fifth column' became nervous international shorthand that sought to excuse the lack of resolve and preparation for war whilst explaining away the effortless conquests of a Germany and Italy with whom Britain was not yet at war. Once Britain was at war, 'the close correlation of fifth column fears and the demand for firmer British action in the subversive sphere in Europe was widespread both in government and public circles'.[1] But not yet. Nevertheless, in the climate of such charged times before the outbreak of formal hostilities, imitation of that which was evidently working for Britain's potential enemy had an immediate, visceral appeal. Kim Philby, the Soviet spy who worked for SIS and who penetrated the highest levels of British intelligence, later wrote: 'When, as a result of the "fifth column" scares in Spain, the potential importance of undercover action against an enemy seeped into what passed for British military thinking, the result was reluctant improvisation.'[2] In fact, there was rather more to it than that. In 1935, a sub-committee of the Committee of Imperial Defence had looked into the question of sabotage attack, but the idea seems to have gone nowhere. In 1938, after the Austrian *Anschluss* and the identification of Germany as the likely enemy of the future, it was re-examined by both Section VI (Industrial) and Section III (Naval) of SIS, who endorsed a recommendation that the matter be re-visited. As a result, Admiral Sir Hugh Sinclair secured from the War Office the temporary secondment of a single officer, Major Lawrence Grand of the Royal Engineers, whose orders were to 'investigate every possibility of attacking potential enemies by means other than the operations of military forces'.[3] Major Lawrence Grand came to SIS – at that stage still merely a gatherer of intelligence rather than a secret organisation given to sabotage and subversion – with no experience of clandestine warfare. Nor, it seemed, had anyone else: 'Probably the reason that sabotage has never been organised is that it is nobody's particular job', recalled one SOE adviser after the war.[4] Kim Philby remembered Lawrence Grand, the carnation-wearing major, as 'Tall and lean ... his mind was certainly not clipped. It ranged free and handsome over the whole field of his awesome responsibilities, never shrinking from an idea, however big or wild.'[5] Bickham Sweet-Escott also worked for Major Grand and what became known as Section D. He remembered:

> What was remarkable about him was the fertility of his imagination, the imperturbability of his character in the most trying circumstances and his gift for leadership; he also had an unusually pretty wit ... What was wrong about the organisation was that there was hardly any machinery whereby his ideas could be sifted and those which we might really be able to do something about translated into action.[6]

Grand may have had big ideas but he had no staff and no budget, and what emerged as Section D was 'born almost in a shed at the bottom of the garden'.[7] There was little office space in the basement of SIS headquarters (HQ) in Broadway House and only the vaguest idea of what he was supposed to do: 'We soon realised that we had come to fill a complete vacuum. There was no real secret communications and there was no organisation for anything except the collection of information. We were starting from scratch with a vengeance.'[8] He added later: 'One felt as if one had been told to move the pyramids with a pin.'[9]

Charged with the task of 'organising and carrying out subversive operations against the Germans', Grand began by writing his own directive for Section D.[10] Dated 31 May 1938, this consisted of little more than a list of potential targets within Germany that might be suitable for demolition by sabotage. Paper, at least, was plentiful. Philby wrote afterwards:

> Grand never had the resources to carry out his ideas. His London staff could fit easily into a large drawing room ... His efforts to get a larger slice of the cake

were frowned upon by the older and more firmly based intelligence-gathering side of the service. The Intelligence people rushed happily to the invalid conclusion that bangs were a waste of time and money, diverting resources from the silent spy.[11]

Evidently, by the summer of 1938, the bureaucratic atmosphere in which SOE would soon be expected to flourish was becoming fouled. The Secret Intelligence Service was already closing ranks against the specific form of clandestine, subversive warfare SOE would be created to conduct. Without funds, Grand compiled his report which included reference to overt abuses of neutrality and the use of what he described as 'moral sabotage'.[12] He proposed that the 'immediate programme' of his unit – the 'D' stood for Destruction[13] – should consist of research into sabotage devices and the production of stocks, an investigation into potential targets, the organisation of depots and the making of contacts in neutral countries. He priced this work at £20,000 and sent the document circulating around the higher echelons of SIS. Here, we are told by the official compiler of SOE's secret history, it was received with 'a combination of alarm and fascination'.[14]

Surprisingly, perhaps, and with the caveat that extreme caution would be necessary to avoid diplomatic incidents in neutral countries in time of peace, Grand's position was confirmed for a further two months with the hint that his posting might be extended until the end of the year. Section D's remit was sabotage abroad, not intelligence-gathering. As such it was supposed to have no contact with Dansey's 'Z' agents in mainland Europe. Grand found the money for his new organisation, not from within SIS but from an American-born tycoon, Sir Chester Beatty, who, for business reasons of his own, decided to fund what became known as the 'sabotage service'.[15]

In the months that followed, Grand hatched a series of ambitious plans, few of which came to fruition, many of which antagonised Section D's parent organisation SIS and all of which were of an 'imaginative and dreamlike quality'.[16] Amongst these was an ambitious plan to impede the flow of Romanian oil to Germany by blocking the Danube Gorge using explosives to bring down a cliff face and making the river impassable. It was, wrote Philby, 'a plan hopelessly out of keeping with the slender resources of Section D'.[17] The plan fell apart and did little to add lustre to the reputation of either Grand's unit or SIS itself. No more did other botched operations in Norway and Sweden, nor the unit's 'muddled and confused' attempts to create clandestine dumps of explosives in remote areas of England and Scotland for the auxiliary units that were to be Britain's stay-behind forces in the event of invasion. In short, 'Section D dug its own grave'.[18] Bickham Sweet-Escott wrote afterwards:

The section's failure to contribute to the defence of Great Britain did not increase its prestige in Whitehall … We had to admit that whatever the reasons, our record of positive achievement was unimpressive. There were a few successful operations to our credit, but certainly not many. As for Western Europe, though there was much to excuse it, the record was lamentable, for we did not possess one single agent between the Balkans and the English Channel.[19]

In the eyes of many, SOE would have its origins in that same organisation that had already created such a bad impression. Yet SIS was not the only department to react to the spectre of 'fifth column' subversion or to the growing threat of Nazi Germany that was becoming ever more apparent. Two further departments would be created that same year, each of which would have influence upon the later development and creation of SOE. Late in March, the Foreign Office set up a new and secret internal organisation called EH, so named after Electra House where it was located. Created initially as the Enemy Publicity Section, its task was to investigate ways in which foreign opinion might be influenced by the use of propaganda. Specifically, it was to investigate ways in which 'Black' or unattributable propaganda could be transmitted into Europe, an area already included in Major Grand's own terms of reference for Section D. Many different organisations vied for its control. The lack of clarity of command, of early terms of reference, was to lead to much acrimony and inter-departmental rivalry on this specific issue alone once war was declared.

The second department to respond to fears of 'fifth columns' and the growing German threat was the War Office which, in the same month that Major Grand took up his responsibilities, created a new department of its own. Initially known as General Staff (Research) or GS(R), its arrival was announced openly in Parliament; its mission 'when so much instruction is to be gained from present events' was to study 'the practice and lessons of actual warfare'.[20] By December 1938 that department – one officer and a typist – was headed by Colonel Jo Holland, Royal Engineers, whose experience of irregular warfare in both India and Ireland suited him to the task. Heeding recent events in China and Spain, Holland began to study the use of guerrilla forces and how they might be applied to modern warfare. Grand and Holland were soon working together and sharing office premises in Caxton Street. They decided between themselves that work which could be admitted by government would be the responsibility of Military Intelligence (Research) or MI(R) – GS(R) now renamed – while Major Grand would take responsibility for that which was unavowable.[21]

Holland made his first report to his superiors in January 1939, as a result of which two officers were seconded to his department. One of these was Major Colin McVean Gubbins, the gunner soldier who would later give SOE the focus and direction it so badly needed. Just how well Grand, the 'volatile dreamer', and

Holland, the 'unsmiling visionary', got on together is open to differing interpretation. [22] Certainly Colin Gubbins, the man who was recruited by Holland and who watched both Section D and MI(R) take their first faltering steps, found the experience of working with both stimulating:

> Like … Holland, Gubbins made fun of Section D's obsession with secrecy and of the eccentricities of its head, Lawrence Grand, with his black homburg hat, dark glasses, tapered cigarette holder and all the paraphernalia of the 'spy master' of popular fiction. Nevertheless, he enjoyed his time in Caxton Street, liked and admired Holland and found the nature of their work exhilarating.[23]

In March of that same year, Grand and Holland produced their first paper. In it they stated that recent German advances into Europe 'for the first time gives an opening to an alternative method of defence, that is a method alternative to organised armed resistance. This defensive technique which must now be developed, must be based on the experience we have had in India, Irak [sic] Ireland and Russia, i.e. the development of a combination of guerrilla and IRA tactics.'[24]

Asking for a total of £500,000 and the posting of twenty-five officers under Colonel Holland, their paper promised they could then arrange 'simultaneous disturbances' throughout German-occupied areas of Eastern Europe within four months. Events now moved fast. Two days later – a week after Hitler had marched into what was left of Czechoslovakia – Grand was seen by the CIGS General Ironside, the Director of Military Operations (DMO), R.H. Dewing, and his deputy, Mr W.E. van Cutsem. Grand and Holland's proposal was approved subject to agreement by the Foreign Secretary, Lord Halifax, who considered the plan the next day. He stressed the importance of secrecy and promised to raise the matter of its funding with the prime minister. Lord Halifax then approved the scheme which he said he 'now intended to forget'.[25] The staff Grand had requested would be provided, promised the CIGS, once the prime minister's approval had been given. There is – perhaps unsurprisingly given its subject matter – no formal record of such approval being given by Prime Minister Neville Chamberlain, although SOE historian Professor Michael Foot records: 'By this decision SOE was begotten; but the child was long in the womb.'[26] Holland followed up with a more specific paper on 3 April 1939, approved by CIGS ten days later, which laid out the objectives of the new section as the study of guerrilla methods and the production of something of a contradiction: a Field Service Regulations instruction manual; the development of destructive devices for use by guerrillas; and the development of a *modus operandi* for such units in the field.

Section D may have belonged to SIS, but Holland's unit came under the control of Military Intelligence despite the fact that its concepts and early origins

came from a pooling of shared ideas. As historian William Mackenzie commented after viewing the original papers, 'The basic ideas of this paper are
recognisably those of Colonel Holland; its style and its unquenchable optimism
are certainly Colonel Grand's'.[27] Yet although the money that funded the new
service came from SIS, Jo Holland was required to report, not in co-operation
with Lawrence Grand, but upwards alone through conventional military channels to the Deputy Chief of the General Staff. This was an arrangement which
lasted until the eve of the outbreak of war, when Holland's section transferred to
the War Office and changed its name to MI(R) because, by this time, claims Foot,
Holland had 'no faith that what he regarded as D's "wildcat" schemes would
ever produce specific achievements'.[28] Yet despite this conflict in temperament
between Grand and Holland, the confusion of demarcation and the overlap of
responsibility between Grand's Section D of SIS and Holland's MI(R) of the War
Office would persist until after the outbreak of war. It certainly did nothing to
prepare the ground for transition between Section D and MI(R) to SOE when
the latter was finally created in July 1940. Neither organisation – not Grand's
Section D nor the superior, more overt and better organised MI(R), which had
'no conspicuous or damning failures'[29] to its name – achieved impressive results
before their amalgamation into the new organisation. 'For all its good men and
good ideas', wrote Professor Foot looking back at MI(R), 'it had only slight actual
achievements to display by the late spring of 1940'.[30] William MacKenzie, the
historian recruited by Gubbins to write the not-for-publication history of SOE
immediately after the war, looked at the early work of Section D and concluded:

> The impression left by a study of D Section's operations is one of great energy
> and ingenuity spread thinly over an immense field ... its demonstrable
> achievements were sadly few ... Relations with other government departments
> were distant and on the whole unfriendly; D Section and all its works were
> a nuisance to the Foreign Office, the Secret Intelligence Service and the War
> Office alike.[31]

If both fledgling organisations had a shared fault it was perhaps that in their
legacy they left little upon which SOE could build and much that would need
repair: thanks to the activities of Section D and MI(R), whether successful or
otherwise, the seeds of suspicion surrounding 'dirty tricks' departments were
now deeply rooted amongst those organisations who had dealt with either
Section D or MI(R), yet whose support would now be vital for the success of
SOE, the subversive newcomer waiting, as yet unformed, in the wings of national
expediency. What was left by their senior sister, SIS herself, was little better.
The German entry into Austria led to the arrest of the head of Vienna station
in spring 1938. The following year the German seizure of Prague triggered the

collapse of SIS operations in Czechoslovakia. Dansey had set up his peacetime network of new 'Z' agents to offer an alternative to those over-exposed SIS agents who were working across Europe through the Passport Control Office system; it was needed. SIS operations in Holland had been penetrated since 1935.[32] Yet not one of Dansey's carefully placed 'Z' agents had given any prior warning of the German occupation of the Rhineland in 1936, nor the union with Austria two years later. This was partly because increasingly stringent security precautions inside Germany made intelligence-gathering harder for sources to predict future developments, while the harsh penalties for those caught spying made the gathering of intelligence increasingly hazardous. Nevertheless, SIS officers were supposed to be in place to give precisely those warnings. Although the situation did improve with better agents in place during the Munich Crisis, the German entry into Prague and the attack on Poland in September 1939 left:

> ... the War Office regularly complaining that the SIS was failing to meet its increasingly urgent need for factual information about Germany's military capacities, equipment, preparations and movements. While in that year the Air Ministry ... dismissed SIS intelligence of this kind as being normally 80% inaccurate.[33]

Professor F.H. Hinsley wrote afterwards: 'the SIS's espionage system and SigInt [Signals Intelligence] were in organised existence throughout the inter-war years and there is no simple explanation of their deficiency during the approach to war.'[34] With the outbreak of that war – and for reasons that remain unexplained – Dansey's 'Z' agents were ordered to operate overtly with those agents who worked within the PCO system even though those same agents were already believed to have been exposed. In The Hague, Holland, that PCO officer was a Major Stevens who, on 8 November 1940, together with 'Z' agent Captain S. Payne Best, was lured over the German border at Venlo on the pretext that a meeting had been set up with anti-Nazis who could give them vital German military intelligence. It was a trap; both SIS officers were captured. Under interrogation they revealed a massive and detailed picture of the whole of the SIS set-up in Europe. Soon the *Abwehr* (German military intelligence) had the names of senior personnel and addresses of nearly all the intelligence officers in Britain as well as of agents in the Low Countries. Thus 'in a single day, the British secret service on the continent of Europe was almost totally destroyed'.[35]

The few agents that did remain undetected in the early months of the Phoney War proved ineffectual and were soon over-run by the rapid German advance. With few radio sets from which to transmit information – another result of chronic pre-war under-funding – they were effectively silenced. By the time the Germans had invaded the Low Countries and France in spring 1940, Britain was left with practically no effective intelligence service in Europe. As a result of having been starved and run-down during the inter-war period, SIS was the object of considerable criticism in senior service circles. The creation of SOE would therefore be seen – by SIS at least – to threaten the very existence of SIS at a time of critical vulnerability; thus the background to the relationship between the two was unpropitious. After the war, former SIS agent Malcolm Muggeridge expressed the relationship in starker terms: 'Though SOE and SIS were nominally on the same side in the war, they were generally speaking more abhorrent to one another than the *Abwehr* was to either of them.'[36] At a very basic level, however, it came down to personalities:

> The head of SIS and SOE hated each other's guts, got on very badly together and didn't care who knew it. SIS resented the cuckoo in the nest and reckoned, correctly, that it was a mistake for two agencies to work on the same ground with such diverse aims.[37]

The creation of something as maverick as SOE was always going to cause resentment and ruffle feathers amongst the established service and civilian intelligence organisations who saw its creation as a threat. But its chances of early survival would have been immeasurably enhanced had its creation not been shrouded in a veil of fumbled origins, botched operations and personal enmity. Those who were now to stand back in the Whitehall shadows, arms folded, and watch with mounting alarm as that 'cuckoo in the nest' tried to take wing were to form, in one sense, a clandestine 'sixth column' of their own.

Notes
 1 Stafford, David, *Britain and European Resistance 1940–1945* (Macmillan Press, London, 1980), p.24.
 2 Philby, Kim, *My Silent War* (Macgibbon & Kee, London, 1968), p.13.
 3 Stafford, *Britain and European Resistance 1940–1945*, p.20.
 4 Seaman, Mark, *Special Operations Executive. A New Instrument of War* (Routledge, London, 2006), p.8.
 5 Philby, *My Silent War*, p.4.
 6 Sweet-Escott, Bickham, *Baker Street Irregular* (Methuen, London, 1965), p.21.
 7 File HS 7/3 at The National Archives, Kew.
 8 Stafford, *Britain and European Resistance 1940–1945*, p.9.
 9 Foot, M.R.D., *SOE: The Special Operations Executive 1940–1946* (Pimlico, London, 1999), p.4.
10 File HS 7/1 at The National Archives, Kew. History of Section D.
11 Philby, *My Silent War*, p.5.
12 Mackenzie, William, *The Secret History of SOE: The Special Operations Executive 1940–1945* (St Ermin's Press, London, 2000), p.5.
13 West, *Secret War*, p.9.

14 Mackenzie, *The Secret History of SOE*, p.5.

15 West, *Secret War*, p.9.

16 Stafford, *Britain and European Resistance 1940–1945*, p.21.

17 Philby, *My Silent War*, p.5.

18 Travers, T. and Archer, C. (eds), *Men At War: Politics, Technology and Innovation in the Twentieth Century* (Precedent, Chicago, 1982), p.122.

19 Sweet-Escott, *Baker Street Irregular*, p.39.

20 Oral Answers, House of Commons Debates, 10 March 1938, Volume 332, Cols 2133–255. Secretary of State for War, Mr Hore-Belisha.

21 Foot, *SOE: The Special Operations Executive 1940–1946*, p.5.

22 Read and Fisher, *Colonel Z*, p.256.

23 Wilkinson, Peter and Astley, Joan, *Gubbins and SOE* (Leo Cooper, London, 1993), p.35.

24 Mackenzie, *The Secret History of SOE*, p.9.

25 Mackenzie, *The Secret History of SOE*, p.9.

26 Foot, M.R.D., *SOE in France* (Frank Cass, London, 2004), p.5.

27 Mackenzie, *The Secret History of SOE*, p.8.

28 West, Nigel (ed.), 'The Guy Liddell Diaries', manuscript kindly loaned to this author by the editor.

29 Mackenzie, *The Secret History of SOE*, p.54.

30 Foot, *SOE in France*, p.7.

31 Mackenzie, *The Secret History of SOE*, p.37.

32 Hinsley, *British Intelligence in the Second World War*, Volume 1, p.57.

33 Hinsley, *British Intelligence in the Second World War*, Volume 1, p.55.

34 Hinsley, *British Intelligence in the Second World War*, Volume 1, p.48.

35 Deacon, *A History of British Secret Service*, p.339.

36 Beevor, J., *SOE Recollections and Reflections 1940–1945* (Bodley Head, London, 1981), pp.75–6.

37 Professor M.R.D Foot, interview with the author, 25 January 2008 at the Savile Club, Mayfair.

CHAPTER THREE

BLITZKRIEG: COMETH THE HOUR ...

Germany's strategic intentions may have been clarified by the outbreak of war but the start of formal hostilities by Britain did not imply an eagerness to join battle with the enemy. For the next eight months a British government led by Neville Chamberlain deluded itself that, perversely, there would be no need to deploy the British Army and that Germany would soon collapse from within. 'I have a feeling that it [the war] won't last very long', confided Chamberlain in September 1939: 'There is such a widespread desire to avoid war, and it is so deeply rooted, that it must surely find expression somehow ... What I hope for is not a military victory – I very much doubt the feasibility of that – but a collapse of the German home front.' Chamberlain, observes historian Maurice Cowling, 'saw no need to *fight* a war, however definitive the declaration'.[1]

Foreign Secretary Halifax echoed the views of his master, telling Lord Lothian, the ambassador in America, 'Time is on our side'.[2] Sir John Slessor, later marshal of the Royal Air Force, reflected in his memoirs: 'How amazing it is to look back upon the illusions and miscalculations of that twilight period.'[3] It was a view shared by leading British journalist Vernon Bartlett: 'One remembers the period of the Phoney War with humiliation – we were so much the victims of wishful thinking. I certainly was. I found it so easy to convince myself that a country which had introduced rationing long before the war could not possibly win.'[4]

Central to that belief was an interlocking trust in two popular misconceptions, neither of which would stand the test of time. The first of these was that 'blockade' – the denial of raw materials by the maritime interdiction of supplies destined for Germany – would be enough to cripple the German economy in the Second World War, just as it had been in the first. Then there had been food riots in 1916 and widespread misery during the 'turnip winter' that followed, with the British trench dead looted for boot leather.[5] In January 1940 the then minister of the newly formed Ministry of Economic Warfare (MEW), Mr R.H. Cross, stated that, after just four months of war, Germany was in the same economic position as she had been after two years of fighting during the First World War. His successor, Hugh Dalton, went further, predicting before Dunkirk that within six months Europe would be 'faced with famine, starvation and revolt and that ... Nazidom will be like a dark pall over all Europe but, after only a few months, it may dissolve like the snow in spring'.[6] His mission, Dalton believed, was to 'strangle Hitler'.[7] Blockade was Britain's secret weapon and economic weapons, he believed, could deliver a knockout blow. Dr Dalton's high-profile optimism would shortly be dismissed by Sir Alexander Cadogan, Permanent Under-secretary at the Foreign Office: 'He [Dalton] the "new broom" talking of taking "vigorous action" due to ignorance and half to egoism.'[8] There was much talk, too, of 'Field Marshal Famine' coming to the aid of beleaguered Britain. The Industrial Intelligence Centre and the Advisory Committee of Trade estimated that Germany probably had reserves of food and raw materials sufficient to last the equivalent of one year's peacetime requirement.[9] Lord Gladwyn wrote:

> One constantly had the impression that, in the Ministry's view, all we had to do was sit tight and the Germans would eventually have to surrender because they would have no more oil, or rubber, or tungsten or whatever it was that they were thought to be incapable of producing or replacing locally.[10]

British planners failed to recognise that to Hitler and his generals, it was the concept of *Blitzkrieg* itself – lightning advance, coupled with the lightning seizure of foreign goods, metals and assets – that would sustain Germany and make nonsense of attrition and any careful estimate of the whittling away of irreplaceable German homeland resources. To Britain, blockade was attractive because it offered an alternative to head-on conflict, a route that might lead to eventual victory at a time when few other ways forward presented themselves. Yet blockade, by any sober, post-war analysis, was never going to be the war winner its advocates hoped it would be:

> Each country deceives itself as much as its opponents in attributing unprovable potentialities to certain of its less understood weapons. Blockade was a familiar enough thing in European warfare but, adorned and transmogrified with a new name and an ill-defined promise, it had become in 1939 Britain's secret weapon.[11]

In fact, too much was expected of blockade and the Ministry of Economic Warfare was then blamed for the over-optimism that ensued. By March 1940 the blockade was said to be 'leaking like a sieve'. No wonder the Ministry of Economic Warfare was being called by some the 'Ministry of Wishful Thinking'.[12]

The second popular misconception that dogged those early days of twilight, Phoney War centred not upon an outdated idea, but upon a country: France. At every stage in strategic planning, France, it was assumed, would hold. There had never been any planning for the possibility that the Western Front might crumble or that German troops would reach the Channel ports and threaten Britain with invasion. Yet it was a comfort, a belief, founded on no more than the past. Secure behind their underground concrete defences, albeit with its flank open to the Ardennes, Belgium and the north, the Maginot Line made France impregnable. That and the phlegmatic courage of the French *Poilu*. Or so it was thought:

> All, Churchill included, retained their blind faith in the French Army, which had taken the worst the Germans could throw at them between 1914 and 1918 and always came back. The *poilus* of this war were the sons of those in the last. Surely they had inherited the same fighting qualities. But they hadn't. Unlike their fathers, they preferred to live.[13]

Churchill had commanded a battalion of the Royal Scots Fusiliers in the trenches beside the French in 1916 and, like many of his Cabinet colleagues, was a confirmed Francophile. However, he may have trusted the French soldiers in their underground bunkers, but his faith in those who governed France had already been severely shaken. In October 1938, France had backed away from her guarantee to Czechoslovakia and had failed to lift so much as a bayonet when German troops crossed the border. And now, in May 1940, the Maginot Line had been side-stepped by German armour through that open flank. France had been overrun, German tanks had halted overlooking the Channel coast and the British Expeditionary Force (BEF) was on the road to Dunkirk. Suddenly, Britain herself faced the prospect of invasion in a month that could lay claim to being perhaps the most significant in British history. Ill-considered intervention in Norway in April without adequate air cover had led to heavy losses of men and warships; there had been strategic errors and the withdrawal of British forces after a muddled campaign hampered by rugged terrain, heavy snowfalls and a confusion of command. The plan of intervention to intercept German supplies of iron ore from Sweden – and thus assist in the blockade of German war supplies – had been the idea of the First Sea Lord, Winston Churchill. Yet, in the heated House of Commons debate that followed the British withdrawals on 30 April, it was not Churchill but the prime minister who was to face the anger of the House of Commons. Even so, it was hardly Churchill's finest hour:

> I have seldom seen him to less advantage. He hesitates, gets his notes in the wrong order, puts on the wrong pair of spectacles, fumbles for the right pair, keeps on saying Sweden when he means Denmark and one way and another makes a lamentable performance. It is a feeble, tired speech and it leaves the House in a mood of grave anxiety.[14]

Nevertheless, the focus remained upon a prime minister who failed to measure up to his hour. To some, the realisation that Chamberlain had little energy for the fight came as a shock: 'it boiled down to nothing more or less than the sudden and paralysing revelation that Chamberlain was a vain old man who had nothing particular up his sleeve.'[15]

Already under pressure for lacklustre leadership, Neville Chamberlain attended a packed House of Commons on 7 May 1940. He looked nervous and dispirited, and 'spoke haltingly and did not make a good case [for Norway]'. From the press gallery, Hilary Kirkpatrick noted that, amidst the jeers, boos and cries, Chamberlain was not allowed to finish a full sentence without interruption. Admiral Sir Roger Keyes, a Tory MP and hero of the First World War, attended the chamber in full dress uniform. The House listened 'in breathless silence'[16] as Keyes delivered a scathing attack on what he saw as the government's lack of nerve in Norway. It was left to Leo Amery, however, to administer the *coup de grâce*. After listening to Chamberlain's halting explanation of the Norway fiasco, Amery said: 'I confess that I did not feel that there was one sentence in the prime minister's speech ... which suggested that the government foresaw what Germany meant to do, or came to a clear decision ... or acted swiftly or consistently throughout the whole of this lamentable affair.' He continued: 'We cannot go on as we are ... for we are fighting today for our life, for our liberty, for our all.' Amery, a keen student of parliamentary history and familiar with the speeches of Cromwell, paused and then delivered his final, telling blow:

This is what Cromwell said to the Long Parliament when he thought it was no longer fit to conduct the affairs of the nation: 'You have sat too long here for any good you have been doing! Depart, I say, and let us have done with you! In the name of God, GO!' [17]

According to historian Graham Stewart, 'like Caesar wilting under the pain of Brutus' dagger, he [Chamberlain] appeared particularly jolted by the words of a former colleague of long and honourable standing'.[18] Churchill was to write later: 'These were terrible words coming from a friend and colleague of many years, a fellow Birmingham Member and a Privy Councillor of distinction and experience.'[19] As First Lord of the Admiralty, Churchill spoke in defence of the Norwegian campaign – and of Chamberlain and the government, attracting as he did so the warning from Lloyd George that he must not allow himself 'to be converted into an air raid shelter to keep the splinters from hitting his colleagues'.[20] He then sided with Chamberlain in the crucial Vote of Censure demanded by Labour MP Herbert Morrison. Amid bitter scenes and accusations of betrayal as Tory members wrestled to align conscience, country and party, the vote was won by the government. However, the Conservative majority was slashed from 250 to just 81. Neville Chamberlain left the chamber to cries of 'Go! Go! Go!' He then summoned Churchill to his office at the Palace of Westminster and told him he was going to resign. Churchill urged him to remain in office. Encouraged, that same evening Chamberlain went to Buckingham Palace to see the King. He went, not to offer his resignation but to share his hopes of forming a government of National Coalition. The next afternoon, 9 May 1940, the prime minister called Churchill and Lord Halifax, the Foreign Secretary, to Downing Street. There he explained that he planned to invite the Labour Party to share government, but if they were unwilling to serve under him then he was 'quite ready to resign'.[21] Labour leader Clement Attlee and Arthur Greenwood then attended Downing Street where they told Chamberlain they thought the party would 'almost certainly' decline to serve under him, but would probably agree to serve under someone else. After they left, Chamberlain conceded that it was 'beyond his power' to form a National Government and that, according to Winston Churchill's recollection, 'the question therefore was whom he should advise the King to send for after his own resignation was accepted'.[22] Chamberlain felt that Halifax was the more acceptable candidate. As a lord, however, Halifax felt that, as he could not lead the House of Commons, he would be in a hopeless position. He wrote afterwards: 'The instinct for self defence is so strong in all the lower animals! I simply don't think it would have been at all a tolerable position for me to get into.'[23] That night, 9 May 1940, Attlee waited for the National Executive, meeting at Bournemouth for the Labour Party Conference, to endorse his views before confirming to Chamberlain that a National Government could only be formed under a new leader.

The next morning Britain awoke to news that Germany had invaded Holland and Belgium. Chamberlain's instinct was to hang on to power 'like a dirty old piece of chewing-gum on the leg of a chair'[24] – an instinct knocked aside by one senior Labour member who drafted a declaration issued over the signatures of both Attlee and Greenwood demanding 'a drastic reconstruction of the government'.[25] At 1530hrs that afternoon the Labour Party National Executive confirmed they were unwilling to serve under Chamberlain. Chamberlain then resigned. Shortly afterwards, Winston Churchill drove to Buckingham Palace to kiss hands with his King. As he did so, German armour was smashing westwards towards the French coast and beginning the early manoeuvres that would soon both outclass and outflank the ponderous BEF, lured into the jaws of the German trap and even then lumbering forward obligingly from carefully prepared positions across the Belgian frontier.

Churchill's accession to the power he had always sought, but which he seemed reluctant to grasp in the closing hours of Neville Chamberlain's premiership, heralded the start of a new realism that rapidly permeated the corridors of Whitehall. It was a realism that pandered to Churchill's strengths as the nation, both within and without Parliament, sensed that what was needed was not a gentleman of the Old School espousing Edwardian values, but a gutter-fighter with a relish for the war of national survival that was now surely inevitable; in the increasing urgency, danger and tempo of the times, the British public seemed prepared to overlook the past misdemeanours and mottled political indiscretions of their new leader. As the BEF fell back towards the coast and the threat of invasion came closer, as sandbagged gun emplacements appeared around government buildings, a senior minister wrote in his diary: 'I examined the organisation for the armed defence of my Ministry. We have a number of old soldiers here. They are to have some rifles and a number of others will bring shot guns and ammunition.'[26] That minister was Dr Hugh Dalton, the man who had drafted the Labour declaration that forced Chamberlain to resign; the man who was soon to run SOE.

Hugh Dalton was the newly appointed minister of a newly created ministry, the Ministry of Economic Warfare, with economic warfare 'a very recent addition to the vocabulary of international coercion'[27] under whose control came the business of blockade and the severing of Germany's supply lines of vital raw materials. It was an appointment that owed little to Dalton's personal popularity and much to Churchill's urgent need to balance the political composition of his newly formed Coalition government.

It owed much also to Dalton's personal scheming ambition. Of all those who took office during the turbulent, dangerous summer of 1940, few caused as much resentment, nurtured as many intractable enemies or attracted such colourful epithets as Hugh Dalton. Calling him 'an able but unattractive renegade', Sir Henry 'Chips' Channon was to write in his diary a little later that same summer: 'I lunched with Alba where I found Dr Dalton, alias Dr Dynamo, who has charm and intelligence but who can on occasions be more offensive than anyone I have ever met.'[28]

Educated at Eton and Cambridge, Dalton belonged to the same clubs as his upper-class colleagues. Yet his doctorate at the London School of Economics in Holborn had been on the inequality of incomes. Loud-voiced, opinionated, impatient, domineering, boorish and served by a 'preposterous conceit',[29] he was regarded with suspicion by the Conservatives and as 'vitriol in an old Etonian flask'[30] by Sir Colin Coote, a colleague. Fellow Labour minister Emanuel Shinwell thought Hugh Dalton was 'the most wicked man in politics I've ever known'.[31] Brendan Bracken MP, Churchill's friend and long-time confidant – once rumoured to be his illegitimate son – described Dalton as 'the biggest bloodiest shit I've ever met!'[32] Dalton admired and respected Winston Churchill. 'He was quite magnificent', he wrote in his diary after a rousing speech by Churchill a little later that month when France stood on the brink of collapse: 'The man, and the only man we have, for this hour.'[33] It was an admiration that was never reciprocated. Dalton was viewed as something of a penance that came with the requirement to form a Coalition government. With Britain facing imminent invasion, Churchill had little time for personal nuance: 'The haste is necessitated by the battle', wrote Churchill to his former leader the same evening he took office. Within minutes of Chamberlain's resignation, Churchill had summoned Labour leader Clement Attlee to his old office at the Admiralty. Once assured that Labour was, indeed, prepared to serve in a Churchill-led Coalition government, Churchill began listing names. He mentioned Bevin, Alexander, Morrison and Hugh Dalton as 'men whose services in high office were immediately required'.[34] A former Secretary of State for Foreign Affairs who spent the early part of the Phoney War shadowing Air Minister Kingsley Wood and Ronald Cross, the then Minister of Economic Warfare, Hugh Dalton, was seen as a powerful, dynamic figure. From the outset, Dalton made it plain to his party leader that he was out for office:

> I should not be interested now in any job which had not got a very close relation to the waging of the war. Nor would I wash bottles for anyone. I am though with that phase. I should prefer the Ministry of Economic Warfare. That is on the border line of economics and foreign policy. Those are the two fields I know best.[35]

Later Dalton told Attlee he would only take the position of Minister of Economic Warfare: 'Failing this, I will stay outside.'[36] Dalton may have had Attlee's ear, but it was Attlee who had Churchill's. In Downing Street, Churchill decided now upon the main Cabinet and ministerial posts in a new government that would see the retention of many old faces. Yet, despite reassurances from Attlee that 'it is as good as settled', Dalton's telephone did not ring.[37]

Notes
1 Cowling, *The Impact of Hitler*, p.352.
2 Stafford, *Britain and European Resistance, 1940–1945*, p.13.
3 Stafford, *Britain and European Resistance, 1940–1945*, p.13.
4 Stafford, John, 'The Detonator Concept', *Journal of Modern History*, Volume 10, Pt 2, 1975, p.190.
5 Holmes, Richard, *Tommy* (Harper Collins, London, 2004), p.69.
6 Stafford, *Britain and European Resistance, 1940–1945*, p.16.
7 Pimlott, *Hugh Dalton* (Macmillan, London, 1986), p.282.
8 Dilks, D. (ed.), *The Diaries of Sir Alexander Cadogan 1938–1945* (Cassell, London, 1971), p.36.
9 Hinsley, *British Intelligence in the Second World War*, Volume 1, p.65.
10 Gladwyn, *The Memoirs of Lord Gladwyn*, p.97.
11 Medlicott, W.N., *The Economic Blockade*, Volume 1 (HMSO, London, 1952), p.xii.

12 Medlicott, *The Economic Blockade*, Volume 1, p.46.

13 Manchester, *The Caged Lion*, p.618.

14 Nicolson, *Diaries and Letters: The War Years 1939–1945*, pp.70, 77.

15 Olson, *Troublesome Young Men*, p.282.

16 Nicolson, *Diaries and Letters: The War Years 1939–1945*, p.77.

17 Oral Answers, House of Commons Debates, 7 May 1940, Volume 360, Cols 1073–196.

18 Stewart, Graham, *Burying Caesar* (Weidenfeld & Nicolson, London, 1999), p.410.

19 Gilbert, *Winston S. Churchill*, Volume V, p.292.

20 Oral Answers, House of Comons Debates, 8 May 1940, Volume 360, Cols 1251–366.

21 Gilbert, *Winston S. Churchill*, Volume V, p.300.

22 Gilbert, *Winston S. Churchill*, Volume V, p.301.

23 Roberts, *Holy Fox*, p.207. In a personal letter to an unnamed friend.

24 Dalton, Hugh, *The Fateful Years* (Muller, London, 1957), p.308.

25 Pimlott, *Hugh Dalton*, p.274.

26 Pimlott, Ben (ed.), *The Second World War Diary of Hugh Dalton: 1940–1945* (Cape, London, 1986), p.29.

27 Medlicott, *The Economic Blockade*, p.17.

28 James, Robert Rhodes (ed.), *Chips: The Diary of Sir Henry Channon* (Weidenfeld & Nicolson, London, 1967), p.264.

29 Pimlott (ed.), *The Second World War Diary of Hugh Dalton: 1940–1945*, p.xii.

30 James, Robert Rhodes, *Bob Boothby* (Hodder & Stoughton, London, 1991), p.333.

31 Seaman, *Special Operations Executive: A New Instrument of War*, p.62.

32 Pimlott, *Hugh Dalton*, p.330.

33 Gilbert, *Winston S. Churchill*, Volume V, p.419.

34 Gilbert, *Winston S. Churchill*, Volume V, p.315.

35 Pimlott (ed.), *The Second World War Diary of Hugh Dalton: 1940–1945*, p.276.

36 Pimlott (ed.), *The Second World War Diary of Hugh Dalton: 1940–1945*, p.277.

37 Pimlott (ed.), *The Second World War Diary of Hugh Dalton: 1940–1945*, p.277.

CHAPTER FOUR

FINGERS IN THE PIE

On the morning of 14 May 1940, Dalton had yet to secure the position of Minister of Economic Warfare under whose umbrella SOE would eventually find shelter. He had heard nothing as he waited at the Labour Party Conference in Bournemouth 'pacing like a caged panther beneath the lounges of the Highcliffe Hotel', wrote Vera Brittain, 'His nervousness became a talking point, the subject of wry amusement'.[1] Finally, the telephone rang. Dalton recalled the conversation verbatim:

> WC [Winston Churchill]: Your friends tell me that you have been making a considerable study of economic warfare. And I think you have been a keen critic of our economic warfare policy. Will you take that Ministry?

> HD [Hugh Dalton]: I should be very glad to. I think I could do that.

> WC: Well, if you will excuse the ceremony, I will have that announced tonight. Time is pressing and it is a life-and-death struggle.[2]

Dalton wrote afterwards:

> Now that I was a Minister of the Crown, I was a dedicated man and a man with power. I was dedicated to one idea – to win the war – and I would use all the power which I commanded to that end … I was impatient of all the better-notters, whether other Ministers, or their advisers, or my own. With my Ministerial colleagues I was prepared to talk it out and if need be, fight it out, with the Foreign Secretary and the First Lord of the Admiralty in particular.[3]

Not only Churchill was rolling up his sleeves.

In May and through June and July, the events that would shape the creation of SOE were gathering pace. That same day, 14 May, the Germans broke through

the French line at Sedan. In France, French and British generals tried to anticipate the main thrust of the German mechanised advance. At 0700hrs the next
morning, Churchill received a telephone call from Paul Reynaud, the French
prime minister. The French counter-attack at Sedan had failed, the road to Paris
was open and 'the battle was lost'.[4] It was a call that said more about the French
leader's appetite for conflict than the plight of French forces on the ground. A
call from Churchill to General Georges revealed that a 15km breach on the front
at Sedan had been plugged, the German advance checked – for now, at least. On
the morning of 16 May German armour broke through the Maginot Line and
French troops began to withdraw. That same afternoon, Churchill flew to Paris
with Generals Dill and Ismay. There they discovered that 'it was obvious that
the situation was far more critical than we had expected ... the Germans were
expected in Paris in a few days'.[5]

At the Quai d'Orsay, the mood was bleak: 'Utter dejection was written on
every face,' recorded Churchill. German armour was pouring through the
French defences; French troops were falling back in confusion; there was a 40km
bulge in the French front line and no strategic reserve to throw into the battle.
Paris herself was being prepared for evacuation and government papers were
being burned in the courtyard of the ministries.[6] The meeting became acrimo-
nious as French demands for yet more British fighters were turned down. The
situation, as Churchill cabled his War Cabinet that evening, was 'grave in the
last degree', emphasising in the same telegram 'the mortal gravity of the hour'.[7]
Churchill and his party returned to London early on 17 May, where General
Ismay announced in private that the French were not just retreating but were
'routed'. Meanwhile, in Belgium, British troops began to retreat. The next day,
conditions in France deteriorated further. On 19 May, Churchill spoke on radio
to the nation for the first time as prime minister and stiffened resolve as he told
the nation of Reynaud's promise that 'whatever happens' France would fight on
to the end. Churchill reassured listeners that Britain could look 'with confidence'
to the stabilisation of the front in France.[8] Yet within hours another meeting took
place, omitted or overlooked by Churchill's official biographer, whose mood and
tenor ran strongly against the grain of such sentiment. It was a meeting of the
Chiefs of Staff to consider the threat of invasion and the implications of a possible French defeat. They studied a paper entitled 'British Strategy in a Certain
Eventuality' – the 'Eventuality' being the collapse of France.[9] It recommended
immediate action against 'fifth column' activities in Britain and concluded that,
with financial help from America, Britain could both survive and bring about
the defeat of Germany through economic pressure augmented by blockade and
the bombing of economic targets. The consequent discontent stirred up over
shortages within German-occupied territories would bring about revolt. Or so it
was hoped. After reviewing Britain's bleak options their report stated:

The only other method of bringing about the downfall of Germany is by stimulating the seeds of revolt within the conquered territories. The occupied countries are likely to prove a fruitful ground for these operations, particularly when economic conditions begin to deteriorate.

A special organisation will be required and plans to put these operations into effect should be prepared and all the necessary preparations and training should be proceeded with as a matter of urgency.[10]

That recommendation was endorsed by the War Cabinet eight days later and was to lead directly to the creation of the Special Operations Executive. It was to be an organisation considered at the time to be little more than 'a hopeful improvisation devised in a really desperate situation'.[11] Five days later and Hugh Dalton, the newly appointed Minister of Economic Warfare, had caught wind of a possible further expansion of his ambitions, writing in his diary for 1 June: 'The D Plan is being concocted.'[12] His manoeuvrings were unsubtle and did not pass unnoticed. Sir Alexander Cadogan, the Permanent Under-secretary at the Foreign Office, wrote in his diary at the end of that same month: 'Dalton ringing up hourly to try to get a large finger in the sabotage pie.'[13] Already, Dalton was referring to Cadogan and all those who worked with him as 'the palsied pansies of the Foreign Office'.[14] It was hardly the most auspicious of beginnings.

At this critical juncture it is difficult for historians to place themselves within the mindset of those who experienced Britain's 'darkest hour' at first hand; to make, as historian Sir Max Hastings has it, 'that leap of imagination' so necessary to reflect accurately the timbre and mood of distant times.[15] It is also easy to forget, when focused upon one particular aspect of strategy – the evolution of Britain's shortest-lived and most unpopular secret organisation – just how small the space its evolution occupied in the wider span of events which framed that summer of 1940.

Within the same two months that SOE changed from an urgently perceived national necessity to an officially sanctioned instrument of subversive warfare – between late May and the end of July 1940 – events of far greater importance were also demanding the attention of Churchill and his newly formed Coalition government: Belgium had surrendered; France, her troops demoralised and routed, edged towards a surrender of vast strategic consequence that would become reality on 22 June; by the end of that same month, Holland, Denmark and Norway would be occupied; more than 335,000 French and British troops would be evacuated from the sand dunes of Dunkirk as German armoured formations closed around a valiant perimeter; the final British evacuation from Norway would be completed with more than 1,500 British casualties; Churchill's War Cabinet would be re-shuffled and his Foreign Secretary, Lord Halifax, would threaten to resign over heated arguments about peace negotiations with Hitler. After much agony of conscience, Churchill would risk war with Britain's recent ally by ordering the British fleet to open fire on French warships anchored at Oran in North Africa to prevent them falling into German hands, whilst the wider world would catch the first glint of steel beneath the rhetoric of Britain's new prime minister.

In the skies above No. II Group in southern England, the RAF and the Luftwaffe would begin the early duels for air supremacy upon whose outcome rested the feasibility of Hitler's plans to invade Britain. It was the likelihood of invasion that dominated the thinking of politician, serviceman and civilian alike during those hot summer months. That meeting of the Chiefs of Staff on 19 May 1940 which had considered the possibility of the fall of France had decided that the new form of economic warfare – subversion from within, leading, it was hoped, to popular revolt in the newly occupied countries – was to be of the 'very highest importance'.[16] It decided, too, that a new organisation was required to run it. But if the Chiefs of Staff believed victory was still possible based upon naval blockade, air bombardment and subversion – if that was indeed what William Mackenzie describes as the 'dominating strategic concept'[17] of that early summer of 1940 – then it had the effect of raising subversion, however briefly, to the same level as any other strategic objective. Yet it was a concept based upon little more than wishful thinking stimulated by the urgency of the times. The difficulty surrounding the creation of that 'new organisation' lay not in the realisation of its need, but in defining its limitations and deciding who should control such a body. It would be a 'Controller', ministers agreed at a meeting on 1 July 1940, who should have 'almost dictatorial powers'.[18] Others, outside government, saw the way forward with equal clarity. One wrote to *The Times* as early as 5 December 1939:

> You have rendered a ... service to the nation by emphasising the necessity of Economic Warfare being undertaken by new methods ... Germany's economic position is her Achilles' heel. We have got to forge an arrow and find an archer and strike her there ... I do not see how this can be achieved unless a minister with real 'drive' be made responsible for the whole problem and be a member of the War Cabinet.[19]

The writer of that letter was Viscount Wolmer, the man who, as Lord Selborne, would replace Hugh Dalton as head of SOE in February 1942. The first Cabinet discussions, in fact, had taken place in January under the auspices of Lord Maurice Hankey, then Chairman of the War Cabinet Committee on German Oil and a man who joined Churchill's Cabinet that summer as Chancellor of the Duchy of Lancaster and minister without portfolio. He was given de facto oversight and co-ordination of all clandestine warfare. What was swiftly decided was that the drive and initiative needed at the head of this new and as yet unnamed organisation could not be provided by a committee – a single man must be put in charge. But was he to be a politician or a soldier? If politician, then that implied direct control by the War Cabinet; if a non-political appointment were to be made then, presumably, he would come from either the War Office or the Foreign Office working through Sir Stewart Menzies, Chief of the Secret Service. Initially, much was unclear. It was to remain so for several weeks, for all were groping in the dark as they attempted to define that which defied conventional definition. There had already been – in the setting up in May of an Inter-services Board – early resolve to provide the machinery for the co-ordination of sabotage and other 'irregular' operations to ensure that 'there is no overlapping or misdirected effort in connection with such projects'.[20] Yet, despite an awareness of the need to work together, there remained at the centre of that uncertainty a fundamental and intractable collision of intention between the diplomacy and subtle manoeuvrings espoused by SIS and the 'big bangs' of unorthodox military activity as advocated by the disciples of MI(R) and Section D. Bickham Sweet-Escott summed up the problem neatly:

> The man who is interested in obtaining intelligence must have peace and quiet, and the agents he employs must never, if possible, be found out. But the man who has to carry out operations will produce loud noises if he is successful, and it is only too likely that some of the men he uses will not escape.[21]

These two conflicting viewpoints, reflected Sir Colin Gubbins at a Royal United Services Institute lecture soon after the war ended, were 'fundamentally incompatible'.[22] None of which prevented a host of different organisations arguing that they should assume control of this new organisation. Perhaps curiously, however, is that at the same time 'it did not appear that either the Foreign Office, the War Office or the SIS were anxious to insist on adding this unlimited commitment to their existing responsibilities'.[23] Despite this apparent contradiction, the first to toss its hat into the ring was the War Office in the form of a paper from Colonel Holland to the Director of Military Intelligence (DMI), suggesting that the responsibilities of MI(R) should be considerably expanded. This became a formal minute on 5 June 1940, four days after Dr Hugh Dalton got wind, probably from Gladwyn Jebb in the Foreign Office, of the possible creation of what would soon become SOE. This suggested that all irregular warfare should be placed under the War Office and would include a 'measure of control'[24] over Electra House, the home of enemy propaganda, and liaison with the Admiralty, the Foreign Office and the Air Ministry. It concluded: 'I recommend therefore the early creation of a separate directorate of the War Office to plan and carry out all operations and activities of an irregular nature.'

Holland took his paper, endorsed by Major General Beaumont-Nesbitt, the Director of Military Intelligence, to the Minister of War, Anthony Eden. The minister passed it forward to the prime minister on or shortly before 12 June. The following day there was the first inter-departmental meeting between Lord Hankey as 'Grand Overseer', Colonel Menzies of SIS and Colonels Holland and Grand from MI(R) and Section D respectively. The meeting was convened to discuss 'certain questions arising out of a possible collapse of France' and focused primarily upon both the necessity and the difficulty of securing information from within enemy-occupied territory.[25] It must have been a meeting which caused Menzies some discomfort: after the collapse of Dansey's 'Z' agent network, SIS had not a single agent in place able to feed back to England vitally needed information about German invasion barges and assault troops gathering on the far side of the Channel.

SIS may still have controlled Signals Intelligence, but that was at this time their only asset. It was, however, considerable, for within the purview of Sir Stewart Menzies, head of SIS, lay the government Code and Cipher School at Bletchley Park. And within that was to lie the biggest wartime secret of all – the breaking of Enigma and the distribution of all 'Ultra' radio traffic. Despite the urgency of the times – German troops were to enter Paris the next day – Lord Hankey's meeting appears to have achieved little of military worth. It did, however, raise an important administrative principle that was to have significant and far-reaching consequences. Having conceded that 'no adequate machinery for such co-ordination at present existed' and taking what appears to have been the War Office line that whatever emerged should be under War Office control, Hankey's draft paper suggested that, in addition to a panel comprising representatives from all three fighting services, SIS and someone from whoever was handling propaganda into enemy territories, the new organisation should answer to its own full-time minister. Dr Dalton's appointment a month later can be traced back directly to that recommendation.

Implicit in Hankey's proposal was also the suggestion that Colonel Grand's Section D, created as part of SIS, should be transferred to the War Office. When that transfer happened a month later: 'Everybody was so busy in the summer of 1940 that nobody remembered to tell "C" that he lost Section D for three weeks. He was livid. It was a bureaucratic oversight that he never forgot and never forgave.'[26] He was not told, in fact, until 4 September 1940. It was further agreed that Lord Hankey should take 'informal soundings' from the individual Chiefs of Staff before turning early thoughts into a formal proposal.[27] There is no trace of that draft scheme nor any surviving record of Lord Hankey's informal discussions with the Chiefs of Staff. Events in any case were moving on apace in directions that were not always convergent: on 15 June 1940 it was decided to create the Directorate of Combined Operations (DCO) under Admiralty control, a directorate whose remit would 'cut sharply across' War Office plans for the new organisation they hoped to run.[28] The directorate was to be commanded by General Sir Alan Bourne RM.

Among his first acts as director was to echo the need for a separate body to liaise between SIS, Electra House, the Admiralty, the Foreign Office and the Air Ministry. General Bourne's paper on irregular activities went on to recommend that the 'raiding' elements of the War Office – MI(R), MI9, Section D and Electra House – should all be amalgamated to form a new directorate under ministerial control.[29] The War Office itself supported the idea of ministerial involvement, but not the creation of a new directorate. This inter-departmental parrying reveals yet another fundamental fissure between military and civilian thinkers at the time. Traditionalists almost to a man, the military believed that all subversive activity must, by definition, lead to rebellion which should only be encouraged to support direct military action. Civilians – and Dalton in particular – disagreed. There was no reason to believe, he stated, that political subversion and economic sabotage could not play an equally important role in undermining the enemy. In a quote that can hardly have endeared him to the War Office, Dalton stated that 'subversive activities are too serious a matter to be left to soldiers'.[30]

In early July 1940, Hankey received a paper on the potential for guerrilla warfare from a small group of MPs calling itself the Guerilla Warfare Committee, organised by a Commander Stephen King-Hall MP.[31] It struck Hankey as 'rather good' and he sent it up into the service chain of command together with his own endorsement.

Not to be outdone, Sir Alexander Cadogan, the Permanent Under-secretary of State at the Foreign Office, had already sent his own paper on subversive activity to Lord Halifax. This attempted to shed light on an area already mottled by many shadows. Claiming he was personally tasked by the new prime minister to keep in touch 'on his behalf' with secret offensive action against the enemy, he asserted: 'The direction of sabotage in enemy and neutral countries, and subversive activities in enemy and enemy-controlled countries, seems to call for review.'[32] He agreed that sabotage and subversion should be concentrated under one control and that they 'should probably be divorced from SIS, which is more concerned with intelligence, and has enough to do in that sphere, and placed under military authority as an operation of war'.[33] Amongst those who received a copy was the Minister of Economic Warfare, Dr Hugh Dalton. His diary of the following day records his reaction: 'It proposes to give too much to DMI [the Director of Military Intelligence, i.e. under War Office control]. I concert [sic] counter-measures and invoke the aid of Attlee. I think it should be under him, with me doing a good deal of it.'[34] Sir Alexander Cadogan's important meeting at the Foreign Office took place three days later, on 1 July. It was attended by Lord Halifax (in the chair) with Lord Lloyd, Secretary of State for the Colonies, Lord Hankey, Dr Dalton, Colonel Stewart Menzies of SIS, Beaumont-Nesbitt, the Director of Military Intelligence, Major Desmond Morton representing the prime minister, Sir Alexander Cadogan himself and his then private secretary, Mr Gladwyn Jebb. It is perhaps significant to note who was not in attendance: representatives from either the Ministry of Information or anyone from Electra House, the home of propaganda in enemy territory and a sphere of operations that was soon to become yet another source of discord and friction to the new organisation about to be created. The meeting furnished further proof, perhaps, that the issue of the day – departmental control and the structure of empires – came at the expense of deeper strategic thinking.

Dalton, certainly, was already working his political circuits and manoeuvring to bring the organisation under his own wing. Nevertheless, the meeting on that date was to shape the structure that was to become SOE. Initially, discussion centred on handing control to either the Foreign Office or the War Office. One of the most articulate during these discussions was Dalton, who spoke scathingly against Cadogan's proposal of War Office control. He wrote in his diary afterwards that evening:

I object to putting everything under the DMI (Director of Military Intelligence). What we have in mind is not a military job at all. It concerns trade unionists, Socialists etc., the making of chaos and revolution – no more suitable for soldiers than fouling at football or throwing when bowling at cricket …

Morton suggests that we should have a single dictator with a status similar to Swinton (placed in charge of Home Defence (Security)). On this broadly we agree. Who should it be? I have in mind Attlee with myself doing a lot of the work. But I do not mention his name in this galere. I afterwards speak to him about it and also write to him and to Halifax.[35]

Dalton claimed there was a clear distinction between 'war from without and war from within', and that the latter was more likely to be conducted by civilians than by soldiers.'[36] The day after that meeting, Dalton wrote to Lord Halifax claiming: 'I am convinced that the potentialities of this war from within are really immense. It is even today one of our best offensive weapons if only we can learn to use it.' He went on to propose control of the new organisation by Attlee, supported by himself, affirming that he would be 'very glad to render such help as I can towards an intensive "war from within"'. He then set out his own vision for a future 'Democratic International' under the control of a Department of Economic Warfare whose role 'has perhaps been defined somewhat too narrowly in the past'.[37] His letter to Lord Halifax is worth quoting at length. It continued:

We have got to organise movements in enemy-occupied territory comparable to the *Sinn Fein* movement in Ireland, to the Chinese Guerrillas now operating against Japan, to the Spanish Irregulars who played such a notable part in Wellington's campaign or – one might as well admit it – to the organisation which the Nazis themselves have developed so remarkably in almost every country in the world.

This 'Democratic International' must use many different methods, including industrial and military sabotage, labour agitation and strikes, continuous propaganda, terrorist acts against traitors and German leaders, boycotts and riots. It is quite clear to me that an organisation on this scale and of this character is not something which can be handled by the ordinary departmental machinery of either the British Civil Service or the British military machine. What is needed is a new organisation to co-ordinate, inspire, control and assist the nationals of the oppressed countries who must themselves be the direct participants. We need absolute secrecy, a certain fanatical enthusiasm, willingness to work with people of different nationalities, complete political reliability. Some of these qualities are certainly to be found in some military officers and, if such men are available, they should undoubtedly be used. But the organisation should, in my view, be entirely independent of the War Office machine.[38]

Returning to his anti-soldier theme, Dalton wrote to Attlee that same day: 'Regular soldiers are not men to stir up revolution, to create chaos or to use all those ungentlemanly means of winning the war which come so easily to the Nazis.'[39] Dalton was pushing uphill, and he knew it: with Labour's Clement Attlee as his ally, he was tilting at the traditional Conservative military establishment and advocating control of what would become SOE, not just by a civilian, but by a Socialist, civilian politician to boot. Already regarded as a class traitor by his Tory opponents,[40] it would not have surprised Dalton – nor would it have dismayed him in the least – to learn that he was already ruffling feathers. However, it was not just his preference for civilians over servicemen that angered the military (whom Dalton detested in turn[41]) – Britain's senior servicemen hated the whole concept of subversion. Indeed, as Professor Foot has pointed out: 'It remains a valid criticism of British war planning machinery that subversion never was fully integrated … into the general strategy of the war.'[42]

In some areas, moreover, Dalton attracted considerable personal dislike. Immediately after the creation of SOE and whilst the future of various SIS departments still hung in the balance that same August, Sir Robert Bruce Lockhart was to write in his diary: 'MI6 officers had preferred to resign rather than be under Dalton.'[43] Meanwhile the following day, 3 July 1940, as the Director of Military Intelligence, Major General Beaumont-Nesbitt, warned the Chiefs of Staff of the imminence of German invasion,[44] Dalton discussed various possibilities for control of the new organisation with Attlee by telephone.

He suggested that Brigadier General Edward Spears should be Chief Executive, himself Minister in Charge and Attlee assuming overall control at Cabinet level. Pitching for Spears was a shrewd move. Decorated, wounded in action four times and invalided out of the army in 1920 after a nervous breakdown, Spears was helped into Parliament in the 1922 General Election by Winston Churchill, with whom he had struck up a lasting friendship. He now remained a strong Francophile and trusted confidant of the prime minister. Attractive though the recruitment of Spears might have appeared to Dalton, opening a path of privileged access to the prime minister, it was a plan that came to nothing and was soon lost in the dust of swiftly moving events.

Others too were jockeying for position at this time, with MI(R) putting in its own paper on 4 July urging the regular and accountable control of irregular operations: 'Irregular operations do not mean unco-ordinated activity. Everything must be done in accordance with a clearly conceived strategic plan … unless action on the lines is taken on a large scale, it is demonstrably impossible to win the war.'[45] If this was a paper that demonstrated anything, it was perhaps that traditional military thinking was indeed too rigid to be applied to the fluidity necessary to meet the demands of the new form of subversive warfare. Now the days dragged by and still no announcement as to who would head the new organisation. Reminded once again that he was not amongst Churchill's favourites and that many of those who were – Desmond Morton and Brendan Bracken among them – might be intriguing against him, Dalton could only chaff at the delay. He was right to be concerned: a diary entry on 31 July shows that Dalton was told whilst being driven home from a dinner party that Brendan Bracken was 'the real cause of the delay in my being given SOE, having ardently pressed upon the PM the view that no minister should be responsible for this particular task.'[46]

On 8 July, Lord Halifax wrote to Churchill confirming their previous evening's decision that Dalton should take over MI(R) and Section D. Unaware of this, the following day Dalton took advantage of a Secret Session at the House of Commons to brief Parliament for ninety minutes on the workings of his ministry and used the opportunity – as prelude to his 'Fourth Arm' argument – to stress that economic warfare was a crucial addition to 'naval, military and air action, and to the flame of revolt in the enslaved lands of Europe which we must seek to kindle and fan'. As Dalton strode to deliver what he himself later immodestly confided was considered his 'great Parliamentary triumph'[47], Attlee passed him in the chamber and told him that 'it is settled and I am to do something additional'. It had, apparently, been agreed that very day; yet still no call from Churchill. The following day, 10 July 1940, saw events move to a climax with three diary entries that spanned three hours:

7.15pm: See Attlee. He says it is all right. M.U.M (Ministry of Ungentlemanly Warfare). I say I should have the same powers as the ex-hyphenate [Swinton, the Minister for Home Defence (Security)] He agrees. Halifax in favour. I say that it is high time I was told officially, so that things can start.

9.00pm: Fletcher says there has been a great to-do today. Beaumont-Nesbitt has been pulling every string. Chiefs of Staff Committee – always apt to be girlish – and Ismay threatening to resign. (I don't believe this). PM a little bothered and reluctant. But it is said, I think by Morton, whom Fletcher knows well, that if Attlee digs his feet in he will win.

10.00pm: See Attlee again. He went straight to PM at 7.45pm from his talk with me and it is true that there has been a strong counter-intrigue … He says he will stand firm. I press for quick decision. Why should Chiefs of Staff object? Beaumont-Nesbitt is another story. Attlee says that he insists that much of what we mean must be done from the Left.[48]

Despite this, records suggest that Churchill was still reluctant to give the new department to Dalton. Crucial support, it appears, came from an unlikely source: the man whose own paper had proposed that the new organisation should be controlled by the War Office. Sir Alexander Cadogan wrote in his diary the following day: 'The PM (put up to it by Morton) is against Dalton taking over and wants to lump the whole thing under Swinton … This is sloppy; we want to get someone to get a grip on sabotage etc., and pull it into shape. I think Dalton the best man. And the meeting agreed to recommend this.'[49]

It must have seemed an incongruous moment: the establishment, in the form of the Permanent Under-secretary of State at the Foreign Office, Sir Alexander Cadogan, putting national survival first and supporting the maverick, renegade Socialist Dr Dalton as the best man for the job. In different times, quite evidently, Dalton would probably have been the choice of few. Now, the very attributes that made him unattractive – aggression, drive, domineering focus – added to his appeal. As one of his close colleagues later noted with a tact redolent of the Foreign Office from which he had been seconded, 'It must be admitted that Dalton was often the reverse of easy'.[50] Gladwyn Jebb continued less guardedly:

He was fairly simple in his reactions, certainly when compared to the ultra-civilised approach of his clever contemporaries at King's College, Cambridge … He admired Churchill immensely and his sorrow was that the feeling never seemed to be reciprocated … Some people found him heavy-handed and a bore and it is true that he had a rather elephantine way of endeavouring to ingratiate himself with people. His eye used to roll round in a rather terrifying way. His voice was always penetrating and even sometimes deafening ... The whole of Berkeley Square House shook with roared insults and ... Unfortunately, not only his voice but his wildly roving eye tended to prejudice people against him. 'You may be right', Frank McDougall once said to me in 1930 after I had been vigorously defending my chief: 'But the trouble about him is his eye. All I can say is that, if he was a horse, I just wouldn't buy him'.[51]

Yet the job was still not Dalton's. Attlee attempted to reassure his impatient colleague: 'It is all right,' he told him the next day, 12 July, 'you are to do it. I have told them that you will be quite tactful in dealing with the brass hats.'[52] Clearly this was not always the case as, after a Cabinet meeting just a month earlier, Sir Alexander Cadogan had confided: 'Dalton very offensive and got everyone's back up.'[53] This, then, was the man who now manoeuvred to control what would become Britain's most sensitive secret department. But desperate times, as noted before, determined desperate solutions. A need for new blood, new thinking and, above all, new vigour in the persecution of a war Britain was on the brink of losing – all these considerations weighted the odds in favour of Dalton. And gave him, at this critical moment, the political weight and attractive, desperate promise that might yet prove him to be, like Churchill himself, the man of the hour Britain needed.

In the final analysis, however, the new Minister of Economic Warfare owed his appointment, confirmed five days later with a visit to Downing Street, not to Cadogan but to Labour leader Clement Attlee. Dalton's diary again tells something of the days of uncertainly and gnawing doubts that were drawing to a close:

13 July: Speak to Morton after Cabinet. 'Who has tried to upset the Cabinet decision of last Tuesday?' I ask. (Concerning the setting up of SOE.) He says: 'No one. It was the PM himself who afterwards had some doubts as to which was the best way to organise it and wondered whether the whole thing shouldn't be under one head, linking up with what Swinton is doing now' ... I say I suppose that D.M.I. had really been at the bottom of the trouble. Morton says he does not think so, though no doubt some of the generals had not liked the idea ... After lunch I go by car to Richmond Terrace with Attlee. He says it's all settled now: 'you are to have it'... I show impatience at the delay.

I hear later in the evening that Morton rang up Gaitskill [then personal secretary to Dalton at MEW] and said that everything was now all right and that I should have a letter from the PM within forty-eight hours ...

15 July: I hear from Gaitskill that Morton told Hall, who lunched with him, that PM's letter to me should go off today! What circumlocutory gossip! Same channel reports that Attlee had 'been very firm'.[54]

The phrase 'Attlee has been very firm' is illuminating. Whatever Churchill may have thought of Dalton personally – he was later to urge aides 'Keep that man away from me. I can't stand his booming voice and shifty eyes'[55] – his hands were tied. He was prime minister and he had appointed himself Minister of Defence without a ministry. He did so without qualms, writing afterwards: 'Power, for the sake of lording it over fellow-creatures or adding to personal pomp, is rightly believed base. But power in a national crisis, when a man believes he knows what orders should be given, is a blessing.'[56]

Churchill may have commanded his government, but the government Churchill led in the summer of 1940 was a National Government of Coalition whose deputy prime minister was Clement Attlee, the Labour leader. Attlee expected – indeed demanded – Socialist representation at the very heart of power to balance against the Conservative Cabinet and ministerial posts of Lord President (Neville Chamberlain), Foreign Secretary (Lord Halifax), Minister for War (Anthony Eden) and Minister for Home Defence (Lord Swinton), as the price of that wartime collaboration. Collaboration, however, did not necessarily mean trust: both men were aware that they were surrounded by former adversaries from the other side of the social and political divide. Morton had long been one of Churchill's allies during his 'wilderness years' and now enjoyed a trust and intimacy Dalton could envy but never hope to emulate. Morton, like Brendan Bracken and Professor Frederick Lindemann, made up Churchill's inner circle, what the excluded Dr Dalton referred to as 'the parasites'.[57]

That same week Attlee warned Dalton that Morton, whilst outwardly friendly and a fellow Director of Dalton's Ministry of Economic Warfare, may well have 'worked on the PM' against Dalton's appointment, adding tartly, 'he wants watching, too'.[58] That meeting on 13 July, claims Morton's biographer, 'set the tone for a battle of wills between Morton and Dalton that the latter never intended to lose'.[59] The Labour leader's support for his minister may have tipped the balance in Dalton's favour, but there were other reasons that made him appear to be the ideal man for the job. Central to these was his role as Minister of Economic Warfare. Setting aside his extravagant claims for the war-winning powers of his own ministry, it was the fondly imagined power of blockade coupled to an erroneous belief in the imminent collapse of an over-extended Germany from within that gave Dalton his decisive and timely appeal in the weeks immediately following the evacuation of Dunkirk. There was yet another reason, too. Crucially, it was the perception that an uprising of the peoples of occupied Europe would be an uprising of Europe's working classes, the Socialists of the Left, that gave compelling logic to passing control of the organisation to a left-wing British politician. Dalton's groundless optimism about Nazism melting 'like the snow in spring' added strength to his claim to title, endorsing as it did a secret Foreign Office report to the prime minister at the end of May 1940 that reported on low German civilian morale. That report concluded rashly that, if Britain could only hold out for just a few more weeks then 'the spearhead of the Nazi attack may be successfully blunted and ... if this occurs there is a very real prospect of disorganisation spreading on the German home front'.[60]

History proved the hope to be nonsense, but it added to the minister's left-wing credibility at a critical time. As his biographer, Ben Pimlott, records: 'Who else would understand labour agitation and strikes, really know about propaganda or create a "Democratic International"? Dalton urged Attlee to tell Churchill that fermenting revolt needed "to be done from the Left".'[61] Yet David Stafford claims in his seminal *Britain and European Resistance 1939–1945* that other fears were also working against Dalton's interests. Stafford maintains that Britain, far from being obsessed solely with national survival post-Dunkirk, was actually already planning for a post-war future of social and economic reconstruction. And that those involved in such planning saw great danger in supporting a left-wing Socialist movement in Europe that could turn against the 'Old Order' once Nazi Germany was defeated: 'Concerns for the present raised urgent questions about the future', claims Stafford neatly.[62]

> It was indeed a paradox that a Tory-led Government should seek to achieve what its predecessors had hitherto actively, and on one occasion, militarily, opposed: namely, popular revolution all over the continent of Europe ... A 'Democratic International' making use of labour agitation, strikes, propaganda, terrorism, boycotts and riots ... was scarcely a recipe for restoring the *status quo ante bellum*.[63]

For Dalton, the waiting was now almost at an end. Churchill never revealed just why he decided to entrust SOE to a new minister, a civilian and a man he actively disliked, rather than to the military or to an established member of the Secret Intelligence Service. With hindsight, three possibilities present themselves. Firstly, that Dalton was indeed his penance, the price he had to pay to keep the Conservative–Labour coalition intact. Secondly, perhaps it was simply that, with a minister in charge whom Churchill knew was keen to please, it would be easy for Churchill, ever the romantic, to keep an eye on his exciting new brainchild. Or thirdly, that Dalton may have owed his appointment to the prime minister's dissatisfaction with the meagre fruits that SIS and Military Intelligence had brought to his table thus far:

> I am not satisfied with the volume or quality of information received ... All Secret Service reports about affairs in France or other captive countries are to be shown to Major Morton, who is responsible for keeping me informed. Make sure this instruction is obeyed. I do not wish such reports as are received

to be sifted and digested by the various intelligence authorities. For the present Major Morton will inspect them for me and submit what he considers of major interest. He is to see everything and submit authentic documents for me in their original form [underlined][64] ... Colonel Menzies should submit a report on what he has done and is proposing to do.[65]

Thus, the focus of attention swung away from the military and from SIS, settling upon Hugh Dalton, the civilian Labour minister in charge of the Ministry of Economic Warfare, whose new organisation might be expected to do better. On 13 July, Churchill asked Neville Chamberlain as Lord President of the Council to prepare a most secret draft paper, outlining the role and remit of the new organisation whose mission was to 'co-ordinate all action, by way of subversion and sabotage, against the enemy overseas'. Chamberlain did so, and gave it a name, too: The Special Operations Executive. It was an irony lost on the British public at the time that the man who would shortly go to his grave,[66] reviled by history for attempting to placate Hitler, would compose, as his last act of public service, what would become known as SOE's Founding Charter,[67] an organisation that was to specialise in the dirtiest forms of warfare. On 16 July, Churchill wrote to Dalton, showed him Chamberlain's draft and invited him to take ministerial charge and become Chairman of SOE. Dalton readily accepted. He received official confirmation of his new additional post the following day. Chamberlain's proposals were given very limited circulation on 19 July and were formally approved by the War Cabinet on 22 July 1940. Dalton was present for the occasion. It was here that Churchill, perhaps remembering Dalton's own choice of emotive rhetoric before the Commons in Secret Session on 9 July, used the famous phrase that is always associated now with SOE. Dalton's own diary records: 'The War Cabinet agreed this morning to my new duties. And now, said the PM, go and set Europe ablaze.'[68] Dalton defined the aims of SOE as 'The corrosion of the Nazi and fascist powers by action from within to be achieved by the careful recruitment and training of agents and meticulous planning during a long preliminary period',[69] although he admitted afterwards:

There would be no public announcement of my new responsibility, and knowledge of the activities of the organisation would be kept within a very restricted circle. As to its scope, 'sabotage' was a simple idea. It meant smashing things up.

'Subversion' was a more complex conception. It meant the weakening, by whatever 'covert' means, of the enemy's will and power of his opponents, including, in particular, guerrilla and resistance movements. It thus included many forms of propaganda.[70]

The job Dalton had long coveted was finally his. Existing SOE historiography appears to gloss over the true cost and consequence of the prime minister's choice of Dalton as chairman and head of SOE. Yet the significance of that choice, of appointing this insensitive man to this most sensitive of positions, can scarcely be exaggerated. The appointment may have been politically motivated and strategically expedient, but, as will be seen, it was also to contribute in large measure to the difficulties, threats and challenges that were about to engulf the fledgling clandestine organisation.

Notes

1 Pimlott (ed.), *The Second World War Diary of Hugh Dalton: 1940–1945*, p.277.

2 Dalton, *The Fateful Years*, p.317.

3 Dalton, *The Fateful Years*, pp.325–6.

4 Gilbert, *Winston S. Churchill*, Volume V, p.339.

5 Gilbert, *Winston S. Churchill*, Volume V, p.349. Churchill to Ismay.

6 Schoenbrun, David, *Soldiers of the Night* (Robert Hale, London, 1981), p.20.

7 Gilbert, *Winston S. Churchill*, Volume V, p.352.

8 Gilbert, *Winston S. Churchill*, Volume V, p.364.

9 Stafford, David, *Britain and European Resistance 1940–1945*, p.23.

10 Stafford, 'The Detonator Concept', p.192.

11 Seaman, *Special Operations Executive: A New Instrument of War*, p.49, citing Bickham Sweet-Escott's *SOE in the Balkans* in Auty and Clogg's *British Policy Towards Wartime Resistance in Yugoslavia* and *Greece*, p.5.

12 Pimlott (ed.), *The Second World War Diary of Hugh Dalton: 1940–1945*, p.33.

13 Pimlott (ed.), *The Second World War Diary of Hugh Dalton: 1940–1945*, p.xx.

14 Pimlott, *Hugh Dalton*, p.294.

15 Hastings, Max, *Overlord* (Michael Joseph, London, 1984), p.14.

16 Files CAB 63/113 & CAB 66/10 at The National Archives, Kew. Deliberations of the Chiefs of Staff.

17 Mackenzie, *The Secret History of SOE*, p.60.

18 Mackenzie, *The Secret History of SOE*, p.65.

19 Letter from Viscount Wolmer to *The Times*, 5 December 1939. Amongst the Selborne Papers at the Bodleian Library, Oxford, in File C.1015.

20 Mackenzie, *The Secret History of SOE*, p.59.

21 Sweet-Escott, *Baker Street Irregular*, p.24.

22 Cookridge, E.H., *Inside SOE* (Barker, London, 1966), p.10. Gubbins RUSI Lecture on 28 January 1948.

23 Mackenzie, *The Secret History of SOE*, p.65.

24 Foot, *SOE in France*, p.8.

25 Seaman, *Special Operations Executive: A New Instrument of War*, p.15.

26 Professor M.R.D. Foot interviewed by the author on 25 January 2008.

27 Mackenzie, *The Secret History of SOE*, p.63.

28 Mackenzie, *The Secret History of SOE*, p.63.

29 Mackenzie, *The Secret History of SOE*, p.66.

30 Mackenzie, *The Secret History of SOE*, p.67.

31 File ADM 223/480 at The National Archives, Kew. Letter from Hankey dated 9 July 1940 to Rear-Admiral J.H. Godfrey, Director of Naval Intelligence.

32 Seaman, *Special Operations Executive: A New Instrument of War*, p.15. Paper of 28 June 1940.

33 Seaman, *Special Operations Executive: A New Instrument of War*, p.15.

34 Pimlott (ed.), *The Second World War Diary of Hugh Dalton: 1940–1945*, p.50. Diary entry for 1 June 1940.

35 Pimlott (ed.), *The Second World War Diary of Hugh Dalton: 1940–1945*, p.52.

36 Mackenzie, *The Secret History of SOE*, p.65.

37 Seaman, *Special Operations Executive: A New Instrument of War*, p.16.

38 Pimlott, *Hugh Dalton*, p.296. Diary entry for 1 June 1940.

39 Stafford, *Britain and European Resistance 1940–1945*, p.24.

40 Seaman, *Special Operations Executive: A New Instrument of War*, p.61.

41 Cookridge, *Inside SOE*, p.8.

42 Foot, *SOE in France*, p.30.

43 Young, *Diaries of Sir Robert Bruce Lockhart*, Volume 2, p.74. Diary entry for 17 August 1940.

44 Gilbert, *Winston S. Churchill*, Volume VI, p.626.

45 Foot, *SOE in France*, p.8. Also CAB 66/10; COS (40) 27 (O), CAB 80/56 at The National Archives, Kew.

46 Dalton, *The Fateful Years*, p.379.

47 Pimlott (ed.), *The Second World War Diary of Hugh Dalton: 1940–1945*, p.56.

48 Pimlott (ed.), *The Second World War Diary of Hugh Dalton: 1940–1945*, p.57.

49 Dilks, *The Diaries of Sir Alexander Cadogan 1938–1945*. Diary entry for 11 July.

50 Gladwyn, *The Memoirs of Lord Gladwyn*, p.105.

51 Gladwyn, *The Memoirs of Lord Gladwyn*, p.105.

52 Pimlott, *Hugh Dalton*, p.297.

53 Dilks, *The Diary of Sir Alexander Cadogan*, p.294. Diary entry for 5 June 1940.

54 Pimlott (ed.), *The Second World War Diary of Hugh Dalton: 1940–1945*, pp.58–9.

55 Seaman, *Special Operations Executive: A New Instrument of War*, p.62.

56 Gilbert, *Winston S. Churchill*, Volume VI, p.327.

57 Bennett, Gill, *Churchill's Man of Mystery* (Routledge, London, 2007), p.261.

58 Pimlott (ed.), *The Second World War Diary of Hugh Dalton: 1940–1945*, p.59.

59 Bennett, *Churchill's Man of Mystery*, p.261.

60 Addison, Paul, *The Road to 1945* (Quarter Books, London, 1987), p.255.

61 Pimlott, *Hugh Dalton*, p.296.

62 Stafford, *Britain and European Resistance 1940–1945*, p.19.

63 Pimlott, *Hugh Dalton*, p.301.

64 Cookridge, *Inside SOE*, pp.8–9.

65 Gilbert, *Winston S. Churchill*, Volume VI, p.667. Churchill to Major General Hastings Ismay, his Chief of Staff and Deputy Secretary to the War Cabinet.

66 Chamberlain entered hospital a few days later. He died of cancer on 9 November 1940.

67 File ADM223/480 at The National Archives, Kew, entitled 'War Cabinet: Home Defence (Security) Executive Special Operations Executive', dated 19 July 1940.

68 Pimlott (ed.), *The Second World War Diary of Hugh Dalton: 1940–1945*, p.62.

69 File HS 7/1 at The National Archives, Kew.

70 Dalton, *The Fateful Years*, p.366.

CHAPTER FIVE

NO TEXTBOOKS FOR NEWCOMERS

Neville Chamberlain's memorandum of 19 July 1940 stated that 'Mr [sic] Dalton' would be assisted by Sir Robert Vansittart from the Foreign Office and 'such additional staff as the chairman and Sir Robert may find necessary'. He further stated that Section D, MI(R) and Electra House, under Sir Campbell Stuart, were all to be brought under Dalton's immediate control. The three directors of Service Intelligence and the head of SIS were instructed to co-operate with the new organisation. Future raids by formal units of British or Allied troops were to remain under military control, but Dalton would be expected to 'maintain touch' with departments planning such raids so that he could help their work through his own channels. Dalton was to co-ordinate the planning operations of underground warfare and to direct which organisation would carry it out. Finally: 'It will be important that the general plan for irregular offensive operations should be in step with the general strategical conduct of the war. With this end in view, Mr [sic] Dalton will consult the Chiefs of Staff as necessary, keeping them informed in general terms of his plans and, in turn, receiving from them the broad strategical picture.'

In view of what was to come, it is interesting to note that Chamberlain's paper made much of the dangers of 'overlapping' between SOE and Lord Swinton's Home Defence (Security) Executive, yet made no reference at all to the dangers of similar duplication between SOE and any of the other organisations who had pitched for control of SOE and whose special pleadings had been so summarily dismissed. Chamberlain concluded: 'The prime minister has requested that Lord Swinton and Mr Dalton should regard me as the member of the War Cabinet who they should consult and to whom any inter-departmental difficulties, should they arise, would be referred.' It was an invitation extended to no one else. Nothing was said, moreover, about the details of that relationship with the Chiefs of Staff, SIS or the Foreign Office – a function one might think today of Chamberlain's preoccupation with his own failing health and of a lifetime's disinterest in matters military or clandestine. Old-school courtesies, together with a certain political pragmatism, had persuaded the new prime minister, magnanimous in personal elevation, to retain both his former enemies, Chamberlain and Halifax, in senior and influential government posts; Churchill, after all, was a prime minister without a party of his own. Now one small consequence of that decision would become clearer in the months of confusion and rancour that lay ahead. For the meantime, however, the mistake lay simply in the omission of busy men, as Nigel West observes: 'The politicians had invented a new body to act as an umbrella for a sabotage and subversion service, but had not provided it with the facilities needed to execute its brief.'[1] Critically, SOE's first chairman would have right of direct access to neither the War Cabinet nor the Chiefs of Staff Committee. As a direct result of this lack of real punch-weight where crucial early decisions were made, rivalries between those organisations and with the Ministry of Information, in charge of propaganda into enemy-occupied countries, were soon to develop renewed vigour. Yet everyone, Chamberlain included, was exploring unknown territory. It was a view endorsed by Lord Selborne, the future replacement for Hugh Dalton:

> Underground warfare was an unknown art in England in 1940; there were no textbooks for newcomers, no old hands to initiate them into the experiences of the last war … lessons had to be learned in the hard school of practice.[2]

Underground warfare was not only an unknown art in Britain in 1940, it was also unavowable. The only caveat the War Cabinet added to Chamberlain's draft memorandum was to remark that 'it would be very undesirable that any [parliamentary] Questions in regard to the SOE should appear on the Order Paper'.[3] SOE, through Dalton, would answer directly to Churchill and the War Cabinet, and to them alone. Secrecy regarding SOE extended far beyond Parliament, however. Indeed, it was to become something of an obsession and yet one more source of friction amongst those who tripped across its shadowed path:

> A dense veil of secrecy was indispensable for SOE, a body for mounting surprise attacks in unexpected places: no secrecy, no surprise. The fact that the body existed at all was for long a closely guarded secret … Some people in high places in other departments knew a lot about SOE; most of them were more or less co-operative, though a few were determined to wreck it. Less dangerous than these, but equally tiresome, were the officials who knew a little about SOE, neither liked nor trusted what they knew, and so were jealous.[4]

From the outset, the problems facing the fledgling organisation appeared almost insurmountable: 'When war broke out the art of underground warfare was unknown in England. There was nothing to build on, no past experience and no precedence.'[5] A new organisation had to be set up from scratch in complete secrecy; premises had to be found, methods of working devised and developed, training regimes established, recruits approached, vetted and selected. Stores, weapons, radios, explosives and equipment had to be developed, tested and procured; and methods of insertion and extraction had to be devised, tested and practised. And all this in a United Kingdom still waiting for invasion, and long before the first SOE agent had even set foot on enemy-occupied Europe. If the concept of SOE and subversive warfare was disliked by the traditional military, the quality and background of those first recruits to SOE did nothing to allay early suspicions:

SOE personnel came from City offices, company boardrooms, university common rooms, Fleet Street and many walks of life. The horrified generals, brigadiers, admirals and air marshals were confronted by men who had never heard a shot fired in anger and who talked about politics, ideologies, psychology and subversion ... Surely one could not give HM the King's commission to accountants, dons, journalists or wine merchants and despatch them with forged papers to fight a secret war in Europe!

However, it was perhaps fortunate that the generals did disown SOE. Although constantly interfered with by half a score of departments, the organisation developed a sturdy independence. On the other hand, the feeling of being loathed by everyone made some of the SOE chiefs arrogant and cocksure. Sometimes this caused errors of judgement.[6]

SOE personnel came in for personal attack, some of which were very personal indeed and included 'not infrequent slurs from outsiders that the organisation was infested by crackpots, communists and homosexuals'.[7] There was, in any event, little time for nuance, for adjustment, for the soothing of ruffled feathers. Churchill himself was a leader in a hurry, impatient for results.

The day after the War Cabinet sanctioned the creation of SOE, the prime minister minuted War Secretary Anthony Eden: 'It is of course urgent and indispensable that every effort should be made to obtain secretly the best possible information about the German forces in the various countries overrun, and to establish intimate contacts with local people, and to plant agents. This, I hope, is being done on a large scale, as opportunity serves, by the new organisation under the Ministry of Economic Warfare.'[8]

However, the gathering of intelligence was the role of SIS or Military Intelligence, not that of an organisation created to perform acts of sabotage and subversion abroad. Yet, from the outset, it appears that SOE was expected to obtain information and pass it to the Cabinet, thus acting in direct competition with both SIS and Military Intelligence who was already smarting from the loss of its own department, MI(R), now part of SOE. Quite deliberately, it seems, the prime minister had 'assigned to SOE a role that went beyond the initially intended task of spreading subversion and carrying out sabotage in enemy-occupied territories'.[9]

As both prime minister and Minister of Defence with a power and autonomy unmatched at any other time in British history, Churchill had few checks on an often inspired enthusiasm that could sometimes lead to meddlesome interference. Churchill was an incurable romantic, a lover of guns, spies and explosives, and was fascinated by the clandestine world of the secret agent. It was a fascination spawned by childhood reading, by his adventures watching guerrilla tactics in Cuba as a young subaltern and by his own escape from the Boers in South Africa almost half a century earlier. The publication of John Steinbeck's *The Moon is Down* in 1942, with its rousing tale of slow-burning resistance to occupation and the dropping of thousands of bomblets to an oppressed population, brought to his attention by Lord Selborne,[10] had Churchill dashing off an urgent memo to the head of SOE demanding to know why similar action could not be attempted in Europe. Yet that book was fiction, and so too, in that summer of 1940, was any early hope that SOE could influence events in occupied Europe overnight.

If the role of SOE in its simplest terms was 'the ultimate delivery to occupied territory of large numbers of personnel and quantities of arms and explosives',[11] then it was a role beset with problems. There was at that stage no network in Europe ready to receive men, weapons and explosives, even if they could have been dropped to them. And in 1940, that too was not possible – SOE had to devise its own role and method of delivery. It thus had much to learn, including its own tradecraft: how to liaise with the RAF to obtain aircraft; how to pack, transport and drop supplies of arms; how to set up reception committees; and how to train its agents in the lethal business of staying alive in enemy-occupied Europe. They were working in the dark, for nothing remotely like this had ever been tried before. As General Gubbins remarked later: 'There was no contact between Britain and any of the occupied countries; nothing was known of the conditions inside those countries except from occasional reports from the few who still managed from time to time to escape.'[12] Eleven thousand tons of stores might have been dropped into France by the war's end, but in that summer four years before the invasion, occupied Europe might have been the dark side of the moon.[13] It would be May 1941 before SOE dropped its first agent into France and, meanwhile, the pressure during that first year was mounting:

Wrangling held up development through the autumn and winter. It looked for a time as if SOE would be trapped for good in a vicious circle ... because it had no positive achievements to show, it could make no progress against its enemies at home; and because it could make no progress against its enemies at home, it could prepare no positive achievements.[14]

For the moment, however, much of that lay in the future. With Dalton placed at last in the position he had long coveted, he now set about attempting to consolidate his empire and enhance the perception of what it might achieve. In the two months of maximum threat to Britain, between July and late September 1940 when the threat of German invasion had receded and calmer, more realistic strategic perceptions prevailed, Dalton made much of the potential of his new brand of subversive warfare. He saw a direct and complementary relationship between his own Socialist left-wing beliefs and the wider war aims of the government he served. To that end, his ambition was to mobilise left-wing opinion in the occupied countries and turn dissent into a spontaneous uprising of the people.

Dalton appeared to believe that 'occupied Europe was smouldering with resistance to the Nazis and ready to erupt at the slightest support or encouragement'.[15] It was a belief – or at the very least, an argument – that he played to maximum personal advantage as he attempted to persuade the Vice Chiefs of Staff that subversion 'by which I mean not just propaganda, but subversive activities in the widest sense' was 'an essential element in any large-scale offensive action'. In his paper entitled 'The Fourth Arm' dated 19 August 1940, Dalton stated:

> My last conclusion (which is really elementary) is that no one of the Fighting Services is in a better position than another to run 'Subversion'. It seems to follow from this that Subversion should be clearly recognised by all three Fighting Services as another and independent service.[16]

That 'seems to follow' appears disingenuous now; a chain of dubious logic stretched a thought-bridge too far. Perhaps the best that can be said of Dalton's 'elementary conclusion' is that he was a generation or two ahead of his time. The worst, that by concentrating entirely upon left-wing revolt he alienated the potentially useful right and that, simply put, he was just too big for his left-wing political boots: SOE had been tasked with sabotage and fanning the flames of revolt in enemy-occupied territory. It was a mission of vital complementary support, assuredly, but hardly one that carried the same weight and responsibility as the three traditional fighting services. Subversion – that dangerous, exciting and immoral new concept – was never going to win the war on its own. Nor, indeed, was subversion ever going to be SOE's exclusive preserve. Yet, underlying arguments about control and status lay a more disturbing truth, for Dalton was simply and fundamentally wrong. As guilty of wishful thinking as were those who heeded his words, Europe was not 'smouldering with resistance to the Nazis and ready to erupt at the slightest support or encouragement', far from it. Mark

Seaman states that such an assumption was 'a gross miscalculation of the actual situation'. Quoting John Lukacs' *The Last European War*, he writes:

> All of those who attempted to record, and later to reconstruct, the state of public opinion and of popular sentiment in the summer of 1940, agree: The majority of the peoples of Western Europe were willing to adjust their thoughts to the new order of things, and to embark on some kind of political collaboration with the Third Reich – with what it was, and with what it seemed to represent.[17]

Dalton's essentially romantic ideas of a dark continent on the cusp of revolt appeared increasingly implausible as summer wore on and Britain moved slowly away from the immediate likelihood of invasion. Dalton was an idealist, not a strategist. Indeed, he admitted as much in that 'Fourth Arm' paper, stating: 'I have no views on strategy as such and I shall certainly not attempt to formulate any.' Yet he was listened to, albeit briefly, because his words, his energy and his simple attack filled a vacuum that had not been filled by others:

> His mental and physical vigour was refreshing. I found him very receptive to new ideas, decisive and quick in action, and a tiger for work. We christened him Dr Dynamo, and he deserved the compliment. Given full control and undivided time, he would, I think, have made a first-class job of what was almost an impossibility.[18]

That paper of Dalton's of 19 August 1940 led, nine days later, to the appointment of Sir Frank Nelson as Executive Director or 'CD' and, early that autumn, to the fortuitous recruitment of Brigadier Colin Gubbins, a former member of MI(R) in Poland who would go on to become the military mainspring of SOE: 'Gubbins' arrival really put a professional backbone behind SOE. Without him in my opinion, or someone like him, [SOE] would certainly have gone the way of Section D and disappeared in fantastic dreams and fury among the military establishment in Whitehall.'[19] Gladwyn Jebb, SOE's Chief Executive Officer (CEO), agreed. In his swan-song assessment of SOE, its purpose and achievements, he wrote: 'But, above all, to Colin Gubbins credit is due. I have seldom met a more vigorous and a more inspiring soldier, or incidentally, one possessing more "political sense". There is no doubt that he is the lynchpin of the existing machine.'[20] That same month of Gubbins' recruitment, Dalton was making it quite plain that if 'certain of the particularly gifted junior officers' of MI(R) could find their way towards his own organisation 'nobody would be more pleased than I'.[21] Somewhat less pleased, one presumes, would be the War Office whose men he intended to poach. Dalton's own back was being watched by Gladwyn Jebb, a career diplomat seconded from the Foreign Office who now became Dalton's CEO. It was a back that needed watching:

> Naturally combatant, he [Dalton] was primarily a politician. He felt that his role as one of the initiators of SOE entitled, indeed obliged him, to fight for it in the political jungles that he moved in, and he did much hard work that guarded it against a number of attempts to nibble away its independent status. But his manner in controversy could not be described as endearing; and though he made SOE respected, he did not make it liked. On the contrary, his doctrinaire tone made enemies.[22]

It would be wrong, however, to dismiss 'Doctor Dynamo' simply as a loud-mouthed troublemaker; a mastiff kept on a short leash by Jebb, his more urbane and sophisticated subordinate. Without the raised profile Dalton brought to his post, it might be argued that SOE would have remained little more than an ill-thought-out idea born of urgent national necessity, yet destined to fade with all Peter Wilkinson's 'fantastic dreams and fury' into oblivion. Instead, SOE grew into a formidable, quasi-military organisation that did much to smooth the way for the invasion of Europe. The man who began that process of growth was Hugh Dalton: 'Dalton had a definite policy; he encouraged SO2's [SOE's] ambitions and pressed for continuous activity so that eventually the organisation created a job for itself. Above all, he generated a sense of urgency and importance.'[23] Perhaps partly because of Dalton's volatile character, the rows that engulfed SOE from the very day of its creation did not diminish. Indeed, in the next few months they were to reach a dangerous intensity that was to undermine SOE's very existence. In August 1941, Bruce Lockhart, the Deputy Under-secretary of State in charge of what was eventually to become the Political Warfare Executive (PWE), reflected on the past year. In a frank and pessimistic minute to Halifax's successor, Anthony Eden, he wrote:

> It is the plain truth which will be denied by no person inside our various propaganda organisations that most of the energy which should have been directed against the enemy has been dissipated in inter-departmental strife and jealousies.[24]

By early autumn 1940, SOE had managed to struggle to its feet. Its direction, control and oversight had finally been ensnared by Dr Hugh Dalton, the newly appointed Minister of Economic Warfare. His essentially abrasive and questionable suitability for the task ahead now lay masked behind political necessity and the false promise of the contribution his 'Fourth Arm' would make to the undermining of the German war effort. In the face of imminent invasion, inter-departmental feuding over empires, the jostle for power and control of the new organisation had helped cloud the clarity of thinking that might have anticipated and resolved future conflicts of interest. In place of that linear clarity espoused by a far-sighted General Bourne, SOE had no direct access to Cabinet and there was confusion as to operational demarcation over intelligence-gathering and the mounting of *coup de main* operations on the enemy coast. The exigencies of wartime operations would soon lay bare these fundamental inadequacies.

Notes

1 West, *Secret War*, p.22.
2 Stafford, *Britain and European Resistance 1940–1945*, p.27 and WP (44) 570, CAB 66/56.
3 Mackenzie, *The Secret History of SOE*, p.70.
4 Foot, *SOE in France*, p.13.
5 File HS 7/1 at The National Archives, Kew. Historical overview report.
6 Cookridge, *Inside SOE*, p.19.
7 Pimlott, *Hugh Dalton*, p.301.
8 Cookridge, *Inside SOE*, p.9.
9 Cookridge, *Inside SOE*, p.9.
10 In File HS 8/924 at the National Archives, Kew. It seems to have been an interest of Lord Selborne's for some while. On 6 September 1939, at the start of the Phoney War and leaflet raids, Churchill received a letter from Selborne which stated: 'I very much hope that when our planes are dropping leaflets on Germany they are also dropping little IRA sticks of gelignite. We ought to produce millions of little packets of high explosive charge plus fuse, plus instructions, each attached to a little parachute so they descend gently … the suggestion is so obvious I feel sure it must have been thought of a long time ago.' Source: the Selborne Papers at the Bodleian Library, Oxford, File D. 450.
11 Cookridge, *Inside SOE*, p.13.
12 Foot, *SOE in France*, p.137.
13 File HS 7/1 at The National Archives, Kew. This lists total numbers of RAF SOE sorties flown by year and the quantities of supplies and agents dropped or air landed. RAF sorties: 1940: (none listed); 1941: 43; 1942: 248; 1943: 1,949.
14 Foot, *SOE in France*, p.137.
15 Seaman, *Special Operations Executive: A New Instrument of War*, p.65.
16 Mackenzie, *The Secret History of SOE*, pp.84–5.
17 Seaman, *Special Operations Executive: A New Instrument of War*, p.65.
18 Lockhart, Sir Robert Bruce, *Comes the Reckoning* (Putnam, London, 1947), p.97.
19 Bailey, Roderick, *Forgotten Voices of the Secret War* (Ebury Press, London, 2008), p.23. Quoting Major Peter Wilkinson, SOE Staff Officer, SOE HQ London.
20 Jebb, Gladwyn, *The Techniques of Subversion*. In File HS 8/251 at The National Archives, Kew.
21 Mackenzie, *The Secret History of SOE*, p.71.
22 Foot, *SOE in France*, p.17.
23 Pimlott, *Hugh Dalton*, p.308.
24 Garnett, David, *The Secret History of PWE* (St Ermin's Press, London, 2002), p.79.

CHAPTER SIX

A COCKTAIL OF ENEMIES

From early autumn 1940, the newly formed SOE struggled to secure its place amid a diversity of conflicting departments, quasi-military organisations and traditional fighting services. Yet, as SOE sought to establish its own areas of responsibility for sabotage and subversion, the early fissures of inter-ministerial rivalry that resulted from a lack of early clarity were beginning to develop into the structural fault lines that would tear SOE in two. Whilst examining the early climate of distrust, hostility and resentment that surrounded SOE in its formative days, and the pressure for results experienced by its chairman, Dr Hugh Dalton, it is also worth considering SOE's relationships with the Foreign Office, the Ministry of Information, the Royal Air Force and the Secret Intelligence Service at a critical time when, with hindsight, it can be seen that SOE's overall strategic mission as defined by the Chiefs of Staff was deeply flawed.

The first few months after SOE's creation in July 1940 was a time dogged by a series of compounded, inter-related problems and frustrations. These problems did nothing to improve relations with those other organisations, both secret and overt, with whom SOE would have to co-exist if it was to become effective.

First, foremost and perhaps most obvious, SOE was secret. Unlike its parent organisation, the Ministry of Economic Warfare, it had no official status in the hierarchy of government departments. It was unaccountable to Parliament and answered only to the prime minister through Dalton, his Minister of Economic Warfare. SOE existed therefore at the whim of the prime minister. Yet it could neither recruit allies in the corridors of Whitehall nor defend itself in public against those who resented its creation and strove to undermine its existence. And resented it was, as former head of SOE, Major General Colin Gubbins, wrote after the war:

> The creation of a new and secret organisation with such an all-embracing charter aroused suspicions and fear in Whitehall. At the best, SOE was looked upon as an organisation of harmless backroom lunatics which, it was hoped, would not develop into an active nuisance. At its worst, it was regarded as

another confusing excrescence, protected from criticism by a veil of secrecy. So SOE went ahead rather on its own.[1]

The fight for its own survival, like the subversive operations it hoped to mount in occupied Europe, would be protracted, prolonged and clandestine. Secondly, SOE's mission had yet to be clarified: tasked by Churchill (one suspects, almost on whim) with collecting intelligence – a role that traditionally fell within the remit of SIS – SOE existed to co-ordinate all action by way of sabotage and subversion against the enemy overseas. Yet that early charter was vague about the precise relationship with the Foreign Office and other ministries.[2] As a result, those early months were hallmarked by a lack of demarcation, most critically in matters relating to propaganda, and this lack of clarity would have significant consequences. It would lead ultimately to a split within SOE, an end to Dalton's 'Fourth Arm' concept, and his own sudden and unanticipated removal from his position as Chairman of SOE two years later. There were other areas, too, where clarity was significantly lacking:

To be unready for subversive war is part of the price that free societies sometimes have to pay for their freedom. It is really less easy to excuse the continuing indecision about what SOE's role ought to be, after it had been set up. Most of its first year was wasted in arid and intricate disputes about what it ought to do. Its roles in relation to military intelligence, political warfare, propaganda, coastal raiding operations and indeed grand strategy were all unclear, all open to dispute and all for a time the prey of contending parties of officials outside it who felt their vested interests were threatened. Wrangling held up development through the autumn and winter.[3]

But the complex problem that vexed Dalton most, as summer stretched into autumn in that first year of 1940, was one he simply had to resolve if SOE was going to survive at all: how to bring SOE to a point of recognised prominence that would justify the huge amount of arms, personnel and equipment it would need if it was ever to make the impact Dalton kept promising his superiors as he championed ambitious claims of parity with the three fighting services.[4]

Yet, at the outset, SOE had only one agent in Western Europe – and he was in a Swedish jail.[5] In the belligerent, occupied and so-called neutral countries of Central and Western Europe, no field staff existed. 'SO2's problem is to get the horse in after the stable door has been shut; and first of all the horse must be found. Recruitment of agents is far from a simple affair'.[6] This report, surveying the dismal lack of achievement that hallmarked that first autumn and winter of SOE's existence, continued:

2. FRANCE

This section has been engaged for the most part in the laborious process of reorganisation and recruitment. Recruitments of agents intended to operate in France is made more difficult by the existence of the De Gaulle organisation which rightly tends to attract enterprising Frenchmen of the better type ... Nevertheless, two men have been engaged to act as organisers in France, and a number of other agents-designate are at present under training. None has yet actually passed into France, though an attempt was made during the night of 11 October to land two by torpedo boat and to drop one by parachute on the 14 November ... Until these visits materialise, there can be little opportunity to push the investigation of lines of communication with France very far.[7]

The revelation that 'two men have been engaged to act as organisers', in the whole of France, is hardly impressive. What was needed now was the early success of a mission that would put SOE on the map. However, it would be a while coming. SOE recruited some of its early members from the old SIS Section D – men whose reputations as the meddlesome troublemakers of pre-war Europe simply confirmed to its jaundiced critics that SOE would bring nothing but trouble. To all intents and purposes, SOE was starting from scratch, its early character defined not by Neville Chamberlain's charter, nor by its Socialist chairman, but by the preferences, contacts and nascent clandestine instincts of those who filled its senior posts and who recruited that first tranche of subversive operatives. First amongst the former was Gladwyn Jebb, later Lord Gladwyn, that career Foreign Office civil servant now seconded to SOE. In theory, he reported to Dalton's Chief Diplomatic Adviser, Sir Robert Vansittart, but in practice he reported to Dalton alone. Jebb was a former private secretary to Sir Alexander Cadogan and had once been Dalton's private secretary when the latter was parliamentary Under-secretary for Foreign Affairs in Ramsey MacDonald's Labour Cabinet of 1929–31. Now, once again, his career was on the rise:

It was with the greatest joy that I received an invitation to be his Chief Lieutenant in the task of 'setting Europe ablaze' ... Technically Van[sittart] was to be the Chief Lieutenant but nobody really expected the Chief Diplomatic Adviser to leave the Foreign Office and to do anything except give advice. I myself was to get a (temporary) double promotion from First Secretary to Assistant Under-Secretary of State and to be installed next door to the minister in Berkeley Square House disguised as 'Foreign Policy Adviser', the rumour being put about for security purposes that I had been appointed to keep a sharp Foreign Office eye on the doings of the 'Dynamic Doctor'.[8]

Jebb, in Dalton's words, was now 'definitely *bien vu* by the service blokes who matter'.[9] At a time when Dalton was accused of 'setting Whitehall ablaze',[10] it was Jebb who kept the conflagration of inter-departmental resentment under control:

> Dalton encouraged, pushed, shouted, stormed and paid careful attention to advice. Jebb entertained his minister with a dry wit, fascinated him with acid appraisals of Whitehall personages, listened patiently to Ministerial outpourings and treated Dalton as one might a large and highly strung pet, dangerous if allowed to get out of control, but useful, if skilfully handled, for barking at hostile strangers. It was an unusual, though on the whole successful, arrangement.[11]

Jebb's cover was that of Foreign Policy Adviser to the Ministry of Economic Warfare. Again, however, it appears that there was no formal office protocol setting out the remit of his duties. That quote from Jebb's memoirs reveals more than he probably intended about the secret organisation he had joined. First, that whilst he and his minister shared offices at the Ministry of Economic Warfare in Berkeley Square, SOE itself was housed elsewhere: an act of physical separation of leaders from those they were leading that was to have far-reaching consequences. It reveals, too, just how little the Foreign Office trusted Jebb's new minister: that 'rumour' Jebb quotes may not have been true, but the sentiments of distrust it reveals undoubtedly were. In those early weeks, as SOE struggled to find its feet in offices first in St Ermin's Hotel, Caxton Street and then, in October, at 64 Baker Street and other premises nearby under the anodyne cover name of the Inter-Services Research Bureau, those drawn in by Jebb and his fellows reflected their own contacts and preferences in the pre-war City. Bankers, solicitors, businessmen, journalists, academics, wine merchants – all were recruited by discreet word of mouth, old school friendships and professional pre-war networks to the new organisation known to insiders as 'The Racket'. What is surprising perhaps, given Dalton's declared intention to mobilise Europe's Socialist Left, is just how many of those first recruits came from the establishment Right. Even so, many doors remained firmly closed. Peter Wilkinson, a former officer in the Royal Fusiliers and later a member of MI(R) who joined SOE in 1940, remembered:

> You were separated from the mainstream of Whitehall … One way and another it was an uphill fight because it was top secret. I remember going down to try and cadge some arms from a member of my old regiment and rather laughingly, when he was asking what it was for, I said 'my lips are sealed' and he said 'so are the doors of the armoury'. Altogether there was a general feeling that, well, to put it quite shortly, SOE was a racket.[12]

Dalton might have recruited Gubbins from MI(R) to be his Director of Operations in November 1940, but it would be some months before Gubbins had any operations to direct. The introduction of a top-secret report entitled 'Survey of SOE Activities October–December 1940' catches the flavour and urgency of its times. Written by an unknown author, it spells out the creation of SOE as a 'necessary experiment' and records:

> Early in October 1940 a secret document under the heading 'subversion' was issued for limited distribution … Embodied in the paper is a memorandum submitted by Mr Dalton, the Minister of Economic Warfare, to the Chiefs of Staff on 20 August at the time of his appointment by Cabinet decision to the control of all subversive activities. The phrase 'Fourth Arm' is his.
>
> It must remain to be seen whether this decision to attempt to beat the Germans at their own game has been taken too late for effective action; whether it will be possible to introduce agents in large enough quantities into the stringently policed countries of Nazi Europe; whether established Departments of State at home during a time of mental and physical stress will be capable of sufficient elasticity of outlook to permit the Fourth Arm to take its place alongside the other three.
>
> Whether it fails or succeeds, SOE is a necessary experiment: at best it may prove to be nothing less than the introduction of an ultimately decisive factor in the conduct of the war.[13]

That first winter SOE was untried, unbloodied and distrusted; thus, wrapped in its cloak of secrecy, without a closely defined mission that precluded tactical uncertainties, without friendly contacts on the Continent, without the tradecraft skills that would later keep agents alive, without the radios in place, the weapons they needed or the dedicated aircraft and pinpoint navigation aids and skills to transport their agents to enemy-occupied territory, SOE made little impact. The same could be said – though with rather less excuse – of its parent organisation, the Ministry of Economic Warfare. Begun under the ineffectual leadership of its first minister, Ronald Cross, on the day that war was declared, the new ministry suffered from the political inertia of its times; when Chamberlain's government pinned its hopes on blockade and the economic collapse of a Germany they were reluctant to actually fight, the MEW earned its sobriquet as the Ministry of Wishful Thinking. That might have changed with the arrival of the 'Dynamic Doctor', but MEW was still far from effective. Germany had expanded her frontiers: her occupied territories – and thus her sources of raw materials – now stretched from Norway to Spain. Russia, at this stage of the war, was still a German friend, if not an ally, and supplied materials to her bellicose neighbour. 'Blockade' was thus a flawed concept based upon the assumption that the stoppage of any German imports would contribute to her ultimate defeat and that 'the ultimate unendurable scarcity of many things would bring about an economic breakdown rather than the absolute lack of any one or two specific commodities [and that] if Germany be no Achilles with a single vital spot, she is vulnerable and can be bled to death if dealt sufficient wounds'.[14]

However, this was not 1918, and by 1940 the effective blockade of Germany and the slow strangulation of her supply lines was a policy that was virtually unenforceable. Side-stepped by Germany's dazzling victories, thwarted by out-of-date concepts regarding maritime prize law, the Ministry achieved little. 'In the summer of 1940,' wrote the ministry's official historian, Professor W.N. Medlicott, 'it needed some persistence and faith to maintain the blockade at all.'[15] Yet in 1940, and months before 'Doctor Dynamo' had been placed in charge of SOE, Cross and his ministry were antagonising the Admiralty with repeated requests for spot checks on merchant shipping at a time when the stopping of Axis blockade runners was never going to figure highly on the Royal Navy's list of wartime priorities. A shortage of Royal Navy warships and the size of the ocean itself made the concept of 'stop and search' more myth than reality: between October 1940 and February 1941, only eight out of 108 French vessels passing through the Straits of Gibraltar were actually intercepted.[16] 'Hence the blockade of French ports was at first little more than nominal: leaking, not like a sieve, but like a bottomless bucket.'[17]

Confronted by opposition from the Admiralty and objections from the Foreign Office, who feared that the stopping and searching of supposedly neutral shipping would damage delicate foreign relations, the first Minister of Economic Warfare, Ronald Cross, backed down. He left little impression upon his successor, who described him as 'a well-mannered man, of good presence. But he was not a commanding figure, and I doubt whether he carried great weight in the Cabinet or with his colleagues individually.'[18] Hugh Dalton, however, was forged from stronger metal. The man whose self-declared task as the new Minister of Economic Warfare was to 'strangle Hitler' stated: 'It is not my job, as I see it, to put a brake on the Foreign Office but rather to act as a spur. Or, in other words, it is not my duty to walk about with a watering can, but rather to light the fires and let the Foreign Office extinguish them if they must.'[19]

A little over two months later, in August 1940, Hugh Dalton was tackling fires of his own nearer home, and doing so with characteristic energy and lack of subtlety. The source of his troubles this time lay not within his Ministry of Economic Warfare, but deep within SOE itself. Lawrence Grand, that 'volatile dreamer', the former head and creator of the now eclipsed Section D, had assumed that he would lead the new organisation which had been formed to usurp his own. Instead, Dalton brought in Sir Frank Nelson as CD and Executive Director. Nelson was a former Conservative MP with links to SIS; a man whose appointment had the support of Claude Dansey,[20] the *éminence grise* of clandestine warfare and de facto Chief of the Secret Intelligence Service. Nelson had been one of Dansey's 'Z' agents and had worked for him in Basle, Switzerland. Within weeks Nelson was advising Jebb, his CEO, that, whilst he was 'impressed' by Grand, he recommended that he be placed 'outside the organisation'. Jebb, however, had already formed his own opinions:

> The so-called D Section of the Secret Service under the impressive but rather theatrical and James Bondish leadership of Colonel Grand, was a problem because it had already made itself pretty unpopular in Whitehall and spent much of its time conducting subversive operations less against the enemy than against a rather similar outfit operating under the War Office known as MI(R).[21]

About Grand himself he was even more scathing, writing to Sir Alexander Cadogan, his former superior:

> His [Grand's] judgement is almost always wrong, his knowledge wide but alarmingly superficial, his organisation in many ways a laughing stock, & he is a consistent, fluent and unmitigated liar … to pit such a man against the German General Council & the German Military Intelligence Service is like arranging an attack on a Panzer division by an actor mounted on a donkey.[22]

Another colleague remembered: 'Grand was as mad as a hatter. He'd blow up anything given half a chance!'[23] Nelson noted that no project of Grand's was 'anywhere near completion' and that what remained of Section D needed a 'radical overhaul'. The suggestion is that Grand fatally damaged his own assumptions of professional survival by disingenuously asking Claude Dansey, the man who lived and breathed secrecy in the highest echelons of SIS, if he would pass on his own carefully nurtured contacts in foreign industry so they could be recruited by Grand's rival organisation.[24] Grand, stated Dansey in a damning report that ended his chances, was 'galloping about the world at his own gait'.[25] Dalton may have had a nickname, but he had one for Grand too – 'King Bomba', named after King Ferdinand II of Italy who bombarded his own cities in 1849.[26] Dalton's diary entry for 18 September 1940 records that Dalton decided to dismiss 'King Bomba' for gross disloyalty to his superior, Sir Frank Nelson, the newly created CD. Section D had been created under the overall control of the Foreign Office, so Dalton ordered Jebb to see Eden, Lord Halifax's successor, 'to rid me and yourself of this lousy shirt quickly'.[27] Grand, however, did not go without a fight. Dalton fired back on 25 September 1940:

In reply to your letter of 20 Sept, I do not propose to give you any reason for the
decision I have taken regarding yourself, except that it was taken in the interest
of the efficiency of the 'D' organisation. Moreover, since my appointment of Sir
Frank Nelson some weeks ago, you ceased to be head of the 'D' organisation.
Hugh Dalton.[28]

The following month, Dalton wrote to Sir John Dill, urging the CIGS to post
Grand to India, adding in longhand: 'I get [sic] rid of him partly on direct evidence and partly on the basis of adverse reports and I believe that my decision
was welcomed by the service departments. It is now most urgent that this most
tiresome question should be finally disposed of.'[29] An anonymous member of
Dalton's ministry wrote on a minute the next day: 'a pretty drastic letter of dismissal! I should have thought a word of thanks would not have come amiss.'[30]

Dalton took some satisfaction from his growing reputation as a man of
strength and decisive action. Indeed, it was for some months the only way his
new organisation could gain anything of a reputation. Meeting Brendan Bracken
outside the Cabinet room later that autumn after Grand's dismissal, Bracken
greeted him with: 'There is that great brute who, like his friend Mr Bevan, tram-
ples all opposition in the mud. He has no Liberal sentiments at all!'[31] The rumour,
Brendan Bracken told Dalton spitefully, was that the manner in which he had
treated Grand was an outrage and that Churchill himself should be told. Dalton
gave almost as good as he got. Yet, despite the show of outer confidence, he felt
uneasy at the encounter. And at the spiteful, public-school cruelty of his persistent
adversary and the less-than-subtle admonition that he, Bracken and not Dalton,
had their leader's ear. It was a painful reminder, once again, of the power of that
club he could never join, of that inner circle of close confidants to Churchill, the
leader he admired but who held him so persistently at arm's length.

Dalton called that inner circle of Brendan Bracken, Professor Frederick
Lindemann and Major Desmond Morton, the one-time head of the Industrial
Intelligence Centre and a former Director of Dalton's own Ministry of Economic
Warfare, 'The Brains' Trust'. Their arrival at Downing Street in early May 1940
on the back of Churchill's coat-tails was compared by John Colville, Churchill's
private secretary, to that of the 'Horsemen of the Apocalypse'.[32] There may have
been only three 'Horsemen' and they may only indirectly have been the harbingers
of War and Death, Famine and Conquest, but they belonged to a club that, for
a time, wielded significant and powerful influence. To the prime minister, all
three were friends of proven loyalty, men who had stood by Winston Churchill
throughout his 'wilderness years'. Now they enjoyed a measure of trust, access
and influence that others could only envy. That influence was never more evident
than in these early days of Churchill's tenure as prime minister, during which
much needed doing with great urgency and there was, as yet, no established

network of research and support to lessen the intense pressure that fell upon the new leader as he fought to fan the flickering flames of Britain's war effort:

> He called on Bracken, Lindemann and Morton for information and action on whatever was uppermost in his mind at the time, bombarding them with minutes and scribbled notes, summoning them to his presence at all hours of the day and night and inviting them to dine with him or spend the weekend at Chequers.[33]

It would be March 1941 before Dalton himself was invited to Chequers and, although he then found the prime minister well briefed, he would complain bitterly that Churchill 'did not focus well on SOE'.[34] Morton received *carte blanche* from Churchill to peer into matters relating to all the intelligence services, including SOE. When, in February 1941, Jebb discovered that Morton had been talking to members of SOE without his knowledge, he objected. Morton, the former member of SIS, vented his anger down the telephone to CD Sir Frank Nelson, who recorded:

> The sense of which was that the prime minister hated Dalton, hated Jebb, hated me, hated the entire organisation and everybody in it and that it was only through the efforts of Major Desmond Morton (who felt that the organisation was an important one and was serving an important purpose) that it had been allowed to continue as long as it had.[35]

Sir Frank Nelson records that Major Morton referred to his CEO's letter as 'one of Jebb's usual tactless communications' and added, 'at another juncture he asked if I was aware that "we had not a friend in the world"'.[36]

In early autumn 1940, however, that outburst from Morton was still some months away. Major Morton never quite lost an earlier allegiance to the SIS that had trained him; he would agitate in the winter of 1943/44, after the comprehensive penetration of SOE circuits in Holland by Major Herman Giskes' *Englandspiel*, for the return of the control of all special operations to SIS. Yet if, in February 1941, Morton did indeed feel that SOE was serving an important purpose, it may have been because he was privy to two special operations whose timely short-term success in March and April 1941 had given SOE the breathing space and a little of the kudos it so badly needed.

The first of these was pure subversion: a plan – ordered by Churchill himself – to engineer a *coup d'état* in Belgrade, Yugoslavia, and so prevent the pro-Axis government of the day from signing a pact with Germany. They were too late. The plan failed, the Yugoslav government signed, but two days later Prince Paul and his government in Belgrade were ousted in a short-lived *putsch* that was

soon eclipsed by the German invasion of that country. No matter, for SOE had
bared its teeth, showed a little of what it could do and Dalton took full credit.
The second operation involved sabotage, but not subversion: the sinking of half
a dozen barges in the Danube to block the river and so disrupt oil supplies from
Romania. The river was only blocked for a few weeks and made a negligible
impact on the flow of Romanian oil, but, once again, SOE had been – and had
been seen to have been – effective. In the wider scheme of things, however, both
these limited and fleeting successes came at the end of a first autumn and winter
in which success of any kind had been conspicuously absent.

Notes

1 Pimlott, *Hugh Dalton*, pp.306–7.
2 Stafford, *Britain and European Resistance 1940–1945*, p.26.
3 Foot, *SOE in France*, pp.136–7.
4 Foot, *SOE in France*, p.137.
5 Sweet-Escott, *Baker Street Irregular*, p.123.
6 File HS 7/211 at The National Archives, Kew. A paper reviewing the creation of SOE and
   its possible evolution, p.3.
7 File HS 7/211 at The National Archives, Kew. Report and review on early progress and
   development, p.25.
8 Gladwyn, *The Memoirs of Lord Gladwyn*, p.102.
9 Pimlott, *Hugh Dalton*, p.303.
10 Wilkinson and Astley, *Gubbins and SOE*, p.75
11 Pimlott, *Hugh Dalton*, pp.303–4.
12 Stafford, David, *Secret Agent: The True Story of the Special Operations Executive* (BBC,
   London, 2000), p.22.
13 File HS 7/211 at The National Archives, Kew, p.3.
14 Medlicott, *The Economic Blockade*, p.47.
15 Pimlott, *Hugh Dalton*, p.282.
16 Pimlott, *Hugh Dalton*, p.288.
17 Pimlott, *Hugh Dalton*. p.288.
18 Bennett, *Churchill's Man of Mystery*, p.203.
19 Pimlott (ed.), *The Second World War Diary of Hugh Dalton: 1940–1945*. Diary entry for
   16 May 1940.
20 Cookridge, *Inside SOE*, p.46.
21 Gladwyn, *The Memoirs of Lord Gladwyn*, p.101.
22 Bennett, *Churchill's Man of Mystery*, p.261, citing Jebb to Cadogan, 13 June 1940, PUSD
   files, FCO.
23 Read and Fisher, *Colonel Z*, pp.256–7.
24 File HS 7/3 at The National Archives, Kew. History of Section D.
25 Philby, *My Silent War*, p.18.
26 Pimlott (ed.), *The Second World War Diary of Hugh Dalton: 1940–1945*, p.83.
27 Pimlott (ed.), *The Second World War Diary of Hugh Dalton: 1940–1945*, p.104.
28 In the Dalton Papers at the library of the London School of Economics and Political
   Science. File DP 7/3.
29 Letter in the Dalton Papers at the library of the London School of Economics and
   Political Science. File DP 7/3.

30 Seaman, *Special Operations Executive: A New Instrument of War*, p.19.
31 Pimlott, *Hugh Dalton*, p.306.
32 Bennett, *Churchill's Man of Mystery*, p.227.
33 Bennett, *Churchill's Man of Mystery*, p.227.
34 Seaman, *Special Operations Executive: A New Instrument of War*, p.49.
35 Copy of both Gladwyn Jebb's original letter to Desmond Morton (15 February 1941) and Sir Frank Nelson's detailed note on the telephone conversation with Morton two days later in File HS 6/309 at The National Archives, Kew.
36 File HS 6/309 at The National Archives, Kew.

CHAPTER SEVEN

TERRITORY WITHOUT MAPS

Enemies, not just within Churchill's inner circle but in the wider establishment at large, were certainly a factor during this early period. Pre-war fears of the Bolshevik 'Red Menace' may have been eclipsed temporarily by war with Nazi Germany, but fears about the Left – and its influence on post-war Europe – dominated establishment thinking and that of a Foreign Office 'unaware that whatever the outcome of the war, the sun of its favourite puppets had set forever'.[1] Kim Philby, the Communist spy burrowed deep in their midst, claimed:

> By and large, the British government had accustomed itself to supporting the monarchs and oligarchs of Europe … Dalton was having his troubles with the Foreign Office.
>
> It … often appeared that the British wanted a simple return to the status quo before Hitler, to a Europe comfortably dominated by Britain and France through the medium of reactionary governments just strong enough to keep their own people in order and uphold the *cordon sanitaire* against the Soviet Union. This view of Europe was incompatible with the very existence of SOE.[2]

Another former SOE officer wrote: 'The instincts of SOE – like those of MEW – were offensive; the instincts of the Foreign Office seemed to have changed little since peacetime. The impression in SOE was that the Foreign Office wasn't really in the war. They were carrying on being the FO, seeking to maintain pre-war diplomatic standards through the crisis with their convictions undisturbed.'[3] Dalton agreed, saving a little of his frustration for his memoirs:

> Someone said: 'The FO is like a chameleon that has grown tired. It has sat so long on the dull appeasement stone that now it can't brighten, even on red granite or green jade.' Poor old FO! It was full of fidgets in those days, suspecting the worst of everyone. They were most unsympathetic to many of my plans for sabotage. There were some sharp disputes towards the end of 1940. I had

some plans, attractive I thought, against the enemy's oil. But I could not get agreement. I said to Halifax: 'Whenever I try to blow up anything anywhere, I am always caught up in some diplomatic trip-wire!'[4]

Professor Foot, writing twenty years later, found evidence to support Dalton's frustration: 'In the early days the Foreign Office's negative influence was often felt; one or two promising schemes put up by MI(R) and several from SO2 [SOE] were banned by a flat declaration that reasons of state rendered them undesirable.'[5] Certainly, the Foreign Office displayed little sense of wartime urgency. Even in 1940, it still began its working day at 1100hrs.[6] At the outset, the Foreign Office may indeed have appeared remote, almost quiescent about the existence of an SOE staffed by people who had once been, and sometimes still were, closely involved with SIS and the Foreign Office. Dalton, for all his faults, had been one of theirs as a former Under-secretary of State for Foreign Affairs; his adviser, Sir Robert Vansittart, was a former Permanent Under-secretary, whilst his senior aide, Gladwyn Jebb, was an active member of the Foreign Service seconded to SOE. Yet the two organisations were on a collision course:

> There was scarcely a point at which SOE's action did not involve considerations of foreign policy: and each problem was approached by SOE and by the Foreign Office from opposite points of view. From the Foreign Office point of view SOE was an intrusive nuisance with an infinite capacity for diplomatic mischief.[7]

The distain was mutual. Dalton thought of Eden, the man who replaced Halifax as Foreign Secretary in December 1940, as 'that wretched Eden, posing before the looking glass'.[8] Gubbins, too, harboured a particular dislike for the new Foreign Secretary, who he believed viewed SOE with 'ruthless hostility'.[9] 'The Foreign Office regard us as nasty people who run around with explosives and they do not really understand what subversive warfare entails.'[10]

It was an accusation that would not fade with time for, post-war, SOE historian William Mackenzie would concur: 'The Foreign Office regarded SOE as an interloper in diplomacy; it interfered only to prevent SOE from acting. The Foreign Office as a whole never grasped how SOE could help it.'[11] Working closely between both camps, Foreign Office civil servant Gladwyn Jebb witnessed the inevitable clash between SOE and his erstwhile masters in the FO:

> In the nature of things there was bound to be some tension between a body like SOE and the Foreign Office but I certainly think that many members of the FO were quite unduly suspicious of SOE. If, looking back, I blame myself for anything during this period, it is for not having succeeded in convincing the critics and the inquirers that, intelligently used, SOE had war-winning potentialities

and further that it was even, on occasions, of positive use to our diplomacy ...
I often wished that those members of the service who regarded SOE first of
all as a joke and then as a menace could have at least tried to understand what
SOE was.[12]

It was not just the perception of SOE by the Foreign Office that was at fault, for
that was merely the outward evidence of a much deeper and intractable divide
between the two organisations – a divide of culture and training that was never
to be bridged:

Nearly all the earlier recruits [to SOE] lacked the habit of subordination to a
regular hierarchy; were disciplined by no mandarin ethos; and were impatient
or even contemptuous of the bureaucratic conventions of the diplomatic service and its auxiliaries. To the diplomats they often appeared brash, ignorant
of things which diplomats were trained to regard as important, and at times a
positive menace.[13]

In the closing days of Dalton's control of SOE in early 1942, the Foreign Office
would draw up a detailed and informal 'Treaty' between itself and SOE that
would attempt to muzzle SOE and reduce it to some form of subsidiary department controlled by a senior Foreign Office official. Mackenzie observed: 'It is
singular that their approach to the problem of subversion, now that it was forced
upon them, was to devise a document laying down at great length what SOE
should not do.'[14]

Although the Foreign Office, deeply entrenched in its pre-war ways, may have
felt irritated but essentially unthreatened by the irksome newcomer, the same
cannot be said for SIS, the senior pre-war intelligence service. On the same day
that SOE was created, 19 July 1940, Lord Swinton, Minister of Home Security,
had been given 'operational control over all the activities of MI6 in Great Britain
and Eire'.[15] Although Sir Stewart Menzies, the head of SIS, expressed no interest
in running the new organisation, he warned of the 'grave disadvantages of running two sections of the Secret Service, with ultimately interlocking interests,
under two masters'.[16] It was a prophetic remark. Both SIS and SOE were soon
to have in place mirror networks of agents throughout occupied Europe 'which
inevitably led to unnecessary confusion and rivalry in the field and much friction in London'.[17] Relationships would only deteriorate in the months ahead:

Relations during 1941 and the early part of 1942 were a continual story of
friction and recrimination. From SIS point of view SOE was an upstart organisation staffed by amateurs not one of whom understood the elements of secret
work. It was invading SIS's territory with much sound and fury and could not

in its first two years expect to achieve anything proportionate to the disturbance which it caused. SIS Intelligence, scant though it might be, represented a concrete gain for the Allied war effort, and there was no reason why it should be endangered by bungling amateurs.[18]

If SOE found itself caught in the double bind of a 'vicious circle', where it was unable to win friends at home until it had gained success in the field abroad – and *vice versa* – the same now applied to SIS. First the humiliating Venlo incident and the capture of British intelligence officers, then the internal struggle between Menzies and others – including, possibly, Desmond Morton – for succession to Sir Hugh Sinclair, the head of SIS, and finally the German invasion of the Low Countries which had rolled up all SIS agents-in-place. These three separate but interlinked developments had left SIS vulnerable. So too had the Hankey inquiry into the Secret Services, ordered by the prime minister in December 1939. This indicated 'the depth of dissatisfaction felt within the War Cabinet at the performance of the agencies during the first few months of the conflict'.[19] It revealed something also about the manner in which the gathering of intelligence and 'ungentlemanly warfare' were still viewed by those within the establishment. Churchill's minister without portfolio, Maurice Hankey, prefaced his passage on Section D with the observation: 'At first sight the natural instinct of any humane person is to recoil from this undesirable business as something he would rather know nothing about.'[20]

Upon taking his new post as head of SIS, Sir Stewart Menzies found himself faced with a series of complaints from the service ministries at the quality and quantity of intelligence received. Until the provision and analysis of SIS intelligence improved, SIS would not be given the weight and political deference to which it believed itself to be entitled; yet SIS could not establish a reputation for reliability until it was taken seriously. MI5's Guy Liddell recorded:

> I had a long discussion with Stewart Menzies. He tells me that every sort of intrigue is going on by those who want to take over the organisation and that criticisms are being made from every quarter by ignorant people. There is no doubt that SIS is going through a very difficult time.[21]

And now, suddenly and as if out of nowhere, there was a new and wide-shouldered rival: SOE, the advocate of 'big bangs' determined to set Europe ablaze, stepping out in heavy boots on to the same flimsy stage as the men of SIS whose instinct was to move in soft-slippered silence. Jebb was certainly aware of the need for friendly co-operation between SIS and SOE. He conceded, however, that both organisations were probably on a collision course and that 'a project may quite possibly be good for purposes of Subversion, but bad for purposes of intelligence'.[22] Small wonder then that for SOE, SIS 'must perhaps also be reckoned among the enemies'.[23] Yet the battle was not entirely one-sided. In his memoirs, Professor R.V. Jones, Britain's leading intelligence scientist, recalls being summonsed to Sir Claude Dansey's office a little later in the war to find Dansey 'almost incoherent with indignation about those buggers in SOE'. It transpired that SOE had sent a paper to the Chiefs of Staff suggesting that they should take over the Secret Intelligence Service.[24] Dansey's hatred of SOE ran deep, and it endured. In 1943, Suttill's SOE-sponsored resistance network in France, code-named 'PROSPER', collapsed. When he heard, Dansey 'marched in, clapped his hands and declared: "Great news, Reilley. Great news ... one of the big SOE networks in France has just blown up!"'[25]

SIS may have been under the nominal charge of Sir Stewart Menzies, but it was Claude Dansey, his deputy, who was its true operational leader. He too was one of those who had hoped that SOE, like MI9, the escape and evasion service, would come under his control. When Dansey discovered he had been outwitted by Dalton, his interest in control of SOE did not end, but merely diverted on to a more oblique course. The endorsed appointment of Sir Frank Nelson as CD/CEO reflected that ongoing interest, for it brought with it an expectation, initially realised, that Nelson would co-operate fully with SIS, his former employer. Thus, early SOE agents expected to be deployed to neutral countries were interviewed and briefed by Dansey himself. He instructed them to contact SIS agents in those countries, but not to recruit anyone else or to 'make any moves'[26] without consulting SIS agents in the field. It was an arrangement of early goodwill and malleability that was unlikely to last, and Dansey knew it. His next move was to propose that SOE should use SIS's own signals, coding and communications organisation since it was already in place; it was a master-stroke, from the master of subterfuge:

> For the next two years, until the volume of traffic became too great, a copy of
> every signal that was sent or received on behalf of SOE was placed on Dansey's
> desk ... Since hardly anyone in SOE was aware of this, it made a most valuable
> source of information for Dansey, not only on SOE activities but also on its
> agents' attitudes and intentions regarding SIS as well as the common enemy.[27]

That wireless link, whether or not run and monitored by SIS, was indispensable to SOE. Gubbins wrote later: 'The most valuable link in the whole of our chain of operations consisted of single agents with short-wave Morse W/T [wireless telegraphy] transmitters, communicating from the field to stations in the Home Counties in cipher. Without these links, we would have been groping in the dark.'[28] Whatever constraint the bond of Sir Frank Nelson's SIS service, friendship and pliant affability may have had upon Dansey's trumpeted dislike of SOE, it did not last. Sir Frank Nelson was to retire due to ill health in early 1942, and those that followed Nelson in post – Sir Charles Hambro in 1942 and Brigadier Colin Gubbins in 1943 – had no intention of letting their SOE be subsumed by 'Uncle Claude' Dansey's organisation. Unable to bring them into line, Dansey's antagonism simply became more overt. He publicly referred to SOE as 'Stately 'Omes of England'[29] – a barbed reference to the many manor houses and county seats that SOE commandeered for training schools and reception centres outside London; he gloated upon every leaked setback and phoned the duty officer at SOE to congratulate him on a fire aboard the French passenger liner *Normandie*, referring to it as SOE's latest 'battle honour'; he raised his hat to every junior officer he passed in the corridors at Baker Street, announcing that anyone who managed to stay a junior officer for more than twenty-four hours at SOE deserved a 'congratulatory salutation'.[30] Evidently, relations could not continue at such a tempo. At the end of 1942, General Sir James Marshall-Cornwall, the senior general in the British Army and a former Vice Chief of the Imperial General Staff, was instructed to spend six months with each organisation in turn and attempt to bring both to some form of mutual understanding and tolerance. He spent six months with Gubbins and learnt everything about SOE. He then spent six months with Dansey and learnt nothing at all about SIS. That soured SOE/SIS relationship was to continue, as bad as before, though there were strained efforts at conviviality: 'A dinner was given by CD at Claridges Hotel at which Mr Dalton, Mr Jebb, DNI, CSS and Sir Orme Sargent from the Foreign Office were present together with the four principal officers of SO2.'[31] Hugh Dalton recorded: 'CD gives one of his, as usual, very successful dinner parties this evening, for purposes of co-ordinating the war against the Germans and suppressing the substitute wars in Whitehall'.[32]

In autumn 1940, however, General Sir James Marshall-Cornwall's one-sided investigation and that strained dinner party at Claridges were still in the future. Gubbins took over as Director of Operations and Training on 19 November 1940. A week later he was dealing with the first formal directive to SOE from the Chiefs of Staff, in which they spelt out the tasks and objectives for SOE in the months ahead.[33] Here, finally – though it would prove to be based upon faulty assumptions – was some form of long-awaited clarity: at last, SOE had its mission.

The Chiefs of Staff Committee was made up of General Ismay, Sir John Dill the CIGS (until December 1941), Sir Dudley Pound the First Sea Lord and Chief of the Naval Staff, and Sir Charles Portal the Chief of the Air Staff (a post he was to hold for the duration of the war). That select committee, advised by the Joint Planning Committee who devised strategic planning, reported directly to Churchill and his recently expanded War Cabinet. Churchill, who had appointed himself Minister of Defence, 'with undefined powers', described the creation of that dual appointment – prime minister as Minister of Defence –

as his 'key change' that shortened and made more responsive the formal chain of command: 'Thus for the first time the Chiefs of Staff Committee assumed its due and proper place in direct daily contact with the executive head of the Government, and in accord with him had full control over the conduct of the war and the armed forces.'[34]

That there was faulty assumption in the COS's thinking may be gleaned from the content of that first all-important directive. It stated that, whilst there was no intention to match the German Army in size, there was an intention to provide a striking force that would attack German forces on mainland Europe once morale had been weakened, thus 'undermining the strength of spirit of the enemy forces should be the constant aim of our subversive organisations'.[35] It went on to predict that, thanks to this 'detonator concept', direct and indirect military action against Germany might eventually take place. This would be made possible by popular uprisings, and co-ordinated and organised revolts in the occupied countries. It was a hypothesis built upon little more than Hugh Dalton's reassurances that the oppressed peoples of occupied Europe would soon be ready for revolt: a powder keg of primed, courageous hostility waiting only for the match that would be provided by SOE. It was a warm and comforting illusion that sustained hope when there was little else in a bleak and lonely post-Dunkirk world. Churchill, too, had lifted hearts with his talk of a British Empire that 'will kindle again the spark of hope in the breasts of hundreds of millions of down-trodden or despairing men and women throughout Europe, and far beyond its bounds, and that from these sparks there will presently come cleansing and devouring flame'.[36] Reality, however, was somewhat different:

> The truth was that, partly due to Dr Dalton's exaggerated claims, SOE had become the victim of a widely held fallacy that Occupied Europe was smouldering with resistance to the Nazis and ready to erupt if given the slightest support or encouragement. In reality in those early days, most people in Occupied Europe were still stunned by defeat and, except for a few ardent patriots, asked for nothing except for peace. Compared with the horrors of invasion, the German Occupation, though disagreeable and humiliating, was as yet by no means intolerable, and most people were content for the time being to remain neutral, if only to survive.[37]

It was a perception which Dalton, despite his assurances, must have know about. His own CEO, Gladwyn Jebb, wrote in October 1940 in a special paper entitled 'Subversion': 'The most astonishing feature in Europe today, not only in the occupied areas, but also in Germany and Italy, is the spread of apathy and indifference.'[38] It would be a long road from stunned defeatism and a pragmatic acceptance of German occupation to active resistance. Julian Jackson, Professor of History at Queen Mary College, University of London, has made a detailed and unflinching study of France during the years of the German occupation from the early days when resistance – that 'great battle in the darkness' – was no more than 'an unstructured body of courage'[39] and observes:

> One must cast aside romantic images of groups feverishly deciphering coded messages from London, unpacking parachute drops, or sabotaging trains. In 1940–1941 there were no contacts with London and no parachute drops; most early resisters had no idea how to sabotage a train or the means to do it. Equally, the hackneyed phrase 'he or she joined the Resistance' is entirely inappropriate to 1940–1941. Before it could be joined, resistance had to be invented … Resistance was a territory without maps.[40]

If resistance in France truly was 'a territory without maps' then SOE's newly won territory at home – populated by Foreign Office diplomats, mandarins, officers in all three armed services and members of the Secret Intelligence Service – was already being charted, hatched and shaded by a veritable army of resentful cartographers.

Notes

1 Philby, *My Silent War*, pp.5–6.
2 Philby, *My Silent War*, p.18.
3 Pimlott, *Hugh Dalton*, p.307.
4 Dalton, *The Fateful Years*, p.371.
5 Foot, *SOE in France*, p.29.
6 Olson, *Troublesome Young Men*, p.225.
7 Mackenzie, *The Secret History of SOE*, p.339.
8 Pimlott (ed.), *The Second World War Diary of Hugh Dalton: 1940–1945*, p.128. Diary entry for 20 December 1940.
9 Wilkinson and Astley, *Gubbins and SOE*, p.3.
10 Mackenzie, *The Secret History of SOE*, p.344.
11 Mackenzie, *The Secret History of SOE*, p.750.
12 Gladwyn, *The Memoirs of Lord Gladwyn*, p.103.
13 Stafford, *Britain and European Resistance 1940–1945*, p.38.
14 Mackenzie, *The Secret History of SOE*, p.345.
15 Bennett, *Churchill's Man of Mystery*, p.370.
16 Mackenzie, *The Secret History of SOE*, p.70.
17 West, *Secret War*, p.27.
18 Mackenzie, *The Secret History of SOE*, p.385.
19 Bennett, *Churchill's Man of Mystery*, p.213.
20 Bennett, *Churchill's Man of Mystery*, p.213.
21 West, Nigel (ed.), *Guy Liddell Diaries*, p.118.
22 Jeffery, *MI6: The History of the Secret Intelligence Service 1909–1949*, p.353.
23 Mackenzie, *The Secret History of SOE*, p.339.

24 Jones, R.V., *Most Secret War* (Hamish Hamilton, London, 1978), p.262.

25 Marshall, Robert, *All The King's Men* (Fontana, London, 1989), p.197 & footnote p.297 quoting letter from Sir Patrick Reilly to author dated 15 September 1986.

26 Read and Fisher, *Colonel Z*, p.270.

27 Read and Fisher, *Colonel Z*, p.270.

28 Foot, *SOE in France*, p.95.

29 Rigden, Denis (intrd.), *SOE Syllabus* (The National Archives, London, 2001), p.2.

30 Read and Fisher, *Colonel Z*, p.271.

31 File HS 7/212 at The National Archives, Kew, p.60.

32 Pimlott (ed.), *The Second World War Diary of Hugh Dalton 1940–1945*, p.143. Diary entry for Friday 7 January 1941.

33 Cabinet File CAB 80/56 at The National Archives, Kew.

34 Butler, J.M.R., *History of the Second World War, Grand Strategy*, Volume 2 (HMSO, London, 1957), p.180.

35 Cabinet File CAB 80/56 at The National Archives, Kew.

36 Stafford, *Britain and European Resistance 1940–1945*, p.27.

37 Wilkinson and Astley, *Gubbins and SOE*, p.79.

38 File HS 8/251 at The National Archives, Kew. A paper entitled 'Subversion' by Gladwyn Jebb, dated October 1940.

39 Both from André Malraux's speech at the transfer of the ashes of Jean Moulin to the Pantheon, Paris, on 16 December 1964. Malraux was then France's Minister for Cultural Affairs.

40 Jackson, Julian, *France: The Dark Years* (Oxford University Press, Oxford, 2001), p.406.

CHAPTER EIGHT

MORE COCKTAILS

Without that map, without the invention of the Resistance, without the willingness of European men and women to take up arms and hazard their lives against the German invader, SOE would achieve nothing. In the words of an SOE report a year later: 'SOE's activities cannot be developed at will, in areas where a spirit of resistance does not already exist, no matter how desirable such activity may be on strategic grounds.'[1]

Dalton's aim had always been to mobilise Europe's left-wing working classes into a mass movement of resistance that would rise up and overthrow the occupying forces. To that end, his claim that subversion represented the 'Fourth Arm' of strategic intent added legitimacy to his argument – and that of Lord Selborne who succeeded him – that SOE merited a permanent seat at the table of the Chiefs of Staff and should be kept fully informed of all strategic decisions, not merely brought in when others decided SOE's opinion or advice might be useful. Lord Mountbatten, the future head of Combined Operations (CO), would enjoy such a privilege of inclusion. 'C', the head of SIS, would not, and he, like Dalton, would only attend on specific occasions. This is perhaps another reason why Dalton pushed for a place at that table: if knowledge is power, then knowledge gleaned at the captain's table would inevitably strengthen SOE's arm in the ongoing struggle with SIS. Yet it would be January 1942 before a liaison officer was appointed between SOE and the Chiefs of Staff Secretariat.[2] Dalton's claim for parity on the Chief of Staff's Committee, like the 'Fourth Arm' concept itself, gradually withered in the emerging realisation that the peoples of occupied Europe were not about to rise, and that consequently subversion would never command the same authority as the three fighting services. SOE's relationship with those services appears to have been equally fraught at times, with claims that 'alliances between "C" (SIS) and various service chiefs against SOE were not uncommon, and were on occasion motivated more by a professional and conservative dislike of SOE's activities in general than by a justified objection to any particular operation'.[3]

Records would suggest that the least complex relationship between SOE and the three services was that which existed between SOE and the British Army. In autumn and winter 1940 the British Army was exhausted and short of weapons. It was rebuilding and rapidly expanding in camps across Britain as it recovered from the débâcle in France and the evacuation at Dunkirk. Its dealings with SOE were restricted in the early months of SOE's existence to the loan or secondment of officers further down the command chain who, like Gubbins, would be involved in training and the development of those military skills SOE's agents would need if they were to survive in the field. SOE's complex relationship with the Admiralty and Royal Navy – and with the newly formed Combined Operations Directorate – will be dealt with in later chapters. It was with the Royal Air Force, however, that SOE was to encounter its most intractable difficulties.

It was clear from the outset that, with the denial of easy access to the enemy shoreline and an embargo on landings on the northern French coast,[4] it was going to be aircraft that would hold the key to SOE's operational effectiveness. For without the means of transporting agents, weapons, radios and stores into occupied Europe, SOE's plans, quite literally, could never get off the ground. And plans there were: by April 1941 Britain was actually contemplating the creation of a striking force to attack mainland Europe of:

six armoured and four infantry divisions ... in conjunction with a universal uprising of oppressed peoples ... The harassing and mopping up of the German armed forces will have to be done by irregular bands of nationals of the countries. This means that SOE will have to organise and equip guerrillas on a vast scale.[5]

Part of today's 'given' for any student of the Second World War includes an appreciation of the gigantic strategic importance of both the German invasion of the Soviet Union in June 1941 and the Japanese attack on Pearl Harbor in December of that same year.[6] The sudden and timely inclusion of those two vast arsenals of men, arms and equipment in any future Allied Order of Battle fundamentally altered Allied strategic assumptions. Yet in early 1941, before the German and Japanese attacks on both countries, strategic planning was moving ahead by desperate default, without reliance upon the intervention of either the Soviet Union or America, but upon that meagre strike force of just six armoured and four infantry divisions. By spring 1941, the concept of subversion, on its own, initiating that workers' uprising, appears to have been eclipsed by the more practicable possibility of civilians acting in support of a major ground attack by British forces. That report quoted above, unrealistic though it was and penned by Colonel Anstruther, SOE's planning officer after consultation with the Future Operational Planning Section (FOPS) of the

Joint Planning Committee, brought with it a remorseless and, to senior officers within the RAF, most unwelcome logic: to support such a policy, scarce aircraft would have to be diverted en masse from bombing to the supply of guerrilla bands. There may also have been other reasons for the Chiefs of Staff's reluctance to support SOE:

> The Chiefs of Staff found difficulty in coming to grips with resistance movements at all – they had had no training to do so, for a start – and had little idea of what they might achieve in this field. On the whole, their attitude when faced with the reality of particular operations and requests from SOE was cautious, and this meant that they favoured the demands of the regular services (or SIS) when it came to a question of priorities for supplies.[7]

Working from that initial premise of future operations as envisaged by the Joint Planning Staff (JPS), Brigadier Gubbins, the no-nonsense soldier and Director of Operations for SOE, submitted a paper based upon the logical consequence of that requirement. It was to have, wrote Mackenzie, 'explosive effect'.[8] It has been suggested, post-war, that Gubbins knew his paper was unrealistic and overly ambitious; that it was posited simply as a manner of drawing attention to SOE's future needs. Yet Gubbins' thinking was sound, the basis of his argument incontestable, and it was the reasoned, logical consequences of his deliberations that were to have such an impact.

Gubbins had built his operational model upon the concept of mobilising a citizens' army of secret soldiers and sabotage groups across the breadth of Europe. Assuming each sabotage group might consist of seven armed men, Gubbins envisaged 1,000 such groups scattered across Poland, 700 across Czechoslovakia and 350 across France. Those secret armies would require, if they were to be of significant tactical assistance to Britain's small striking force, eighty-four battalions in Poland, 100 in Czechoslovakia and seventy in France. All of which would need weapons, explosives, radios and supplies, which in turn would require containers, parachute drops and aircraft – many aircraft.

Gubbins' paper envisaged the dropping of 14,000 sub-machine guns and 77 tons of explosives to the sabotage groups alone. The 'Secret Army' battalions would require 125,500 light machine guns, 42,000 sub-machine guns, 132,000 pistols and some 30,000 containers of equipment equating to almost 8,000 separate aircraft sorties into enemy-occupied territory. And this at a time when the RAF, with Germany in its inefficient bombsights, was straining to equip its own home squadrons with the aircraft and crews they needed. The simple mathematics of Gubbins' shopping list, if implemented, would overwhelm any other tactical or strategic response planned by RAF Bomber Command for years to come. Gubbins' plans required the use of 444 aircraft; however, at the time of its submission RAF Bomber Command had just ninety heavy bombers of the type suitable for container drops.[9]

The suggestion that Gubbins was, indeed, playing to the gallery is endorsed by his private admission, in writing to Dalton six months after submitting the report quoted above, stating that the arms that they were being given by the War Office could not be distributed through an 'insufficiency of agents abroad'.[10] By September 1941 there would be just twenty-one agents and organisers on the ground in France, whilst one of those sent to Belgium had been dropped without his radio, straight into a POW camp in Germany! Navigational errors apart, there had already been clashes with the RAF, when SOE's first attempt to drop an agent into France in November 1940 ended in ignominy as the Free French 'RF' Section agent refused to leave his aircraft.[11]

In January 1941, plans had been mooted to drop RF agents into southern Brittany to assassinate elite Luftwaffe Pathfinder aircrew as they travelled by bus from their hotel to their airfield near Vannes. From the outset, however, Operation *Savanna* ran into problems. Not all were of SOE's making: 'The necessary personnel (two officers and six men) was to be recruited from men undergoing a course at de Gaulle's request at an SOE training establishment … When de Gaulle was approached by General Spears he flatly refused to give his consent.'[12] Eventually de Gaulle was won round, though the idea did not find favour either with Sir Charles Portal, Chief of the Air Staff, who informed Gladwyn Jebb:

> I think that the dropping of men dressed in civilian clothes for the purpose of attempting to kill members of the opposing forces is not an operation with which the Royal Air Force should be associated.
>
> I think you will agree that there is a vast difference, in ethics, between the time-honoured operation of the dropping of a spy from the air and this entirely new scheme for dropping what one can only call assassins.[13]

Portal's scruples were eventually overcome, but by this time the Luftwaffe aircrew had changed their travel plans and the attack was abandoned.

Of all the three services, the RAF presented the most difficult problem of co-operation. Brigadier Colin Gubbins minuted in February 1941: 'The situation as regards further operations in the immediate future is now more than acute … unless we have approximately six aircraft and crews available, we shall get into very serious difficulties.'[14] The business of planning and authorising a single SOE aircraft operation over enemy-occupied territory involved, in its final evolution, no fewer than twenty-three different stages and liaison between seven different authorities:

An airman could see there were few people in SOE who had any conception of the technical difficulties involved ... even a dropping operation was like trying to get home in the dark to an aerodrome controlled by irresponsible amateurs; and it was many times worse for landing operations. The aircrews concerned took fantastic risks with great coolness and skill: but it pressed awkwardly on their superiors that they should have to send men on such errands without some guarantee that reasonably 'airmanlike' precautions had been taken.[15]

What pressed upon those superiors hardest of all was the diversion of valuable aircraft away from the main bomber thrust aimed at the heart of Germany. In time – and only after the direct intervention of the prime minister who had been 'door-stepped' in desperation by one of SOE RF Section's field agents, Wing Commander Yeo-Thomas[16] – adequate numbers of aircraft were provided to support operations in the field. However, the provision of aircraft for the dropping of agents, arms and supplies was never guaranteed. Sir Charles Portal objected on principle to diverting precious aircraft from dropping bombs to dropping supplies and agents to the Resistance, as he told Colonel Harry Sporborg, a senior SOE officer:

Your work is a gamble which may give us a valuable dividend or may produce nothing. It is anybody's guess. My bombing offensive is not a gamble. Its dividend is certain; it is a gilt-edged investment. I cannot divert aircraft from a certainty to a gamble which may be a gold mine or may be completely worthless.[17]

To the commander-in-chief of Bomber Command, Air Marshal Arthur Harris, SOE remained, throughout the war, a 'tedious mystery' and one he hardly bothered to comprehend. He 'was not readily persuaded to part with even a few of his precious aeroplanes to carry apparent ragamuffins to distant spots in pursuit of objects no one seemed anxious to explain'.[18] As late as November 1943, the last and greatest of the crises over SOE's aircraft allocation came to a head when, without consulting SOE, Harris abruptly countermanded all SOE air operations in Western Europe. His justification was the final and long-suspected proof that SOE radio operations in Holland had been 'turned' by the Germans; aircraft were being lost and weapons, agents and supplies were dropping directly to German reception committees. Nevertheless, Harris' peremptory decision caused an outcry, his act 'only justified by the relatively high rate of aircraft losses in Holland and by his comprehensive ignorance of the effects of this action on the Resistance in other areas'.[19] The climax to that particular struggle came two months later, in January 1944, but it was symptomatic of the clash of interests that endured throughout the first four years of war as the result of 'a direct incompatibility between the existing bomber policy and subversion on the scale now proposed'.[20]

From the outset of its formation, SOE was in various degrees of conflict with many agencies and personalities: with the prime minister and his coterie of close aids; with the Chiefs of Staff; with the Foreign Office and with Anthony Eden, its new minister ('Eden found Dalton's loud voice and rumbustious heartiness repellent. Dalton for his part thought Eden a stuffed shirt and made no secret of it'[21]); with the War Office; with the Secret Intelligence Service's Sir Stewart Menzies and Claude Dansey; and with Portal, 'Bomber' Harris and Bomber Command. Strained early relations with the Royal Navy and Combined Operations existed too, which will be dealt with in later chapters. There still remained, however, one further ministry with which Dalton was to enjoy fraught relations, and it was one which, ultimately, would prove to be his nemesis. This was the appositely misnamed Ministry of Information. The biographer of red-haired, Irish-born Brendan Bracken, the self-styled Australian fire-orphan, congenital liar, self-made newspaper tycoon and the man Rudyard Kipling called the 'faithful chela of Churchill'[22] claims Bracken described the Ministry of Information as an 'unquiet cemetery',[23] a graveyard of efficiency and personal political ambition. 'Drafted' there initially against his wishes,[24] Bracken would be elevated to the post of minister – the fourth, final and only successful Minister of a Ministry of Information that had seen three others – Lord Macmillan, John Reith and Duff Cooper – come and go in the eight months since December 1940:

> None of them had seriously tried to remedy structural weaknesses, or to disentangle the thickness of red tape which prevented ordered progress. Relations with the Press, the BBC and other ministries had, if anything, worsened under the limp control of Duff Cooper.[25]

One of the ministry's harassed senior officials and assistant to Duff Cooper confided:

> I get horribly depressed from time to time with the burden of this Ministry … At present I feel that the Ministry is flopping badly in its foreign propaganda, and that big changes in personnel must take place to improve the thing, but it is just in this direction I find my master unready to move.[26]

Duff Cooper, the minister himself, agreed. His ministry was 'a monster … so large, so voluminous, so amorphous, that no single man could cope with it'.[27] He, certainly, could not. Hounded by a bad press after his 'Silent column' poster campaign against careless talk became a 'ghastly failure',[28] and ridiculed for his survey team of ministry eavesdroppers unerringly dubbed 'Cooper's Snoopers', Duff Cooper was replaced as minister by Brendan Bracken in July 1941.

The conflict with the Ministry of Information was to lead ultimately to Dalton's removal from SOE and from the Ministry of Economic Warfare. To understand how it came to pass that Dalton fell victim to the politicking of a ministry despised by all as the epitome of bureaucratic inefficiency, it is necessary to look back at the original uncertainty and clouded terms of reference that surrounded SOE at the time of its creation in July 1940:

> SOE suffered from a trouble that also affected the air forces – lack of crystal clear directives; and some of SOE's directives were muddied, as happened in other and even more technical fields, by lack of understanding of the nature and powers of the weapon the force wielded.[29]

On the face of it, Dalton's initial brief could not have been clearer. SOE, under his control as Minister of Economic Warfare, was to 'co-ordinate all action by way of subversion and sabotage against the enemy overseas'.[30] As Minister of Economic Warfare, Dalton was also responsible for the blockade, and if the purpose of blockade was to undermine enemy morale – and it demonstrably was – then covert propaganda and subversion fell logically within his remit. The initial creation of SOE with its two complementary sections – SO1 to deal with propaganda and SO2 to deal with sabotage – had involved assuming responsibility, not just for Section D which had come from the Foreign Office and MI(R) which came from the War Office, but also EH, administered jointly by the Foreign Office and the Ministry of Information. EH, named after its location at Electra House on London's Embankment, was re-created in 1939 after a false start in 1938. It was initially responsible for all propaganda activities and reported first to the Ministry of Information, then, from October 1939, to the Foreign Office, before reverting once again in June 1940 to control by the Ministry of Information headed by Duff Cooper. No wonder Pimlott describes propaganda as the 'Whitehall Orphan' no one wanted[31] – until Dalton. Dalton saw both black (covert) and white (overt) propaganda as part of his remit and could refer to the Chiefs of Staff directive COS (40) 683 of 4 September 1940 which, after some paragraphs devoted to 'Subversive Activities', includes the observation that 'if successful revolts are to be organised in German-occupied territories', one of the conditions to be fulfilled was 'a carefully prepared scheme of propaganda'. But what sort of propaganda – black or white – was not specified. Nor was it specified under which ministry, MOI or MEW, responsibility for that propaganda was to fall: 'It would surely be hard to invent from a practical point of view any less workable arrangement than this division of propaganda policy between two parallel organisations ... both covering the entire field.'[32] That unworkable arrangement was to lead to a rivalry

between SOE and the Ministry of Information which 'escalated from an administrative dispute between officials into a bitter personal row between ministers'.[33]
From the outset, Dalton was characteristically unrepentant:

> There was inevitably a conflict of jurisdiction between myself and successive
> Ministers of Information. They were responsible for 'overt' and I for 'covert'
> propaganda, but there could be much argument as to where the dividing line
> should run. Were leaflets dropped from aircraft, for example, overt or covert?
> It was ruled that they were covert, and therefore my responsibility.[34]

One ruling, however, did not resolve a basic, intractable problem: what was
'black' propaganda? The solution – if it could be called that – was the appointment of the Lord President, Lord Anderson, to adjudicate between the two
rival ministries. The Anderson Award, finally agreed in May 1941, gave secret
propaganda to Dalton. It gave Duff Cooper overt propaganda and passed
responsibility to ensure co-ordination to Dalton, Cooper and Eden, the new
Foreign Secretary, all of whom were supposed to work together. The Anderson
Award merely confounded confusion. There were other problems for Dalton,
too. SO1 – the propaganda arm of SOE – was intended to support the work
of SO2, thereby adding strength in depth to Dalton's claim for a 'Fourth Arm'
that embraced all forms of subversive warfare. However, when Dalton appointed
Foreign Office mandarin Rex Leeper to take charge of SO1 and that promotion
coincided with the physical removal of SO1 from its brother branch in central
London, intended harmony began to turn into fratricide:

> The original idea was that the SOE was to be divided up into SO1, Subversive
> Activities and SOE which would take charge of all the 'black' propaganda side
> including leaflets, rumours and secret radio transmitters. As originally con-
> ceived, I was going to be, under the minister, the man in charge of the whole
> organisation; but unfortunately Dalton was persuaded, by Vansittart, to
> appoint Rex Leeper to be the head of SO1. The consequences of the decision
> rapidly made themselves felt and it became more and more apparent when
> the SO1 HQ moved in November from London to Woburn. As a result largely
> of physical separation, subversive propaganda was thus conceived of as some-
> thing apart from subversive action: separate loyalties followed and whereas
> SO1 tended to regard their colleagues as rather bungling amateur assassins,
> SO2, equally unjustly, began to think of SO1 as half-baked theorisers who were
> not to be trusted for reasons of security.[35]

Getting straight answers from Leeper, confided Dalton, was 'like trying to
pull teeth out of a sheep'.[36] The real problem, however, lay not in the physical

separation of two arms of the same ministry but in a clash of personalities and professional ambition: 'Dalton and Leeper rapidly discovered that they would be united only by mutual antipathy.'[37] When Leeper moved SO1 out to Woburn Abbey in Bedfordshire, Dalton claimed it was because he was frightened of the bombing; Leeper told writer and journalist Robert Bruce Lockhart that it was because 'Dalton was driving him mad'.[38] There was worse blood, it appears, between Rex Leeper and Gladwyn Jebb, Dalton's doubly promoted CEO and a career Foreign Office diplomat twelve years Leeper's junior: 'Rex and Jebb are fighting. Whole thing is disgusting. Hours, days and weeks and wasted on these personal questions, and no work is done.'[39]

When Dalton had fallen out with Grand over Section D, he had Grand removed to India. Now Dalton tried to persuade Leeper to accept an offer of the ambassadorship in Rio, which would allow him to promote Jebb to head of SO1 in his place. The ruse failed. In time, SO1 would be subsumed into the Political Warfare Executive and its creation would mark the formal death of Dalton's 'Fourth Arm' concept. This dismal story of squabbles and petty inter-ministerial intrigues drifted on for almost a year. As that frustrated officer wrote to Foreign Secretary Anthony Eden: 'If our war effort is not to suffer it is of paramount importance that our propaganda machine should be put in order at the earliest possible moment.'[40] There was worse to come. Duff Cooper and his cumbrous ministry were mauled in debate in the House of Commons on 3 July and Duff Cooper was sacked: 'It was good of you to write. I confess I was rather taken aback by my abrupt dismissal from the MoI and I mind losing it very much.'[41] No sooner had Brendan Bracken been appointed Minister of Information in Duff Cooper's place than he was proposing the creation of a new Department of Political Warfare 'with the right to create and lay down policy for every government organ concerned with political warfare'.[42] The new department would be supervised by a committee of three; it would not be controlled by Dalton. The plan quickly won approval and Dalton found himself out-flanked. Plans for the department would be endorsed by September 1941, leaving Dalton running second in a two-horse race. Now he was engaged in a struggle with a man who was his equal, a man whose influence he feared. And, already, he had lost the first round: 'When Cooper was Minister of Information, Dalton made the running and the situation was containable. The arrival of Bracken, by contrast, rapidly drove Dalton to the edge of despair. Dalton saw Bracken as a rootless Tory adventurer; Bracken regarded Dalton as a Socialist careerist and intriguer.'[43] Bracken's biographer observes:

A distinctive temperamental incompatibility ruled out any chance of an understanding between Dalton and Bracken from the outset. Churchill's friend showed scorn for the air of 'omniscient superiority' assumed by his antagonist, an ex-economics don and writer who gave a uniform impression of looking down his nose at this new arrival as an impossible *arriviste*.[44]

The prime minister sat back and watched developments. It was a significant error of leadership. Earlier that year Dalton had circulated a witness statement complaining that Brendan Bracken had been criticising him at semi-public gatherings. Presented by Dalton to Labour leader Attlee, the complaint made its way to the prime minister who challenged his protégé. Far from contrite, Bracken dined out on the story for months: 'WSC sends for Brendan: "Is it true that at dinner the other night you attacked SO2 and Dalton's work?" "What I said was that Dalton was the biggest bloodiest shit I've ever met!" Winston laughed.'[45]

That last sentence suggests the prime minister never rated the issues associated with propaganda very highly on his list of priorities. The head of the Political Warfare Executive wrote after the war: 'Much of our teething trouble would have been modified if only the prime minister had been interested in political warfare. Unfortunately for us, this great man, himself our greatest war propagandist, attached at best a secondary importance to all forms of propaganda. Yet words counted.'[46] Churchill could have stepped in. He could have ended in a moment the wasteful infighting between the younger man he liked and the older man he did not. He chose not to, and so the mutual antipathy between those two powerful men, Hugh Dalton and Brendan Bracken, was permitted to drag on, even finding its way into formal correspondence:

> This resulted in one of the most appalling 'demarcation' disputes that I have ever witnessed. The correspondence which had started 'Brendan' and 'Dear Hugh' and passed 'Bracken' and 'Dear Dalton' ended up with communications of pure invective between the 'Dear Minister of Information' and his 'Dear Minister of Economic Warfare'. I must say I rather hope this interchange has been preserved somewhere as it really is a classic example of the 'Whitehall War' consequent on the establishment for war purposes of large and powerful organisations.[47]

The bickering continued throughout that summer and winter of 1941 with Bracken gradually gaining the upper hand in 1942. In those two years, Dalton would bring SOE to a certain prominence and notice. But he would also ensure that, as Europe's clandestine war got into its stride, the Special Operations Executive would be surrounded not just by foes abroad but by a cocktail of enemies at home as a prime minister, busy elsewhere, simply watched.

SOE was a new organisation, its methods and remit were shrouded in mystery, its very existence resented by clandestine 'friends' and service allies alike who saw no reason to welcome the new boy into their midst. While such initial resentment and dislike was perhaps inevitable, its month-in, month-out perpetuation was not. Yet that resentment, that dislike, would endure. And it would do so nurtured by that lack of strategic clarity and operational separateness that had surrounded its hasty creation at a time of unprecedented national desperation.

Notes

1 Stafford, *Britain and European Resistance 1940–1945*, p.42. COS (43) 212 (O) in CAB 80/69.
2 Mackenzie, *The Secret History of SOE*, p.348.
3 Stafford, *Britain and European Resistance 1940–1945*, p.37.
4 Richards, Sir Brooks, *Secret Flotillas* (HMSO, London, 1996), p.82.
5 Mackenzie, *The Secret History of SOE*, p.349.
6 Randolph Churchill visited his father at Admiralty House on the morning of 18 May 1940. There, as Churchill shaved, his son asked how Britain was to win the war: 'By this time he had dried and sponged his face and turning round to me said with great intensity: "I shall drag the United States in".' Source: Hastings, Max, *Finest Years* (Harper Press, London, 2009), p.18.
7 Stafford, *Britain and European Resistance 1940–1945*, p.40.
8 Mackenzie, *The Secret History of SOE*, p.350.
9 Mackenzie, *The Secret History of SOE*, p.352.
10 Stafford, *Britain and European Resistance 1940–1945*, p.71.
11 Foot, *SOE in France*, p.138.
12 Files HS 7/212 and HS 6/309 at The National Archives, Kew, reveal a detailed description of the de Gaulle/*Passy*/General Spears political aspects of this operation.
13 Foot, *SOE in France*, p.140.
14 File HS 8/251 at The National Archives, Kew. This file contains copies of Jebb's papers on 'Subversion' together with Gubbins' evaluation of the critical situation regarding aircraft availability in early 1941.
15 Mackenzie, *The Secret History of SOE*, p.364.
16 Marshall, Bruce, *The White Rabbit* (Pan, London, 1952), p.96.
17 Stafford, *Britain and European Resistance 1940–1945*, p.62.
18 Foot, *SOE in France*, p.15.
19 Mackenzie, *The Secret History of SOE*, p.416.
20 Stafford, *Britain and European Resistance 1940–1945*, p.61.
21 Wilkinson and Astley, *Gubbins and SOE*, p.99.
22 Boyle, A., *Poor, Dear Brendan* (Hutchinson, London, 1974), p.105.
23 Boyle, *Poor, Dear Brendan*, p.65.
24 Bracken to his friend 'Top', then Lord Wolmer, soon to be Lord Selborne, 23 July 1941: 'My Dear Top – When the PM drafted me to MOI he had the hardihood to say that it was worse than running a bomb disposal unit!' Source: the Selborne Papers, File C.1015 at the Bodleian Library, Oxford.
25 Boyle, *Poor, Dear Brendan*, p.266.
26 Lord Birkenhead, *Walter Monckton* (Collins, London, 1969), pp.185–6.
27 Olson, *Troublesome Young Men*, p.251.
28 McLaine, Ian, *Ministry of Morale* (George Allen & Unwin, London, 1979), p.82.
29 Foot, *SOE in France*, p.383.
30 West, *Secret War*, p.20.
31 Pimlott (ed.), *The Second World War Diary of Hugh Dalton: 1940–1945*, p.xxii.
32 Mackenzie, *The Secret History of SOE*, p.97.

33 Pimlott (ed.), *The Second World War Diary of Hugh Dalton: 1940–1945*, p.xxii.
34 Dalton, *The Fateful Years*, p.378.
35 Gladwyn, *The Memoirs of Lord Gladwyn*, p.102.
36 Pimlott (ed.), *The Second World War Diary of Hugh Dalton: 1940–1945*, p.270. Diary
   entry for 21 August 1941.
37 Pimlott, *Hugh Dalton*, p.321.
38 Pimlott, *Hugh Dalton*, p.321.
39 Young, Kenneth (ed.), *Diaries of Sir Robert Bruce*, Volume 11 (Macmillan, London,
   1980), p.85. Diary entry for 26 November 1940.
40 Garnett, David, *The Secret History of PWE* (St Ermin's Press, London, 2002), p.79.
41 Duff Cooper to Wolmer, later Lord Selborne, dated 22 July 1941. Source: the Selborne
   Papers, File C.1015 at the Bodleian Library, Oxford.
42 Mackenzie, *The Secret History of SOE*, p.100.
43 Pimlott (ed.), *The Second World War Diary of Hugh Dalton: 1940–1945*, p.xxiv.
44 Boyle, *Poor, Dear Brendan*, p.271.
45 Pimlott, *Hugh Dalton*, p.330.
46 Lockhart, *Comes the Reckoning*, p.127.
47 Gladwyn, *The Memoirs of Lord Gladwyn*, p.104.

CHAPTER NINE

FIERCE YOUNG ANIMALS

Those who start fires usually do so at arm's length. It follows that if the prime minister wanted Hugh Dalton's SOE to 'set Europe ablaze', then the first requirement was proximity to the seat of possible conflagration. To be able to start fires in Europe, however, SOE needed access to, and communications with, enemy-occupied territory, accurate intelligence, potential resisters and knowledge of conditions in Europe that would make their work possible. Gubbins was to write:

> SOE operations are dependent to a very large extent on the creation of subversive organisations in enemy-occupied territories. The establishment of communications is the pre-requisite for forming these organisations or employing existing ones.[1]

However, in the summer of 1940 and in the immediate aftermath of the chaos and retreat from Dunkirk, there was no easy way back to the enemy shore for Britain's clandestine services anxious to establish communications with 'the other side'. Yet this was a time when Britain's very survival depended upon the timely detection of enemy intentions. Invasion appeared imminent. SOE may have been charged with setting fire to Europe, but it was the Secret Intelligence Service that was ordered by the Directors of Naval, Military and Air Intelligence to provide at least a seventy-two-hour warning of a German invasion.[2] But SIS, its European intelligence-gathering operations decimated by *Blitzkrieg*, was effectively starting again from scratch. Other agencies also needed access to an as yet poorly defended central enemy coastline that stretched from Brest to the Hook of Holland. With no radio links into France – the suitcase wireless set was still in development and would remain so until later that winter – and with the concept of insertion by air still in its infancy, access by sea offered the only way back for those fringe organisations anxious to place their agents on occupied soil. It would be so for some time to come. In March 1941, Gubbins wrote: 'All the parties of men we are now training may well have to be landed by sea as no other means exist.'[3]

It is tempting to suppose, because there are now tidy, post-war histories of the conflict written with hindsight, that the war itself in those early days was a struggle fought to a neatly choreographed sequence of ordered and inevitable events. It was not. A study of the history of those early months reveals that chaos was never far beneath the surface. That near-chaos was a condition compounded by secrecy, rivalry, obstruction, duplication, chronic shortages and hand-to-mouth desperation as Britain's clandestine forces struggled to react to events orchestrated by a victorious enemy that appeared invincible. In that midst was an SOE that existed not only to bring sabotage, subversion and disruption to the occupying forces, but which adhered to a creed which included the vigorous deployment of *coup de main*[4] forces in raids on the enemy coast. This was a policy which appeared to conform to Churchill's desire for there to be that 'hand of steel' which came out of the sea to pluck German sentries from their posts.[5] Churchill's vivid rhetoric apart, the struggle with SIS over access to the enemy shoreline *by sea* was a struggle that SOE was destined to lose.

> There was a conflict of interest certainly from the beginning because the intelligence world wanted the coast left as private as possible to come and go, whereas SOE at the time thought that the only type of target they would be able to attack would be the ones nearer the coast because they hadn't got aircraft or parachutes to land them and (submarines) weren't going to be available. Consequently what use the two services would be able to make of the French coast was very much in debate.[6]

Professor Michael Foot believes that such a debate might have been triggered by a darker motive:

> Active SOE coastal operations, in fact, might imperil other work of different and perhaps greater strategic importance; and in any case, Combined Operations Headquarters had been set up specifically to undertake coastal raids, so there was no need for SOE to duplicate its work. It would seem as if the sound excuse for preventing raiding – that raids would stir up the Germans – was extended, beyond what it would reasonably cover, to prevent the infiltration of agents from a rival firm.[7]

It is a view not shared – or at least not recorded as being shared – by Sir Brooks Richards. In his seminal work *Secret Flotillas*, Richards, a distinguished post-war diplomat, elaborated on what he described from first-hand personal experience as simply 'a grave complication':

The trouble, from SIS's point of view, was that SOE, not content to wait for resistance to develop spontaneously, saw itself as a striking force whose blows would help convince opinion in occupied Europe that Great Britain was fighting on and was neither beaten nor cowed. This was why they planned small-scale raids on targets accessible from the sea as well as landing agents and cargoes of arms and explosives for subsequent use.[8]

SIS, meanwhile, was under pressure to get their agents into enemy-occupied territory and provide that early warning of plans for a German invasion. Sir Stewart Menzies set up two new SIS staff sections to produce intelligence on targets in France. One of these, to be independent of Free French forces, was under a Commander Wilfred Dunderdale, the former head of SIS's Paris Section until the fall of France. The second section, under Commander Kenneth Cohen RN, was tasked to work with General de Gaulle's embryonic Free French units. At the same time – and reflecting the close links that always existed between SIS and the senior service – an Operations Section was created to establish physical communications by air and sea between Britain and occupied Europe. This Operations Section of Naval Intelligence Division, NID(C) – the 'C' stood for clandestine – was commanded by Frank Slocum, a retired navigation specialist brought back into uniform as a commander RN at the outbreak of war. Air operations may have been within Slocum's remit – for now – but it would be some while before the RAF was ready to provide air transport for clandestine operations. Until then, sea was the only way into Europe. Early, chaotic days and fine, settled weather saw a rash of ad hoc missions to France, Holland and Belgium by a variety of agencies in a variety of small, unsuitable craft as British intelligence in its various guises tried to peer over the far side of the hill: Slocum's first SIS agent went ashore from a French motor torpedo boat (MTB) near Brest on the night of 20 June 1940 and was picked up and brought home eleven days later. At that same time, Commanders Dunderdale and Cohen of SIS, working independently from Commander Slocum, were starting to use French fishing boats to run clandestine missions to France. Dunderdale, working out of Mylor Creek upstream from Falmouth, was busy setting up the JOHNNY network which was soon providing vital intelligence on German shipping movements:

We had the *Scharnhorst* and *Gneisenau* bottled up in Brest and SIS has managed, through the Free French, to organise an intelligence circuit extending into the naval dockyard in Brest where they had got a highly placed French naval engineer as their agent. This group was able to report every time *Scharnhorst* and *Gneiseneau* came within three or four weeks of being ready to sail, so another big bombing raid would be carried out and this kept them bottled up in Brest, I think, for nearly a year.[9]

SOE also wanted to get its own agents into France and they too based their early operations on the south Cornish coast. Suitable boats, however, were hard to find from traditional sources, and submarines, though ideal, were in desperately short supply and could seldom be risked in low-value, shallow-water operations. Commander Slocum may have gained an early reputation as the unbending autocrat in Royal Navy uniform placed there to thwart SOE's operational intentions in favour of those of SIS, but he too had his difficulties: six new MTBs, built at Southampton for the eclipsed French Navy and now earmarked for Slocum's exclusive use, were commandeered over his head by Coastal Forces. It would be 1943 before Slocum was allocated his own flotilla of Dartmouth-based motor gun boats (MGB) for the clandestine missions of SIS, SOE and MI9 (the organisation responsible for the return of evaders). Until then, finding suitable boats for all those who came to him for passage to France proved a continual difficulty. But now, in early autumn 1940, worse was to follow.

Of the thirty-two missions Slocum attempted between June and October 1940 when the onset of winter weather called a halt to further quixotic trips in small, unsuitable boats, only three achieved results, whilst another – an ill-thought-out request by the newly formed Combined Operations to rescue Commandos erroneously believed to be stranded on Guernsey – was a pin-prick raid described by Churchill as a 'silly fiasco'.[10] As for the rest: of those thirty-two attempted landings, ten had been on behalf of SOE. Thanks to bad weather, poor planning, inexperience and enemy action, not one had been successful.[11] Those ten failed missions of SIS under Commander Slocum directly followed SOE's own attempt to side-step the Slocum/SIS boat queue by taking their agents across to France by sea themselves.

In early August a slow, noisy Belgian motor yacht lying at Newlyn was requisitioned, fitted out and despatched towards Primel, near Morlaix in Brittany, with three SOE agents on board. En route they ran into a German convoy and came under fire. The mission was abandoned and they were all lucky to return to Penzance unscathed. But not every mission escaped so lightly:

We were a good deal occupied by how to give ourselves a little protection against machine-gunning if we were caught in the area where we had no business to be as fishermen … I wanted to get hold of some non-magnetic armour and they said: 'Oh, far too expensive. That'll cost about £600.' However, a couple of well-bestowed bottles of whisky on the Petty Officer in charge of the naval side of dockyard repairs at Falmouth got us some non-magnetic armour put in place … Well, we were barely twenty miles off the Scillies. At the right time an aircraft appeared and came in towards us, so we fired the recognition signal but instead of firing the recognition signal back, as we expected, we were strafed from end to end by 20mm cannon. It was in fact a German Focke-Wulf

… and he came round and gave us a second dose. Fortunately, Gerry and I were able to take shelter behind the wheelhouse armour and consequently we were perfectly all right. One chap on deck was killed. He didn't die immediately but he was dead by the time we got into the Scillies.[12]

'Gerry' was the officer in charge of early operations, Gerry Holdsworth, a former member of Section D. Holdsworth had worked pre-war for SIS helping survey the Norwegian coastline under the cover story of the Royal Cruising Club:[13]

I was summoned to London and having arrived there my boss, who was Laurence Grand, the head of Section D, said there was an urgent requirement for a Frenchman to be taken from somewhere in the west country, not specified, to some area of France that he would know. Since I knew the French coast quite well, he thought I would probably be the chap to do it. I came to the conclusion that the obvious place to try this from would be the Cornish peninsula … somewhere like Newlyn and make for the Brittany coast, perhaps somewhere in the area of Brest.[14]

Transferred into the Royal Navy and then into SOE, Holdsworth's critical after-action report on the aborted Morlaix mission strengthened SOE's determination to run its own sea operations across to France. Holdsworth recommended strongly that SOE set up its own 'transport outfit' because, as he put it with a characteristic lack of tact, 'other people keep letting us down'.[15] Holdsworth would always make waves. Brooks Richards' younger brother Robin, who also served with the Flotilla, recalled:

Holdsworth was a very independent, tough-minded fellow and he regarded Slocum with great distrust and Slocum regarded him as a hothead and with great mistrust. Gerry Holdsworth was a buccaneer, a strong character. Although he was in naval uniform and had a naval rank he was very informal in his methods in the sense that if he wanted anything he would use any method that he could to accomplish it.[16]

Holdsworth's personal file would record: 'A most forceful personality. An expert in clandestine warfare in all its aspects. Never spares himself. Somewhat mercurial in temperament but with careful handling will give most loyal and conscientious service.'[17] Holdsworth's maverick, forthright character and his personal conflict with the unbending Commander Slocum in the months ahead would be a significant element in the thwarting of SOE's maritime ambitions. In October 1940, Holdsworth was authorised to find ships, recruit personnel and set up a suitable base. His plan – copied, one may assume, from leaks and whispers about the success of Dunderdale's and Cohen's SIS fishing boat missions out of Mylor a little further east along the coast – was to use SOE-crewed French fishing boats to mingle with the genuine article off French shores, exchange information and, eventually, land weapons and supplies for the nascent Resistance. This boat work would be unrelated to that of SIS. However, unknown to Sir Stewart Menzies and strictly against the rules, Commander Cohen was soon co-operating with F Section:

> The liaison with SIS started on a personal basis by periodical visits by F [Buckmaster] to Commander Cohen to read SIS files. This interesting experience had to be done 'sub rosa' and every Wednesday morning for nearly a year F crept into the Registry at Broadway with the connivance of Commander Cohen and [name blanked out] and studied the latest reports. The unwritten rules were that F could copy anything that interested him from a sabotage angle, but must not take the reports away. F spent many hours, pencil in hand, copying drawings which were frequently of great use here.[18]

That blanked out name is intriguing. Evidently it refers to some even more sensitive 'mole' within SIS prepared to help the fledgling SOE. Thus at local 'country section' level it appears that relations between SOE and SIS were significantly better than between their chiefs. Buckmaster did not join SOE until early 1941 and therefore it is unlikely that secret access to Cohen's SIS files helped Holdsworth in his very early work in Cornwall. However, although there is no record to this effect, it is quite possible that Holdsworth's work for SIS in Norway before the war had brought him into contact with Commander Cohen and that, at a local level, information about Cohen's operations from Mylor was simply exchanged between old friends. That would certainly be in keeping with Holdsworth's maverick disregard for the rules.

Finding a French fishing boat in wartime England in 1940 turned out to be the easiest of Holdsworth's tasks: many had crossed the Channel laden with refugees after the German invasion and were lying unmanned and abandoned in a dozen south coast ports. Boats found and requisitioned, Holdsworth would later obtain permission from the Naval Officer in Charge at Falmouth to set up his own small base on the Helford River between the Lizard and Falmouth: a secluded, deeply cleft, sheltered creek framed by thick oak woods that lay within striking distance of the enemy shore. In the light of what was to follow, the date of that meeting with the Falmouth admiral was propitious: 5 November 1940.[19]

Holdsworth next needed a shore base from which to run SOE operations from the Helford estuary: 'I was introduced to Mrs Bickford-Smith who owned a very charming house on the Helford River named Ridifarne. It was surrounded by trees and had its own little steps down to the foreshore and was in fact just opposite the deepest part of the river and altogether suitable.'[20] Ridifarne was requisitioned for the duration of hostilities without demur from its civilian owners. Gerry Holdsworth's glamorous blonde wife Mary, herself a Section D agent with distinguished service in Norway, was released from work in London to run the domestic side of Ridifarne and her husband was free to set up SOE Helford:

> We used fast craft to the north Breton coast where we had eight or nine hours of darkness because I could get from Helford over to the Breton coast by midnight, leaving our side about five-thirty in the afternoon, spend an hour ashore meeting my friends and delivering whatever it was, dynamite and things of that sort, stores, possibly collecting one or two people who the French were very keen to get back to hear what was going on and so on. And possibly, after they'd been in England a fortnight, they might return to me and at the first opportunity I'd take them over again.[21]

Gerry Holdsworth was having a good war, although it was not to last. The 'over there' that intelligence agents crossed to for both SIS and SOE offered contrasting coastlines and very different tactical approaches to those wishing to land agents, stores and weapons in occupied France. One option was simply to cross over at high speed at night in poor weather, make landfall on the rocky north coast of Brittany somewhere between St Brieuc to the east and L'Aber Wrac'h to the west, land and embark agents and stores and then withdraw swiftly before daylight. The second, longer option involved slower boats and stronger nerves: the use of camouflaged and requisitioned French fishing boats officered and crewed by British seamen. These boats would mingle with the real French fishing fleets on the banks south of Ushant and down past Pointe du Raz towards Audierne, Guilvinec and the small fishing ports beyond. In the absence of fast, seaworthy MTB craft that might or might not be available on loan from the Admiralty, Gerry Holdsworth looked for and found two French vessels abandoned by refugees: *Mutin*, a 60-ton yawl, and *Denise-Louise*, a small motor long-liner from Normandy. With Admiralty permission, he next recruited twelve volunteer crewmen from the Royal Naval Patrol Service Depot at Lowestoft. Peacetime fishermen and yacht-hands to a man, they welcomed the opportunity to work in civilian clothes and shed the conformity of regular naval service.

While Holdsworth began organising the SOE base at Helford, Commanders Dunderdale and Cohen of SIS had already stolen a march on SOE. In June a French MTB had delivered their first SIS agent to Brest, and another mission had followed in early July when HM submarine *H43* had landed an agent on Guernsey. At the end of that same month, Dunderdale had landed and recovered a French SIS agent at Guilvinec. A further operation was mounted to Morlaix on 30 July and four more SIS agent-landing operations were completed between August and early October 1940.

SIS also dropped its first agent into France by parachute in October. An account of that mission reveals just how much both SOE and SIS had yet to learn about the novel business of clandestine insertion and recovery by air. The mission began badly, deteriorated quickly and ended in farce. The SIS agent chosen was Philip Schneidau, aka *Felix*. Flown to the drop zone (DZ) by a Whitley bomber, the drop was aborted five times. On the sixth attempt, with two homing pigeons wrapped in socks (the pigeons were his only means of communication) *Felix* made his historic arrival on French soil on the night of 9 October 1940. Ten days later, missing his original rendezvous (RV) with the aircraft that was supposed to take him home, Schneidau released his pigeons with the message that he was at Fontainbleu awaiting transport. Twenty-four hours later a Lysander aircraft arrived from RAF Tangmere; Schneidau boarded and the aircraft took off. It was shot at by rifle fire on departure and the compass knocked out of action. Without any navigation aids, a waterlogged wireless set, an open rear cockpit and a jammed elevator, the Lysander lumbered towards home in the teeth of a south-westerly gale. Without compass or radio they became hopelessly lost. The pilot, Flight Lieutenant W.R. Farley, feared they might be over occupied Belgium, perhaps even Holland. Six hours later, at 0655hrs the next morning and with fuel gauges indicating empty, the engine cut. Farley ordered his passenger to remove all his civilian clothing as they were about to land in enemy territory: if dressed and captured, Schneidau could be shot as a spy. Schneidau undressed, and when they crash-landed he was lying in the back, stark naked. They crashed near Oban in western Scotland, having flown almost the entire length of the British Isles. Much would have to be learned by both SIS and SOE in the months to come.

Yet still – no missions by sea from Helford to France for Gerry Holdsworth and SOE. A month later, in November 1940, SOE undertook adventures of a different kind, this time involving a submarine – HMS *Talisman* – and a Royal Naval Volunteer Reserve (RNVR) officer seconded to Naval Intelligence named Merlin Minshall, who took five Free French RF SOE agents with him to settle an argument and establish once and for all whether German U-boats were using French Biscay ports.[22] In his own book about the exploits, Minshall implies that he acted alone.[23] It was not his only error. Attributing his actions to the mouth of the Gironde, HMS *Talisman* in fact surfaced off Ile de Croix, 160 miles to the north. They seized a French 60ft ketch-rigged tunneyman, the *Marie*. They impressed half the crew, trans-shipped the remainder to the submarine and then used the *Marie* as a platform upon which to spend six days observing U-boat movements as they charted pennant numbers, routes and armament. For a mission described in SOE's War Diary as 'colourful and extremely successful',[24]

Minshall, whose book makes no mention of the other five SOE agents with whom he shared the enterprise, received a Mention in Despatches (MID). Quite what five SOE agents were doing on a mission of pure intelligence-gathering led by an RNVR officer working for Naval Intelligence who had nothing whatever to do with subversion was never made clear. It was not the first time SOE was to stray on to another department's jealously guarded territory. This from a Combined Operations/SOE liaison officer's report a few months later: 'ACO have again received remonstration from Service Intelligence departments that SOE are NOT an intelligence organisation. They therefore viewed my recent enquiry on the extent of coastline on which they require domestic information with considerable misgiving.' In the margin of the paper an unnamed superior has written: 'I am not surprised. I have told Wyatt to keep off this or we shall be in trouble.'[25]

Arguably, they already were. Charles Morgan wrote in a paper entitled 'SOE – Teething Troubles':

Early in the year the newly-organised special operations executive (SOE) became a thorn in the flesh. It was created to undertake the subversive activities which had formerly belonged to Section 'D' of 'C's organisation and, being very young, was a little blinded by the cloak and dazzled by the dagger. Its relations with C are not our concern but its energies were for a time a source of considerable embarrassment to N.I.D. itself ... Some time was to pass before the fierce young animal became house-trained.[26]

Charles Morgan's neat use of words in that undated paper illuminate more than just the irritation of Naval Intelligence at SOE's seafaring ambitions. It reveals too how SOE continued to be viewed and patronised as a meddlesome, junior player and unequal partner in that wider game of clandestine maritime warfare.

Notes

1 Foot, *SOE in France*, p.59.
2 Richards, *Secret Flotillas*, p.24.
3 Foot, *SOE in France*, p.61.
4 File HS 8/203 at The National Archives, Kew: 'The object of a *coup de main* is to attack an important target with a party landed in the country for the specific purpose.' Undated SOE Objectives Board Memo from SOE HQ file covering period July 1942–February 1943. Memo entitled: 'Notes on the Selection of Targets for *Coup de Main* Parties and those Operating from the Field.'
5 Binney, Marcus, *Secret War Heroes* (Hodder & Stoughton, London, 2005), p.122.
6 Interview with Sir Brooks Richards by the author at Dartmouth in August 2001. Sir Brooks Richards DSC and Bar died in September 2002.
7 Foot, *SOE in France*, p.64.
8 Richards, *Secret Flotillas*, p.91.

9 Interview with Sir Brooks Richards. Sound Archive No. 9970 at the Imperial War Museum, London.

10 Fergusson, Bernard, *The Watery Maze* (Collins, London, 1961), p.49.

11 Richards, *Secret Flotillas*, p.29.

12 Bailey, Roderick, *Forgotten Voices of the Secret War* (Ebury Press, London), p.79. Audio interview with Brooks Richards.

13 File HS 7/4 at The National Archives, Kew, contains a detailed twenty-two-page report on the 'landing possibilities' on the Norwegian coast identified by Holdsworth and his companions.

14 Sound Archive interview, No. 12304 with Gerry Holdsworth at the Imperial War Museum, London.

15 Richards, *Secret Flotillas*, p.91.

16 Bailey, *Forgotten Voices of The Secret War*, p.77. Quoting Sub Lieutenant Robin Richards in audio interview.

17 Gerald Holdsworth personal file HS 9/7692 held at The National Archives, Kew.

18 File HS 7/121 at The National Archives, Kew entitled 'F. Section History' written by Colonel Buckmaster, p.19. The report is undated.

19 Richards, *Secret Flotillas*, p.102.

20 Direct quotation attributed to Gerry Holdsworth in private papers passed to this author by a former member of Slocum's irregular forces.

21 Sound Archive interview, No. 12304 with Gerry Holdsworth at the Imperial War Museum, London.

22 Richards, *Secret Flotillas*, p.92.

23 Minshall, Merlin, *Guilt Edged* (Bachman & Turner, London, 1976).

24 Foot, *SOE in France*, p.138.

25 File HS 8/819 at The National Archives, Kew. Report dated 5 December 1941.

26 File ADM 223/480 at The National Archives, Kew, p.257. Morgan's rank and responsibilities are not mentioned. The paper is undated.

CHAPTER TEN

A SEA OF TROUBLES

Merlin Minshall's November 1940 mission to Brittany was perhaps nothing more than yet another example of random, seized opportunity and of the chaos and confusion that dogged those early months of SOE's existence. Operation *Shamrock* did, however, yield results:

> The information procured by personal observation and by the interrogation of the French fishermen proved of great value to the Navy and the RAF and it is understood that successful operations based on this information were shortly afterwards undertaken.[1]

Meanwhile, back in Helford, nothing is recorded of any attempts by Holdsworth and his crew to use his newly refurbished and reconditioned French and Belgian fishing vessels for agent and arms' delivery drops across the Channel. This, despite the fact that MTBs on loan from Coastal Forces were used on five unsuccessful attempts between May and June 1941 to land three SOE agents near Anse de Brehec in support of the AUTOGYRO network. Two of those five missions failed because of bad weather. The other three failed because the agents concerned refused to land. At this time Holdsworth took possession of RAF 360, a small 41ft seaplane tender on loan from the RAF, who hoped Holdsworth might use it to help rescue RAF airmen ditched in the Channel. He didn't. Instead, on 11 September and 14 October 1941, he and Brooks Richards, his second-in-command, completed two missions in a vessel that Brooks admitted was 'really too slow, too small and too vulnerable for the work Holdsworth hoped to carry out for SOE'.[2] The first of these missions was to collect intelligence reports for SIS from Ile de Batz, off Roscoff, the second to land two SOE agents near Aber-Benoit to the west. Improbably, both missions were successful, that first run to Ile de Batz representing the first successful operation to France by high-speed craft for thirteen months.[3] Brooks Richards claims they were simply 'lucky' – unusually, bright moonlight and calm seas were on their side. Upon their return,

Commander Slocum, in effect their area commander, ruled that RAF 360 must in future only be used for summer crossings, perhaps deliberately overlooking the logical consequence of such an edict: that RAF 360's limited range and slow top speed would preclude a return trip to the enemy coast in the short hours of summer darkness. Despite repeated requests from Holdsworth, no larger boats were forthcoming. That same winter Gerry Holdsworth proposed an SOE raid across to Guernsey to capture a German E-boat. 'General idea approved, and E-boat is badly required by the Admiralty', records a report.[4] To be followed by: 'Both C and G3 Admiralty have replied that they cannot supply the necessary craft for this operation.' With no boat, the idea went nowhere and, with *Mutin* in major refit, left SOE without an operational carrier and Holdsworth was reduced to the role of boatwork officer on a vessel commanded by someone else. Brooks Richards wrote delicately: 'This change of status was by no means congenial to a man of a highly independent disposition who had previously commanded his own ship on operations.'[5] Holdsworth's and Richards' frustration might have been sweetened by the knowledge that two subsequent attempts by others to make the same RV for SIS both failed[6] and that two further attempts by borrowed MTBs for SIS on 13 and 15 October, the first to embark an agent – Joel le Tac, one of the those involved with Operation *Savanna* – and the second to pick up intelligence reports, failed also. The first failed because of enemy action, the second because of the weather. Moreover, the latter, Operation *Polish III*, failed with Slocum's second-in-command, Lieutenant Commander E.A.G. Davis, aboard as navigator. Davis was a peacetime Cunard-line navigating officer aboard the luxury liner *Queen Mary*.

At this remove, the phrase 'because of the weather' slips past almost without notice. Yet weather, in all its cruel and sudden variables, was the deal-breaker for missions for both SOE and SIS. Trips to the coast of North Brittany were made to pinpoint RVs, at night, in silence and darkness to a rock-fanged, unlit and inhospitable enemy shoreline scoured by 6 knot (kts) lateral currents and a tidal range of 30ft between high and low water springs. In peacetime, that northern coast of Brittany could be a graveyard for unwary shipping. In wartime, its hidden, timeless dangers were multiplied tenfold. That highly experienced Cunard navigator, Lieutenant Commander Davis, advised in his after-action report to Slocum after Operation *Tenderly* to lay sonar buoys near Triagoz and Ile Losquet for SIS:

> ... of all the festering collections of rocks on this rotten coast, the Ile-Losquet area wins the hamburger. Not one of the islands on the chart could be distinguished. The swell here was most uncomfortable and its action on the outlying reefs was most impressive. It would start as a white break with a rumble and develop as a white express train with about the same volume of sound.[7]

Pinpoint navigation to a hostile, dangerous winter shore, at night, was the key to the success of every mission that crossed to the northern coast of Brittany. One of the most successful of such navigators for SOE was David Birkin, a sickly, shore-based telegraphist promoted to RNVR lieutenant after exploiting a peace-time acquaintance with Brendan Bracken[8] to wrangle an attachment to Slocum's irregular navy. Beset with blurred vision, bleeding lungs, recurrent sinus head-aches and the guaranteed certainty of violent seasickness on even the calmest of days, Birkin was later awarded the Distinguished Service Cross (DSC). Seldom have medals been harder earned. David Birkin died in 1991 but left a detailed description of the Breton shore and his work as navigating officer crammed into a tiny chartroom behind the wheelhouse of one of Slocum's MTBs:

> There can be few less hospitable coastlines than that of North Brittany where the Atlantic joins the English Channel in the Western Approaches. It is rugged, wild, and romantically sinister with its masses of offshore islands and islets, reefs and rocks, some just submerged at high water, others towering above the surface like gigantic icebergs, often miles out to sea.
>
> Even in fine weather, a long low swell rumbles in from the Atlantic, breaking into white foam on anything in its path. But when a south westerly wind blows – and it is apt to reach gale force in a disconcertingly short space of time – the effect is devastating. The whole coastline becomes a cauldron of boiling surf as the breakers race shorewards with the speed and noise of an express train.
>
> The chart room was a model of idiotic planning. It was as though the designers had put their energy and brains into constructing as near a torture chamber as possible, and with considerable success … Over the chart table a feeble electric lamp just illuminated half a normal-size chart … a voice pipe over the table connecting with the bridge … I would never have believed the movement of an MTB's chart room could have been so horrible. It was like being shut in a hen coop attached to a universal joint placed in a high-speed lift operated by a madman. The table was an indescribable mess of rusty water cascading down the voice pipe from the bridge, sick and blood from the bash-ings of my head against every kind of projection.[9]

The secret of Birkin's success, mission after mission, was the painstaking draw-ing on a chart of the levels of exposure of every large rock close inshore that he might expect to pass on passage at all states of the tide. Birkin navigated with pinpoint accuracy on twenty-eight missions for SIS, SOE and MI9, primarily to the area around L'Aber Wrac'h. This author has kayaked amongst those same inhospitable offshore islands in poor weather when what David Birkin achieved, at night, in winter, in wartime and with only the most basic of navigational aids, takes on an impressive significance impossible to capture on the printed page.

Despite Slocum's lack of success, other boats were crossing to France. Commander Dunderdale mounted five missions from Mylor to northern France between July 1940 and spring 1941, before the entrapment of his French fishing vessel *L'Emigrant* off Plouha on 19 April 1941 brought his fishing-boat activities to an abrupt end. In February, another of his vessels, *Marie-Louise*, had also been arrested and towed into Brest. From now on, Commander Slocum would exercise direct control of all SIS surface-sea operations.[10] There were other carriers too for, despite expectations, submarines at this time were carrying agents and observers across to France, their secondary task of agent collection and delivery sanctioned by their strategic primary mission to keep watch off Brest for the possible breakout of the German battlecruisers *Scharnhorst* and *Gneisenau*.

One of those submarines was HMS *Sealion* which brought out a young Frenchman whose contribution to Commander Slocum's clandestine endeavours for SIS would sound the death-knell on SOE's hopes of penetration to the enemy shoreline. Daniel Lomenech, aged 19 and whose parents owned a tunny fish cannery south of Concarneau, had helped set up Dunderdale's JOHNNY circuit. He then escaped from France by fishing boat in mid-September 1940: 'He was very bright, very impetuous for an intelligence agent, rather rash, immensely brave and I mean, for a teenager to come out when he did like that showed he was very determined'.[11]

Arriving in England and swiftly recruited into SIS, Daniel Lomenech was dropped back on to the French coast near Pont-Aven to assess the strength of German forces along the coast and return to England. After several more trips to the coast of France by submarine acting as conducting officer,[12] Lomenech went to Slocum with what seemed to him to be an original suggestion. In fact, it was the same idea that had occurred to both Dunderdale and Holdsworth:

> What you want is one of the local trawlers that are working and behaving like a Frenchman ... these little trawlers have permission to stay out three or four days at a time and if we could get another one of them we can lurk about and instead of the agent ashore having to fit in with our plans entirely, we can fit in with when he can deliver.

Commander Slocum agreed. Lomenech, together with another of Slocum's officers, Stephen Mackenzie, were ordered to find a suitable boat. They did so and, in the months that followed, *N51 Le Dinan* was re-engined and fitted out. On 15 December 1941 Lomenech sailed for France aboard the French fishing boat *La Brise*. Her destination was Iles Glenan where she was to land and hide food and stores for RAF evaders. Operation *Hatchet* was never completed: Lomenech's captain, a Scots RNR civilian trawler skipper, found courage in a bottle on the voyage down Channel and ran the boat on to rocks off Ushant.

'I heard a row in the crew's quarters. I went in and what did I see? The Captain who was really drunk, standing up with a grenade in each hand and telling the men he was going to throw them at them if they did not agree to surrender vessel and crew to the Boches.' Nineteen-year-old Daniel Lomenech assumed command, locked his captain in the hold and turned the boat back out to sea. As Lomenech told the story at the formal inquiry afterwards:

> While we were under way I heard an explosion which came from the hold. I opened it up and saw the Captain sitting down, looking dazed. His head was flopping from right to left, his eyes looked at me reproachfully. He must have primed a grenade which had exploded under him. Then, bang! He died without saying a word.[13]

Lomenech brought *La Brise* back to the Scillies. In February 1942 *Le N51's* refit was complete and she was ready for operations. Again, however, early days did not run smoothly: her skipper had to be replaced after endangering his crew. Richard Townsend was on board. An experienced peacetime sailor, he was nevertheless on a month's probation as Slocum's newest recruit:

> I checked over his workings and found that he had made some elementary blunder, pointed out that our present course would eventually put us back on the French coast and that all he had to do was to steer north and make a landfall. So we arrived back in Dartmouth, all of us seething in discontent and total lack of confidence in our CO.[14]

The officer was transferred and Daniel Lomenech was appointed in his place: 'He was obviously the man for the job and we all had a great respect for his seamanship and drive. The ship's company was devoted to him and would have done anything with him aboard. We were, for security purposes, called the Inshore Patrol and N51 was painted grey like any warship.'[15] Richard Townsend was appointed first lieutenant and, with Lomenech, would work for SIS, not SOE.

It was the outstanding success of this working relationship between Lomenech, Mackenzie and Townsend that was both to frustrate and hobble SOE's maritime ambitions on the French coast. Fuelling the intractable SOE/SIS tactical argument, it would also push SOE's maritime role at Helford to the margins of operational viability. Back on the mainland, Townsend's boat sometimes shared moorings with SOE on the Helford River. John Garrett remembered:

> SOE had offices ashore. They were periodically visited by what struck us as wild young men with an unhealthy way of playing with explosives. I remember one who was given to leaving exploding pencils around the place. More certain

was an SOE exploit that gave us grounds for worry. One of their MFVs [Motor Fishing Vessels] went down to Scilly on a training exercise and managed to hit a rock in the harbour and the boat became a total loss. We felt that on no account should SOE be allowed to trespass on our ground in the Bay of Biscay, which was becoming familiar territory.[16]

Lieutenant John Garnett served with both Richard Townsend and Daniel Lomenech on the Helford Flotilla. He too was unimpressed with what he saw of SOE: 'These two organisations [SOE and SIS] were utterly split from top to bottom, right down at even the most local level. On the whole, although many plans were made, in the years that I was [at Helford] SOE did nothing very much as far as I could discover, other than practice and prepare boats.'[17]

A little harsh, perhaps, but it was the impression that endured into unpublished post-war memoirs. This author has been struck, when searching official records for successful SOE crossings to the shores of northern France, by the fact that many months appear to elapse with little of significance to report. Helford and its SOE personnel appear to have spent much time running assault courses, learning pistol shooting and doing ship painting, repair and maintenance; they practised stalking, unarmed combat, escape and evasion drills and silent approaches to a dark shoreline by dory and mother craft. But there were few operations using the requisitioned boats from Helford. Three Operation *Overcloud* agent landing/embarking operations were mounted in late 1941 and early 1942, but none of them appear to have involved Holdsworth nor any of the boats from Helford. The same holds true for SOE Operations *Pickaxe*, *Waterworks* and *Rowan* in January and February 1942, all three of which used MGB 314, usually sailing from either Falmouth or Dartmouth, to land and embark agents east off Roscoff.

That reference to the Isles of Scilly in Townsend's recollections hints at the role those islands played in the missions of both SOE and SIS. For it was there, in New Grimsby Sound, that those commandeered French fishing boats underwent a sudden, dramatic and colourful transformation:

On the French coast we had to look like any other local fishing boat with our port of registration numbers painted in large and flamboyant lettering on the bulwarks.

Each port had its own style and it was necessary to get the design right as well as choose a plausible number. The Breton fishermen who had escaped and were working out of Newlyn were a useful source of such information. The fishing fleet over in France were very short of material, especially paint, so the boats looked incredibly worn and scruffy. We had to paint ours in the bright and cheerful colours dear to the Bretons but at the same time hide the fact that the paint was new …

Not only did the ship have to look right, so did we. We were issued with canvas trousers and smocks as well as peaked caps so that we looked more or less like Breton fishermen … We were, of course, scarcely armed. We were issued also with Tommy guns, colt revolvers, hand grenades, commando knives etc. Our only hope in the case of being challenged was to get alongside the challenging vessel, shoot away its aerial, lob hand grenades into the radio room, wheelhouse and engine room and take the ship by storm. This plan, luckily, was never put to the test.[18]

It was not long before *N51*, commanded by Mackenzie with Lomenech as first lieutenant and Townsend as junior officer under training, was ready for operations. Their first mission, in April 1942, was to:

Plant boxes for posting mail at various points along the coast. We were given submersible steel canisters with chains to attach them to the pillar buoys which are all along the main thoroughfares of the French coast … On our way down we stopped alongside two or three of the huge pillar buoys which marked dangers. The weather was quite exceptionally calm and we had no difficulty in attaching our canisters.

In May 1942 *Le Dinan* received orders to sail to collect an intelligence agent and his family who would RV with *Le Dinan* by fishing boat off Iles de Glenan. At the last minute, however, Operation *Marie Louise* was delayed. Mackenzie received permission to sail on reconnaissance anyway. Their trip was successful and they tried a second time on 20 May 1942, waiting for their target boat, *Les Deux Anges*, to make the RV. It failed to do so and they returned to the Isles of Scilly and their secret anchorage in New Grimsby Sound. There, *Le Dinan*'s newly painted bright colours were over-painted yet again in drab Admiralty grey before she returned to the mainland. In June 1942 they were ordered away again – this time there was to be no mistake. The mission turned out to be hugely important. Its verbatim report, written first hand, is worth quoting at length:

1630: We reached the position with half an hour in hand and proceeded to steam up and down as though we were trawling. Five o'clock, six o'clock passed while our hopes gradually faded away. Another failure; another voyage for nothing. A little after six, black smoke appeared on the southern horizon, quickly followed by the appearance of five German corvettes steaming up the convoy route towards us. We held our course watching them anxiously, for they would pass all too close.

As the corvette came on Jasper, the Cox'n, nudged my arm and pointed towards the islands. A tiny white sail had appeared there, too far off to identify but clearly making out to sea. The excitement grew intense. The corvettes lent the final touch of colour to the situation. We reached the end of our run and turned, letting them overtake us to starboard … We could see the Captain examining us through glasses from the Bridge. Then they were past, the casual inspection over.

We watched the white sail tacking to and fro till the corvettes had disappeared. At last it steadied on a seaward course, making directly for us. We made our signal, identified ourselves and went alongside.

One thing puzzled me: on the deck of *Les Deux Anges* stood only three persons, all obvious fishermen. Yet we expected to see three passengers at least besides the children. It was not until the two ships were fast alongside, heaving up and down unevenly in the light swell, that they appeared. It seemed amazing that so many people could be hidden in that little cockleshell of a boat. They certainly had been hidden, and had survived a German inspection when the vessel left harbour. Now they emerged in lengthy succession: a woman three children ranging between eleven and five years old, a man with several suitcases and finally M. Raymond himself with a bag full of papers in one hand and in the other – an eighteen months old baby.

Rapidly they were helped on board, choosing the moments when the deck of *Les Deux Anges* heaved up to our gunwhale. The stores we had brought for the fishermen handed over – petrol, oil and some food and tobacco. In five minutes it was all over, the warps were cast off and *Les Deux Anges* turned away in a wide circle. I felt deeply moved by the sight we had seen: four young children and their mother helped to safety, their smiles of thanks, their obvious confidence of security in our hands. Jasper was at the wheel staring straight ahead. His voice when he spoke was gruffer, his language more picturesque than usual. After a few moments I left him and went out on deck. Cookie Nash, still grasping his coffee pot, was gazing at the retreating coast and there were tears in his eyes. This is no exaggeration: there was not a man among the crew that did not feel the sentimental strength of that dramatic meeting.[19]

The next day they made landfall at New Grimsby Sound on the Isles of Scilly:

All was friendly, welcoming, unchanged. We had already signalled the Admiralty the happy result of the expedition and had expected to find a gunboat waiting to take our passengers to the mainland. Within half an hour of our making fast we heard the drones of her engines beyond the point and we waited idly for her coming …

Agent *Raymond* takes up the story:

The water was wonderfully green and clear. The bottom, which was at least eight metres under our hull, could be seen in the minutest detail. I could not resist the desire to dive in. I borrowed a pair of swimming trunks and jumped into the water which was as icy as it was beautiful. While I was swimming I heard a fanfare coming from the other side of the trawler. The children were calling me to come back on board quickly, quickly. I lost some time trying to find the rope ladder and I missed the spectacle. Edith described it to me: a fast patrol boat of great beauty, long and white, shining in the sun, the crew standing *to attention* [his emphasis] on the foredeck, all the flags flying, the sound of music (I learned later it was a gramophone record playing through a loud speaker) playing a military march, the officers on the bridge standing to attention and saluting … a truly royal reception.[20]

Raymond – also alias *Remy*, real name Colonel Gilbert Renault – had earned his salute. He was the leader of what was destined to become one of the most influential and effective of all Free French intelligence networks in France – *Confrérie de Notre-Dame* (CND). The papers he brought with him to England aboard *Le Dinan* contained drawings of all German defences along the Normandy coast from Cherbourg to Honfleur – the area that, in two years' time, would become the D-Day invasion beaches. Operation *Marie Louise* had been a resounding success. Now the threatened sea link to Brittany was secured. *Remy* would be returned to France by *Le Dinan* in October and that vital SIS sea-line to *Remy*'s network would be maintained until October 1943.

After the collapse of Dunderdale's SIS networks, SIS had become critically dependent upon CND's output. It became Slocum's mission to ensure that nothing – especially not SOE operations – risked endangering that intelligence source and its sea route back to England. Post-war, Slocum would claim that he 'never entirely succeeded in convincing SOE that he was not prejudiced in favour of SIS'.[21] It is not surprising for the evidence suggests that he manifestly was. And that his primary loyalty, perhaps understandably, was always to Rear Admiral J.H. Godfrey, Director of Naval Intelligence (DNI), who insisted that 'the collection of intelligence in regard to the enemy and the safeguarding of the means of collecting this intelligence in the future must always have priority over other subversive activities'.[22]

Even while Operation *Marie Louise* was being planned back in April 1942, Slocum was already moving towards a decision that would ensure that SIS, effectively, had the sea to themselves. Having reviewed the suitability of vessels approaching the German-occupied French coast, he concluded that only the smallest of boats would be suited to escape German observation and reported:

To employ *Denise Louise* [an SOE vessel] would be running a considerable risk. *Mutin* could work as a tunny boat between May and October. Under no conditions, however, could *Mutin* operate outside the tunny season. The situation as it stands at present is therefore:

The Helford River Flotilla, being composed of large ships, is not suitable for carrying out operations in close proximity to the French coast.[23]

Mutin and *Denise Louise* were too large; RAF 360 was too small. SOE Helford, it appeared, was running out of both ships and friends. Referring to another mission, *Engineer II*, thwarted by Slocum, Gubbins went on record as thinking: 'it was really another case of obstruction. SOE could, of course, always put off *Engineer II* until December when Slocum would find some other objection to doing it, and so on.'[24] Yet support was at hand. Five days after Slocum penned that report, on 15 April 1942, the flotilla was watched at exercise by a senior officer who reported: 'In spite of what Slocum may contend, Holdsworth assures me – and from the little I could see he was amply justified – that she [RAF 360] has first class sea-going qualities and in expert hands should be perfectly capable of carrying out an operation in Brittany. I think we have a case for a further attack on Slocum to allow Holdsworth to use her when the situation arises.'[25] Now Slocum planned to visit the Helford Flotilla himself. On 22 April 1942, a week later, Stephen Mackenzie warned Holdsworth from Slocum's London office:

The enclosed intelligence report on the French fishing fleet vessel situation – March 1942 – has been received from Slocum. Attached to it Slocum sent me a minute, the gist of which is as follows:

He stated that his main preoccupation was the suitability of your ships for their intended work ...

All the above seems to lead him gravely to doubt the ability of your ships to enter the Bay of Biscay and operate unsuspected by the enemy. Maybe there is something in all this, but doubtless you know the answers better than anyone this end. I have therefore set it all out in some detail so that you may be prepared to shoot down Slocum's arguments when he comes to see you.[26]

Gerry Holdsworth fired back an angry response three days later:

Dear Mac,
Answering your letter of 22nd April – I have read the 'intelligence' report and return it herewith. It contains nothing that we didn't know before, except a few inaccuracies. Most of it was supplied to Blow'ard by Peake and Pierre when he worked here with us months ago ... Whatever Capt Slocum and his experts (?) think of their craft or, for that matter, of ours, concerns me not at all. Once again I tell you that we have got ourselves the finest collection of sea-going,

working, typical Breton fishing vessels capable of covering ALL seasons that is to be had in this Country and this War. It doesn't matter a bugger if they're built in Havre or Honolulu so long as when we've finished with them they look 100% Breton. Pierre says they do! No, the facts are we're being written-down so that we can be bought up cheap, and I for one am just about sick of it. It's perhaps worth bearing in mind that SOE personnel Richards and Holdsworth don't want to be bought up cheap, or for that matter, dear, by the first TOM, DICK or HARRY who comes swaggering down Whitehall. And what's more I'm going to take damn good care it doesn't happen. SOE – or, as it was then, D Section – told me to get on and fix them up a transport outfit to operate to Brittany because Slocum kept on letting them down. Well, it's been done and on those occasions when it's been used it hasn't once failed. I confirm again and for the last time that our ships are the right type for Brittany, south of the Chasse de Seine RIGHT NOW.

Gerry[27]

A month later, Slocum was still attempting to gather information about the Helford Flotilla. A request from NID(C) in London for Holdsworth to forward on photographs and dimensions of all Helford vessels was met with the frosty: 'Phoned Captain Slocum and told him Holdsworth had left and therefore photographs could not be produced.'[28]

Attempts were already in hand to bring the three 'Irregular' flotillas – requisitioned French fishing boats and MTBs at Dartmouth, Falmouth and Helford – under single, unified, accountable command in which the fleets of SIS and SOE would be amalgamated, all operational vessels would be taken over by the Royal Navy, the post of NID(C) would be abolished and a newly promoted Captain Slocum would assume a new title: DDOD(I), Deputy Director Operations Division (Irregular). This move entirely supported, if not actually orchestrated, by Slocum, was to come to fruition in the spring of 1943. In the autumn of 1942, however, Holdsworth found another way of taking his men to the enemy shore: he devised a series of 'Lardering' operations – missions in which weapons, stores and equipment were taken across to the French shore and buried in watertight containers in the sand at low water for later retrieval. Of the six *Carpenter* missions in October, only one succeeded in landing and burying weapons. The rest failed in bad weather. Three further attempts between January and March also failed; one was cancelled. A final attempt – *Carpenter III* – to land half a ton of SOE stores and bury them in sand near Ile Stagadon also failed: Robin Richards was on that last 'Lardering' mission:

The intention was to build up stores or warlike arms in sealed camouflaged containers on the north coast of Brittany. We started from Dartmouth in a Fairmile gunboat. The gunboat dropped anchor, we landed our ton of stores on one of the islets, tried to bury them, found there was no soil and simply had to camouflage them as best we could with seaweed and branches, got barked at by a dog, and by the mercy of providence managed to find our way back to our gunboat.[29]

It was an inauspicious end to an unsuccessful series of operations created by Holdsworth to find a mission for his men after the Admiralty vetoed his plans for an independent SOE sea-line into Brittany. Reviewing progress in October 1942 after three of the first four *Carpenter* operations had ended in failure, D/Navy had written to Gubbins through D/CD(O) (Deputy CD (Operations)):

The result of SOE's attempts to transport stores by sea in recent months has been very unsatisfactory. This naturally gives rise to the question as to whether the operational control is satisfactory, and the fact that this control is not in SOE's hands makes us wonder if we could not do better ourselves.

Larder Operations on the West Coast of France: these have given unsatisfactory results because:

Insufficient suitable fishing vessels are available and –

There is a conflict of interests between SIS and SOE imposing a restricted programme upon the latter.[30]

The officer who compiled this report goes on to suggest that the officer who until then had controlled SOE's maritime activities had been 'over-cautious' and had been 'slow' to produce the new craft SOE needed. The letter is tactful and concedes that the present system of operational control whereby SOE had to apply to NID(C) for permission before mounting any operation of its own was 'clumsy'. The Deputy Director of Operations to whom his report was addressed did not mince his words. Writing to Gubbins four days later, he recorded:

I cannot agree with D/Navy's opinion of Captain Slocum. Under a charming exterior and constant profession of being all out to help us in every way he can, he has succeeded through his wiles in almost entirely defeating our attempts in having any sea contact with the North and West coasts of France. On almost every occasion we have tried to do something there has been to him some good and adequate reason why the operation was impossible, and he unfortunately has the last say ...

I agree that the present system of operational control is clumsy, but I am sure that you will agree that to put both SOE and SIS naval sections under the same naval officer would spell ruination for us, and I still think that one day we shall get our way if we only batter on against the wall.[31]

In that summer of 1942, a new officer in London took over control of SOE Naval Section. One of the first tasks of Captain Simpson was to tackle Slocum's reservations about the physical suitability of Holdsworth's fishing fleet. With NID(C) approval of the type of vessels he chose, Simpson requisitioned a further four French fishing boats and had them converted for stores' carrying. The first of these was ready for operations in autumn 1942 and Gubbins and Simpson visited Holdsworth at Helford to discuss a new mission using those boats approved by Slocum: 'At the last moment, however, when all details had been worked out, a ban was placed by Slocum on all SOE operations to the west coast of France for fear of compromising the SIS fishing-vessel mail service.'[32]

Colonel *Remy* and the fishing-boat exploits of Lomenech, Mackenzie and Townsend were to take absolute precedence. For Holdsworth, it was the last straw. He handed over command of the base and sailed for Africa with *Mutin* and most of the Helford operational personnel: 'Gerry lost the battle with Slocum. Slocum finally achieved his overall control of clandestine traffic in the Channel and so Gerry Holdsworth stuck two fingers up, said "bugger that" and got into *Mutin* and pushed off to Gibraltar and North Africa to make a new career for himself.'[33]

Files detailing the exchanges and volleys of minutes and memoranda between Captain Slocum and Gerry Holdsworth remain untraced. Two letters have been found, however, which give some indication as to the heat and venom of their exchanges. A letter dated 14 February 1943 discussing future posting for Gerry Holdsworth when he returned from Africa states bluntly: 'We cannot let him down by expecting him to serve under Slocum.'[34] A letter from Captain Simpson of SOE's Naval Section, signed the following day on 15 February 1943, records: 'Lt Commander Holdsworth has been severely admonished by his Commanding Officer and has since proceeded abroad on operational duties. It is therefore suggested that the Admiralty letter to him calling for a report be not forwarded.'[35]

With Holdsworth in Africa, the amalgamation of the SOE and SIS flotillas went ahead without incident in summer 1943. With pressure from the Flag Officer in Charge at Falmouth to see affairs within his command centralised, the senior naval officer and the SOE commander in Helford were now formally required to:

... work in the closest co-operation and draw up a mutually agreed periodical period of training. The operations, whether for 'C' or SOE to be initiated as hitherto and Operation orders to be issued from NID(C) Headquarters in London in collaboration with the SOE, Naval Staff, London, and Helford

River. The above proposed organisation should remove all difficulties regarding the different duties required of the present SOE and 'C' crews.[36]

The new system appears to have worked. Lieutenant Commander Bevil Warington-Smyth, Holdsworth's successor, recorded:

> It [the amalgamation] enabled everyone to get to know each other, and it came as a source of great surprise to more than one Officer (and to some of the more intelligent ratings) to discover that – contrary to what they had been educated to believe – the principal enemy was Hitler and not their opposite number on the sister organisation.[37]

An end to the in-fighting between SIS and SOE at Helford rang down the curtain on a period of 'needless waste':[38] twenty months from February 1942 to October 1943 when not one SOE agent had entered or left France by sea via the north and west coasts. SOE Helford was to enjoy a final blaze of glory almost ten months later when, on Christmas Day 1943, their boat-handling, dory-landing and recovery skills were enlisted by SIS to help with the evacuation of twenty-eight evaders from the off-lying island Ile Taric, Aber Benoit. It was, undoubtedly, SOE Helford's finest hour. But it had very little to do with setting Europe ablaze.

The ban on SOE activities on to Breton beaches initiated by Slocum on behalf of SIS hampered the development of SOE *réseaux* on a vital shoreline at an important time. Existing historiography[39] leaves unresolved the question as to whether that ban was justified by the results achieved. It also side-steps the darker, more political motive for the frustration of SOE's legitimate maritime ambitions to land agents in northern Brittany. Yet the conclusion seems inescapable: the work of CND was important, assuredly. But it was important in large measure because of the absence of other networks. If SOE had been trusted, if SOE had been permitted clandestine access to that forbidden and forbidding coastline, its agents could perhaps, in the later stages of this period, have helped create more *reseaux* at a time when the people of France were just beginning to stir; just beginning to shrug off that air of pragmatic defeatism that had been the hallmark of Pétain's new regime and at least begin to contemplate the possibility of armed resistance. Yet, in the final analysis, SOE's freedom of action and independence, its ability to support Britain's wider intelligence effort, was deliberately out-manoeuvred and thwarted by internal politics and by the convenient higher strategic priorities of rival SIS and its surrogate, NID(C).

Notes

1 Foot, *SOE in France*, p.138.
2 Richards, *Secret Flotillas*, p.103.
3 Richards, *Secret Flotillas*, p.109.
4 File HS 8/819 at The National Archives, Kew. Liaison officer's report November 1941–December 1942.
5 Richards, *Secret Flotillas*, pp.116–7.
6 Richards, *Secret Flotillas*, p.309.
7 Richards, *Secret Flotillas*, p.155.
8 Personal letter to David Birkin from Brendan Bracken loaned to the author by his widow, Judy Birkin. She died in June 2004.
9 David Birkin's personal papers loaned to the author by his widow, Judy Birkin.
10 Richards, *Secret Flotillas*, p.81.
11 Interview by the author with Sir Brooks Richards at Dartmouth, August 2001.
12 Personal papers passed to the author by former members of the Helford Flotilla.
13 Verbatim account of this incident recorded by Colonel Gilbert Renault, alias *Remy*, and recorded in his own *Memoires d'un Agent Secret de la France Libre* and passed to this author by veterans of the Helford Flotilla.
14 Townsend, Lieutenant R.U.D., DSC, 'Reminiscences of N51'. Amongst unpublished papers loaned to this author by his widow, Mrs Ursula Townsend.
15 Townsend, 'Reminiscences of N51'.
16 Townsend, 'Reminiscences of N51'.
17 Personal recollection. Papers passed to this author by veterans of the Helford Flotilla.
18 Townsend, 'Reminiscences of N51'.
19 Personal papers. An extract from *Operation Marie Louise*, a personal account of this operation by Steven Mackenzie and passed to this author by veterans of the Helford Flotilla.
20 Extract from notes from *Memoires d'un Agent Secret de la France Libre* by Colonel Gilbert Renault, alias *Remy*, alias *Raymond*.
21 Richards, *Secret Flotillas*, p.162.
22 Jeffery, *MI6 The History of the Secret Intelligence Service 1909*–1949, p.354.
23 File HS 8/770 at The National Archives, Kew. Memo written by Slocum on 10 April 1942.
24 File HS 7/245 at The National Archives, Kew. SOE Minutes October–December 1942.
25 File HS 8/770 at The National Archives, Kew. Memo written by Slocum on 10 April 1942.
26 File HS 8/770 at The National Archives, Kew.
27 File HS 8/770 at The National Archives, Kew.
28 File HS 8/770 at The National Archives, Kew.
29 Bailey, *Forgotten Voices of the Secret War*, pp.77–8. Audio recording with Sub Lieutenant Robin Richards.
30 File HS 8/823 at The National Archives, Kew.
31 File HS 8/823 at The National Archives, Kew.
32 Richards, *Secret Flotillas*, p.146.
33 Excerpt from Sound Archive interview with Robin Richards No. 27462 held at the Imperial War Museum, London.
34 File HS 8/823 at The National Archives, Kew.
35 Found in Holdsworth's personal file in HS 9/729/2 at The National Archives, Kew. No further details have come to light.
36 File HS 8/770 at The National Archives, Kew.

37 Foot, *SOE in France*, p.65
38 Richards, *Secret Flotillas*, p.239
39 Foot, *SOE in France*, p.64

CHAPTER ELEVEN

COMBINED OPERATIONS:
TO THE ENEMY SHORE

The Special Operations Executive was not the only major British organisation that was born out of the fear, chaos and confusion of those sweeping, early German victories in summer 1940. Like SOE, Combined Operations would be created to meet a specific and hitherto overlooked strategic need. It too would have to weather a similar climate of suspicion and entrenched early disapproval. Unlike SOE, however, that initial hostility would be eroded by success and by the drive, charm and leadership of a man whose style would contrast sharply with that of the boorish, Socialist politician who headed SOE. Combined Operations would prosper too in the gathering momentum and increasing sophistication of the war itself; a momentum married to the inescapable realisation that, in the absence of Britain's defeat, the war could only be concluded after the successful landing and retention of Allied troops upon the shores of occupied Europe. An irony whose significance has been overlooked thus far in the historiography of both SOE and Combined Operations is that whilst both organisations came into being during the same summer of 1940, both also shared early chiefs whose personal style, animus and political ambition hampered and obscured the development of the organisation they led. Thus a poorly chosen appointment by Churchill at the head of Combined Operations during its early, formative months was soon to have external consequences and a direct impact upon Combined Operations' relationship with SOE. Three disparate but soon-to-be complementary ideas converged in that summer of 1940 to bring about the creation of Combined Operations: the resurrection of the Inter-services Training and Development Centre (ISTDC), the creation of the independent strike force that would be known as the Commandos and an impatient series of memoranda from the new prime minister who was determined to lean forward into Europe.

Between the wars, Combined Operations as a concept – the transportation of ground troops to a hostile shore supported by the Royal Navy and the Royal Air Force – had been haunted by the bloody failure of the Allied landings at Gallipoli in 1915: a botched, long-delayed and long-signalled landing that had resulted in more than 140,000 Allied casualties. That preoccupation with historic failure was brought to an end by a far-sighted paper of review in 1936, written by Captain Bertram Wilson of the Royal Naval Staff College at Greenwich.[1] He gathered together the lessons that had been learned from the last war, warned that lack of forward thinking would shackle Britain to the same mistakes in the next, and briskly recommended the steps that should be taken to plan for and anticipate Combined Operations in the future. Two years passed before another well-argued paper arrived on the desks of the Chiefs of Staff, this time from Sir Ronald Adam, Deputy Chief of the General Staff. Persuaded by the clarity of the arguments no less than the gathering momentum and urgency of events in Europe, the Chiefs of Staff created the Inter-services Training and Development Centre to investigate all aspects of Combined Operations. In keeping with the austerity of the times, ISTDC consisted of four officers, a small clerical staff, a free hand and £30,000.[2] Importantly, they also had access to both the Deputy Chiefs of Staff and the Joint Intelligence Committee. In the immediate weeks after their creation, ISTDC's four officers prepared far-sighted reports on suitable craft for landing tanks, beach organisation, floating piers, headquarters' ships, amphibious tanks, underwater obstacles and the logistical problems attendant upon landing stores, ammunition, water and petrol on an enemy shore. Much of those early days were spent working out what sort of mother ships, landing craft and support vessels would be suitable. Another paper was prepared and, with brutal clarity, pressed the case for a £350,000 assault craft-building programme. That was in June 1939. War was declared in September and ISTDC was inexplicably disbanded, with Britain's only team of Combined Operations specialists dispersed. Restored to life before the end of 1940, much that it had recommended in the last months of peace was to become the basis of a sound and huge expansion in war.

Meanwhile, elsewhere in the War Office, Brigadier Dudley Clarke, brought up in the Transvaal on stories of the Boer Commandos in the South African War at the turn of the century, wondered to his superior officer, General Sir John Dill, if British amphibious troops could not be raised and trained for a similar role.[3] It was a timely suggestion. On 4 June 1940, Churchill told the House of Commons that Britain 'would not be content with a defensive war'.[4] Returning to his office that same afternoon, he minuted General Ismay, his newly appointed Chief of Staff, urging him to adopt an offensive habit of mind:

Enterprises must be prepared with specially trained troops of the hunter class who can develop a reign of terror first of all on the 'butcher and bolt' policy. I look to the Chiefs of Staff to propose me measures for a vigorous enterprising and ceaseless offensive against the whole German occupied coastline.[5]

Dill took Clarke's suggestion to the Chiefs of Staff Committee. They approved the concept, placed Clarke in command and ordered him to organise a small raid across the Channel at the earliest opportunity; in an otherwise disastrous campaign, the fighting in Norway had already revealed just how effective small-scale raiding parties could be behind an extended enemy front line. It is an irony not lost to military historians but one which passed unnoticed at the time that these small raiding parties were recruited from the newly formed independent companies created by Jo Holland, the then head of MI(R). And they were commanded by Brigadier Colin Gubbins, who, via the command of Britain's Stay-behind Auxiliary Units, would become, in November, SOE's Director of Operations and Training. Less than a week later, on 11 June 1940, the Chiefs of Staff were proposing the appointment of a commander, offensive operations, to 'prepare, as a matter of urgency, plans which he should subsequently execute'.[6] In his book *Grand Strategy*, Butler claims the directive was approved and Lieutenant General A.G. Bourne, Royal Marines, was subsequently appointed. Others, notably Fergusson,[7] claim Bourne's appointment was made without Churchill's approval; a fact which perhaps accounts for his short tenure in office. For the moment, however, Lieutenant General Bourne was appointed 'Commander of Raiding Operations on coasts in enemy occupation, and Adviser to the Chiefs of Staff on Combined Operations'.

Bourne was promised the six independent companies raised for Norway together with the 'Irregular Commandos', which were then being raised. Paratroopers too were pledged when they became available. Whilst his Combined Operations role specified he was to advise on the organisation of opposed landings, supervise training and the development of whatever specialised craft would be needed, it was raiding that was the early priority; and raids there were. On 24 June 1940, the day immediately after France surrendered, 115 officers and men of No. 11 Independent Company crossed the Channel in eight RAF air-sea rescue launches. They landed at three sites around Boulogne, killed two Germans near Le Touquet and returned without loss.

A month later and five days before the prime minister gave Dr Dalton his potentially conflicting instructions to 'set Europe ablaze', there was another raid, this time against Guernsey. Confusion, navigational errors, out-dated intelligence and a rising sea that left three non-swimmers behind on the enemy shore was not the sort of high-impact dividend Churchill had been hoping for. 'Let there be no more silly fiascos like those perpetrated at Boulogne and Guernsey,' he pronounced. 'The idea of working all these coasts up against us by pin-prick raids is one to be strictly avoided.'[8] From there on, it was, and it would be nine months before Britain's raiders set foot again on the enemy shore. In a minute to Eden, his Secretary of State for War, Churchill outlined the broader picture: a series of 'medium raids' by between 5,000 and 10,000 troops. Two or three of these raids might be 'brought off' on the French coast during the coming winter. Detailed plans could be started just as soon as the immediate threat of invasion had receded. Once those medium raids had taken place there would be 'no objection ... to stirring up the French coast by minor forays'.[9]

The Guernsey raid took place on 14 June 1940, and even while it was being planned Churchill was thinking about General Bourne's replacement. For weeks an old friend, Admiral of the Fleet Sir Roger Keyes, the hero of Zeebrugge, now aged 68, had been pestering him for a position of responsibility in the New Order. Earlier that summer, in full naval dress uniform, Keyes had addressed the House of Commons on the failings of the Norwegian campaign and, in a halting, poorly delivered speech as powerfully remembered for its angry, spell-binding sincerity as the 'Cromwell' speech of Leo Amery, flayed both Chamberlain, the prime minister, and the Admiralty – with Churchill at its helm as First Lord – for perceived failings of leadership, strategy and clarity of intention. The debate, wrote one of Churchill's later biographers, was 'one of the most memorable in British history'.[10] In a devastating attack, Keyes accused former friends and allies at the Admiralty of a lack of nerve during the failed Norwegian campaign. Later still, recorded Fergusson, 'He once told the assembled Chiefs of Staff that they were "yellow"'. It was, commented Fergusson dryly, 'an opportunity that comes the way of few'.[11]

Now, with the shameless exploitation of friendship and past favours, the old war horse was pushing for one last charge. The man who had written to Churchill in April 1940 urging 'For God's sake put your trust in me and don't waste any more time', and who had been promised by Churchill when First Sea Lord that he would, in time, 'find a mission for me worthy of my abilities',[12] wrote to Churchill on 4 July 1940:

I am told that my speech was decisive in helping you to get the freedom and power you needed ... Apart from considerations of friendship, which has been steadfast from my side, is the Country so flush of people with the experience I possess and the qualities you so handsomely attributed to me ... that you can afford to continue to ignore me at this critical hour?

Three days later Bourne had gone. Churchill wrote in his memoirs: 'In July I created a separate Combined Operations Command under the Chiefs of Staff and Admiral of the Fleet Sir Roger Keyes became its chief. His close personal contact with me and with the Defence office served to overcome any departmental difficulties arising from this unusual appointment.'[13]

The appointment was more than just unusual: it smacked of nepotism. Certainly, General Hastings Ismay, Churchill's Chief of Staff, and John Colville, Churchill's assistant private secretary, thought so.[14] Churchill's final sentence, too, was not borne out by the reaction of those senior naval officers who found themselves working with an elderly naval officer who had retired from active duty as commander-in-chief Portsmouth in 1931. Keyes, they felt, was out of touch with the realities of modern warfare. He was a man, most certainly, who had little time for nuance or diplomacy. If a diplomat was needed to smooth relations with the Chiefs of Staff and with senior officers in all three services – and it was – then Keyes was a strange choice. Bourne moved aside without protest, however, bowing before the prime minister's personal compliment:

> General Bourne should be informed that, owing to the larger scope now to be given to these operations, it is essential to have an officer of higher rank in charge, and that the change in no way reflects upon him or those associated with him. I formed a high opinion of this officer's work as Adjutant-General Royal Marines.[15]

Evidently the possibility of simply elevating Bourne to the rank required was an option Churchill chose not to exercise. Bourne's parting gift to the organisation he commanded for exactly one calendar month was a prescient warning. There was, he believed, 'Too much overlapping between several service and Government departments, all concerned with the one aim of undermining the enemy, causing confusion'.[16]

His recommendation to the Chiefs of Staff, made in the week before Dalton was appointed to head of SOE and MI(R), Section D and Electra House, who found themselves absorbed into the new subversive organisation, was that all these activities should be co-ordinated under a single Cabinet minister. It is at least arguable that, had General Bourne's advice been heeded at the time, much of the rivalry, confusion and wasteful duplication that followed might have been avoided. As it was, Bourne was relieved and Keyes took over. He did so at a delicate time: 'Combined Operations began in an atmosphere of controversy and acrimony. They were hated by all three established services, and came in for special loathing from the Admiralty.'[17] The Royal Navy, claimed Hollis, who was secretary to the Chiefs of Staff Committee and deputy head of the Military Wing of the War Cabinet, were traditionally jealous of what they imagined might become a rival concern. Other sources echo that impression:

> The Admiralty showed its contempt for Combined Operations by foolishly relegating it to a Cinderella of the Services, giving it as personnel officers those it wished to be rid of and ratings who were either Active Service men so undisciplined that they could not be controlled in a battleship, or the poorest material among the Hostilities Only entries.[18]

Philip Ziegler, biographer of Lord Louis Mountbatten, arguably the most successful of all commanders of Combined Operations, reported that Combined Operations was 'seen by the Admiralty and, indeed, the rest of Whitehall, to be little more than an exotic naval by-blow ... The Chiefs of Staff – indeed, almost all of the principal military figures of the day – viewed Combined Operations with distrust if not dislike'.[19] With General Bourne dismissed, Keyes swept into power, telling a colleague that Churchill had always meant the job for him but had been thwarted by the Chiefs of Staff whose choice Bourne had been.[20] Keyes wrote to Churchill on 22 July 1940:

> I must tell you how happy I am – and that I am most grateful to you for giving me this opportunity of proving that I am not as useless as my detractors, whoever they may be, would have you think.
>   I am your very devoted
>   Roger[21]

Churchill may have been glad to get him; the Chiefs of Staff to a man were not. Many thought he was simply, and dangerously, too old for active service in a new and young man's war. One of those, Admiral Sir Dudley Pound, First Sea Lord, wrote to Admiral of the Fleet Sir Andrew Cunningham on 12 December 1940: 'I pointed out to the PM that the employment of an officer of Roger Keyes' age on a job of this kind was entirely opposed to the policy which we were urged to adopt of only employing young officers at sea. However, the PM is as pig-headed as a mule over these things and his reply was that RK was full of the flame of war etc.'[22] The principal problem, wrote Pound's biographer, Robin Broadhurst, was 'Keyes' rampant ego'.[23] One of Keyes' friends, the commander-in-chief Portsmouth, Admiral Sir William James, wrote:

> He [Keyes] is thrilled with the new job Winston has given him. He is to raise an independent force for Combined Operations and – this is the strange feature – to be responsible only to the prime minister. I do not see how he is to get his men, material and boats unless through the Chiefs of Staff or launch an operation without their concurrence, and said so. But he is in 'full flight' and sees no difficulties. Time will tell.[24]

It was an astute observation by an admiral who warned a little later: 'He [Keyes] sees no breakers ahead.'[25] The prime minister, in fact, had ordered Keyes to establish contact with the service departments, not through him, but through General Ismay representing the Minister of Defence – Churchill himself.[26] It was to prove an ultimately fatal distinction which Keyes was to ignore at his peril: 'For the moment, and to a degree which was never to recur, he was his own master: subject, according to the directive which he had inherited, only to the Chiefs of Staff; subject, as he saw it, only to the prime minister.'[27]

Someone else who was also observing the new head of Combined Operations was Hugh Dalton, the head of one of those 'service and government departments' with whom Bourne had warned there might be 'a good deal of overlapping with the risk of confusion in execution' unless all were co-ordinated under the control of a single Cabinet minister.[28] Hugh Dalton noted shortly after his appointment on 19 July 1940:

> Fletcher to lunch ... I ask him to keep things sweet between the First Lord [Pound] to whom he continues to be PPS, old Keyes and me – a sort of triangular liaison. He says that Keyes has been saying that he has 'sailed into action' against my new appointment, but I understand that, having seen the PM, he sailed out again![29]

The 'Fletcher' Dalton refers to is Commander Fletcher MP, who was to sit on the newly formed Special Operations (SO) Board as the representative of the Director of Combined Operations. Significantly, that SO Board 'disappeared'[30] in February 1941 and was not replaced, leaving in its absence a vacuum of formal liaison between the two new organisations that would not be filled until Keyes' replacement by Lord Mountbatten.

Despite the recognition of the need for close liaison, there appears to have been no entry in either man's diary about any meeting early in Keyes' tenure. In the New Year, Keyes would write to a colleague in reply to his correspondent's disparaging remarks about an earlier operation: 'I thoroughly agree with you in all you say about these little side-shows. It was inspired by Dalton's party and arranged while I was in Scotland training troops and crews for Assault Landing Craft for a *real* [Keyes' emphasis] Combined Operation'.[31]

Diary entries apart, it is hard to envisage much warmth and friendship between the Socialist minister who knew Admiral Keyes had lobbied unsuccessfully against his appointment and a restored firebrand Conservative admiral who appeared to consider any request for co-operation from 'Dalton's party' to be beneath the serious consideration of Combined Operations. The territory between their two organisations was 'ill-defined and potentially unlimited' with plenty of scope for conflict if Keyes had coveted Dalton's sphere of operations. It appears he did not and, by December 1940, both men had worked out a 'rather vague but amicable' agreement that attempted to set down lines of demarcation. Keyes had his hands full with his inheritance from General Bourne. His request had been approved for the allocation of four ships to be landing-craft carriers and depot ships, 200 landing craft, 100 motor boats, ten independent companies of 200 men each and a further ten Commando units of 500 men. There was also to be a parachute training centre and enough converted Whitley bombers to carry 720 fully armed men.

By 6 August, Keyes was reporting that arrangements had been made for combined operations training in Inveraray in western Scotland; that four of the ten independent companies were now trained, twelve Commandos had been raised and a further 500 specially trained volunteers were undergoing parachute training. And there, in September 1940, things halted: all independent companies and Commando forces were placed at the disposal of Home Forces to assist in repelling the anticipated German invasion. SOE was not so constrained. If the creation of Combined Operations went some way to nullify the claim of both army and Royal Navy/Royal Marines that raids to the enemy shore lay within their area of expertise, SOE felt no such inhibition. In any event, they too, like Combined Operations, were fumbling to define the perimeters of their own role. It would be early 1942 before SOE and Combined Operations 'agreed to co-operate rather than squabble over demarcation'.[32] Initially, matters appear to have proceeded amicably enough. Gladwyn Jebb wrote to Dalton on 8 August 1940:

> I saw Commander Fletcher this morning and discussed with him the question of our liaison with the DCO [Directorate of Combined Operations]. Commander Fletcher and I agreed that it would be extremely difficult to lay down any hard and fast rule for distinguishing between a 'combined' operation and a 'D' Operation. Obviously, something involving two or three hundred men would come within the former category, but the exact number could hardly be laid down in advance. As Commander Fletcher remarked, to do so would be like trying to make a precise distinction between a large heap of stones and a small heap of stones, the difference being one stone! We agreed, therefore, that in practice the thing to do would be for me to tell him, from time to time, in confidence, of projects on the coasts of Europe which we might have in mind to carry out. He would then pass this information on to Admiral Keyes who would decide whether he was, *prima facie*, interested or not.[33]

Such casual informality may have been well-meant between two professionals anxious to work together to the mutual advantage of their new organisations, but its 'from time to time' vagueness would lead to the very confusion the now-departed General Bourne had counselled against. Less than a fortnight later, such potential for further duplication between SOE and Combined Operations was committed to paper in a secret SOE report:

> In addition to the expansion of those revolutionary organisations which will be required for the eventual underground counter-offensive against Germany, a trained body is required capable of undertaking sabotage projects on and

near the coast of occupied territory. Such a body will consist of specially selected individuals of mixed nationalities under a carefully chosen director and will carry out such sabotage projects as may from time to time be remitted to it. Such acts are purely local attacks and are not part of the eventual revolutionary movement. They may, however, contribute to our knowledge of the enemy in the various countries and provide us with papers and experienced saboteurs, who may be invaluable later.[34]

Towards the end of that same month – August 1940 – Keyes led his staff out of the Admiralty to new, larger and independent offices in Richmond Terrace, off Whitehall. It was a move calculated to affirm the independence of Combined Operations and establish Keyes' new command as a genuinely inter-service organisation without binding ties and obligations to the senior service. Within days Keyes and his staff were considering 'many brave options'[35] to keep faith with the prime minister's urging to carry out raids. Plans submitted for approval to the Chiefs of Staff, however, met with an increasingly hostile reception:

None of the earlier plans put up by Combined Operations had been noticeably successful, but since Keyes had the ear of the prime minister, they had to fall in with his wishes and examine all his proposals. Indeed, this gallant old Admiral continually bombarded them with new ideas and plans for attack. They soon groaned when they saw his name on any new folder.[36]

Wherever else Admiral Keyes was searching for glory – he proposed, amongst several others, a raid on the island of Pantellaria between Sicily and Tunis which he intended to lead himself – he did not appear to covet that which his friend and mentor the prime minister had handed to Dalton. Stuck in a mental time-warp of his own by-gone age, Keyes had little time, it appears, for meetings of co-ordination with 'Dalton's party'. On 4 September 1940, a major reported to Dalton:

I had a telephone message from Commander Fletcher this morning regretting that the DCO [Director of Combined Operations: Admiral Keyes] could not arrange for the two meetings with SO2 [SOE] which had been agreed upon for Monday next. It will be recalled that these meetings were to deal respectively with questions concerning training and the advisability of organising, at this stage, small raids on the coastline held by the enemy. Commander Fletcher gave no explanation for this postponement, beyond the fact that the DCO was not yet in a position to give his views.[37]

On the bottom of that note, Dalton has written in his own hand: 'This non-co-operative attitude is very unfortunate. The JPC [Joint Planning Committee] have tried to help, but have not succeeded so far.'[38] There would shortly be a more concerted attempt to lay down established guidelines for co-operation between SOE and Combined Operations. Yet the files show that, almost three years later, Admiral Lord Louis Mountbatten, chief of a hugely expanded Combined Operations, was still attempting to set up some form of formal liaison mechanism that would prevent overlapping between his Commandos in Combined Operations and the agents of SOE:

> I am writing to confirm our conversation yesterday when we discussed the creation of your new Commando and the possibility of overlapping with SOE in raiding operations from this country onto the coast of Western Europe. Personally, I believe that very little overlapping can occur provided there is close liaison at the planning stage so that each project can be judged on its merits. I would suggest, therefore, that in order to ensure co-ordination in general, Neville[39] should get in touch with Brigadier Mockler-Ferryman[40] and work out a *modus operandi* for approval, the main objective being to ensure that any plans for small raiding operations are properly co-ordinated between the two organisations to the greatest discomfort of the enemy.[41]

Mountbatten's memorandum was written on 23 June 1943, and it is quoted here at length in a passage concerned with the unfolding events of autumn 1940 to illustrate that, despite what might be formally recorded in the minutes of various meetings aimed at improving co-operation between the two organisations, the problems of liaison between Combined Operations and SOE persisted far into the war. Extant SOE files and minutes reveal something else too: that whilst Admiral Keyes made much of the inaction and operational timidity of others, his directorate too came in for criticism from SOE in the months immediately after his appointment.

An undated paper from the same period reviews the scope for Combined Operations to take the fight to the enemy. It bears the official Admiralty watermark, together with a stigmata of confessed failure and operational pessimism which is confirmed in an SOE report on a joint meeting on 16 December 1940 at which 'DCO maintained that raids on the western seaboard as far as they were concerned were very limited. A) On account of lack of craft; B) On account of German vigilance.'[42] That Admiralty paper referred to in the SOE report of 16 December 1940 listed a long series of possible raids. Each was followed by a pessimistic justification of inaction: 'No action by DCO being contemplated … Not at present being considered by DCO … Small chance of success … No raid being contemplated … has not been executed owing to the improbability of success in the face of anticipated opposition.' Someone in SOE – the handwriting appears to be Dalton's – has underscored these twenty excerpts in red ink and then added at the top of the page: 'a cemetery of tiny hopes.'[43] The unidentified author of a report on that same meeting reported back to SOE's Gladwyn Jebb:

> The atmosphere of course, was very cordial although no-one quite knew why the meeting had been convened, there was no agenda and my paper, in fact, formed the basis for discussion.
>
> It was clear that the DCO is now paralysed as far as raiding parties from this country to the western seaboard are concerned, and these will be carried out in future by SO2 with foreigners.
>
> This, of course, places a large responsibility on our shoulders and we shall have to sharpen our weapons as regards recruitment and training of desperadoes, the establishment of a proper intelligence and planning department and an increase in our sea transport facilities.[44]

Dalton added to this in ink: 'Very interesting. But this should be carefully discussed with SO2 before we undertaken to conduct these coastal raids. I am all for them – when we are ready – and I hope this may be soon – but not before.'[45]

If not one of raids, then December 1940 was at least a month of papers and meetings: on 14 December Major Davies of SOE put up a paper entitled 'Raiding Parties'.[46] It began by recognising the distinction between DCO raids – 'substantially those where fairly large bodies of troops are concerned, namely, from 50 upwards, and where it is the intention to withdraw the raiding party later' – and those of SO2,[47] 'primarily concerned with raids involving acts of sabotage on specific objectives with foreign personnel, and up to fifty in number'.[48] Major Davies felt it essential that DCO and SO2 should collaborate over the selection of targets, that they should provide mutual assistance regarding both communications and transport, and that SOE could be 'called upon by DCO to effect forward reconnaissance in respect of any raids which DCO may have in mind'. It was a recommendation which would come to nothing, as SOE would mount no 'forward reconnaissance' raids for DCO or anyone else.

Davies' forward thinking was nearer the mark, however, when he wrote: 'Although SO2 cannot exclude the possibility of a smash and grab raid, their chief role will be the infiltration of small bodies. They will also not only confine themselves to coastline sabotage, but also to raids in the interior.'[49]

Slowly, at one meeting after another, SOE was groping towards evolving a definition of its own role. But no mention yet of insertion by air: or of parachutes, DZs, secret radios, 'Reception Committees' or *réseaux*. Papers of vision and foresight from attached majors were not the same as face-to-face inter-departmental liaison. As far as Dalton's diary was concerned, early that month: 'There is no liaison with DCO. We don't know what he is up to.'[50]

Something appeared to change. A fortnight later the DCO and SO2/SOE, together with Commander Arnold-Foster from SIS, met to discuss relations between all three organisations and Major Davies' paper on 'Raiding Parties'. SOE were in attendance despite the earlier private reservation that DCO appeared to be 'paralysed' where raiding was concerned. The meeting agreed – in principle at least – that in 'certain' (but unspecified) operations, 'DCO and SO2 could help one another'. They agreed that DCO, SOE and SIS 'will always keep each other informed at an early date of any project under consideration'.[51] It was to prove a fond hope. SIS was already signalling alarm at the declared raiding intentions of both DCO and SOE – raiding which must, they believed, disrupt the peace and quiet on the enemy shore that was essential if SIS's agents were to go about their work collecting secret intelligence secretly:

> The Representative of 'C', Commander Arnold-Foster, stated that while this organisation recognised the necessity for raids, he wished it to be recorded that raids on the Atlantic seaboard (including Channel and North Sea) were detrimental to the collection of intelligence by his department.[52]

Brooks Richards commented later: 'The implication was clear: Commando raids and SOE attacks on coastal targets might imperil work of a different and perhaps greater, strategic importance.'[53] Gerry Holdsworth, the firebrand commander of the Helford Flotilla and Admiral Keyes, the firebrand commander of Combined Operations, had common cause.

Notes

1 Fergusson, *The Watery Maze*, p.37.
2 Fergusson, *The Watery Maze*, p.38.
3 Aspinall-Oglander, Cecil, *Roger Keyes* (The Hogarth Press, London, 1951), p.381.
4 Oral Answers, House of Commons Debates, 4 June 1940, Volume 361, Cols 787–98.
5 Allan, Stuart, *Commando Country* (National Museums Scotland, Edinburgh, 2007), p.84. Cabinet Records CAB 120/414 at The National Archives, Kew.
6 Butler, J., *History of the Second World War, Grand Strategy*, Volume II (HMSO, London, 1957), p.259.
7 Fergusson, *The Watery Maze*, p.51.
8 Fergusson, *The Watery Maze*, p.49.
9 Gilbert, *Winston S. Churchill*, Volume VI, p.676.
10 Manchester, *The Caged Lion*, p.654.
11 Fergusson, *The Watery Maze*, p.85.
12 Halpern, Paul (ed.), *The Keyes Papers*, Volume III: '1939–1945' (George Allen & Unwin, London, 1981), p.8. Keyes to Admiral Sir William Reginald Hall.
13 Churchill, Winston S., *The Second World War*, Volume II: 'Their Finest Hour' (Cassell & Co., London, 1949), p.219.
14 Broadhurst, Robin, *Churchill's Anchor* (Leo Cooper, London, 2000), p.187.
15 Fergusson, *The Watery Maze*, p.51. Memorandum from the prime minister to General

Ismay and Sir Edward Bridges, 17 July 1940.

16 Butler, *History of the Second World War, Grand Strategy*, Volume II, p.259.

17 Leasor, James and Hollis, General Leslie, *War at the Top* (Michael Joseph, London, 1959), p.119.

18 Deacon, *A History of British Secret Service*, p.347.

19 Ziegler, Philip, *Mountbatten: The Official Biography* (Book Club Associates, London, 1985), p.155.

20 Halpern, *The Keyes Papers*, Volume III: '1939–1945', p 91.Keyes to Tomkinson, 29 July 1940.

21 Aspinall-Oglander, *Roger Keyes*, p.384.

22 Broadhurst, *Churchill's Anchor*, p.187.

23 Broadhurst, *Churchill's Anchor*, p.187.

24 James, Admiral Sir William, *The Portsmouth Letters* (Macmillan & Co., London, 1946), p.77.

25 James, *The Portsmouth Letters*, p.93.

26 Cookridge, *Inside SOE*, p.4.

27 Fergusson, *The Watery Maze*, p.53.

28 Butler, *History of the Second World War, Grand Strategy*, Volume II, p.260.

29 Pimlott (ed.), *The Second World War Diary of Hugh Dalton: 1940–1945*, p.62. Diary entry for 22 July 1940.

30 Mackenzie, *The Secret History of SOE*, p.94.

31 Halpern, *The Keyes Papers*, Volume III: '1939–1945', p.156. Keyes to Tomkinson, 29 July 1940.

32 Ziegler, *Mountbatten: The Official Biography*, p.166.

33 File HS 8/818 at The National Archives, Kew. Dated 8 August 1940.

34 File HS 8/818 at The National Archives, Kew. Dated 20 August 1940.

35 Leasor and Hollis, *War at the Top*, p.120.

36 Leasor and Hollis, *War at the Top*, p.121.

37 File HS 8/818 at The National Archives, Kew. Dated 4 September 1940.

38 There appears to be some confusion as to the origins of this note. At the paper's head there is the date '4.9.40'. At its foot, beneath Davies' signature, the date is recorded as '7th December 1940'.

39 General Sir Robert Neville KCMG CBE, Royal Marines. Assistant Director of Naval Intelligence.

40 SOE Chief of Intelligence.

41 File HS 8/818 at The National Archives, Kew.

42 File HS 8/818 at The National Archives, Kew.

43 File HS 8/818 at The National Archives, Kew.

44 File HS 8/818 at The National Archives, Kew.

45 Foot, *SOE in France*, p.182.

46 Foot, *SOE in France*, p.182, Footnote 6.

47 There still existed at this time SO1, the MEW's propaganda arm. SO2 was the 'action' arm soon to be become SOE with the demise of SO1.

48 File HS 8/818 at The National Archives, Kew.

49 Foot, *SOE in France*, p.182, Footnote 6.

50 Pimlott (ed.), *The Second World War Diary of Hugh Dalton: 1940–1945*, p.113. Diary entry for 2 December 1940.

51 File HS 8/818 in The National Archives, Kew.

52 File HS 8/818 at The National Archives, Kew. Meeting of 16 December 1940.

53 Richards, *Secret Flotillas*, p.91.

CHAPTER TWELVE

FIREBRAND ADMIRAL

The new year, 1941, began with increasingly bitter feuds between Keyes and the Chiefs of Staff, Admiralty and War Office over the organisation, overseas deployment and 'splitting up of his splendid force'[1] as three Commandos were detached from Combined Operations and sent for possible operational deployment in the Middle East. Keyes' anger was fuelled by an Admiralty signal that cut him and his HQ out of the command and communications loop regarding the onward deployment of 'his' Commandos. True to form, Keyes said 'harsh and bitter things' to those in authority over him. He described Churchill's advisers as 'craven-hearted',[2] bombarded the prime minister with minutes and clamoured for an interview.

SOE, meanwhile, was pressing ahead with plans for a maritime operation of its own, plans that would provide a timely reminder of SOE's potential to those watching the slow progress of the fledgling clandestine organisation that had yet to drop its first agent into France.

Operation *Rubble*, staged at the end of January 1941, involved the violation of Swedish neutrality and the spiriting away, under cover of nightfall, a heavy snowstorm and with Swedish connivance, of five unarmed Norwegian merchant ships, all of which were laden with steel and ball-bearings vital to the British war effort. With them too came British and Norwegian merchant seamen who had been trapped in Sweden, together with Royal Navy survivors from British ships sunk during the Norwegian campaign. SOE engineered the successful extraction of the ships through the German blockade of the Skagerrak and across the North Sea to safety in Kirkwall in the Orkneys. It was 'a major coup'[3] that earned knighthoods for the two SOE officers who arranged it, George Binney and Charles Hambro.

On 10 February 1941, seven officers and twenty-two men from 'X' Troop, 11th Special Air Service (SAS) Battalion, took part in Britain's first airborne attack, Operation *Colossus*. The men, seconded from Keyes' No. 2 Commando, were dropped at night in southern Italy together with an Italian interpreter named Picchi. Their target was a fresh water aqueduct near Calitri. The aqueduct was blown up (and rapidly repaired).

Operation *Colossus* was hallmarked – as first operations so often are – by a series of errors in navigation, equipment delivery failure and extraction planning that ended in the ambush and capture of most of those who took part. Only one officer escaped capture whilst the Italian interpreter was captured, tortured and executed. As a raid, the operation achieved little beyond providing a brief fillip for public morale as Britain was seen to take the fight to the enemy. More importantly perhaps, it was seen as a benchmark, a starting point, for British airborne operations. Many lessons were learned that would be put to good use later, but its execution cut across plans already in train with SOE. Dalton wrote shortly after news of *Colossus* was trumpeted in headlines across Britain:

> Newspapers full of British parachute descent in the heel of Italy. This is the DCO's Operation in favour of which ours against the toe was postponed. All we did was to lend the DCO one Italian. The thing seems to have been a pretty good failure and the PM didn't know it was to happen and was furious. I hear that Keyes is now refused admission to the PM. Previously he was always in and out. He writes long, wordy papers and is thought by the Chiefs of Staff to be half-way between a menace and a lunatic.[4]

Insane? Probably not. Incautious? Most certainly. On 4 February Keyes had written a six-page letter to Churchill suggesting, *inter alia*, that the prime minister should 'throw overboard' the Chiefs of Staff Committee and let him, Keyes, 'share your burden' as Under-secretary for Defence or make him the prime minister's Chief of Naval Staff. He wrote: 'I would give the ardent spirits who are spoiling for a fight a chance.'[5] Churchill replied the next day: 'It is quite impossible for me to receive a letter of this character, I am sure it would do you a great deal of harm if it fell into unsympathetic hands. I therefore return it to you with its enclosures.'[6]

Lower down the command chain others too, this time within SOE, were pushing for a chance to flex their muscles and carry the war to the enemy shore regardless of and oblivious to any restraint or limitation SIS might wish to impose upon cross-Channel raiding. One of these was a young gunner subaltern, Gustavus March-Phillipps, who had been sent to Scotland for Commando training with the newly formed Combined Operations and then, by devious means, found himself transferred into SOE on the coat-tails of Brigadier Gubbins, the newly appointed Director of Operations and Training. Gubbins' previous work during the Norwegian campaign and his own researches into irregular warfare had 'demonstrated the value of small raids from local fishing vessels as a means of disrupting communications behind the enemy lines'.[7]

Now, in March 1941, Captain March-Phillipps put up his own scheme to help develop resistance movements in France by establishing personal contact with patriots and bringing back information. It was a scheme that, like Gerry Holdsworth's Helford River base of operations set up the previous autumn, had Gubbins' full support. SOE agent Peter Kemp recalled:

> He told us his plan was to mount a series of small raids across the Channel, to attack German strong points, signal stations on the Brittany coast and the Channel Islands with the idea of scaring [the Germans] and secondly, causing them to divert more and more troops to garrison duties to prevent these raids, and in this way, hoped eventually to mount raids all the length of occupied Europe from Biarritz up to Norway.[8]

The direct consequence of March-Phillipps' paper was that presently he and a friend, Geoffrey Appleyard, were authorised to set up a base of their own under the cover name of No. 62 Commando, near Poole in Dorset. Like Holdsworth a few months previously, they found that clandestine, unaccountable operations had some unanticipated fringe benefits. Geoffrey Appleyard wrote:

> Gus and I drove down to Dorset to spend a day house-hunting. We located a magnificent house about seven miles from Wareham and ten from Poole. It's a large and very beautiful Elizabethan manor, and in every way ideal for our purpose, very much in the country, in an excellent training area with beautiful gardens. Initially there'll be about thirty of us living there, nearly all officers.

Captain March-Phillipps wrote to his wife of their new base, Anderson Manor: 'I wish you were here. It's really a marvellous place, and the weather is perfect. Every morning I ride out through the woods full of primroses and bluebells and violets with the dew still on them, and the sun shining through the early morning mist.'[9] But it was not all primroses and early morning mist. Soon March-Phillipps and Geoffrey Appleyard had spotted three vessels in Poole harbour – one of them a 65-ton Brixham trawler, the *Maid Honor*, which they were impatient to requisition, refit and arm for their self-styled intruder missions across to France.[10] Although Brigadier Gubbins had been present at the Richmond Terrace meeting on 16 December 1940 at which Commander Arnold-Foster of SIS had stated that raids to exactly that part of the enemy coast were 'detrimental to the collection of [SIS] intelligence',[11] there is no evidence that March-Phillipps was prepared to pay that restriction much heed. Indeed, he was about to sail into that same Admiralty minefield encountered by Holdsworth a little further down the coast:

It became clear that there was a conflict of interest between SOE's naval interests as they envisaged them at the time and those of SIS as they perceived them. Gus took this boat over [*Maid Honor*] and proceeded with his unit to try her out and fit her out and sail her. And when he was in the middle of this, Captain Frank Slocum, who was head of SOE's effective Naval Section known by the acronym NID(C) and who had overall responsibility for SOE and SIS cross-Channel operations said to Gus March-Phillipps: 'What on earth are you going to do with that boat you're fitting out?' And March-Phillipps said: 'Well, I'm going to lie off a French port like Cherbourg with her and wait til the Germans come to investigate and then when they get close enough to me I shall sink them because I've got a secret weapon on board.'[12] Slocum said: 'You're certainly not going to do that in the English Channel!' And so poor Gus was rather crestfallen and there was a haggle between SOE and SIS and finally it was agreed and Gus said: 'Well, I've got this ship: what on earth can I do with her?' And they said take her out to West Africa. So Gus and his unit found himself invited to go to Port Harcourt or Lagos and get lost as far as the English Channel was concerned.[13]

Gus March-Philipps would indeed sail *Maid Honor* to Africa where he would lead the successful Operation *Postmaster*, a cutting-out operation involving merchantmen moored at the Spanish island of Fernando Po. The success of the mission 'boosted SOE's reputation at a critical time and demonstrated its capacity to plan daring, difficult, Commando-style secret operations'.[14] Seven of the officers involved in *Postmaster* received medals, Gus March-Phillipps among them. Brigadier Gubbins wrote in his official recommendation:

> Captain Gus March- Phillips displayed military qualities of a very high order in his successful execution of this very difficult task which secured for the British government a 10,000 ton liner carrying a cargo valued at several hundred thousand pounds ... I strongly recommend him for the award of the DSO.[15]

March-Phillipps DSO and his team returned in triumph to home waters. When he did so, it was to find that his early raiding plans and his '*Maid Honor*' unit had been formalised into the creation of the 'Small Scale Raiding Force' (SSRF). Sanctioned by the Chiefs of Staff,[16] SSRF was to be under joint Combined Operations and SOE control with operational command resting with Combined Operations 'as it must be in order to get the necessary authorisation to sail and other facilities'.[17] SOE's task was to provide the raiding party of up to forty men. SOE was also to provide the operational and training base and its staff, any special landing craft that might be required and whatever arms, ammunition, explosives and special stores SSRF might require. Half a dozen 'butcher and bolt' raids of aggressive reconnaissance and prisoner-taking from the enemy shore ensued. Indeed, Geoffrey Appleyard's parents were later to claim their son took part in seventeen raids to enemy-held territory, including Operations *Brandford*, *Barricade*, *Fahrenheit* and *Dryad*.[18] The last of these was Operation *Basalt*, a raid on the Channel Island of Sark on 3/4 October 1942 in which a disputed number of German prisoners were killed with their hands tied behind their backs. Lord Louis Mountbatten recalled:

> I specially told Major Appleyard (if my memory serves me right) before he undertook the raid on Sark that he was not to tie the hands of any of his prisoners. Unfortunately this order was disregarded ... One of the prisoners gave out a great cry for help and ran away in the dark. The Commandos shot him as he ran. The others were brought back safely with their hands bound. Their hands were immediately untied when they got into the boat. As soon as the Germans discovered a prisoner with his hands tied behind his back, who had been shot dead through the back, they made a tremendous affair of this in their political warfare broadcasts ...[19]

This execution – or executions, for the actual number remains disputed – gave rise in turn to Hitler's infamous 'Commando Order' of 18 October 1942 which stated that all captured Commando forces, whether in uniform or not and including those who might have surrendered, were to be summarily executed. That order was to have tragic consequences later relating to Operation *Frankton*.

Despite his earlier restriction upon just such minor raids, Churchill now supported SOE and Gus March-Phillipps' endeavours to keep German coastal defences at full stretch. As has been shown elsewhere, not everyone in SIS nor the Admiralty shared Churchill's view of the efficiency or necessity of such raids. Nor, it appears – Captain Slocum apart – did senior officers in the Royal Navy. Lieutenant Freddie Bourne commanded MTB 344, the boat used to ferry members of March-Phillipps' unit to their target. After the war he remembered March-Phillipps with an 18in-long cook's carving knife slipped down his trouser leg and another officer coming on board MTB 344 carrying a bow and arrows which were used for the silent killing of guard dogs and sentries.[20] Other enemies, however, could not be despatched so efficiently:

> I was called before Admiral Hughes-Hewitt. He made it absolutely clear to me – which I got very cross about – that he felt all these pin-prick raids on the French coast which I had been partly responsible for were a total waste of war effort. That was his personal view. He said it to me. I'll never forget that.[21]

Major March-Phillipps was killed with several of his men on Operation *Aquatint* whilst raiding the Normandy coastline in September 1942. The SSRF was later disbanded in 1943 after suffering significant losses. Geoffrey Appleyard died in an air crash serving with the SAS.

March-Phillipps' thwarted attack on German shipping with a Spigot mortar 'which had been invented by the SOE boffins' together with SOE's requirement to support the new SSRF with whatever equipment they might require, reveals a further dimension of potential co-operation between Combined Operations and SOE: the provision of specialist stores, expertise, arms and equipment:

> SOE's main contribution to Combined Operations was technical. Its research and devices sections were far ahead of anyone else's, for the special purposes of raiding techniques, and commando parties were often equipped with snow-shoes, silenced weapons, delay fuses and so on of SOE design. Commanders of such bodies … often visited SOE's research stations to be shown what was being done there and placed large orders for special equipment and stores.[22]

Professor Foot, one may assume, was writing about SOE in the fullness of its years rather than in its early period of struggle. The principle, however, held good: stores and special equipment for special operations were the domain of the Special Operations Executive. In addition to its HQ at 64 Baker Street under the cover name of the Inter-services Research Bureau with its cluster of nondescript requisitioned offices scattered around the western end of Marylebone Road and Portman Square,[23] SOE had developed a series of technical out-stations dotted across the outskirts of northern London. These were quite distinct from the agent-training bases that served the four-stage training plan that progressed and screened potential agents through 'Preliminary', 'Paramilitary' and SOE 'Finishing' schools in the Home Counties, Scotland and Beaulieu, Hampshire. These seventeen Research and Development Stations – identified by a number in Roman rather than Arabic numerals – came under the control of SOE's Director of Scientific Research, Dr Dudley Newitt. Principal amongst these was Station IX, a requisitioned 'large, hideous Victorian house'[24] and former private hotel named The Frythe in Welwyn Garden City. This was the seat of four main lines of research: physical-chemical, engineering, operational and camouflage. Elsewhere other SOE schools handled weapons, clandestine wireless set production, packing and despatch, forgery, concealment, photography and make-up. 'Physical-chemical' related to fuses and the devices that would be used to detonate them; chemical research led SOE scientists into the dark void of poisons, sleeping draughts and suicide pills; whilst the Engineering Department embraced everything from the design of silenced and easily hidden personal weapons to the development of the magnetic 'limpet' explosive bomb.[25] The needs of Special Operations both within and without SOE may have caused many to find their way to places like The Frythe, Bride Hall, near Ayot

St Lawrence in Hertfordshire and The Thatched Barn at Borehamwood,[26] but those who actually worked there found themselves in a highly secure, restricted environment. John Brown, a wireless set designer at The Frythe, remembered:

> Security was very tight. I remember being told that whatever I needed to know to do my job I would be told, enough and no more, that if I wanted to ask questions of anyone I should address my questions only to my immediate boss.[27]

Obsessive security, it seems, was not only the preserve of those who worked in Research and Development. It was endemic within SOE in Baker Street too – and a cause for considerable friction between members of SOE and Combined Operations:

> There was inevitably some jealousy and tensions between the two staffs, whose strategic roles were sometimes close together, whose needs and methods overlapped, who competed with each other for staff, for fighting men, and for fields of operations … much of such friction as was generated stemmed from an insistence upon security precautions by SOE that sometimes appeared schoolboyish to Combined Operations' officers, who did not see why (for example) CD's officers found it necessary to use one surname in Baker Street and another in Whitehall.[28]

In March 1941 Combined Operations mounted its first major assault on the enemy shore. Unlike many of those that would follow, Operation *Claymore* had no need of 'special stores' from The Frythe, but it was a raid that took with it some of the earliest Norwegian recruits to SOE. Since the German invasion of Norway in April 1940, Norwegians had been escaping to Britain by sea via Shetland. Many of those new arrivals had now been scooped up into SOE by a Captain Martin Linge, a Norwegian actor turned army officer, who was appointed SOE liaison officer by the Norwegian government-in-exile. His force, Norwegian Independent Company 1 (soon to be renamed *Kompani Linge* after Linge was killed in action leading a second raid in December 1941), accompanied the main force to the Lofoten Islands off the north-west coast of Norway 100 miles north of the Arctic Circle. The operation involved three warships and a naval escort of five destroyers, plus 500 men of Nos 3 and 4 Commando. Its objective was to destroy Norwegian fish oil factories and so reduce German glycerine production. It was an unqualified success that met with little resistance and sustained no casualties. The raiders destroyed eleven factories, 800,000 gallons of fish oil and returned with more than 200 German prisoners and sixty Norwegian collaborators. The true value of Operation *Claymore*, however, lay elsewhere: Lord Lovat was a junior officer on that raid:

What was the significance of Lofoten? From the commando angle, the short-term answer was simple: although there had been no fighting, any action was better than no raid at all. At top level, Lofoten was hailed as a considerable success and a necessity for survival. Had it failed, or the raid been cancelled, Chiefs of Staff would inevitably have disbanded Sir Roger Keyes' private army.[29]

That may, indeed, have been justification enough, though the far greater and top-secret benefit of Operation *Claymore* lay in the recovery of a set of spare rotors for a German Enigma coding machine from the whaling trawler *Krebs*. With 'all the guts in the world'[30] this small German requisitioned trawler with a single small gun on her foredeck and a single heavy machine gun aft attempted to take on the British Tribal Class destroyer HMS *Somali*, which promptly blew her apart. Grounded on a nearby island, the wrecked *Krebs* was boarded by three naval officers, one of whom found 'two black discs about the size of hockey pucks'[31] in a locked cupboard. These turned out to be the spare Enigma rotors. Their unexpected discovery and top-secret delivery to Bletchley Park, together with accompanying code tables, inadvertently provided all the justification Operation *Claymore* needed and enabled the Codes and Cipher School to read all German naval signals' traffic for February 1941.[32]

However, it was not only the gallant Captain Hans Kapfinger and his puny trawler *Krebs* that sailed recklessly into danger in March 1941. That same month a new directive had been sent to Keyes from the Chiefs of Staff. This spelt out Keyes' duties with unambiguous clarity and placed him firmly 'under the direction of the Minister of Defence and the Chiefs of Staff'.[33] It could not be plainer: Keyes was being brought to heel. On the surface, Keyes appeared to take the demotion meekly enough. As spring turned to summer, however, relations with senior officers and the Chiefs of Staff deteriorated still further with a disastrous Combined Operations Exercise *Leapfrog* in the western highlands, witnessed by His Majesty the King. This proved the last straw for senior commanders determined to preserve an orderly chain of command. Lieutenant General Sir Henry Pownall, Vice Chief of the Imperial General Staff, wrote:

> Roger Keyes is a great nuisance. As Director of Combined Operations, a post invented by Winston, he butts in continually. Keyes continually interferes with the Chiefs of Staff. Keyes continually criticizes the strategical aspect of the whole thing, and this is no business of his whatsoever. But Winston put him in and it's the devil of a job to get him out. Not that Winston has any real faith in him, I'm sure. But his nominees, good or bad, remain.[34]

September brought another directive from the Chiefs of Staff, which began by stating 'two outstanding principles' of command and control: the proffering of advice to the prime minister, the War Cabinet or the Defence Committee 'must rest with the Chiefs of Staff'; once commanders had been appointed for an operation, 'the planning, training and execution of that operation must be the responsibility of those officers'. Both points cut directly across Keyes and his assumption of direct access to the prime minister. Worse, however, was to come. The Chiefs of Staff recommended the creation of a special 'Inter-Service Organisation' to assist Combined Operations under the control of an adviser on Combined Operations – Admiral Keyes. The memorandum was signed by all three Chiefs of Staff: Dill, Portal and Pound, his one-time subordinate. Churchill wrote to Keyes on 30 September 1941:

> I hope you will find yourself able to come to an agreement with the Chiefs of Staff upon the modification of your original directive. Your title of 'Director' does not correspond with the facts ... the responsibility for advising the Defence Committee and the War Cabinet can only lie with the Chiefs of the Staff. These are facts which must be accepted. I trust therefore that you will fall in with the plans which have now taken shape.[35]

Admiral Keyes, hero of Zeebrugge, had no intention of falling in with the plans which had taken shape. He replied to the prime minister, his one-time mentor: 'Although it would be easier and pleasanter for me to fall in with your wishes, it would be rotten of me to do so because I know that, under the organisation which Pound and the Naval Staff have been intriguing to force on me since last August 1940, we should drift on as we have been doing, inviting disaster.'[36]

Keyes' previous letter to Churchill had run to eight foolscap pages and had included the categorical assertion: 'I have tried to make it clear to the Chiefs of Staff that I cannot accept such a sweeping reduction in status and an absurd title that means nothing.'[37] Keyes' following letter to Churchill of 4 October 1941 had ended: 'I know I am destined to play a decisive part in helping you win this war. Why postpone the day?' Churchill did not share his friend's conviction. His letter of dismissal ran to just five lines. It was a letter, claims Hollis, which was written with the greatest reluctance and only at his, Hollis', specific recommendation. Hollis further claims Churchill then had second thoughts, calling him later to say: 'You didn't despatch that letter, I hope? We have been too hard, much too hard. I don't want it to go.'[38] But the letter had gone. And thus, so too, had Keyes.

The First Sea Lord Dudley Pound greeted the news with jubilation: 'He never had much brain and what he has got left is quite addled.'[39] The same man had written earlier: 'I am sorry to say it but I firmly believe that the only thing he cares for is the glorification of Roger Keyes.'[40] Hugh Dalton did not mourn his passing: his published diary makes no mention of his departure. More than a month later, however, he gossips:

Fletcher says that Keyes dismissal was his wife's fault. A satisfactory agreement had been reached with the Chiefs of Staff and Keyes had accepted it, but his wife persuaded him to write a five-page letter to the PM going back over all the old ground.[41]

Even then, it appears, Keyes did not go quietly. Churchill wrote to him in August the following year: 'I certainly understand how you feel about not having an active part to play. I can only say that I acted in what I considered was the public interest and that I do not think it likely that any fighting post will be open to an officer now over 70.'[42] Keyes died in December 1945.

On the far side of the world, Captain Louis Mountbatten, the newly decorated hero of HMS *Kelly* and cousin of King George VI, was in Los Angeles waiting for repairs to be completed to his new command, the aircraft carrier HMS *Illustrious*. Ordered to fly to Washington, he was told to report to London to take up some post connected with Combined Operations: 'We want you here at once for something which you will find of the highest interest', confided Churchill in a private telegram.[43] That 'something' was promotion to commodore and elevation to the post Admiral Keyes had despised to the point of dismissal: adviser on Combined Operations. It was a promotion that would bring Mountbatten, like his predecessor, into close contact with SOE and the Minister for Economic Warfare.

Keyes is credited with nurturing the *esprit de corps* and *élan* for which Commando units later became famous. His other contribution to the Second World War was less beneficial. Like Dalton at SOE, Keyes at Combined Operations had obscured, with the veil of his own bombastic, egotistical personality, the essential clarity of vision that should have revealed and laid bare to its leader the dangerous flaws of omission, overlap and confusion that lay in the path of Combined Operations. Instead, that confusion and duplication of tactical role remained perceived in the abstract but essentially unresolved in practice. Now, more than two years after the outbreak of hostilities, SOE and Combined Operations found themselves still working the same side of the street. And such competitive duplication, as General Bourne had both warned and predicted, was to have significant and tragic consequences.

Notes

1 Fergusson, *The Watery Maze*, p.77.

2 Aspinall-Oglander, *Roger Keyes*, p.399.

3 Binney, *Secret War Heroes*, p.52.

4 Pimlott (Ed.), *The Second World War Diary of Hugh Dalton: 1940–1945*, p.160. Diary entry for 17 February 1941.

5 Halpern, *The Keyes Papers*, Volume III: '1939–1945', pp.147–52. Paper 71. Keyes to Churchill.

6 Halpern, *The Keyes Papers*, Volume III: '1939–1945', pp.147–52. Paper 71. Churchill to Keyes.

7 Richards, *Secret Flotillas*, p.94.

8 Binney, *Secret War Heroes*, p.124.

9 Binney, *Secret War Heroes*, p.124.

10 File HS 8/806 at The National Archives, Kew.

11 File HS 8/818 at The National Archives, Kew.

12 The author Nevil Shute served in the RNVR and worked in the Directorate of Miscellaneous Weapons Development. He wrote a novel, *Most Secret*, based precisely upon this scenario. It was first published by William Heinemann in 1945 and is still in print today.

13 Excerpt from interview with Sir Brooks Richards. Sound Archive No. 27462 at the Imperial War Museum, London.

14 Binney, *Secret War Heroes*, p.121.

15 File HS 9/1283/3 at The National Archives, Kew. Gus March-Phillipps' personal file.

16 File HS 8/198 at The National Archives, Kew. Headquarters File November 1941–July 1942. Meeting of SO Council report, 23 March 1942.

17 File HS 8/818 at The National Archives, Kew. '*Most Secret*' file dated 18 March 1942.

18 Foot, *SOE in France*, p.168.

19 Letter from Lord Louis Mountbatten at the Broadlands Archive, Hartland Library, University of Southampton. Ref. MB1/B58.

20 Bailey, *Forgotten Voices of the Secret War*, pp.80–1.

21 Excerpt from Sound Archive interview with Freddie Bourne No. 11721 at the Imperial War Museum, London.

22 Foot, *SOE in France*, p.166.

23 Piekalkiewicz, Janusz, *Secret Agents, Spies & Saboteurs* (David & Charles, Newton Abbot, 1974), p.47.

24 Sweet-Escott, *Baker Street Irregular*, p.21.

25 Rigden, Denis (Intrd.), *SOE Syllabus* (The National Archives, London, 2004), p.19.

26 Boyce, Frederic and Everett, Douglas, *SOE: The Scientific Secrets* (Sutton Publishing, Stroud, 2003), p.289.

27 Bailey, *Forgotten Voices of the Secret War*, p.68. Quoting Sub Lieutenant Harvey Bennette in audio interview.

28 Foot, *SOE in France*, pp.165–6.

29 Lovat, Lord, *March Past* (Weidenfeld & Nicolson, London, 1978), p.215.

30 Kahn, David, *Seizing the Enigma* (Arrow, London, 1996), p.132.

31 Kahn, *Seizing the Enigma*, p.135.

32 Hinsley, *British Intelligence in the Second World War*, Volume 1, p.337.

33 Halpern, *The Keyes Papers*, p.159. Paper 78.

34 Halpern, *The Keyes Papers*, p.83. Paper 78.

35 Halpern, *The Keyes Papers*, p.201. Paper 107.

36 Halpern, *The Keyes Papers*, p.208. Paper 109.

37 Halpern, *The Keyes Papers*, p.202. Paper 108.

38 Leasor and Hollis, *War at the Top*, p.125.

39 Ziegler, *Mountbatten: The Official Biography*, p.155.

40 Ziegler, *Mountbatten: The Official Biography*, p.154.

41 Pimlott (ed.), *The Second World War Diary of Hugh Dalton: 1940–1945*, p.317. Diary entry for 19 November 1941.

42 CHAR 20/96B at the Churchill Archives Centre, Churchill College, Cambridge. Letter from Churchill to Keyes dated 14 August 1943.

43 Ziegler, *Mountbatten: The Official Biography*, p.151.

CHAPTER THIRTEEN

CLOAKS AND RUBBER DAGGERS

If SOE were indeed created in 1940 as a desperate solution to desperate times then, by late 1942, the imperative that led to its creation had lost something of its urgency. For by then, bare-cupboard wishful thinking by a Britain standing alone had been replaced by coherent three-power strategic planning, the linchpin of which was to be a landing on enemy-occupied soil by a large multi-national army. That invasion of June 1944 might still be some way over the horizon, but the fact that there was now the realistic prospect of a large Allied army to disembark on to the enemy shore was one of the central precepts which had altered both the strategic balance and the light in which SOE was now regarded by those who controlled its destiny. Yet, throughout this period of 1941 and 1942 of 'pawn moves'[1] as SOE's early development was concluded, significant events took place within the ambit of SOE's relations with others which both weakened and altered the strategic role of SOE whilst making that distrusted, nascent organisation an indispensable element in Allied plans for that European invasion. An examination of the evolution of that paradox and the growing pressures these events placed upon SOE has identified five separate areas of conflict, change and exclusion which, taken together, ensured that SOE's early sense of encirclement had diminished little by the end of 1942. The first three of these will be dealt with in this chapter:

1. The 'Muddle East' débâcle which provided SOE's enemies with welcome ammunition with which to snipe at the rival organisation.
2. The demise of Dalton's much-vaunted 'Fourth Arm' concept.
3. The paucity of operational results as defined by SOE agents-in-place.

The final two points in that list of five which contributed to SOE's continuing sense of beleaguered isolation up to the end of 1942 – the eclipse of Hugh Dalton and the explosive growth of Combined Operations – will be addressed in the next chapter.

In addition to these five areas – if not of stasis then at least of obstructed progress – that same period would also see the culmination of Dalton's doomed struggle with Foreign Secretary Anthony Eden and Brendan Bracken, the newly appointed Minister of Information, for control of 'black' propaganda. The creation of the Political Warfare Executive and the loss of SO1, the political in-fighting with former ally Rex Leeper whose 'mischief-making stuff against me'[2] was souring Dalton's already unpopular reputation, the realisation that SOE would not now control nor orchestrate every aspect of subversion and the bruising personal exchanges with Bracken himself would wear Dalton down and culminate in a diary entry that confided: 'I just cannot go on like this.'[3] It would be written less than three months before Dalton found himself, without warning, 'passed to a higher office'.[4] Yet, just a year earlier, matters had begun auspiciously as Dalton received fulsome praise from the man whose approval he sought most – the prime minister.

In the Balkans, SOE had been instrumental, though not in both instances directly responsible, for two coups which became, in retrospect, perhaps the high watermark of Dalton's achievements within that organisation. The first was an act of pure subversion; the second, an act of straightforward sabotage. At the end of 1940, Churchill ordered SOE to undermine the pro-Axis government in Yugoslavia and thwart moves by that regime to sign a Tripartite Pact with Hitler. It was, said Churchill, 'the acid test for SOE'.[5] However, the attempt failed when the pact was signed on 25 March 1941. SOE immediately diverted its attentions away from policy change and towards the engineering of outright coup. Two days later a coup ousted Prince Paul and his government in Belgrade: 'What a day! Gladwyn comes into my room this morning with a smiling face and says, "There was a *coup d'etat* early this morning at Belgrade". As the day goes on, we hear more detail, and it is clear that our chaps have done their part well.'[6]

Post-war research suggests it was not SOE but more probably the British Air Attaché who prodded disgruntled Yugoslav patriots into action but, no matter: the Defence Committee 'graciously conveyed an expression of appreciation'[7] to the Minister of Economic Warfare and Dalton was delighted:[8] 'More congratulations upon my Jug achievement. Letter from Ismay on behalf of PM and Defence Committee. We are well on top!'[9] Less than a month later SOE agents sank six barges in the Danube, thus blocking German access to Romanian oil. By mid-June, however, the river had been cleared and was once more open to traffic. Dalton recorded the words of the prime minister: 'Never mind. You blocked it for two months. That was good.' Earlier Churchill had written to Dalton:

> Pray press on with any useful scheme to cause trouble to the enemy in his own country or occupied territories. Should you meet opposition from any of your colleagues in regard to any special scheme about which you hold strong views,

I shall always be glad to give the matter my personal consideration if you will bring it to my notice.[10]

Such closeness of support, such privileged access to the ultimate untier of inter-departmental and ministerial knottage, however, was to remain more chimera than reality and thus a source of intense frustration to Churchill's beleaguered Minister of Economic Warfare. Churchill may have disliked Dalton,[11] and wished him kept at arm's length, yet the business of clandestine warfare, of sub-version and subterfuge, exerted an enduring if amateurish attraction. According to No. 10's intelligence chief, Major Desmond Morton:

Winston adored funny operations. Unfortunately he seemed unable to con-nect up funny operations with the great strategic plans, or see the effect of one upon the other. He addressed his mind to them as the managing director of a vast railway might have, as a hobby, a miniature railway in his garden.[12]

It is a view endorsed by other examples of Churchill's impulsive and often short-lived enthusiasms. In 1942, John Steinbeck wrote *The Moon is Down*,[13] a play about the igniting of resistance amongst the oppressed and occupied people of Europe. The passage below gives a flavour:

MAYOR: Tell them how it is. We are watched. Any move we make calls for reprisal. If we could have simple weapons, secret weapons. Weapons of stealth. Explosives. Dynamite to blow out rails. Grenades if possible. Even poison … This is no honourable war. This is a war of treachery and murder. Let us use the methods they have used on us. Let the British bombers drop their great bombs on the works, but let them also drop little bombs for us to use. To hide. To slip under rails. Under trucks. Then we will be secretly armed and the invader will never know which of us is armed …[14]

As a young subaltern, Churchill had marched to the sound of guerrillas' guns in Cuba[15] in the dusk-days of the nineteenth century, heard shots fired in anger for the first time on his twenty-first birthday. He had fought Pathan tribesmen on the North West Frontier and had been an evader himself during his escape from a POW camp in South Africa. His heart, if not his sentiment, was with the under-dog. Now Churchill read *The Moon is Down*. Excited by its potential, inspired by its timely, stirring heroism, Churchill commended the book and its premise – the random dropping of 'simple weapons such as sticks of dynamite which could be easily concealed and are easy in operation'[16] to Lord Selborne on 27 May 1942. Operation *Braddock* resulted in the manufacture of 50,000 'attack packs' con-taining grenades, pocket incendiary devices and a crude one-shot, pressed-metal

.45 pistol, before what is delicately referred to as a 'diminution of enthusiasm' resulted in the abandonment of the project in September 1943.[17] Others may have lost enthusiasm for the casual method of *Braddock*'s delivery and the wider strategic implications of scattering weapons willy nilly across Germany and half of Europe, but Churchill remained lucid about the overall objective:

> We shall aid and stir the people of every conquered country to resistance and revolt. We shall break up and derange every effort which Hitler makes to system-ise and consolidate his subjugation. Subjugated peoples must be caused to rise against their oppressors, but not until the stage is set. The 'attack from within' is the basic concept of such operations. The Patriots must be secretly organised and armed with personal weapons to be delivered to them by air if necessary.[18]

Words, of course, were always Churchill's forte. David Stafford, however, agrees with Morton's 'miniature railway' analogy: 'Dalton had complained in October 1941 that Churchill did not "focus well" on SOE affairs, for it should have been obvious to Churchill had he been focusing at all on the question, that SOE policy had been to discourage isolated and undirected civilian direct action resistance for fear of provoking German reprisals.'[19]

Obvious or not, what is not in dispute is Churchill's belief that the people of Europe should play a vital part in their own eventual liberation. What was at issue was his ability to focus long enough upon the role, impact and jurisdiction of the new organisation he had created to provide a clear definition of its respon-sibilities and delineation. Throughout those early formative years, and in 1941 and 1942 in particular, Churchill's interest, fascination, meddling involvement and fickle, emotional enthusiasm for SOE was a constant background presence; one more cockpit of threat, support or 'indispensable salvation'[20] for Dalton, Jebb, Selborne and Gubbins to watch, court, nurture and guard against. With hindsight, however, it should perhaps surprise no one that SOE's organisational and hierarchical complexities were to find so little space in the busy, scheming mind of a war leader who strove to combine the roles of prime minister and Minister of Defence and thus become his own de facto Defence Committee.

Churchill's occasional patronage, however, could offer Dalton little support when it came to problems in the Middle East – problems which threatened to smother the infant SOE before it had hardly caught first breath. Soon after the qualified success of the two Balkans operations, Dalton received reports of inef-ficiencies and internal feuding between SO1 and SO2 in SOE's Cairo office. One of those in the SOE team sent from London to investigate wrote afterwards: 'Nobody who did not experience it can possibly imagine the atmosphere of jeal-ousy, suspicion and intrigue which embittered the relations between the various secret and semi-secret departments in Cairo during that summer of 1941, or for that matter for the next two years. It would be quite beyond my powers to describe it.'[21] One of those officers in Cairo wrote a report for his superiors entitled 'Notes on Organisation of SOE in Middle East' and confided:

> What may be called the general morale of the organisation and confidence in its leadership is very low. It is freely said that lives have been lost through amateurish bungling in preparation for raids. There seems to be a wide-spread delusion that you can become a Lawrence of Arabia by sitting in offices and bars in Cairo and Jerusalem.[22]

Captain Bill Stirling of the Scots Guards (brother of David Stirling, who founded the Special Air Service Regiment) went further. That same day he formalised a devastating critique of SOE Middle East. In a report entitled 'Report on Certain Aspects of SOE Middle East' he stated:

> This brief report aims to be constructive and to face squarely an unpleasant issue in order to secure drastic and immediate reform ... The ventures of SO2 may be described as a series of inspirations by different persons in the UK and Middle East, which are put into effect on no known plan, with no financial or disciplinary check and often without reference to GHQ policy at the time ... Large sums of money have been wasted through gross incompetence, on projects that were obviously futile ...

> CONCLUSIONS:

> The organisation of SO2 in the Middle East is thoroughly rotten: its personnel is incompetent, or worse, its methods are wasteful and in action it is completely ineffective ...
>   Reform is urgently needed ... A far more radical reform is necessary than any yet proposed ...[23]

Those who resented SOE seized their opportunity. Whilst Hugh Dalton's diary describes events in Cairo mildly as 'undoubtedly a bad tangle' and an environment wherein existed 'muddle, extravagance, gossip and intrigue in great quantities',[24] senior service officers took more formal steps. General Sir Claude Auchinleck, who succeeded Wavell as commander-in-chief Middle East, and Air Marshal Sir Charles Portal, the Chief of the Air Staff (the officer who had vigorously opposed Operation *Savanna*), denounced SOE to the prime minister as a 'bogus, irresponsible, corrupt show'. Similarly, Field Marshal Archibald Wavell, commander-in-chief Middle East before 'The Auk', described SOE to Sir John Dill, CIGS, simply as 'a racket'.[25] Wavell actually went further, recruiting a

Cairo SOE secretary as a spy and persuading her to make copies of internal SOE papers she thought 'worrying' and pass them on to his Chief of Staff, General Arthur Smith. He picked the right woman. Just three months earlier Hermione Ranfurly had confided in her diary:

> I am now sure there is something wrong with my office. Security is almost non-existent. We spend money on a fabulous scale but it's difficult to trace results. Secretary Peggy Wright said laughingly to me in the office today: 'Hermione, sometimes it's difficult to know whose side we are working for – British or German'.[26]

Heads rolled. Men in charge of both SO1 and SO2 in the aptly named 'Muddle East' were recalled, but in many eyes the damage was done. Archie Lyall remarked over drinks in London's Cavendish Hotel to his friend Lord Lovat:

> I have recently designed a coat of arms for SOE. This is it: surmounted by an unexploded bomb; a cloak and rubber dagger, casually left in a bar sinister. The arms are supported by two double agents. The motto: *nihil quod tetigit non* (made a balls of it).[27]

However, there was rather more to it than that. Historian Saul Kelly has noted: 'It was well known in the summer of 1941 that a bloodthirsty internecine warfare was going on and had been going on for some little time between two parts of the same entity, *viz* SO1 and SO2 who should have been SOE.'[28] This state of 'open warfare'[29] over the control of propaganda between SO1 and SO2 in Cairo mirrored the bitter concurrent argument in London between Leeper, Bracken, Eden and Dalton. Its origins in the Middle East, however, lay in a failure at the top to ensure that the streamlining of what Sweet-Escott describes as the 'elaborate and ramshackle'[30] machinery that had existed before the creation of SOE and the amalgamation of the Foreign Office's Electra House, the War Office's MI(R) and SIS's Section D was replicated in Cairo. The result was bitter, not-so-private inter-departmental feuding and a consequent lack of confidence amongst those with whom SOE was supposed to work. Distance, poor communications, confusion of responsibility, attempts by the military to take over SOE's charter[31] and a series of botched sabotage operations did little to enhance SOE's local reputation. Oliver Lyttelton, the Minister of State in the Middle East, was charged with investigating the warring agencies. There he found 'chaos in the field of subversive activities and propaganda. I was disturbed, in particular by the lack of security, waste of public funds and the ineffectiveness of SOE. I frankly exposed to him [Dalton] by telegram the deplorable conditions of this service, of which I had incontestable proof, and urged him to clean it up.'[32]

Accordingly, on 10 July 1941 Dalton received this telegraph from the Minister of State:

Preliminary enquiries which I have made into the activities of SO2 organisation in Middle East point to alarming state of affairs. Information in the possession of HQ Middle East reveals inefficiency, extravagance and even corruption.

It is essential that a senior and responsible officer, preferably head of SO2 organisation itself, should come to Cairo at once to investigate.[33]

And so Sir Frank Nelson – Dalton's CD – boarded a plane and flew to Cairo. An anti-SO2 Dossier compiled by SOE's critics was investigated. Nelson reported that drastic action was needed to restore confidence. He recommended the immediate replacement of the head of SO2 and a subordinate. Nelson's report back to Dalton did not pull its punches:

Senior personnel of SO2 have lost confidence of all British authorities. As a result, work of SO2 is stultified. Inquiry was therefore urgently necessary and drastic action must be taken at once … the position has been greatly exaggerated by intrigues on all sides, facilitated by parallel communications, by clashing of personalities, by slinging of mud and by orgy of gossip. Behind this, I believe the truth to be:

1. Results are inadequate

2. There has been extravagance, and probably some improper expenditure

3. Control has been lax and ineffective

4. In any case and above all, situation is now out of hand because confidence has been largely impaired.[34]

Nelson recommended the dismissal of two senior officers of SO1. In London, Dalton immediately sanctioned Nelson's recommendations without questioning the SO1 officers involved, a move considered typical of the abrasive 'Doctor Dynamo'. In doing so, Dalton immediately added fuel to Leeper's resentment for both failing to consult him over the dismissal of senior officers within his department and for weighting much of the penalty for what Leeper and his colleagues saw as SO2's errors and extravagances against their organisation, SO1. It was office politics on a grand scale.

Notes

1 Foot, *SOE in France*, p.162.

2 Pimlott (ed.), *The Second World War Diary of Hugh Dalton: 1940–1945*, p.329. Diary entry for 1 December 1941.

3 Pimlott (ed.), *The Second World War Diary of Hugh Dalton: 1940–1945*, p.329. Diary entry for 3 December 1941.

4 Mackenzie, *The Secret History of SOE*, p.341.

5 Stafford, *Britain and European Resistance 1940–1945*, p.52.

6 Pimlott (ed.), *The Second World War Diary of Hugh Dalton: 1940–1945*, p.176. Diary entry for 27 March 1941.

7 Pimlott (ed.), *The Second World War Diary of Hugh Dalton: 1940–1945*, p.329. Diary entry for 1 December 1941.

8 The coup was swiftly nullified by the German invasion of Yugoslavia on 6 April 1941.

9 Pimlott (ed.), *The Second World War Diary of Hugh Dalton: 1940–1945*, p.178. Diary entry for 28 March 1941.

10 Mackenzie, *The Secret History of SOE*, pp.92–3. Letter dated 20 January 1941.

11 Long after the war's end, in December 1947, Winston Churchill still describes Hugh Dalton as 'the dirty Doctor' to his wife in a private latter. Source: Soames, Mary (ed.), *Winston and Clementine: The Personal Letters of the Churchills* (Doubleday, London, 1998), p.548.

12 Roberts, Andrew, *Eminent Churchillians* (Weidenfeld & Nicolson, London, 1994), p.63.

13 Steinbeck, John, *The Moon is Down* (English Theatre Guild, London, 1943).

14 Steinbeck, *The Moon is Down*.

15 Russell, Douglas S., *Winston Churchill: Soldier* (Brassey's, London, 2005), p.122.

16 Boyce and Everett, *SOE: The Scientific Secrets*, p.243.

17 It was revived briefly as *Braddock II* in September 1944 when 200,000 'Braddock' incendiary devices were dropped on Frankfurt and Mainz. There was another brief *Braddock* operation in February 1945.

18 Hastings, *Finest Years* (Harper Press, London, 2009) pp.451–2.

19 Stafford, *Britain and European Resistance 1940–1945*, p.100.

20 Seaman, *Special Operations Executive: A New Instrument of War*, p.59.

21 Sweet-Escott, *Baker Street Irregular*, p.73.

22 File HS 3/192 at The National Archives, Kew. The report, dated 30 June 1941, is unsigned.

23 SOE File HS 3/192 in The National Archives, Kew

24 Pimlott (ed.), *The Second World War Diary of Hugh Dalton: 1940–1945*, p.267.

25 Pimlott (ed.), *The Second World War Diary of Hugh Dalton: 1940–1945*, p.215. Diary entry for 26 May 1941.

26 Ranfurly, Hermione, *To War with Whitaker* (Mandarin, London, 1995), p.79. Diary entry for 27 February 1941.

27 Lovat, *March Past*, p.164.

28 Kelly, Saul, 'A Succession of Crises: SOE in the Middle East 1940–1945', *Intelligence and National Security*, Volume 20, No.1, March 2005, p.123.

29 File HS 7/220 at The National Archives, Kew.

30 Sweet-Escott, *Baker Street Irregular*, p.65.

31 Mackenzie, *The Secret History of SOE*, p.174.

32 Lyttelton, Oliver, *The Memoirs of Lord Chandos* (Bodley Head, London, 1962), p.239.

33 Mackenzie, *The Secret History of SOE*, p.178.

34 File HS 3/193 at The National Archives, Kew. Sir Frank Nelson's report to Hugh Dalton on the state of affairs within SOE Middle East. Visit made between 30 July and 20 August 1941. Report by CD to SO 21 August 1941.

CHAPTER FOURTEEN

HUNGRY MOUTHS

As Minister of Economic Warfare, Dalton may have been able to ride roughshod over the sensibilities of Rex Leeper, his subordinate, but he, like the late-departed Admiral Keyes of Combined Operations, was required to take his strategic direction from the Chiefs of Staff. It was this triumvirate – Dill (replaced by Brooke in December 1941), Pound and Portal – who issued directives and thus determined the shape of SOE's war. The first of such papers appeared as an annex to a document on 'Future Strategy' dated 4 September 1940. Approved by the War Cabinet at the end of that same month, it focused on the possibilities of revolt in occupied Europe and devoted some paragraphs to the discussion of 'Subversive Activities'. In earlier times – in late May 1940 directly before the fall of France – the Chiefs of Staff had told the War Cabinet: 'The only method of bringing about the downfall of Germany is by stimulating the seeds of revolt within the conquered territories. In the circumstances envisaged, we regard this form of activity as of the highest importance.'[1] The later paper of 4 September 1940 may have been more restrained, but it nevertheless revealed just how seriously the Chiefs of Staff were still taking both the potential and the possibility of armed popular revolt:

> The stimulation of the subversive tendencies already latent in most countries is likely to prove a valuable contributory factor towards the defeat of Germany … A general uprising, coinciding with major operations by our forces, may finally assist to bring about his defeat.[2]

That revolt as perceived 'was to be single, sudden and complete; it was to break out everywhere at the chosen moment without warning or rehearsal'.[3] Yet, despite the importance the Chiefs of Staff appeared to place upon the role of the prime minister's new brainchild, SOE had no direct input into the deliberations of the Chiefs of Staff and was only ever invited to their meetings as a favour, never as a right. It was a source of irritation and a pointed reminder of the

inherent distrust with which SOE was viewed that was to persist for the duration
of the war:

> SOE's successive heads each maintained that they ought to have sat with the
> Chiefs of Staff, permanently, instead of being summoned to the Chiefs' meet-
> ings only when SOE's affairs were on the agenda.
>   There was complaint that chances were thus missed because SOE was not
> consulted in the formative stage of discussion: and at intervals SOE reasserted
> the view that it was the Fourth Arm of modern war, and could not be effectively
> used unless it were given full membership of the COS, the JPS and the JIC.[4]

There was at least one occasion – 12 November 1940 – when SOE's Sir Frank
Nelson addressed the Chiefs of Staff about the work and potential capabilities of
SOE, yet the practical effect of this general exclusion was to deny SOE a voice at
high table and leave them the often mute recipient of a policy and set of strategic
priorities they were powerless either to influence significantly or to predict. The
same restraint was not extended to Lord Louis Mountbatten. Churchill wrote to
President Roosevelt in late March 1942:

> For your personal and secret eye I have made him [Mountbatten] Vice
> Admiral, Lieutenant-General and Air Marshal some weeks ago. Have put
> him on the Chiefs of Staff of Combined Operations. He is an equal member
> attending whenever his own affairs or the general conduct of the war are
> under consideration.[5]

Mountbatten's inclusion was an illustration of shifting strategic priorities, and
of the good fortune and rising ascendancy of one of those fortunate few who
had managed to catch and retain the prime minister's approval. Dalton, however, was not among them.

SOE was not kept entirely in the dark, however, and in autumn 1940 the
Chiefs of Staff had issued their first general directive. Entitled 'Subversive
Activities in Relation to Strategy', its aim was to guide SOE 'as to the direction in
which subversive activities can best assist our strategy' and acknowledged that
'our strategy and current plans should take account of the contribution which
subversive activities should make towards the military and economic offensive'.
After emphasising the importance of consultation and liaison between the Joint
Planning Staff, the Director of Combined Operations and the Air Staff, COS (40)
27(O) spelt out a strategy of attrition for 1941 and continued: 'On a long view,
it should be the particular aim of our subversive organisation to prepare the
way for the final stage of the war when, by co-ordinated and organised revolts
in the occupied countries and by a popular rising against the Nazi party inside

Germany, direct and decisive military operations against Germany herself may be possible.' Looking out over a bleak and deserted European battlefield with not an ally under arms in sight, the Chiefs of Staff continued in that directive of November 1940:

> We are, however, very conscious of the important and even decisive part which subversive activities must play in our strategy. In the circumstances we feel that if we are to exploit the use of subversive activities to the full, these activities must be planned on a very big and comprehensive scale.[6]

With hindsight, this directive represents perhaps the high point of Dalton's hopes for his 'Fourth Arm' concept, that brief window of time when both he and the Chiefs of Staff perceived that subversion in all its guises might just be the new and decisive element in British strategy that might hold the ring, make up for all those vast slogging Wehrmacht legions. It was a concept of wishful thinking, of strategic convenience, that endured longer than it deserved. As late as April 1941, the Future Operations Planning Section of the Joint Planning Staff was still writing about 'a universal uprising of oppressed peoples'[7] that would erupt in support of some under-powered British strike force; a popular rising whose guerrillas would have to be equipped by SOE on a vast scale. Tall orders indeed, and quite beyond the reach of the fledgling SOE with not an agent in enemy-occupied Europe.

Spring 1941 was what David Stafford has called the 'nadir' of Britain's wartime fortunes with Greece and Crete lost and the British bombing offensive failing as pilots struggled to place their bombs within 5 miles of targets[8] which were sometimes quite unaware they had even been the subject of a determined air attack.[9] At the same time the U-boat offensive gathered strength in the Atlantic, merchant shipping losses rose exponentially and half a dozen great British cities buckled beneath the weight of their own cavalry as, night after night, German bombers pounded them into ruin. Viewed from SOE's singular perspective, there was little to set against the scale of such losses. Sir Alexander Cadogan confided: 'News everywhere as depressing as usual. Can't see any daylight.'[10] He was writing on 8 April 1942, but could have written the same entry precisely a year earlier.

In early March 1941, and as Combined Operations launched Operation *Claymore*, a raid of little consequence against the distant Norwegian Lofoten Islands, further south SOE was busy training its first crop of agents for operations in France. By late spring 1941, twenty had completed final training at Wanborough Manor on the Hog's Back outside Guildford, with the first F Section agent dropping 'blind' into France on the night of 5/6 May 1941 at a time when the Joint Planning Staff's 'Review of Future Strategy' in June that year was still wedded to the idea of the rising of a 'People's Army':

Gentleman warrior. Lieutenant Richard Townsend DSC RNVR. (*Ursula Townsend*)

Daniel Lomenech, French exile, fierce patriot and Skipper of *N51*: 'The ship's company were devoted to him and would have done anything with him on board.'

Major David Wyatt RE on his wedding day in 1940. A popular and conscientious liaison officer between Combined Operations and SOE, he was killed on the Dieppe raid in August 1942. His bride had no idea he had been recruited into SOE. (*Jonathan Wyatt*)

Lord Louis Mountbatten found time to pen this handwritten letter to Major Wyatt's wife Patricia four days after her husband was posted missing after Dieppe. (*Jonathan Wyatt*)

COMBINED OPERATIONS HEADQUARTERS,
WAR CABINET ANNEXE,
1a, RICHMOND TERRACE,
WHITEHALL, S.W.1.

Telephone :
WHItehall 5422.

23rd August 1942

Dear Mrs. Wyatt,

I am so distressed that your husband has been reported missing after the Dieppe raid and although we all hope he may turn out to have been taken prisoner

much I feel for you.

As you know he was engaged in particularly important & secret work on my staff. He volunteered to take part in this raid, together with a large number of others from this headquarters and I feel sure that one day we shall hear how gallantly he fought.

He was so popular here and I cannot tell you how

Major 'Blondie Hasler'. Professional Royal Marine, peerless leader and meticulous planner. The man who led Mountbatten's 'Cockleshell Heroes' into legend. (*Trustees of the Royal Marines Museum*)

Corporal George Sheard. His body was never found. (*Barbara Roche and the late Peter Siddall*)

HMS *Tuna*. Passage boat for Operation *Frankton*.

HMS *Tuna* and her crew. Her commander, Lieutenant Dick Raikes DSO RN is in the centre of five seated officers.

The cargo vessel *Tannenfels* pictured before Hasler's attack. (*Deutsches U-Boot Museum, Cuxhaven-Altenbruch*)

Damaged blockade runners alongside Bordeaux docks the morning after Hasler's attack. (*Deutsches U-Boot Museum, Cuxhaven-Altenbruch*)

Ridifarne house on the banks of the Helford estuary. Idyllic setting, clandestine purpose. Gerry Holdsworth's requisitioned headquarters for SOE's Helford Flotilla, Cornwall.

Lieutenant Jack MacKinnon. The coal merchant's clerk and former corporal who came near the top of his class in officer training. (*Judy Simms*)

Marine David Moffatt.
Washed ashore on Ile de
Re. (*David Moffatt*)

Replica Cockle Mk II. Flat
bottomed, yet stable and
surprisingly seaworthy.

Bordeaux docks near Cafe Chartrons today.

Cockle Mk I being passed through the forward torpedo hatch of a submarine.

Lord Louis Mountbatten of England arrived at Gatow Airport in Berlin, Germany, for the Potsdam Conference. (*NARA*)

Marine Robert Ewart.

Marine Bill Mills.

Marine Eric Fisher.

Marine James Conway.

Sergeant Sam Wallace.

Lieutenant Jack MacKinnon.

'Blondie' Hasler in Spanish clothes in Barcelona during the evasion phase of Operation *Frankton*.

Corporal Albert Laver.

Two-man kayaks afloat in a non-tactical situation! (*Replica reconstruction*)

Lieutenant Colonel 'Blondie' Hasler (*left*) and ex-Corporal Bill Sparks DSM visiting Bordeaux after the war.

Pritchard-Gordon and Lambert in Cockle Mk II following a canoe of another unit. Note the stylish paddling with 'feathered' paddles.

A rigid type of canoe is carried up the esplanade wall at Southsea during comparative trials.

At Southsea a Cockle Mk II follows canoes of another unit.

Lieutenant David Birkin DSC. The brilliant, painstaking MTB navigator who was plagued by seasickness every time he crossed the Channel. (*Jane Birkin*)

In areas where German power has become sufficiently weak, subjugated peoples must rise against their Nazi overlords. The armed forces at the patriot's disposal must be sufficient to destroy the local German forces. The attack from within will be the basic concept of such operations.[11]

Yet everyone was groping in the dark. What exactly was required to arm and equip patriot armies? No one knew. In response to a request from the Joint Planning Staff's Future Operations Planning Section for a more detailed estimate of SOE's requirements to sustain an all-out guerrilla war, Gladwyn Jebb produced his paper 'The Prospects of Subversion'. This stated, *inter alia*:

As the time for a general uprising was still far distant, it was necessary to prepare and at the same time to encourage sabotage and passive resistance. In this work SOE was at present greatly handicapped by the shortage of arms, aircraft and transport facilities.

If SOE were to perform their function they would have to train and infiltrate large numbers of agents during the coming year, a process which required large numbers of aircraft of suitable design and adequate facilities for communications. The Chiefs of Staff have already been approached on these points but it would be helpful to know if they agreed with the policy recommended in the paper and, if so, whether they were prepared to make available the necessary men and material for its execution.[12]

General Ismay replied to Gladwyn Jebb on 24 April 1941:

Much as we may deplore it, the COS are at present faced with the problem of having to feed many hungry mouths with bread, on which the butter has to be spread very sparingly. To sum up, I feel sure that the COS would agree, in principle, with your paper, but I am positive that they would not be prepared to give you the *carte blanche* for which you ask.[13]

Ismay's reply led in turn to Brigadier Colin Gubbins' detailed and explosive report submitted on 21 May 1941[14] on just what would be needed if Britain were to support those secret armies in enemy-occupied territory (see Chapter 8). Yet even the basic supply of the 'Sabotage Groups' and 'Secret Armies' on the modest scale Gubbins proposed would require 8,000 aircraft sorties at a time when the operational strength of Bomber Command was ninety heavy bombers: 'There could not be a less favourable time at which to talk of the diversion of aircraft from the attack on Germany.'[15] The unanswerable mathematical logic of Brigadier Gubbins' paper, the sheer scale of minimal support needed to make resistance viable – they would require 55 per cent of the bomber force in a planned uprising in which 'the Allied contingents in Britain would be retrained as airborne troops and parachuted in to assist the revolt' – brought into sharp focus the whole question of SOE's strategic purpose and realistic capabilities; capabilities that must be weighed against the demands of the daily bomber offensive against Germany. Taking Gubbins' figures in the round:

> To equip a force of 200,000 underground fighters throughout Europe would require, if the SOE figures were correct, not less than 12,000 sorties, or six months effort by the entire command; and this diversion would have to be made during the next year or eighteen months, while the command was passing through the most critical phase of its expansion. There was thus a direct incompatibility between the existing bomber policy and subversion on the scale now proposed. The Allies could pin their faith to one or the other; but they could not afford, at least in 1941, to support both on an equal scale.[16]

Therein lay its demise. For neither Churchill nor his Chiefs of Staff would ever be persuaded to place the uncertainty of subversion and the hope of a one-off popular uprising throughout Europe, a popular uprising that, by definition, could never be rehearsed and could only be guaranteed if backed up by the support of ground forces in such strength as to make it redundant, above what Portal had described as the 'gilt-edged investment' of his bombing offensive.

It was a question that had no sooner been posed than the paper it sprang from was overtaken by the German invasion of Russia on 22 June 1941 – Operation *Barbarossa*. Here, at a stroke, was the arrival of an ally that meant Britain was no longer alone – the 'something else' that made redundant further talk about organised revolts in occupied countries; sabotage and subversion in occupied territory were to be supported, assuredly, but the 'detonator concept' with secret armies as its keystone was abandoned. It was a concept that died slowly, stifled by default and neglect. It was referred to occasionally, sometimes by Churchill himself, but such references were simply 'the last flickerings of a concept that had been extinguished by its own internal contradictions, the scarcity of resources and the rapidly approaching promise of the intervention of large Russian and American armies in the field'.[17]

Despite offering Churchill a revised paper in which he had significantly reduced his ambitions for SOE, Dalton was once again caught on the back foot. Excluded from both the COS and the Defence Committee, what hurt Dalton most was the fact that throughout the crucial weeks of debate about the importance of resistance, sabotage and subversion to British war strategy, there had been no personal word of inclusion or explanation from the prime minister. Such an admission was 'eloquent testimony to the low priority subversion and sabotage now played in the long-term plans of British strategy, and to SOE's relationship to the war leadership and the prime minister'.[18] The writing was on the wall; very soon it would become clearer still. At the First Washington 'Arcadia' Conference between British and US Chiefs of Staff in December 1941, immediately after the Japanese attack on Pearl Harbor, the role of the Resistance and secret armies in Europe was mentioned only briefly. The 'Arcadia' document listed the methods to be used for the undermining and wearing down of Germany's war effort in order of priority. The organisation of subversive movements and the nurturing of the spirit of revolt came last on the list.

Popular armies and the uprising of civilian populations were no longer perceived to hold the key to ultimate victory. Dalton the pragmatist might have reduced the breadth of his ambitions in an effort to keep SOE in line with the latest strategic thinking, but with SOE effectively denied sea access to the coast of northern France, agents in whatever numbers would still need aircraft to deliver them and their supplies to occupied Europe. Yet so few were available to SOE that Gubbins had minuted on 18 March 1941: 'All the various parties of men whom we are now training may well have to be landed by sea as no other means exist.'[19] The only aircraft that could be made available to what remained of that 'war from within' were bombers diverted from Portal's strategic bombing offensive: 'This essential clash of interests, so often nearly fatal to SOE, was to occupy Gubbins during 1942 and 1943 more than any other issue.'[20]

It occupied others too and appears not to have diminished with time. Bruce Marshall, the biographer of respected RF Section agent Wing Commander Tommy Yeo-Thomas, alias *The White Rabbit*, claims his subject was driven by desperation to door-step Churchill himself just a few months before D-Day to plead for the supply aircraft needed by agents in the field. Granted unusual access to the prime minister by Major Desmond Morton, Yeo-Thomas:

> ... started in right away on the Secret Army and the *Maquis*. He spoke of their appalling lack of arms and equipment. He spoke of the need for aircraft to drop supplies. Panting, breathless, he threw a potted version of the whole sad story at Mr Churchill and hoped that his hero would understand. His hero did ... The wand which Mr Churchill had waved was a powerful one: within forty-eight hours RF Section had at its disposal twenty-two Halifaxes, twelve Liberators, thirty-six Stirlings, six Albermarles and a number of small aircraft for pick-up operations.[21]

By early 1944, however, aircraft were available in quantities only dreamed of in 1941 when shortages of aircraft and more urgent strategic priorities dictated a far more modest waving of prime ministerial wands. From mid-1941 – and long before 'Arcadia' – it was made abundantly plain by the Joint Planning Staff that the strategic bombing offensive must always assume priority and that SIS was to enjoy priority over any SOE aircraft requirement:

> Subversive activities are mainly a complement to bombing and secret armies can never operate until bombing has first created suitable conditions. It would be unsound therefore to sacrifice the effectiveness of our bombing effort to those activities. It is essential that provision of sorties for SO2 should not be allowed to interfere with the requirements of SIS.[22]

It could not be clearer. Both Bomber Command and SIS were to have priority over Dalton, SOE and his 'Fourth Arm'. Dalton's wings may have been clipped but there was one immediate and welcome result that flowed from this critical scrutiny: the Special Duties Flight that had been allocated to SOE was expanded into a full squadron, reflecting the Chiefs of Staff belief that whilst the supply – and, crucially, the airdrop – of weapons should be cut to just 25 per cent of what Dalton and Gubbins had requested, the full requirement to support both propaganda and subversive activities should be met. Aircraft allocation was now to reflect those adjusted priorities. Up until then – and from February 1941 – No. 1419 Flight had been based at Newmarket racecourse and consisted of three Whitley bombers, one Lysander and one Maryland aircraft to service the needs of both SOE and SIS. Now, as from 25 August 1941,[23] 1419 became No. 138 Squadron. By November 1941, SOE had use of nine Whitleys and three Halifax bombers which, Gubbins told Dalton, 'were more than sufficient for all his prospective operations'.[24] There would be further expansion to Tempsford in Bedfordshire in early 1942.

By mid-1943 the demand for aircraft and airdrops would have expanded significantly; however, with just twenty-two aircraft at SOE's disposal, Sir Charles Hambro, then CD, would tell the Chiefs of Staff that, over four months, more than 300 requests from agents on the ground for re-supply had gone unanswered due to a shortage of aircraft.[25] All of which perhaps takes this account too far forward for, in early 1941, SOE's need for aircraft, despite the small number of agents deployed to mainland Europe, was already pressing. Gubbins minuted on 19 February 1941: 'The position as regards air facilities for SO2 both for transport of staff and agents, and for operations, is acute.'[26]

Gladwyn Jebb was despatched to plead for more aircraft to Major General Hastings Ismay, Churchill's Chief of Staff. Ismay wrote to Chief of the Air Staff Sir Charles Portal on 22 February 1941: 'Jebb came to see me the other day in some distress over the decisions recently taken by the Vice Chiefs of Staff in regard to the supply of aircraft for SOE purposes.'[27]

Jebb, it appears, was actually part of the problem. His tone and approach did not sit well with 'Bomber' Harris. Jebb was moved aside and Sir Frank Nelson became chief SOE aircraft negotiator. Harris wrote: 'I think now that Sir Frank Nelson is dealing with us instead of Gladwyn Jebb we shall be able to progress better from the point of view of amicable co-operation and in understanding each other's difficulties. I am dining with Mr Dalton next week and I hope that I shall be able to impress on him that our needs and requirements are at least as urgent as his.'[28] Elsewhere Harris had already gone on record as describing SOE operations as 'sidelines and comic departments' which had got entirely out of control.[29]

Dalton, meanwhile, had also entered the battle for more aircraft for SOE. After a long-awaited luncheon at Chequers with the prime minister on 2 March 1941, Dalton noted: 'I had three quarters of an hour with him alone. I pressed very strongly my need for more aircraft.'[30]

Three days later, and perhaps on Churchill's advice that it might be worth Dalton's while building bridges to the man under Portal whose supply or retention of his precious bombers could make or mar anything SOE might attempt to achieve in Europe, Dalton and Harris dined together: 'This is a good move. We must keep in touch with this Air Marshal', recorded Dalton in his diary. He may have thought Harris could be won round by dinner and lumbering charm, but the record shows otherwise: Harris described Dalton's Ministry of Economic Warfare as 'amateurish, ignorant, irresponsible and mendacious'.[31]

Harris and Dalton were to clash repeatedly. SOE's demands were practically without limit and represented, at their simplest, a diversion of resources: 'Harris was not readily persuaded to part with even a few of his precious aeroplanes to carry apparent ragamuffins to distant spots, in pursuit of objects no one seemed anxious to explain.'[32]

Once again, it seems apposite to peer into the future to assess that critical relationship between SOE and Bomber Command for, in November 1943, after Dalton's departure and whilst Bomber Command was suffering punitive losses during the Battle of Berlin, Harris would take it upon himself to cancel all SOE flights to Western Europe. He would do this in the wake of the discovery that, for almost two years, SOE had been the unwitting victim of *Der Englandspiel* – The England Game – the highly successful head-to-toe *Abwehr* penetration of SOE radio and agent circuits in Holland by Major Herman Giskes that was to cost the lives of fifty-four SOE agents. *Der Englandspiel* débâcle would come to represent one of SOE's most significant, damaging and shameful crises and it would provoke Major Morton, Churchill's intelligence adviser, to lobby the prime minister to fold SOE as an independent organisation and hand its activities lock, stock and barrel to SIS. That peremptory cancellation of all SOE flights was an act Harris justified 'only by the relatively high rate of aircraft losses in Holland, and by his comprehensive ignorance of the effects of this action on the Resistance in other areas. The paper war which followed was fought with quite exceptional bitterness …'[33] William Mackenzie, ever the diplomat, goes on to suggest that the row 'is perhaps not worth now recording in detail', although his footnote indicates that General Hastings Ismay, Clement Attlee the deputy prime minister and SOE's Lord Selborne all entered into the fray. The full investigation into the work of SOE that followed *Der Englandspiel* débâcle, conducted by outsiders in an atmosphere of aggressive hostility, led to a further attack on the very existence of SOE and the reassertion of old arguments between 'Fourth Arm' proponents within SOE and the Foreign Office/SIS opinion that '[SOE] had no right to separate existence and should be abolished in short order'.[34]

Not for the first time it would be the intervention of the prime minister – on this occasion just a few months before D-Day – that would ensure the continuation of SOE's fragile independence.

Notes

1 Mackenzie, *The Secret History of SOE*, p.60.
2 Mackenzie, *The Secret History of SOE*, p.87. COS (40) 683 (Extract).
3 Gwyer, *Grand Strategy*, Volume II, p.44.
4 Mackenzie, *The Secret History of SOE*, p.348.
5 Churchill to Roosevelt. Undated letter from 'former Naval Person' in CHAR 20/73 at the Churchill Archives Centre, Churchill College, Cambridge.
6 COS (40) 27 (O) in CAB 80/56 (microfilm) at The National Archives, Kew, dated 25 November 1940.
7 Mackenzie, *The Secret History of SOE*, p.349.
8. In June and July 1941, an investigation revealed that one-third of all bombers despatched returned after failing to find their primary target. Of those that claimed success, photographic evidence revealed only one-third bombed within 5 miles of their aiming point. Source: Hastings, Max, *Bomber Command* (Pan, London, 1981), p.128.
9 Bishop, Patrick, *Bomber Boys* (Harper, London, 2008), p.70.
10 Dilks, *The Diaries of Sir Alexander Cadogan*, p.445. Diary entry for 8 April 1942.
11 JP (41) 444 in CAB 79/12 (microfilm) at The National Archives, Kew, dated 14 June 1941.
12 'Prospects of Subversion' paper dated 21 April 1941 by Gladwyn Jebb. In File HS 7/215 at The National Archives, Kew, p.686.
13 Mackenzie, *The Secret History of SOE*, p.350.
14 In file HS 8/319 at The National Archives, Kew. Report entitled 'Outline Plan of SO2 Operations from 1 September 1941 to 1 October 1942'.
15 Mackenzie, *The Secret History of SOE*, p.352.
16 Gwyer, *Grand Strategy*, Volume II, p.46.
17 Stafford, *Britain and European Resistance 1940–1945*, p.66.
18 Stafford, *Britain and European Resistance 1940–1945*, p.68.
19 Foot, *SOE in France*, p.61.
20 Wilkinson and Astley, *Gubbins and SOE*, p.99.
21 Marshall, Bruce, *The White Rabbit* (Pan, London, 1954), p.97.
22 Report JP (41) 649 by the Joint Planning Staff entitled 'Special Operations Executive' and dated 9 August 1941. In CAB 79/13 at The National Archives, Kew.
23 Foot, SOE in France, p.165.
24 Stafford, *Britain and European Resistance 1940–1945*, p.66.

25 Foot, *SOE in France,* p.211.

26 File AIR 20/2901 at The National Archives, Kew. Minute in file.

27 File AIR 20/2901 at The National Archives, Kew. Letter in file dated 22 February 1941.

28 File AIR 20/2759 at The National Archives, Kew. Letter in file dated 27 February 1941.

29 Nicolson, David, *Aristide Warlord of the Resistance* (Leo Cooper, London, 1994), p.186. Undated letter from Air Marshal Harris, C-in-C Bomber Command, to Air Chief Marshal Sir Charles Portal, Chief of the Air Staff. In AIR 20/901.

30 Pimlott (ed.), *The Second World War Diary of Hugh Dalton: 1940–1945,* p.170. Diary entry for 2 March 1941.

31 Deacon, *A History of British Secret Service,* p.394.

32 Foot, *SOE in France,* p.15.

33 Mackenzie, William, *The Secret History of SOE: Special Operations Executive 1940–1945* (St Ermin's Press, London, 2000), p.416.

34 Mackenzie, *The Secret History of SOE,* p.416. Following a JIC investigation in July 1943 recorded in COS (43) 173rd(O)Mtg.

CHAPTER FIFTEEN

APOCALYPSE AS FAMILY PICNIC

In May 1941 a milestone was reached with the despatch of the first agent by air to France. The RAF claimed their first 'Joe' – Georges Bégué, alias *George Noble* – had been dropped with pinpoint accuracy into unoccupied central France some 20 miles north of Chateauroux. Bégué claimed he had been dropped wide by several miles. This, like the agent himself, rather missed the point: it had begun. In London, however, such news provided scant comfort for the Minister of Economic Warfare, who was beginning to react to pressures both real and imagined as SOE senior management began to take shape around a coterie of bankers, former fashion-house executives, public school chums and conservative businessmen whose appointment ran at curious variance to the establishment's ingrained suspicions of SOE's left-wing bias. Dalton wrote on 17 May 1941:

> I row Gladwyn violently both before and after lunch, on SO2. Too many businessmen; too little political gumption and biases against the left; an inefficient machine wherein my minutes are lost or disregarded; failure to keep me informed on what is going on … too many smooth-faced explanations; failure to get the right man to take over my Middle East show. The truth is the war is going rather badly and all these things show up sharply as a consequence. In the afternoon to West Leaze[1] in a most black mood.[2]

SOE's difficulties at this time were not all related to aircraft allocation, nor to the frustrations and impatience of a Labour minister who found himself at odds with disaffected subordinates and an entrenched conservative establishment. SOE might have despatched its first agent to France, but the recruitment, selection, training and despatch of agents to enemy-occupied territory and, most particularly, their ability to communicate back to London, were causing significant concerns of their own.

Georges Bégué – known ever after in SOE circles as 'Georges the First'[3] – was a trained radio operator and was dropped with his wireless set. Opening up communications with London four days after landing on 5/6 May 1941, he would remain SOE's only radio link with France until his arrest in October.[4] Thereafter there would be no radio link at all until February 1942. Between 5 May and 11 September 1941, operations *Torture, Trombone, Fabulous, Dastard* and *Barter* despatched agents to France for either F or the Gaullist RF Sections.

The first and only Lysander pick-up in 1941 took place on 4 September, whilst the first RAF airdrop of weapons – tommy guns, knives, plastic explosive (PE) and 'limpet' mines for attacks on shipping – were dropped successfully after three abortive attempts over the 300-acre estate of Philippe de Vomécourt in Haute-Vienne on 13 June 1941.[5] De Vomécourt had been contacted by his brother Pierre, who had made his way to London for agent training after the BEF evacuation and the fall of France had signalled the end of his work as an interpreter with a British Army regiment. He and another agent, Roger Cottin, had parachuted into France a week after Georges the First. These were the very first agents whose dangerous mission was to find and recruit others:

> Recruiting for the Resistance was a difficult task. Right from the beginning there were people prepared to do something to oppose the Germans but we needed those for whom there were no reservations, no twitchings of conscience about whether it was right, or proper, or legal to resist ...

Philippe de Vomécourt wrote *Who Lived to See the Day* in 1959 when the memory of what Professor Jackson has called 'The Dark Years' of France[6] was still raw and at a time when post-war France had still to reach an accommodation with the truth of its past. This was a past in which not all Frenchmen and women were heroes of the Resistance and in which, pre-1944, less than 2 per cent of the population became active resisters.[7] This was a past, too, in which pragmatic collaboration with an all-conquering enemy who showed every indication of permanence was not always seen by those *attentistes*[8] as the wartime crime it later became.

Central to those 'twitchings of conscience' was the nation's relationship with France's dominant figure, the venerated and venerable First World War hero of Verdun, Marshal Philippe Pétain. After the German breakthrough at Sedan in May 1940 and the subsequent collapse of French opposition that saw jack-booted Wehrmacht units strutting down the Champs Elysées on 14 June 1940, Pétain came to personify the new legal reality. Two days later the French Cabinet turned down Churchill's offer of a Declaration of Union that would have bound Britain and France together in a 'declaration of indissoluble union and unyielding resolution in their common defence of justice and freedom against subjection to a system which reduces mankind to a life of robots and slaves'.[9] Pétain queried caustically why anyone would wish to 'fuse with a corpse'. Prime Minister Reynaud resigned that evening, 16 June, and Marshal Pétain was invited by President Lebrun to form a government. The next day, Pétain went on French radio and in a thin, metallic voice that author and journalist Arthur Koestler described later as sounding like 'a skeleton with a chill',[10] the 84-year-old marshal announced:

> It is with a heavy heart that I tell you today we must cease hostilities. The fighting must stop.

To many, the full implication of France's looming defeat was lost to a shimmer in the summer heat. On 18 June, Arthur Koestler passed a group of refugees on the road to Perigueux in the Dordogne. He wrote in his diary:

> All the way saw families by the roadside with cars parked off the road on the spot where the last drop of petrol gave out. It is a sort of general stay put. All wait for armistice to be signed and 'everything to become normal again.' They really believe life will be as it was before. Meanwhile, they eat and drink in the sunny meadows and play belotte. The apocalypse as a family picnic.[11]

However, France was ostensibly still at war and had yet to surrender. The same day that Pétain made his wavering speech of imminent capitulation, a French Army general left Bordeaux airport for London with General Spears, Churchill's personal representative to the now ex-French prime minister, Reynaud. This French general was determined to carry on the fight. He carried with him a spare pair of trousers, four clean shirts and a family photograph. History would decide that he carried with him also the honour of France, for his name was Charles de Gaulle. Spears was to write later: 'I realised more vividly than before that there was nothing but this man's courage to kindle into flame the tiny spark of hope he had brought with him; all that was now left of the spirit of France.'[12]

The next day, 18 June, while French families played belotte in sunny Perigueux meadows waiting for the war to end, de Gaulle asked the British government for permission to use BBC radio to broadcast to France. His request was turned down by the Cabinet and only rescinded after the intervention of Churchill and General Spears, who had seen the scale of French collapse for himself and realised that Pétain truly intended to take France out of the war. That evening of 18 June 1940 in a speech no one bothered to record for posterity, de Gaulle reached out across the Channel to the French people:

> I, General de Gaulle, now in London, call upon the French officers and soldiers who are or who may find themselves on British soil, with or without their weapons, I call upon the engineers and the skilled workers in the armaments industry who are or who may find themselves on British soil, to join

me. Whatever happens, the flame of French Resistance must not and shall not die.[13]

On 22 June 1940 France surrendered and Marshal Pétain signed the armistice with Germany. France was divided into two, with Germany having control and physical occupation of the north and west – including Paris and the Atlantic coastline – whilst the remaining two-fifths remained unoccupied but governed from the town of Vichy in central France. Paris remained the *de jura* capital. Shaking hands with Hitler, co-operating willingly with an invader intent upon sucking France dry, proclaiming anti-Semitic laws that would send more than 75,000 French Jews to Auschwitz, standing by whilst thousands of fellow citizens were shot as hostages and raising not a finger in protest as 650,000 civilian workers would be compulsorily shipped out to work in German factories,[14] Pétain signed away – with the legal approval of the National Assembly – what he saw as the decadent Third Republic. It was replaced by the bucolic, paternalistic, inward-looking State of Vichy with himself as *Chef de l'Etat Français*. Gone was the stirring battle cry of the Revolution, as *Liberté! Egalité! Fraternité!* became the stolid *Travail, Famille, Patrie* – Work, Family, Fatherland. Marshal Pétain embodied the conservative, authoritarian legality of the new state: 'The programme of the French state was simple: a "national revolution" designed to root out the Freemasons, communists and Jews who were deemed to be the root of France's woes.'[15]

What General de Gaulle was advocating now from London was illegal, and nothing less than treason. Not that, in mid-June 1940, it seemed to matter particularly: few outside the French military had even heard of the junior general who had once served directly under Pétain, been his military protégé, even named his son after him in admiration of the man whose constitutional legality he now openly defied. For his part, Pétain appears to have distanced himself from de Gaulle who, he claimed, 'has no friends in the army. No wonder, for he gives the impression of looking down on everybody.'[16] General de Gaulle's initial call to the colours appears to have made little impact:

In the main, De Gaulle's declaration fell on deaf ears. The French population was bitter, depressed, cynical. Calls to arms from a nobody had little purchase on people who no longer trusted their military leaders.[17]

One French soldier, Georges Sadoul, listened to de Gaulle's speech on the radio surrounded by a group of fellow soldiers. His reaction was hardly what the general must have hoped for:

Go fight yourself, you bastard. You've got your arse in an armchair and you want other people to go on getting themselves killed.[18]

Less than a month later a court martial in Toulouse sentenced de Gaulle *in absentia* to four years in prison. In August that same year a second court martial sentenced de Gaulle to death for treason against the Vichy regime.[19] Author Andrew Shennan claims that one of the first people who rallied to de Gaulle's side challenged the general as to the precise legal status of his Free French movement, and to which he claims General de Gaulle replied, with characteristic hauteur: '*Nous sommes la France*' ('*We* are France').[20] It was an aloofness, a necessary arrogance, that Churchill understood and appreciated:

> He also felt it to be essential that he should maintain a proud and haughty demeanour towards '*Perfidious Albion*' although an exile, dependent upon our protection and dwelling in our midst. He had to be rude to the British to prove to French eyes that he was not a British puppet. He certainly carried out this policy with perseverance.[21]

Those Frenchmen who made their moral choice about continuing the fight against the Nazis without the elderly marshal's permission made their way to London where they found themselves enjoying a brief stay under guard at the requisitioned Royal Victoria Patriotic School on Wandsworth Common. Here they were screened and vetted by interrogators skilled in the art of weeding out German infiltrators. Volunteers from other countries endured the same process either in Wandsworth or Camberley before those candidates showing early promise found themselves signing the Official Secrets Act and being interviewed for secret work that might involve foreign travel.

SOE's core operations were based around 'Country' sections with each section representing territory under German occupation. Each was anxious to recruit those nationals who could be inserted back into their homeland to carry out clandestine work. Yet the very nature of that work meant that they could hardly advertise for recruits:

> In one way at least, SOE was like a club, for membership was by invitation only. Entry was so largely a matter of accident that there was nothing which deserved the name of a recruiting system though there was system enough to prevent people from inviting themselves to join and simply walking in …[22]

The situation regarding France, however, was more complicated than any other. Very quickly it was established that there would be two French 'Country' sections. Sharing an initial degree of mutual suspicion and enmity worthy of SOE's relationship with SIS, F Section was run by the British whilst RF Section, though relying upon Britain for training, stores, arms, aircraft and radios, worked in co-operation with General de Gaulle who, within days of his arrival, had formed the Free French Committee and surrounded himself with other French officers in exile. On 28 June the British government recognised de Gaulle as 'Leader of all Free Frenchmen, wherever they may be, who rally to him in support of the Allied cause'.

From the outset, General de Gaulle insisted – and received Churchill's assurance – that French men and women would not be recruited by F Section. Instead, they would, if selected, join RF, the SOE section whose clandestine activities General de Gaulle delegated to Major *Passy*, André Dewavrin, the newly appointed head of what would evolve into the Free French *Bureau Central de Renseignement et d'Action* (BCRA), the office of security, intelligence and offensive action. Yet – as with so much to do with the arcane politics of SOE – there was to be a hidden sting in the tail: SOE might pay lip service to the idea of wholehearted co-operation with the Gaullist section of SOE, but Baker Street did not trust de Gaulle, his political ambitions or his internal security. As it turned out, General de Gaulle was wise not to trust SOE either. Wise, not simply because F Section sometimes poached potential agents earmarked for RF Section, but because, after raising plans for both 'sides' to work together in the closest harmony with the common aim of placing agents in France, the exchange of vital information was not so forthcoming. Sir Frank Nelson minuted Dalton on 11 October 1940:

> The ideal is to allow the Gestapo and the De Gaulle staff to think we are co-operating 100% with each other – whereas in truth, whilst I should wish you to have the friendliest day-to-day relationship and liaison with the De Gaulle people, I should wish you at the same time to tell them nothing of our innermost and most confidential plans, and above all, such bases as you may establish in France must be our bases and known only to us. The whole of our HQ organisation and its field organisation would be entirely concealed from the French.[23]

Dalton wholeheartedly agreed, although it was an unsubtle subterfuge and it did not last long. The discovery of such blatant deception left de Gaulle and RF Section 'exceedingly angry'.[24]

Eric Piquet-Wicks was the half-French fusilier captain seconded to RF Section who ended up running that organisation until August 1942. He wrote a well-regarded book about his wartime experiences and observed: '*Passy* felt frequently that he was fighting on three fronts: the home front and red tape; the enemy and, regrettably, what the Free French looked upon as a rival organisation, the French Section.'[25] Jealousies between both sections often 'raged with virulence', wrote Professor Michael Foot, who witnessed it first hand:

Each of the two sections was sure that its own men and methods were sound, while the rival's were not; each thought the other was unfairly favoured, either by the rest of the SOE machine or by politicians outside it. Most of this jealous feeling was froth though occasionally it had some impact, usually harmful, on operations.[26]

Denied official access to exiled Frenchmen earmarked for RF Section and de Gaulle, British F Section recruited from amongst men and women who were not French citizens but who had been born, brought up or worked in France and who could pass as native.

The practical effect of this separation of sources was an unconscious replication of pre-war class divisions: F Section recruits tended to be officer class; those of RF, blue collar. And it was blue-collar artisans who would bear the brunt of the dying in the clandestine war in the long, dreary months that stretched ahead:

They were of every class, category and size, and common to them all was an unflinching determination to regain their country. Few were regular soldiers, or sailors or airmen; frequently they were non-commissioned officers who had been clerks or garage hands – the little people of France.[27]

Recruitment, from any class, came with its own difficulties:

Recruitment was difficult because it was impossible ever to be absolutely sure of your man. It was hard enough in England, where the new organisation was looking for men and women who could be taught how to use weapons, how to undertake efficient sabotage, and how to pass on their knowledge to the French.

These agents had to speak French fluently – and some did not and should not have been sent – and they had to be capable of a flawless impersonation of a Frenchman, an impersonation so perfect that it would not break down no matter what the stress to which it was subjected. The agent needed courage, intelligence, and a profound self-sufficiency and resourcefulness.[28]

Those who volunteered for SOE – often without knowing or being told where that act might lead them – followed a selection and training programme that altered little throughout the war. Devised by Major Davies of pre-SOE MI(R), this consisted of a four-stage training regime built around periods of time spent under continual assessment at different Special Training Schools (STS) scattered between the remote wilds of western Scotland, genteel Hampshire and the Home Counties of southern England. The course began with a two- to four-week 'Preliminary' course of basic military and physical training that helped weed out the unfit and unsuitable. These were held in one of six 'Group A' country houses requisitioned by SOE in the Home Counties. Here – without being told precisely what SOE actually did – students learned weapon handling, unarmed combat, elementary demolitions, map reading, fieldcraft and basic signalling.[29]

From here potential agents moved to the 'Paramilitary' schools in Scotland, based around ten shooting lodges in the Arisaig and Morar areas of Inverness-shire. Amid some of the most spectacular – and wettest – countryside in Britain, agents learnt silent killing, knife work, rope work, boat work, pistol and sub-machine gun training with British and German weapons, more fieldcraft, more mapwork, elementary Morse code, advanced raiding tactics, practical railway demolitions and living off the land. They also and always did a great deal of hard marching across broken country, both by day and by night.

Mandatory parachute training at Ringway, near Manchester, then followed and each candidate was required to complete five jumps, one at night. They then returned south to the 'Group B' 'Finishing' schools in the New Forest, Hampshire. Here, all pretence of the Commando training cover story was dropped and agents learnt the trade-craft skills of clandestine movement, coding and cipher-ing, industrial sabotage, observation and urban concealment intended to keep them operational, effective, unnoticed, unwatched and uncaught in enemy-occupied territory. Finally, those deemed suitable for missions abroad went to operational holding schools where they might remain for a few hours or even a few weeks waiting for that opportune moment when, weather permitting, train-ing gave way to operations:

> To be dropped in Occupied France was not a great adventure, nor was it an exciting pastime – it was a deadly struggle against a ruthless and savage enemy, most often with death as a reward.[30]

Hugh Dalton reflected after the war:

> Many of these agents of SOE showed great heroism, often a very lonely courage. Some met death in direct combat, some through misadventure, some through privation, some following long torture. To be the minister responsible for all this brave striving towards victory and freedom made me feel very humble.[31]

By the contemporary standards of wartime attrition, an SOE agent's chances of survival were good. Told they had a fifty-fifty chance, the rate was actually higher than that: of 450 F Section agents despatched to France, a quarter did not return; against which, only ten in every hundred crews flying raids for 'Bomber' Harris could expect to complete a first tour of thirty operations. Many of those who completed SOE's four-stage series of demanding courses emerged feeling supremely capable of looking after themselves:

Just back from the north of England where my training had ended, I was conscious of the new man I had become, of my new fitness and physical strength. Although I was thirty-five, the exceptional training I had undergone had made me as strong and as healthy as I had ever been or ever shall be. I knew that I could fight far more intelligently and efficiently than the majority of men and that, single-handed, I was capable of blowing up a bridge, of sinking a ship, of putting a railway engine out of action in a matter of seconds with a mere spanner, or of derailing an express train with my overcoat. I had been taught to drive a locomotive, how to kill an enraged dog with my bare hands, to jump from a fast-moving train, how to throw a horse, to decode a message, to make invisible ink, to receive and transmit Morse. I had finished my five regulation parachute jumps and, although I hated it each time a little more, I was proud of having done it.[32]

Yet still, the trick remained elusive: how to insert agents into Vichy and German-occupied France and make them operationally effective; how to gauge the national mood; how to link up with potential Resistance members; and how to establish and maintain radio links with London from a France that had suddenly become unknown territory. It was also a land in which the concept of armed resistance was something that most French men and women had yet to grasp.

Many historians date the dawn of that realisation to 20 October 1941 when a Lieutenant Colonel Karl Hotz, Nazi military commander of Nantes, was gunned down crossing a square by Spartaco Guisco and Gilbert Brustlein, two members of the *Jeunesses Communistes* charged with directing German repression away from Paris. They succeeded in their aim, but the murder of the urbane, sophisticated Hotz was deeply unpopular among the people of Nantes who feared German reprisals. They were right to do so: two days later forty-eight hostages were executed.[33]

Professor Michael Foot believes those first executions had far-reaching consequences: 'For every Frenchman or Frenchwoman that reprisal executions of this kind frightened into acquiescence, a score were shocked into opposition – in their hearts at least – and so became ripe for recruiting.'[34] Yet not every historian agrees that reprisal stiffened resistance: that same evening a German military adviser was killed in Bordeaux. The following day fifty more hostages were shot. Between October 1941 and October 1942, 814 more hostages were executed, thus 'further weakening public support for an armed struggle most people found bewildering'.[35]

That 'armed struggle' appears hardly worthy of the name. In 1941, fewer than fifteen Germans were killed throughout France. It was a year of small paces rather than giant strides. One of those who saw just how small those early steps were was Maurice Buckmaster, a pre-war manager with Ford in Paris, who joined SOE in London in May 1941 as an information officer in the days of bare offices and 'a deserted atmosphere' when he was told that 'everything is highly embryonic'.[36] In September that same year he would take over F Section. He would command it for the rest of the war, but was felt to be 'frightfully naïve and far too nice for his job. And not tough enough.'[37]

From the start, Buckmaster claims to have been unimpressed with progress. In a colourful and self-serving autobiography whose accuracy has not withstood the test of time, Buckmaster describes an early conversation with Sir Charles Hambro, Sir Frank Nelson's second-in-command:

'What's being done'?

'Well', he said: 'We've got a small nucleus in training already, including about ten men preparing to get back into France and see what it's all about. The important thing is to move fairly slowly at first.'

'Well, we certainly seem to be doing that,' I observed, 'has anyone gone yet?'
He said: 'They're in training'.

'Good Lord!' I said: 'It's nearly a year since we were chucked out of France!'

'Now look here, Buckmaster, these things take time. In 1940 we had to concentrate on real essentials – Defensive essentials. We're only just beginning to get our breath back'.[38]

Six agents followed Georges Bégué into France in mid-September and a further eight, four by boat to Barcares north-east of Perpignan[39] and four by air as part of the CORSICAN mission that dropped near Bergerac on 10/11 October.[40] Thereafter a wave of arrests followed, described as 'the beginning of the dark age for F Section'[41] with all four of the CORSICAN mission arrested within ten days of arrival, leaving just five agents at large in Vichy France. Other arrests in occupied France followed, including that of the second W/T operator, Pierre Bloch. This left Robert Leroy, an SOE agent critical to this story, alone in Bordeaux and F Section with no radio link to London from occupied France. Sabotage, too, had been negligible.

In September 1941, Dalton had to report to Churchill that only twenty-one agents and organisers had been sent to France[42] and a further thirteen had been recruited locally. Two agents were in Belgium awaiting stores and two more had been dropped into Holland from whom nothing further had been heard. Further afield, SOE had only been able to find a single Italian prepared to go back into Italy – SOE's black spot – as an agent. In all, 385 agents were under training; a further 115 had been rejected as unsuitable, whilst ten had been rather darkly recorded as 'handed to security'.[43] In March 1941, in an earlier, more confident and combative mood, Dalton had pressed Churchill for more aircraft, asking for 'more tools' so they could start setting Europe ablaze. Eight months on, however,

and Gubbins was admitting to Dalton that the weapons given to SOE by the War
Office could not be distributed as fast as he wished because there was an 'insufficiency of agents abroad'.[44] Those grand 'Fourth Arm' ambitions of Dalton's,
indulged and explored for a brief while by the Chiefs of Staff during Britain's
months of extreme danger, had been thwarted by logistics and by Hitler's decision to invade Russia. Perhaps it was just as well. Now, as 1941 drew towards
its close, old animosities began to re-assert themselves as the arguments with
Brendan Bracken over control of propaganda moved to a new level of embittered acrimony. Over the next few months:

> Disagreement turned to hostility, and hostility to fury. Bracken, however, was
> the aggressor. Though he had less experience than Dalton he was younger,
> fresher and determined to win his spurs in this, his first engagement. By con-
> trast, Dalton fought with a growing desperation, his anger reflecting a weary
> loneliness. Never in his public life did he feel so persecuted as during the winter
> of 1941–42 and never so unhappy.[45]

It was not just Brendan Bracken who was unsettling Dalton. SOE itself was also
causing serious concerns:

> Apart from the trouble with Bracken, our Operations now are few and far
> between. Our last reports have been most bare, long tales of what has not been
> done. We are living on the past. I tell Gladywn that just now I am particularly
> anxious for a successful operation or two.[46]

Other enemies were also beginning to circle. A week earlier Dalton recorded that
the faithful Jebb had told him:

> Ronald Tree told de la Warr, who told it back to him, that I was a most sinister
> figure and was organising a Gestapo of my own staffed with members of the
> Labour Party. Also that Hood gave Gladwyn the impression that the talk in the
> Ministry of Information was that they should take it all over and that what was
> left of SOE could be done by 'the military' or C [SIS]! We want allies very badly.[47]

Dalton added to his diary that same day: 'What is all this worth? Sometimes I feel
that I should be much happier outside it all.' A little later he would add: 'Going
to bed, I think that we just don't deserve to win the war. We are all fighting each
other instead of the enemy and with such zest.'

The year 1941 had witnessed significant changes for SOE: the German invasion of Russia in June and the Japanese attack upon Pearl Harbor six months
later had dramatically altered the global strategic picture. *En passant*, the conse-

quence of those attacks had stripped SOE of much of its untested promise and unique strategic potential. The 'militarisation' of SOE might have gone some way to ensure its survival, but it would now be in a supporting rather than a leading role. Difficulties in organisation, in training, knowledge of enemy territory and clandestine trade-craft, in aircraft supply and deployment and selection of personnel had all conspired to prevent SOE sending agents to occupied Europe in the sort of numbers that might have impressed its critics. The existing SOE historiography overlooks the accumulative impact of these disparate developments in 1941, yet they placed SOE and its chairman in a position of increasing vulnerability. Now Dalton himself felt beleaguered and under pressure, as those who wished him ill sensed weakness and began to close in. For Britain, for Dalton and for SOE, 1941 had been a bleak year. It drew now to a bleak close.

Notes

1 His Wiltshire home.
2 Pimlott (ed.), *The Second World War Diary of Hugh Dalton: 1940–1945*, p.210. Diary entry for 19 May 1941.
3 De Vomécourt, Philippe, *Who Lived to See the Day* (Hutchinson, London, 1961), p.38.
4 Contradicted by Foot who claims George Bloch dropped with a radio on 6/7 September. Foot, *SOE in France*, p.156.
5 De Vomécourt, *Who Lived to See the Day*, p.45.
6 Jackson, Julian, *France: The Dark Years 1940–1944* (Oxford University Press, Oxford, 2001).
7 Cobb, Matthew, *The Resistance: The French Fight Against the Nazis* (Simon & Schuster, London, 2009), p.3.
8 Wait-and-see.
9 Spears, E., *Assignment to Catastrophe* (Heinemann, London, 1954), p.292.
10 Koestler, Arthur, *Scum of the Earth* (Collins, London, 1955), p.180.
11 Koestler, *Scum of the Earth*, p.175.
12 Spears, *Assignment to Catastrophe*, p.323.
13 Cobb, *The Resistance: The French Fight Against the Nazis*, p.34.
14 Jackson, *France: The Dark Years 1940–1944*, p.1.
15 Cobb, *The Resistance: The French Fight Against the Nazis*, p.27.
16 Spears, *Assignment to Catastrophe*, p.85.
17 Cobb, *The Resistance: The French Fight Against the Nazis*, p.34.
18 Cobb, *The Resistance: The French Fight Against the Nazis*, p.34.
19 Five years later Charles de Gaulle, then President of the Provisional Government of France, commuted Marshal Pétain's death sentence for treason to life imprisonment. Reduced to senility on Ile d'Yeu, Pétain died in 1951, aged 95.
20 Shennan, Andrew, *De Gaulle* (Longman, London, 1993), p.27.
21 Churchill, *The Second World War*, Volume II: 'Their Finest Hour', p.451.
22 Foot, *SOE in France*, p.41.
23 Mackenzie, *The Secret History of SOE*, p.230.
24 Foot, *SOE in France*, p.22.
25 Piquet-Wicks, Eric, *Four in the Shadows* (Jarrolds, London, 1957), p.22.
26 Foot, *SOE in France*, p.23.

27 Piquet-Wicks, *Four in the Shadows*, p.21.

28 De Vomécourt, *Who Lived to See the Day*, pp.42–3.

29 Rigden, *SOE Syllabus: Lessons in Ungentlemanly Warfare World War II*, pp.2–3.

30 Piquet-Wicks, *Four in the Shadows*, p.142.

31 Dalton, *The Fateful Years*, p.372.

32 Langalaan, George, *Knights of the Floating Silk* (Hutchinson, London, 1959), p.81.

33 Cobb, *The Resistance: The French Fight Against the Nazis*, p.80.

34 Foot, *SOE in France*, p.161.

35 Cobb, *The Resistance: The French Fight Against the Nazis*, p.84.

36 Cookridge, *Inside SOE*, p.101.

37 Professor Foot interviewed by this author on 25 January 2008.

38 Buckmaster, Maurice, *They Fought Alone* (Panther, London, 1960), p.15.

39 One of these was Robert Leroy, a merchant seaman, who made his way from the ZNO to Bordeaux. His intelligence-gathering in the docks there features prominently in the chapter that follows.

40 This team, consisting of Captain Jack Hayes, Captain Clement Jumerau, Lieutenant Charles le Harivel and Lieutenant Daniel Turberville was dropped to act as sabotage instructors within the ZNO. All were captured within ten days.

41 Foot, *SOE in France*, p.157.

42 Dalton report to Churchill, September 1941. In Dalton Papers 7/3 at the library of the London School of Political and Economic Science.

43 In Dalton Papers 7/3 at the library of the London School of Political and Economic Science.

44 Dalton to Gladwyn Jebb 'Most Secret and Strictly Confidential' Memo dated 19 December 1941 recounting meeting with Gubbins on 3 November 1941. In Dalton Papers 18/2 at the library of the London School of Political and Economic Science.

45 Pimlott, *Hugh Dalton*, p.331.

46 Pimlott (ed.), *The Second World War Diary of Hugh Dalton: 1940–1945*, p.329. Diary entry for 1 December 1941.

47 Pimlott (ed.), *The Second World War Diary of Hugh Dalton: 1940–1945*, p.323. Diary entry for 24 November 1941. Ronald Tree (1897–1976) Parliamentary private secretary to the then Minister of Information; H.E.D.B. Sackville (1900–76) 9th Earl de la Warr; Samuel Hood (1910–81), private secretary to the then Minister of Information.

CHAPTER SIXTEEN

POISON FOR THE DOCTOR

It is arguable that, without Dalton's drive, aggression, political agitation and bullying manner, and that, to a lesser extent, of his CEO, Gladwyn Jebb, the Special Operations Executive would never have struggled to its feet. The concomitant of that supposition, however, is that it was the same character and its defects which caused Dalton, Jebb, Nelson and SOE many of the problems that were to stalk SOE's operational development and reputation throughout the winter of 1941 and spring of 1942. Although it may have been the 'militarisation' of SOE's strategic role in the build-up to the invasion of Normandy that brought SOE closer to the ambit of conventional military thinking, it is surely no coincidence that Dalton's replacement in February 1942 by the conservative and emollient Viscount Wolmer (soon to be Lord Selborne) ushered in a period of placatory, inter-departmental harmony, albeit one in which the threat to SOE's very existence merely took on a less abrasive texture.

From the outset, Dalton believed passionately in the concept of the 'unity of subversion', yet we can see with the wisdom of hindsight that he critically omitted to ensure, in the urgency of his new appointment in July 1940, that the Ministry of Information and therefore both 'black' and 'white' propaganda came under the control of his newly created Ministry of Economic Warfare. Thus Dalton, himself at that stage still in charge of SO1, the arm of his new organisation whose remit was also propaganda, found himself in immediate conflict with the ineffectual Duff Cooper: 'I have seldom known two men more naturally antipathetic to each other', commented Anthony Eden, with whom Dalton's own relations were soon to become so bad that they led to a 'virtual severance' between SOE and the Foreign Office by mid-1941.[1] Duff Cooper was replaced by Brendan Bracken in July 1941.

That disrespected Ministry of Information may have proved to be Duff Cooper's political graveyard, but Bracken had every intention of succeeding in this, his first ministerial post. Central to his plans was the exclusion of Dalton and his ministry from anything to do with propaganda, black or white.

Bracken had youth and energy on his side, and something else, too: the security of 'belonging' to his class and – jewel beyond price – the enduring 'wilderness years' friendship of the prime minister, 'an asset which, like a priceless gem, needed only to be displayed to exert its influence'.[2] Three days into his appointment and Bracken had already identified Dalton as a Whitehall enemy: 'At 5pm saw Brendan who was very friendly. Made little attempt to conceal his desire to get rid of Dalton.'[3]

From the start, surrounded by the safety of his conservative, like-minded friends, Bracken launched a sniping war of attrition aimed at wearing down and belittling his Socialist opponent. Dalton's biographer observes astutely that whilst the diaries of both Sir Alexander Cadogan and Sir Robert Bruce Lockhart often refer to Bracken as 'Brendan', Hugh Dalton is referred to simply as 'Dalton'. He was the outsider; the Eton-educated class renegade. As such, he found himself 'ringed by people who regarded him privately with contempt'.[4] Lockhart recorded: 'Dr Dalton seems to have few friends. At least, Richie Calder[5] who is a Labour man, says he is a very unpopular man in the Labour Party.'[6] Now the bully found himself bullied by Bracken, the man Jebb had described as a '*Firbolg*, or bog squatter, an aboriginal inhabitant of Ireland clear both from his features and from his conduct' whose 'moonish, cherubic face topped by a shock of crinkly, flaming-red hair belied a caustic determination'.[7] His confidence continually eroded and belatedly made aware of the prime minister's personal dislike, Hugh Dalton 'had to be coaxed to make even the most essential calls to No. 10'[8] whilst 'Churchill's supposed "Camarilla" took to meeting frequently at Chequers where they worked themselves into a lather of vilification of SOE denouncing Dalton's "secret show" and reaffirming that it should be taken from him'.[9]

The diary of Sir Robert Bruce Lockhart, the chairman and soon-to-be Director General of the newly formed Political Warfare Executive supports such a view. Lockhart wrote that same month: 'Had a few minutes with him [Beaverbrook]. Told me he had heard Dalton's secret show attacked at Chequers on Saturday evening. It was to be taken away from him. Advised me to back Bracken.'[10] Notwithstanding the prime minister's episodic dabbling in the activities of SOE, if Churchill's interest in SOE appeared at times to waver it may have been because of his dislike of Dalton himself rather than the organisation he championed so abrasively. John Colville, one of Churchill's private secretaries, observed:

> The Special Operations Executive and other clandestine organisations, however effective, did not attract his attention. He knew less than he should of the gallantry and initiative of British agents. This was because he saw as little as possible of Dalton, under whose broad authority most of them came, and there was no direct contact with No 10 on these matters.[11]

It was an attitude not lost on Hugh Dalton who complained bitterly to Labour leader Clement Attlee: 'The PM took no interest in this particular branch of my work and regarded it as a bloody bone which has been thrown to me in order to appease the Labour Party.'[12] But it was Bracken, not Dalton's unpopularity or his doomed attempts to ingratiate himself with the prime minister, that was to prove Dalton's ultimate undoing as superficial cordiality between the two rival ministers turned to hostility and then to outright hatred. A Hambro-hosted dinner in early October was 'Not a success. Bracken was rude, assertive, ignorant, inconsequent, stupid, angular and unreceptive', wrote Dalton.[13] Sir Alexander Cadogan, Permanent Under-secretary at the Foreign Office, observed a few days later: '3.45. Meeting of PWE. Dogfight between Dalton and Bracken. Inconclusive. Dalton became white to the top of his bald head with rage.'[14]

Much of their anger, however, was committed to paper. A selection of excerpts from Dalton's diary in chronological sequence between mid-October 1941 and early February 1942 shows the scale and escalation of the animosity between two of Churchill's senior ministers. Dalton wrote in his diary of Monday, 13 October 1941:

An incredible letter arrives for me today from Bracken – 'Dear Minister of Economic Warfare …Yours sincerely'. What a fool and a nuisance this man is! The result is I have to spend hours – yes, literally many hours – of my own time and that of CEO, AD and ADZ going through old files and making a reply which shall reach this fool before our meeting.[15]

And a week later:

Weekly meeting of PWE. A most infuriating afternoon! Bracken is worse than ever. He brings no papers, has studied nothing, is arrogant, rude, inconsequent, critical, purely destructive. I am told he makes a bad impression on several of those there. I show great restraint, but shall not indefinitely continue to do so.[16]

A month passes and matters do not improve:

The meeting this afternoon goes fairly smoothly till the end when, as usual, Bracken explodes. I merely say that he is wrong, not for the first time, in his facts. I stay behind and talk to Eden. I summon up all my reserves of charm for this vain, feminine creature. Then, turning to Bracken, I say that I shall pour out to Attlee the story of what I have had to put up with during his absence [the deputy prime minister was away in America]. It is quite intolerable that Bracken should always be running around to the PM. Eden says he doesn't think the PM pays much heed to what Bracken says. He doesn't register.[17]

This was manifestly not what Eden believed. Clement Attlee dined with Dalton the day after he returned from his successful trip to America when he had met the president and his advisers. Immediately after dinner, however, Dalton returned to the subject which was foremost in his mind and showed Attlee Bracken's letters: 'He read it all through – though there is now a damned lot of it – snorting with indignation. He said: "This man is not fit to be a minister in the middle of a war".'[18]

Bracken's abusive letters appear to have continued. Dalton wrote on 2 December 1941: 'On returning from the PWE meeting I find Bracken's latest letter. This is so offensive that I decide not to answer it …'[19]

Evidently the problems of Bracken and his letter-writing was not something that resided solely in the minister's imagination. Even Anthony Eden – never one of Dalton's supporters – conceded that one of those Bracken letters of early 1942 was 'the letter of a lunatic'.[20] Dalton wrote on 3 December 1941: 'I have been trying several times to catch Attlee to whom I hand over further papers relating to Bracken[21] and speak with emphasis and indignation. I just cannot go on like this and my patience is exhausted.'[22]

Attlee pressed Dalton's case with the prime minister some time during the following week. On 12 December 1941, Dalton's ally and CEO, Gladwyn Jebb, attempted to lighten the mood: 'Gladwyn says that one of my staff is going to present me with a book entitled "How To Get Rid Of Bracken" but the trouble is that it takes seven years, and then the bloody stuff may grow again.'[23] A week later Dalton wrote a lengthy top-secret report to Jebb, outlining the results of his attempts to make an ally of Major Desmond Morton at No. 10 and recruit his help in the endless battle with Brendan Bracken:

> I said that Mr Bracken, on the other hand, talked everywhere against me and SOE. Of this I had much evidence. I added that Bracken and I both had loud voices, but that we differed in that, just for this very reason, I was very careful what I said. Mr Bracken was the only colleague with whom I had unfortunately found it quite impossible to get on. I dared say that he spoke very wildly and maliciously about me and my affairs to the PM. Major Morton said that he was quite sure that the PM would not be influenced in any way by what Mr Bracken might say on such matters. He said that he hoped it might be possible to end our 'barging match'.[24]

Beyond that Morton would not be drawn, although he then proceeded to unsettle Dalton somewhat by suggesting, in the light of the creation of PWE and 'other developments', that it might be time to revise the initial SOE charter. Clearly, Dalton thought he had been confiding in, if not a friend, then at least an ally:

I did not react much to this and still less to Major Morton's next suggestion, namely that he might help by trying his hand at a first rough re-draft. I said that I did not think he need attempt this ...

Once again, Dalton's maladroit political antenna had let him down. Morton, one of Dalton's Chequers 'Camarilla', was never a friend and was alleged to have represented him, to Dalton's later mortification, 'most amusingly, as a windbag, a careerist, and a witless fool who shouted contradictory objugations [sic] at his officials'.[25] As far back as November 1940, Dalton had been warned by Sir Frank Nelson that Morton 'was no friend of his or G's [Jebb's] or mine, and would much like to discredit our whole show'.[26] Now Bruce Lockhart wrote gleefully about a conversation passed on between Major Morton and a colleague in the privacy of a closed car on the way to London: 'It was anti-Dalton; said Dalton was very tactless, that Winston did not like him. Dalton spoke to me yesterday about Morton. It was quite serious that Dalton knows Morton does not like him, and that he does not like Morton.'[27]

Determined now to find some way to counter Bracken's remorseless intentions to reorganise their two ministries and squeeze Dalton out of the propaganda picture altogether, before Christmas the beleaguered 'Doctor Dynamo' came up with a plan of his own: there should be a new Ministry of Economic *and* Political Warfare. And he, Dalton, should be in charge. He took the idea to Attlee, who supported him and presented Dalton's proposal to the Foreign Secretary. Eden remained non-committal. What Eden did divulge, however, was that Bracken had proposed that he should take over all propaganda and that Dalton's remaining tasks should be absorbed by the Chiefs of Staff. Attlee bridled at this and told Eden that Labour ministers, as part of a working Coalition government, expected to have a proper share of the conduct of the war. Realising that the prospect of Labour resignations from a Coalition government Churchill needed to keep intact was a powerful negotiating tool, Dalton warned Attlee: 'If anything of the kind happened, I should not regard the Ministry of Economic Warfare as a full-time job and should not go on.'[28] Dalton's idea of a Ministry of Economic and Political Warfare went nowhere. Elsewhere, too, there was little change. Diary entries over four consecutive days conclude this squalid, bitter squabble between Dalton and Bracken. Seventy years on, it still comes as a surprise to learn how viciously petty, infantile and time-wasting some of the exchanges were between two senior government ministers of a country that was fighting for its life:

Tuesday, 3 February 1942:

PWE meeting. Bracken back towards his old form – reckless rudeness. He is as Gladwyn says, simply a guttersnipe.[29]

Wednesday, February 4 1942:

Bowes-Lyon to dine. Bracken, he says, is just a very small man who hates me
personally and is therefore prepared to sacrifice everything to scoring off me.
He has heard from Hood today that Bracken has just received a very severe
snub from the PM and has been told to mind his own business and not inter-
fere in other people's.[30]

Dalton had long enjoyed a sense of kinship with the exiled Poles in Britain and
had spent Christmas 1940 inspecting and dining with Polish troops under training at Forfar in Scotland. Now, on 7 February 1942, he asked a Polish nationalist
he had known since the 1920s, Dr Josef Retinger, adviser to the prime minister
of the Polish government-in-exile, General Wladyslaw Sikorski, for his observations on current events:

He gives a very Polish and political interpretation of affairs. His account is
that I have many enemies, partly because I am a Socialist and partly because
I am known to have courage and energy and am thought to be personally dangerous. Therefore, he says, there is sabotage of my work in the Air
Ministry and War Office by all the Blimps, and the PM is just not told of
what I do and no reports are passed on. I have, he says, many enemies in the
PM's entourage.[31]

Dalton was under mounting pressure. Some of it came from much closer to
home; his personal life was in tatters. Wearied by months of distant contact with
a husband of twenty-seven years whose egoism, war work and professional dis-
tractions had left her with an increasing sense of worthlessness, Ruth Dalton left
London in October 1941 to find war work in Lancashire. It would be 1945 before
they were reunited, if not reconciled. That same week, caused perhaps by his
private tensions elsewhere, there was an 'uncontrolled outburst' between Dalton
and Nelson that resulted in Nelson offering his resignation. Exhausted by work,
overwrought, Sir Frank Nelson had resigned once before, in September 1941, as
the battle over the creation of the Political Warfare Executive reached its climax.
That resignation had soon been withdrawn. This time, however, it was personal.
Both Dalton and Jebb had, in the view of Nelson (and others), become insuffer-
able meddlers in the day-to-day management of SOE. Evidently, it was a fiery
exchange both were to regret. Nelson wrote to Dalton:

This letter concerns my resignation as 'Chief' of your SOE organisation. I have
been increasingly aware of late that you may perhaps be better served by someone who is not so adamant in his views as I am as to the necessity of the 'man

in charge' being allowed to deal himself with the staff. I am sorry I permitted myself to be rude in tone in informing you of my intention to resign.[32]

Nelson, dangerously stretched, was seen now by Jebb and Dalton as a loose cannon, someone whose sudden public departure could cause significant damage to SOE at a critical time. His resignation, wrote Dalton back to Nelson that same day, 'could only cause our enemies to shout with joy and give the Whitehall World the impression that the whole show is cracking up and must be avoided if at all possible'.[33] In a memo marked 'Strictly Confidential' Dalton confided to Jebb the next day:

> CD came to see me on the 30.10.41. I began by asking him to wash out from his memory our telephone conversation of yesterday. I was sorry that I had spoken to him so abruptly and no doubt I had not well chosen my words. He said he fully accepted this and asked me to think no more about it. After some general conversation he said that he considered SOE could not go on as it was. His position was being undermined because he could *never* say yes or no but must refer everything up. Nelson then proceeded to suggest three principles of remedy which, if adopted, might enable him to stay. All related to restoring his eroded authority. He hinted that if I did not feel able to accept these 'three principles' he did not feel that he could carry on. He could resign 'without leaving a ripple'.[34]

Dalton himself was partly to blame. Although his ministry office in Berkeley Square House kept him physically detached from SOE HQ in Baker Street, he kept a close eye on Nelson and his activities: 'People didn't like it when the minister overrode them but nobody could deny that he knew in detail (some felt too much detail) what was going on.'[35] Dalton promised to give Nelson's proposals careful consideration and Nelson withdrew his resignation, for the time being, at least. Between 3 November and 5 November 1941, Dalton canvassed Nelson's subordinates on the Daily Council (formed in the winter of 1941–42 to discuss problems of policy and help ease the burden of individual responsibility amongst senior SOE officers), finding that they confirmed Nelson's views. Jebb, the career Foreign Office mandarin with his enduring close links with the FO, came in for particular criticism. The Foreign Office itself was perceived as 'a great danger to the efficient working of such an institution as SOE'.[36]

The conclusions of Dalton's personal enquiry[37] reflected SOE's gradual coming of age as its strategic role became clearer: there was the need for a better distinction between policy and matters operational, for more distance between SOE and the Foreign Office and, paradoxically, closer contact with the Chiefs of Staff and the Joint Planning Committee.[38] Thus Nelson's authority was to be strengthened as the price of the withdrawal of his threat to resign. It was to prove, however, only the shortest of respites. The following day 'CEO has had a further talk with CD after this morning's Council and reports that the latter is looking very ill and feeling very low and conscious of strain. He is now saying that in any case he would like to resign and make way for a younger man.'[39] The next day and another meeting with Sir Frank Nelson; another offer to resign, with this one batted away by Dalton and Jebb conspiring in unison:

> This afternoon I see CD alone. This too goes easily. I begin by getting rid of his offer to resign. I say that, with these new changes, he must go on at least for several months … I then read over to him, having given him a copy, my scheme of new arrangements. And then I send for CEO and tell him we two have agreed on a certain paper which I have shown CD. And CEO, playing up very well, says 'I haven't seen it yet'. And so I give him a copy and he reads it through and then says he agrees too. (Of course, he drafted it for me and I haven't altered his draft much). And so all has gone on swimmingly, but I felt with CD that it was a little bit like doing a major negotiation with a backward child![40]

Dalton and Jebb were not the only Whitehall warriors plotting and scheming behind closed doors, for now the march of world events conspired to give Bracken his opportunity to be rid of the troublesome doctor. In December and early 1942 there were a rash of strategic setbacks abroad. These led, at home, to a major government reshuffle. Lacking air cover, the battleship HMS *Prince of Wales* and battlecruiser HMS *Repulse*, pride of the British fleet, were sunk with the loss of 840 lives on 10 December 1941 as they sailed to the relief of Singapore; the Japanese attacked Hong Kong and the garrison surrendered on Christmas Day; Singapore itself fell in mid-February and more than 80,000 British troops marched into captivity heralding what the prime minister would describe as the worst disaster and largest capitulation in British history. Just a few days earlier a *Kriegsmarine* squadron consisting of the German battleships *Scharnhorst*, *Gneisenau* and *Prinz Eugen* flaunted British domination of the English Channel, evaded the British blockade at Brest, swotted aside British attacks by MTBs and out-dated, lumbering Swordfish biplanes and sailed home to Germany. Churchill may have presented the *Kriegsmarine*'s Channel dash as a camouflaged strategic victory for the British but, in truth, it was anything but. Churchill's soaring rhetoric may have rallied the nation after Dunkirk, but now, twenty months later, they needed more than words. Meanwhile, in the western Atlantic, the German U-boat fleet was enjoying its second 'happy time'. In February 1942 alone, seventy-one ships totalling 384,000 tons were sunk, the German U-boat wolf pack's freedom of manoeuvre assisted by the introduction of a new 'Triton' Enigma wheel and reflector which presented the Bletchley Park code-breakers with a code-breaking difficulty that increased by a factor of twenty-six overnight.[41] Britain could no longer 'read' German U-boat traffic, and it would be ten months before Bletchley Park broke back into 'Shark' decrypts. Set against these reverses, a government reshuffle offered the hope of fresh brains and new energy – the pressure for change was mounting. Pressing his advantage, Bracken wrote to Churchill on 17 February 1942: 'You are being looked upon as a faithful friend of ministers who have outlived their usefulness.'[42]

Rumours of change were rife. Yet just eleven days earlier Jebb had confidently told a colleague that Dalton's position was 'politically so strong that there is no chance of being shifted'.[43] The details of the reshuffle were announced on 19 February with members reduced from nine to seven. Churchill, Attlee, Anderson, Eden and Bevan remained; Cripps became Lord Privy Seal; Oliver Lyttelton became Minister of State for Production. Out went Kingsley Wood, Beaverbrook and Greenwood. 'This really is a large sweep,' noted the editor of *The Times* in his diary, 'capable of re-invigorating the conduct of the war and public confidence.'[44] Dalton wondered if the cascade effect of Churchill's changes would reach his own ministry. He consulted Attlee and asked if he was likely to be moved: 'Certainly not', replied Attlee emphatically. Reassured, Dalton left for a visit to his constituency. But others, it seems, were better informed: 'I hear from A [Anthony Eden] that PM is going to take SOE away from Dalton and divide it between us and Chiefs of Staff! Help! Home as usual and dined.'[45]

Called from a speech to constituents at the Hipperdrome, Shildon, the following day, 21 February 1942, Churchill peremptorily offered Dalton the Board of Trade:

Dalton: 'I suppose the Board of Trade is a very full- time job?'
Churchill: 'Yes, quite full time.'
Dalton: 'So that would mean that I should give up all the other duties which I am now doing?'
Churchill: 'Yes, you would.'[46]

Promotion – of a kind – but not dismissal. Dalton accepted. But why was he moved? Perhaps Churchill wearied of Attlee's intercessions on behalf of the loud, left-wing Socialist he neither liked nor trusted. Two other possibilities present themselves. First, that a prime minister with many graver concerns than propaganda simply bowed to pressure from Bracken and Eden. Churchill, certainly, was weighed down by worries of his own. Just back from that first vital Washington Conference, facing pressure from the House and the public, aware of the need to make changes and move – even hurt – faithful friends like Max Beaverbrook, Lockhart's diary records Bracken told him: 'The prime minister is in a state of great depression and mental agony.'[47] Another diary entry suggests it almost certainly was Eden and Bracken who made sure Dalton's name appeared on a list of proposed changes and that, consequently, his days at SOE were numbered:

A.E. [Eden] saw P.M. this morning when latter promised not to bring out the new list until Monday and not without consulting him about it. A.E. has also seen Bracken who is being helpful in urging P.M. to make drastic changes. A.E. has given Bracken his own list of changes and Bracken is going to take this to P.M. on Monday. It is proposed to move Dalton from M.E.W., possibly to Health.[48]

Professor Michael Foot suggests, however, there may have been a darker explanation for Dalton's sudden and unexpected removal from SOE: 'He was caught by MI5 using SOE's telephone [System] to listen in on his colleagues in the Labour Party.'[49] Professor Foot claims Dalton was caught eavesdropping in January 1942 and was then moved across to the Board of Trade where he could 'do less damage'. Perhaps unsurprisingly, this author has been unable to trace any record to support such a claim in the published records of SOE in The National Archives at Kew or in the Dalton Papers. The year 2009 saw the publication of *The Defence of the Realm: The Authorised History of MI5* by Professor Christopher Andrew. There is no mention of Dr Hugh Dalton in the index and SOE itself is only referred to on four pages.[50] All references in this context are anodyne. Dalton took his phone call from Churchill on 21 February 1942. It was, wrote the now former Minister of Economic Warfare:

A day of goodbyes. I break this news to Gladwyn who is quite dumbfounded and thinks there must be some mistake. He just cannot conceive of Wolmer [the soon-to-be Lord Selborne] running SOE.[51]

Gladwyn Jebb appeared lost without his mentor 'like a sheep without his shepherd', observed Sir Frank Nelson, expressing little sympathy for the man he considered responsible for much of his own professional discomfort. Professor Sean Greenwood noted: 'Gladwyn was shocked by Dalton's departure and morose by the prospect of his chief's replacement by a slightly deaf fifty-five-year-old who seemed older than his years, had no intellectual pretensions and an indifferent political career behind him.'[52]

There remains the tantalising possibility that Jebb was right: Selborne's appointment was a mistake and that he was offered the appointment as a political concession in the near-certainty that he would turn it down. Bracken wrote to Churchill: 'I feel sure that "Top" Wolmer does not want office. And I feel certain he would like to be asked.'[53]

That Dalton's sudden move to the Board of Trade and thus away from PWE, SOE and the front line of subversive warfare represented a victory for Bracken, no one doubted. Bruce Lockhart recorded: 'More changes tonight of which the two most important are the replacement of Margesson [Minister of War] and the transfer of Dalton to Board of Trade. Max says this means triumph for Brendan and removal of Dalton from PWE.'[54] The Political Warfare Executive would now be headed by Anthony Eden as Foreign Secretary, with Bracken attending to administration. Bruce Lockhart would shortly be confirmed as director general and would be knighted in 1943. The dislocation of propaganda from SOE was now complete and Dalton's 'unitary' concept of subversion lay in ruins. Dalton wrote to the prime minister: 'I lay down my responsibilities for the work of SOE with keen personal regret.'[55] He confided in his diary three days later:

Today I hand over MEW. I say many farewells to officials who, nearly all of them, are rather sorry that I am going. I have chased and hunted them about and shouted at many of them, and written splenetic minutes, but faced with the possibility of a minister who may be more inert, I think they are inclined to regret the change.[56]

Gladwyn Jebb, certainly, was regretting Dalton's departure. Since SOE's inception he had matched his combative style of management to that of his dynamic master. Now he was alone and exposed, writing to Dalton in early March: 'I feel rather like a lone wolf, but I think I may get through, with luck.'[57] But to survive, Jebb needed more than luck; he needed friends in high places. And, like Dalton, he now found these in short supply. From the outset he had made enemies amongst those who served the Chiefs of Staff:

Brooks[58] full of diatribes against Jebb who, he says, is finished with the Chiefs of Staff. Jebb was very rude to Hollis[59] about a paper. Hollis, who knows Brooks well, told Brooks that in future Jebb would get no War Cabinet papers.[60]

Jebb asked Selborne outright if he wanted him to stay on. Selborne replied that he did, and that he liked him. Nelson, however, observed that relationship differently: '[they] never got on from the first moment, but were like two cats arching their backs against one another.'[61] Theirs was a clash of style as much as temperament. Jebb, used to the drive, urgency and political danger of working for Dalton, found frustration in the working regime of a man who took long weekends, left his papers at the office, worked a strict 1000hrs to 1800hrs and revealed elements of, to Jebb, appalling political naivety. Still in touch with Dalton – to whom he now, most improperly, leaked secret SOE papers – his relationship with Selborne deteriorated rapidly. Nelson was diagnosed with a duodenal ulcer and retired on grounds of ill health in early spring, to be replaced by Sir Charles Hambro. Jebb's return to the Foreign Office swiftly followed: he was fired by Lord Selborne after a not-unjustified accusation of divided loyalties. It was a painful departure: 'Unpleasant half-hour with GJ [Gladwyn Jebb] who has just been sacked by Selborne. Very sorry for him and think it's a mistake.'[62] In the next few months Jebb would struggle to regain his feet back within the Foreign Office. He would spend much of this bleak and difficult time composing a 'highly personal and rather explosive'[63] thirty-page paper of analysis on 'The Technique of Subversion'. Part treatise, it was also part document of exculpation:

> We must finally dismiss from our minds any lingering thought that there is anything disreputable in subversive activities and replace our old notions, if possible, by the conception of subversion as a noble pursuit, carried out in the field by some of the bravest men in Europe.[64]

His paper went on to review the existing state of SOE and the manner in which he believed the secret organisation had been betrayed by those responsible for its birth. Essentially, however, it altered nothing. Dr Hugh Dalton, his CEO Gladywn Jebb and CD Sir Frank Nelson had all moved on, and so too had SOE. An era had ended.

Notes

1 Stafford, *Britain and European Resistance 1940–1945*, p.76.
2 Pimlott, *Hugh Dalton*, p.330.
3 Young, *Diaries of Sir Robert Bruce Lockhart*, Volume 2, p.110. Diary entry for 23 July 1941.
4 Pimlott, *Hugh Dalton*, p.330.
5 Director, Plans and Campaigns, PWE 1941–45.
6 Young, *Diaries of Sir Robert Bruce Lockhart*, Volume 2, p.129. Diary entry for 3 November 1941.
7 Greenwood, Sean, *Titan at the Foreign Office* (Nijhoff Publishers, Boston, 2008), p.109.
8 Pimlott, *Hugh Dalton*, p.348.
9 Greenwood, *Titan at the Foreign Office*, p.111.
10 Young, *Diaries of Sir Robert Bruce Lockhart*, Volume 2, p.112. Diary entry for 4 August 1941.
11 John Colville, *The Churchillians* (Weidenfeld & Nicolson, London, 1981), p.59.
12 Pimlott, *Hugh Dalton*, p.350. Diary entry for 15 May 1941.
13 Pimlott (ed.), *The Second World War Diary of Hugh Dalton: 1940–1945*, p.292. Diary entry for 9 October 1941.
14 Dilks, *The Diaries of Sir Alexander Cadogan 1938–1945*, p.409.
15 Pimlott (ed.), *The Second World War Diary of Hugh Dalton: 1940–1945*, p.293.
16 Pimlott (ed.), *The Second World War Diary of Hugh Dalton: 1940–1945*, p.296. Diary entry for 21 October 1941.
17 Pimlott (ed.), *The Second World War Diary of Hugh Dalton: 1940–1945*, p.316. Diary entry for 18 November 1941.
18 Pimlott (ed.), *The Second World War Diary of Hugh Dalton: 1940–1945*, p.319. Diary entry for 19 November 1941.
19 Pimlott (ed.), *The Second World War Diary of Hugh Dalton: 1940–1945*, p.329.
20 Greenwood, *Titan at the Foreign Office*, p.124.

21 Clement Attlee's papers are held at the Bodleian Library, Oxford. A search of that archive did not unearth Bracken's letters. It is possible that they were returned to Dalton by Attlee. Or even that the lively venom of their contents ensured their destruction. A search of the Dalton Papers at the British Library of Political and Economic Science was also inconclusive. Several papers cited to exist in the latter archive by earlier historians also appear to have been removed.

22 Pimlott (ed.), *The Second World War Diary of Hugh Dalton: 1940–1945*, p.329.

23 Pimlott (ed.), *The Second World War Diary of Hugh Dalton: 1940–1945*, p.332.

24 Dalton Papers. Memo marked 'Most Secret' and 'Strictly Confidential' to Gladwyn Jebb dated 19 December 1941. In Dalton Papers File 18/2 at the British Library of Political and Economic Science.

25 Pimlott, *Hugh Dalton*, p.348.

26 Bennett, *Churchill's Man of Mystery*, p.262.

27 Young, *Diaries of Sir Robert Bruce Lockhart*, Volume 2, p.91. Diary entry for 24 February 1941.

28 Pimlott (ed.), The Second World War Diary of Hugh Dalton: 1940–1945, p.341. Diary entry for 5 January 1942.

29 Pimlott (ed.), *The Second World War Diary of Hugh Dalton: 1940–1945*, p.358.

30 Pimlott (ed.), *The Second World War Diary of Hugh Dalton: 1940–1945*, p.361.

31 Pimlott (ed.), *The Second World War Diary of Hugh Dalton: 1940–1945*, p.363.

32 File DP 18/2 in the Dalton Papers at the British Library of Political and Economic Science. Letter dated 29 October 1941 from Nelson to Dalton.

33 Greenwood, *Titan at the Foreign Office*, p.121.

34 File DP 18/2 in the Dalton Papers at the British Library of Political and Economic Science. Letter from Dalton to Jebb dated 30 October 1941.

35 Pimlott, *Hugh Dalton*, p.308.

36 Dalton Papers file DP 18/2, p.3, at the British Library of Political and Economic Science. Memo to Jebb from Dalton dated 19 December 1941.

37 One of those Dalton canvassed was Brigadier Gubbins. Despite what both Gubbins and Dalton might say to Air Vice Marshal Harris and others concerning the provision of Bomber Command aircraft for SOE operations, Gubbins confessed to Dalton on 3 November 1941 that he 'did not feel hampered in any way', adding that the aircraft now at his disposal 'were more than sufficient for all his operations'. Source: Memo to Gladwyn Jebb from Dalton dated 19 December 1941. In Dalton Papers DP 18/2, p.2, at the British Library of Political and Economic Science.

38 Stafford, *Britain and European Resistance 1940–1945*, pp.75–6.

39 Pimlott (ed.), *The Second World War Diary of Hugh Dalton: 1940–1945*, p.306. Diary entry for 6 November 1941.

40 Pimlott (ed.), *The Second World War Diary of Hugh Dalton: 1940–1945*, p.308. Diary entry for 7 November 1941.

41 Sebag-Montefiore, Hugh, *Enigma: The Battle for the Code* (Phoenix, London, 2001), p.245.

42 Gilbert, *Winston S. Churchill*, Volume VII, p.63.

43 Greenwood, *Titan at the Foreign Office*, p.125.

44 Gilbert, *Winston S. Churchill*, Volume VII, p.63.

45 Dilks, *The Diaries of Sir Alexander Cadogan 1938–1945*, p.435. Diary entry for 20 February 1942.

46 Pimlott (ed.), *The Second World War Diary of Hugh Dalton 1940–1945*, pp.374–5.

47 Young, *Diaries of Sir Robert Bruce Lockhart*, Volume 2, p.147. Diary entry for 25 February 1942.

48 Harvey, Oliver, *The War Diaries of Oliver Harvey* (Collins, London, 1978), p.100. Cited by Pimlott, *Hugh Dalton*, p.345. Harvey was Anthony Eden's private secretary at this time.

49 Professor Foot interviewed by this author on 25 January 2008.

50 Andrew, Christopher, *The Defence of the Realm: The Authorised History of MI5* (Allen Lane, London, 2009). SOE is mentioned on pp.251, 278, 287 and 655. The 'Dalton' listed is another.

51 Pimlott, *Hugh Dalton*, p.380. Diary entry for 21 February 1942.

52 Greenwood, *Titan at the Foreign Office*, p.126.

53 Undated letter from Bracken to Churchill in file CHAR 20/34 12–15 at the Churchill Archives Centre, Churchill College, Cambridge.

54 Young, *Diaries of Sir Robert Bruce Lockhart*, Volume 2, p.143. Diary entry for 22 February 1942.

55 In Dalton Papers, File DP 7/3, p.3, at the British Library of Political and Economic Science. Dalton to Churchill, 22 February 1942.

56 Pimlott (ed.), *The Second World War Diary of Hugh Dalton: 1940–1945*, p.383. Diary entry for 24 February 1942.

57 Greenwood, *Titan at the Foreign Office*, p.127.

58 Brigadier Dallas Brooks commanded the military wing of PWE at Woburn.

59 Brigadier (later General) Sir Leslie Hollis, Secretary to the Chiefs of Staff Committee and Deputy Head of the Military Wing of the War Cabinet. Later Commandant-General, Royal Marines (1949–52).

60 Young, *Diaries of Sir Robert Bruce Lockhart*, Volume 2, p.79. Diary entry for 23 September 1940.

61 Greenwood, *Titan at the Foreign Office*, p.127.

62 Dilks, *The Diaries of Sir Alexander Cadogan 1938–1945*, p.447. Diary entry for 20 April 1942.

63 Greenwood, *Titan at the Foreign Office*, p.131.

64 'The Technique of Subversion' by Gladwyn Jebb in File HS 8/251 at The National Archives, Kew. Undated, but must be spring 1942.

CHAPTER SEVENTEEN

BUILDING BRIDGES

Dalton had owed his 1940 appointment to political expediency and to the mood of desperate times in which much was pinned upon the possibility of economic blockade. His removal now took with it in large measure the fear of the establishment that SOE's secret remit was internal subversion and that, under Dalton's Socialist leadership, the battle for wartime liberation would somehow turn into post-war, left-wing, pan-European political insurrection. Lord Selborne was a life-long conservative and personal friend of both Churchill and Bracken. Selborne also had what Dalton so conspicuously lacked: 'the knack of making people like and trust him. His appointment made SOE's relations with many other departments at home a good deal smoother.'[1] He made his own views plain when he wrote to Foreign Secretary Anthony Eden enclosing a paper from Nelson stating that it appeared:

SIS's overall attitude was to delay rather than expedite the natural expansion of SOE. Whereas SIS initially saw SOE as a rather ineffective and ridiculous collection of amateurs who might endanger SIS if not kept quiet, they now seem to regard SOE as dangerous rivals who, if not squashed quickly, will eventually squash them. This is because we have outstripped them in many directions and proved ourselves in many directions to be a more efficient organisation. It is nonetheless both foolish and deplorable since the last thing SOE wants is to obstruct SIS in the slightest degree.[2]

Perish the thought. The man who had reorganised the Post Office and spent the early part of the war rejoicing beneath the distinctly unglamorous title of Director of Cement at the Ministry of Works in charge of pill-box construction, appeared, after Dalton's insensitive fumbling, to offer a safer pair of neatly gloved hands altogether; Lord Selborne even went on record stating that he did not approve of pursuing a policy at variance with that of the Foreign Office.[3] Such comments may have gone some way towards placating the FO, yet the threat and challenge to SOE's existence remained very real. Just eight weeks earlier, in December 1941, General de Gaulle had voiced his long-held suspicions of SOE and told Eden that, as far as he was concerned, SOE could be dispensed with entirely. The Norwegian, Belgian and Polish governments-in-exile also had reason to be unhappy with SOE; the Belgian, 'one of the weakest of the Allied governments-in-exile',[4] because, by their lights, SOE was working against the national interest by promoting continuous sabotage and building up a Secret Army. These were actions which, it was believed, would result in reprisals and the arming of those who opposed the political stance of the Belgian government-in-exile. These delicate relationships between SOE and exiled governments were something SIS did not hesitate to exploit to its own advantage:

> As late as autumn 1944 I've found in the archives 'C' getting hold of members of governments-in-exile in London saying 'you mustn't let this, that or the other happen because they [SOE] are dangerous'. On no sound ground at all, simply because he was jealous. I think SIS raised a great many quite unnecessary obstacles to SOE and could have been a great deal more helpful than they were.[5]

As perhaps was to be expected from a man who traded in shadows and dissembled untruths, Dansey had once told Sir Stewart Menzies, his nominal superior at SIS: 'If we cannot kill it [SOE] and I do not think we can, let us for the sake of work and war effort try to live on and work on friendly terms. I for one counsel collaboration.'[6] Yet two years later, Gubbins was writing to senior intelligence officer Sir William Stephenson:[7] 'Since I told you about the Dansey menace in May and you talked with Stewart [Menzies] about it, Dansey has somehow accelerated his jabbing interference to the point when I am losing good men. I should be grateful if you would help me put a stop to his actions.'[8] For Lord Selborne, Claude Dansey was simply another problem, like Belgium, that he had inherited.

In Norway the situation was more active, more complex. Since 1940 SOE had been running agents and radios, arms and equipment into Norway by fishing boat. By spring 1942 those small fishing boats – the *Shetland Bus* – working only in the foulest of dark, winter weather, had made forty trips, dropping off and picking up agents and landing 150 tons of equipment. Perhaps because the great length of the indented Norwegian 25,000km coastline permitted both organisations to operate without cramping one another's style, both SOE and SIS, at that tactical local level, appear to have worked without significant conflict but with considerable frustration – for SOE, at least:

> No matter how hard the Norwegian Section [of SOE] tried, and it tried 'something' hard, it could never get to grips and work in accord with the opposite section in SIS. There was frequent inter-communication between the

two sections, weekly meetings were tried, but were a total failure. Information of any interest was passed immediately to SIS and all too frequently unused or written down.[9]

In Norway, as in Helford, elements of SOE's 'private navy' proliferated in mirror image maritime operations under development by more conventional units. Utilising their own small boat, canoe and Folboat[10] training facility in western Scotland, which involved night-time exercises and the newly developed 'limpet' mine,[11] SOE was to launch a series of successful attacks by *Kompani Linge* 'limpeteers' in kayaks on shipping in Norwegian waters and harbours under the *Vestige* serial of operations which began in September 1943. Many of these attacks on shipping were conducted by a single saboteur, Max Manus.[12]

Not every mission by SOE in Norway, however, was a success. Plans to assassinate Himmler at Oslo railway station collapsed when Himmler changed his schedule and failed to show on the platform decked out for his arrival.[13] There were arrests but no deaths. That team was lucky, for sometimes missions that failed exacted a terrible price from the civilian population. Operation *Penguin*[14] was the first of these. On 17 April 1942 the same landing place near Nesvik was used by both SIS and SOE *Kompani Linge* agents within a few days. The consequences of this piece of carelessness were predictable: the SOE party was betrayed and a gun battle ensued in which three Germans and one SOE agent were killed. Eighteen Norwegians in nearby Televaag were executed in reprisal, none of whom had anything to do with Operation *Penguin*. Hundreds of others were sent to a concentration camp and 300 buildings were razed.[15] SOE's Operation *Archer* resulted in a gun battle with the Germans on 6 September 1942 at the tiny village of Majavatn. Another thirty-four Norwegians were executed in reprisal. Operation *Bittern*[16] did further significant damage, this time not just to SOE relations in London but to SOE's relationship with Milorg, the nascent Norwegian Home Army. In October 1942, four SOE agents were dropped north of Oslo; their mission was to assist Milorg in the assassination of Norwegian informers and collaborators. The mission had not, however, been sanctioned by Milorg. Early negotiations revealed SOE had arrived with a London-selected 'hit' list of sixty-two names including not just informers and Quislings (collaborators), but local Nazi politicians as well. Fearing reprisals similar to the massacre carried out at Lidice in response to the assassination of Reinhard Heydrich, Milorg downgraded the *Bittern* mission from assisting in assassination to military training and the SOE team was split into two. This division of resources led to heavy drinking and significant security lapses. *Bittern* was recalled in disgrace, leaving a rift between SOE and Milorg that endured for some time.

Six months earlier, in April 1942, General Sikorski, the Polish leader-in-exile, asked Churchill to set up an Allied General Staff of all exiled nations to oversee future insurrection in occupied countries, thus in effect side-stepping SOE altogether. He did so in a mood of mounting frustration at SOE's chronic and continuing inability to supply his Secret Army in distant Poland with the weapons and supplies they needed. The request, turned down emphatically by the Chiefs of Staff on 6 May 1942, proved to be of small enduring consequence. Its only long-term result, ironically, was to force those who opposed SOE to recognise, despite its shortcomings, the validity of SOE's role in the struggle that lay ahead:

> For all that SOE appeared to the Foreign Office and Chiefs of Staff to be an unruly sixth-form schoolboy unable to keep his grubby fingers off the table-cloth while constantly demanding second helpings when there were none, they were forced to recognise that he was indispensable in keeping the smaller boys in order.[17]

Now General Sikorski's demand was yet another straw in that gale of cold wind blowing around Baker Street. Others noticed it too: 'There was certainly in the air early in 1942, a feeling that something must be done about SOE.'[18] Bickham Sweet-Escott confirms Dalton's departure to the Board of Trade 'coincided with one of the periodical waves of feeling in Whitehall that it was time to give SOE a real shake up'.[19] Leading the charge – unsurprisingly, perhaps – was SIS, who launched a vicious whispering campaign hinting at incompetence and misman-agement at Baker Street. This was aimed at bringing SOE under stricter control whilst, at the Foreign Office, Cadogan talked, albeit unrealistically, about 'having to crash [sic] SOE altogether'.[20] He claimed Churchill was considering winding up SOE and dividing its work between the Chiefs of Staff and the Foreign Office. The new minister acted swiftly. Lord Selborne abolished Jebb's post as CEO and replaced it – and him – with Mr Harry Sporborg, a former City solicitor and head of SOE operations, Western Europe, as his principal private secretary, a post more in keeping with traditional Whitehall hierarchies. Reporting first impressions to the prime minister on 10 April 1942, Lord Selborne stated:

> Since taking office I have made as thorough an inspection of SOE – its personnel, offices and its schools – as time has permitted. I have discussed its work with every minister, government official or organisation that has had dealings with SOE. I have also endeavoured to trace to their sources various rumours which I have heard. I have no hesitation in reporting that these are baseless calumnies.
>
> The fair and true comment on the above is, that if you attempt to create a world wide organisation under war conditions in a hurry, some appointments and arrangements are likely to be less successful than others. The significant fact is that the failures have been very much fewer than the achievements.[21]

In a paper that went on to state that 'SOE must and will play for the team', Lord Selborne reported that he had found much evidence of friction between SOE and SIS. To ensure the current rumours ceased, he intended to commission a fundamental review of SOE's organisation and method of operation by 'an impartial person of sufficient authority and experience' who would report back to him personally. 'If SOE is to function, it must receive fair play as well as give it,' he wrote, adding: 'I hope my colleagues will accept my assurance that much good work has been performed by zealous and patriotic men, and for this purpose I should be grateful if you could see your way to circulate this report to the War Cabinet.'[22]

A fortnight later, sensing perhaps a vacuum of intent within MEW under a new minister of deceptive mildness who had yet to make his mark, the Joint Intelligence Committee weighed into the fray with a report recommending a closer dove-tailing of interests between SOE, SIS and Combined Operations because 'the activities of SOE increase the alertness of the local authorities and greatly hamper the work of our intelligence'.[23] The JIC report was accepted by the Chiefs of Staff on 1 May 1942 who went on to recommend the amalgamation of both SIS and SOE into a single service under the direction of themselves, the Chiefs of Staff. Now, once again, it was Churchill who saved SOE from extinction. He rejected the Chiefs of Staff's recommendation outright and set in motion the creation of an SOE/SIS liaison committee under Sir Findlater-Stewart which, in the event, achieved nothing. Lord Selborne, meanwhile, saw off Major Morton's sly suggestion to Churchill that SOE should be removed entirely from ministerial control and that he, Morton, should lead an inquiry into SOE. Instead, on 12 May 1942, as he had promised, Selborne commissioned his own inquiry into allegations of waste and mismanagement within SOE. This he entrusted to a Bank of England director, John Hanbury-Williams, and a senior Treasury official, Eddie Playfair, who would report back in mid-June. Playfair's surname – one might like to think in the light of Lord Selborne's earlier comments to the prime minister – was taken as the title of the ensuing report. Churchill's emphatic defence of SOE and his outright rejection of the Chiefs of Staff's recommendation had startling and immediate results. The same day that Selborne commissioned the 'Playfair Report', the Chiefs of Staff, galvanised by both the prime minister's emphatic defence of SOE and, one may presume, their own clarity of focus upon an invasion of mainland Europe that was planned, at that stage, for as early as spring 1943, produced their own directive: 'SOE Collaboration in Operations on the Continent'. Although SOE's role was to be secondary and supportive to the main military thrust of that invasion, this amounted to a vote of confidence in the continued existence of SOE and the role it would contribute to that assault from some of its severest erstwhile critics. With Churchill's endorsement, SOE was now part of the Order of Battle; it was on the map and here to stay – for the moment, at least (there would be two further concerted attempts by SIS and Bomber Command to emasculate SOE in July and December 1943). In the meantime, SOE was required to:

> … conform with the general plan by organising and co-ordinating action by patriots. Particular care should be taken to avoid premature large-scale risings of patriots. SOE should endeavour to build up and equip paramilitary organisations in the area of the projected operations.
>
> The actions of such organisations will in particular be directed towards the following tasks:
>
> 1. Prevention of the arrival of enemy reinforcements by the interruption of road, rail and air transport.
> 2. The interruption of enemy signal communications in and behind the battle area generally.
> 3. Prevention of demolitions by the enemy.
> 4. Attacks on enemy aircraft and air personnel.
> 5. Disorganisation of enemy movements and rear services by the spreading of rumours.[24]

Hard on the heels of this formal directive from the Chiefs of Staff Committee came an important agreement with the Foreign Office – part uneasy truce, part informal treaty – signed three days later on 15 May 1942. Negotiated by Hugh Dalton in the dog-days of his watch, the 'Treaty' attempted to codify the vexed working relationship between SOE and the Foreign Office whenever and wherever SOE's explosive intentions clashed with Foreign Office policy, which was often. It was a document of significance in that SOE's role was again identified, downgraded, strengthened and clarified, although Sir Frank Nelson recorded just before he stood down:

> My personal view is that the Foreign Office do not wish to be burdened with the responsibility for SOE; but wish to control it by means of a 'Treaty' and by means of steadfast and settled obstruction, until it has been reduced to an innocuous bomb disposal squad.[25]

In essence, the treaty that was never signed by either Eden or Selborne, the two ministers involved, formally recognised that SOE was an executive, operational body rather than one engaged in the making of policy. As such, it would defer strategic interests to the Foreign Office. Just how free SOE would be to operate abroad would depend in turn upon the area of operations. It sounded cumbersome and it was. The Foreign Office was attempting to quantify and regularise elusive subversion. Nailing down quicksilver might have proved easier:

> It is impossible to believe that the Treaty did anything to improve the conduct of business, and major rows were not much less common than before. But on the whole the minor friction decreased. This was partly due [to] Lord Selborne [who] made it a cardinal point of his policy that SOE should go along with the Foreign Office in all cases where co-operation was possible.[26]

Reporting back a month later on 18 June 1942, the 'Playfair Report' acquitted SOE HQ of all the major charges of 'nepotism, waste, corruption and incompetence which had been freely circulated'.[27] SOE emerged 'as much sinned against as sinning'.[28] The same cannot be said for SIS. The report concluded:

> There is nothing to worry about there, with one notable exception: SOE's relations with SIS which are more at arm's length than should ever be the case between two organisations which must be so closely connected. We hope that in future a friendlier spirit may prevail; but it is not a matter which we can pass over in silence. Having seen a couple of week's correspondence between officers of SIS and SOE on day-to-day matters, we are much disturbed by the tone of petty bickering and sniping which one finds in SIS communications.
>
> Whether or how far SOE were to blame in the past, we cannot say. At the present, all officers appear to be doing their best to cooperate. But if things do not improve on the SIS side, they are bound to get worse on the SOE side.
>
> *Cet animal est très méchant*
> *Quand on l'attaque il se défend*
>
> [An old French witticism: 'This animal is very wicked; when you attack it, it defends itself']
>
> These bad relations are perhaps not of the same importance now that SOE (having at last completely separated communications) have become so largely independent of SIS. But that they lead to inefficiency, wasted effort, some duplication and it may be at times danger to life and liberty to devoted men is not open to doubt.
>
> Having seen one side of the picture only, we find it difficult to make any positive suggestion for bettering this lamentable state of affairs.[29]

Churchill would express the same view to General Hastings Ismay in February 1944: 'The warfare between SOE and SIS is a lamentable but perhaps inevitable feature of our affairs.'[30] The 'Playfair Report' largely vindicated SOE's battered reputation and provided much needed ammunition in the fight for SOE's continued independence; Lord Selborne found the report 'immensely satisfactory'[31] and lost no time sending a copy to Churchill who ordered copies sent to the War Cabinet and Defence Committee.[32] Even Foreign Secretary Anthony Eden conceded that the 'Playfair' inquiry showed there was nothing wrong with SOE that could not be put right[33] whilst the duplicitous Major Morton, perhaps sensing the way the wind was blowing, wrote from Downing Street: 'I am so glad that the report is satisfactory and supports your conclusion which many people hold, that SOE while not pretending to be perfect, has in the past done very good work.'[34] Lord Selborne also found time to send a copy of the report to his predecessor, Hugh Dalton: 'As you were the architect of the whole edifice, perhaps you may care to have this little tribute from an admirer of your work.'[35] It was a gracious, thoughtful note from the desk of a busy man.

Notes

1 Foot, *SOE in France*, p.18.

2 Jeffery, *MI6: The History of the Secret Intelligence Service 1909–1949*, p.356.

3 Mackenzie, *The Secret History of SOE*, p.347.

4 Mackenzie, *The Secret History of SOE*, p.296.

5 Interview with Professor Foot by the author on 25 January 2008.

6 Jeffery, *MI6: The History of the Secret Intelligence Service 1909–1949*, p.354. Conversation between Sir Stewart Menzies and Claude Dansey on 1 May 1941.

7 Senior diplomat and western spymaster, aka *Intrepid*, Head of British Security Co-ordination in New York and sometimes, as here, a liaison link between SOE and SIS.

8 Marshall, *All The King's Men*, p.236. Also: 'It was common knowledge in the intelligence community that Dansey was intent on destroying the SOE' (Footnote 3, p.302). Marshall quotes a separate telex from Stephenson in response to that call for help from Gubbins: 'I came to the conclusion that a warning from Menzies to Dansey in May 1943 ... resulted in Dansey intensifying his attacks on the SOE'.

9 In File HS 8/818 at The National Archives, Kew. Report on SOE Operations in Norway.

10 Folboat: early folding kayak.

11 Boyce and Everett, *SOE: The Scientific Secrets*, p.50.

12 Manus, Max, *Underwater Saboteur* (Kimber, London, 1953). The dates of the *Vestige* operations are listed in Files HS 2/208. HS 2/209, HS 2/210 at The National Archives, Kew.

13 In File HS 7/174 at The National Archives, Kew.

14 In File HS 2/166 at The National Archives, Kew.

15 Details of Operation *Penguin* in File HS 2/266 at The National Archives, Kew.

16 Details of Operation *Bittern* in File HS 2/200 at The National Archives, Kew.

17 Stafford, *Britain and European Resistance 1940–1945*, p.86.

18 Mackenzie, *The Secret History of SOE*, p.340.

19 Sweet-Escott, *Baker Street Irregular*, p.124.

20 Stafford, *Britain and European Resistance 1940–1945*, p.77.

21 File HS 8/251 at The National Archives, Kew. A report dated 10 April 1942 from Lord Selborne to the prime minister.

22 File HS 8/251 at The National Archives, Kew. A report dated 10 April 1942 from Lord Selborne to the prime minister.
23 JIC Report (42) 156(O) (Final) 29 dated April 1942 in CAB 84/85 at The National Archives, Kew.
24 COS (42) 133(O) in File CAB 80/62 at The National Archive, Kew. Reproduced in full in Mackenzie, *The Secret History of SOE*, pp.766–9.
25 Sir Frank Nelson in CD/OR/550 on 7 April 1942. Cited in Mackenzie, *The Secret History of SOE*, p.344.
26 Mackenzie, *The Secret History of SOE*, p.347.
27 Mackenzie, *The Secret History of SOE*, p.342.
28 Sweet-Escott, *Baker Street Irregular*, p.124.
29 In File HS 8/252 at The National Archives, Kew. SOE 'Playfair' report by John Hanbury-Williams.
30 In File PREM 3 185/1 at The National Archives, Kew. Churchill to General Hastings Ismay on 10 February 1944.
31 In File HS 8/924 at The National Archives, Kew. Lord Selborne reaction to 'Playfair Report'.
32 Seaman, *Special Operations Executive: A New Instrument of War*, p.55.
33 File HS 8/252 at The National Archives, Kew.
34 File HS 8/924 at The National Archives, Kew. Major Desmond Morton letter to Lord Selborne dated 2 July 1942.
35 File DP 7/3 in the Dalton Papers at the British Library of Political and Economic Science. Letter from Selborne to Dalton on delivery of the 'Playfair Report'.

CHAPTER EIGHTEEN

ONE-WAY STREETS

The 'Playfair Report' had strengthened Selborne's hand with the prime minister. Lord Selborne now began sending Churchill quarterly progress reports on SOE activities worldwide, thus exploiting a long-standing friendship and a direct ease of access Dalton could never have hoped to realise. Churchill replied: 'My Dear Top – Thank you so much for sending me the quarterly report on SOE activities. It is encouraging to learn of the steady increase in scale and in achievement of the work being done by these brave men.'[1] The first of these reports reached Churchill's desk in mid-July 1942. It covered the period March–June 1942 and stated that:

> Its [SOE's] active operations are all planned in conformity with higher strategy. As the temper and hopes of oppressed Europe rise, however, and as SOE organisation instils courage into groups and provides them with arms, a rising tide of sabotage is increasingly impeding the enemy.[2]

Ten Norwegian ships had attempted to run the German blockade in Gothenburg, Sweden, and two of these had succeeded in slipping through the Skagerrak; Norwegian patriots had blown up a power station in Bardshaug; six others had commandeered a Norwegian coastal steamer of 600 tons and sailed it across the North Sea to Aberdeen. SOE fishing vessels operating out of Shetland had made fifteen trips to Norway and landed eight agents and 71 tons of arms and 'devices'. In France, sabotage had included the assassination of Germans, train derailments, the cutting of high-tension cables and the destruction of goods destined for Germany. In the Reich itself, the Berlin–Konigsberg express had been derailed and an aircraft assembly shed containing thirty-five fighter and transport aircraft had been destroyed. In that same period 138 agents had been inserted into enemy-occupied territory, together with 211 containers which each held 300lb of arms and explosives. Twenty-nine radio sets had been parachuted into enemy territory. The report listed SOE activities in Belgium, the Balkans, Poland and

Madagascar. In Czechoslovakia, claimed Lord Selborne, two SOE assassins had, as he phrased it, 'earned the gratitude of mankind' by killing Reinhard Heydrich during Operation *Anthropoid*. Heydrich was head of Nazi Security Police and Governor of Bohemia-Moravia.[3] Overall, the impression given by Selborne's first report to the prime minister is one of upbeat steady progress upon a broad international canvas. In Selborne's second summary compiled personally for the prime minister for the period July to September 1942, Lord Selborne stated: 'Occupied Europe is seething with the spirit of revolt and revolution. In all this turmoil SOE have been the moving spirit.'[4]

In truth, the field successes, in France particularly, were meagre. By the end of summer 1942, Buckmaster, the head of F Section, reported that in the two different 'Zones' of France there were:

Zone Occupée:
Preparations made for receipt of stores;
6 organisers installed;
1 courier
2 W/T operators (only one in contact)[5]
No stores.

Zone Non-Occupée:
25 SOE trained organisers
19 local recruits
6 wireless operators (4 in contact)
64 containers delivered
24 containers scheduled for September drop
2,000 lbs of stores scheduled for delivery by sea.[6]

Much scheduled and promised, but little realised. Historian William Mackenzie commented of those times when F Section's own men in the field were few and their equipment negligible:

Wireless communications were still on too narrow a base to be very safe but they had improved greatly in the last few months. There were at least eight sets in operation, mainly in the unoccupied Zone. Apart from wireless sets, the supply position was bad and the amount of stores dropped was too small to have any practical significance. This was a source of ceaseless worry.[7]

Shortly after Dalton's departure in February 1942 there had been an important technical victory when, the following month, SOE finally managed to wrest control of its own wireless operations from SIS. Until then, under a long-defunct

1940 agreement, all SOE messages had been vetted, routed and, when it suited them, intercepted, delayed or withheld, by SIS. In late 1940 the communications situation between SOE and SIS had been 'regarded as so serious as to make CD's activities in many cases almost impossible'.[8] This dependence upon SIS lasted until 1942 and gave rise to probably well-founded suspicions that SIS exerted its rights under the 1940 agreement and often obstructed SOE operations of which it disapproved. Colonel, later Brigadier, Gambier-Perry, the head of SIS communications, 'disliked and was alleged to have obstructed SOE'.[9] In August 1941 SOE had recorded:

> Experience has taught us that Gambier-Perry does not live up to his promises in regard to the deliveries of W/T sets for agents. We have grave reasons to doubt that his attitude will be very much changed as regards the future. Gambier-Perry frequently makes personal attacks on our staff, both in London and at Station IX, which are totally unjustified and greatly resented by us at Headquarters.[10]

In December that same year, Gambier-Perry felt 'most strongly that we must face a complete show-down with SOE that we either absolutely control their communications, including the manufacture and supply of equipment, training, preparation of operations or we cut completely adrift and let them wallow in their own mire!'[11] He would go on to describe SOE's communications plans as 'extravagant, insecure, fatuous and very dangerous'. In January 1942 CD had written to Jebb stating:

> We are moving fast towards a crisis in our relationship with SIS. I shall be very grateful if you will wade through this paper so that we may perhaps consult together on the line that I think we ought to adopt, not only on detail matters like communications but the general attitude of obstruction and deceit which I am afraid there is no gainsaying we experience every day and every week from various members of C organisation. I ought to say at this juncture that I view with the greatest possible gravity the position into which we are drifting in regard to communications – to say nothing of the many low-level attempts on the part of C's employees to get us in wrong with the various authorities and generally belittle our organisation and the work we are doing.[12]

A further flurry of internal exchanges between Gubbins, Jebb and Dalton before the latter's removal show that SOE bitterly resented both SIS's meddling in SOE affairs and their patronising attitude towards their rival and 'junior partner'. Referring to an amended SIS annex, Dalton wrote in red ink: 'I have gone through this most carefully a number of times and my personal view is that it is

utterly unacceptable even as a basis for discussion. It has an undertone of conde-
scending patronage bordering upon the impertinent.'[13]

However, in early 1942, with SOE sending three or four agents into the field
for every one despatched by SIS,[14] the anticipated volume of SOE wireless traffic
into enemy-occupied territory in the build-up to invasion demanded SOE to
take control of its own codes, ciphers and signals' traffic.[15] Yet that deep hostility
and distrust between SOE and SIS made the duplication of a signals' directorate
inevitable: 'This was wasteful of manpower and material. Doing it yourself is a
satisfying pastime, but it would be interesting to know how much time, effort
and money would have been saved if an amicable arrangement could have been
reached between the two of us.'[16]

That same early quarter of 1942 saw a general improvement in communications and liaison elsewhere: in early January, a lieutenant colonel was appointed
as SOE's first permanent liaison officer to the Chiefs of Staff Secretariat; whilst in
the month before he was abruptly moved to the Board of Trade, Dalton hosted
two unexpectedly successful meetings that were to deliver significant dividends
after his departure. The first of these, on 6 January 1942, was a luncheon with
the new CIGS and Chairman of the Chiefs of Staff, General Sir Alan Brooke
(promoted field marshal in 1944), who replaced Sir John Dill. Dill had opposed
SOE but now Brooke brought to his new appointment a more positive attitude
towards SOE and the supply of arms and equipment to resistance groups across
Europe, recording in his diary: 'Dined with Dalton and discussed with him his
sabotage activities in Europe. There is a great deal to be done in this direction at
present and I don't feel we are doing anything like enough.'[17] The second of these
successful meetings was with the adviser on Combined Operations, Lord Louis
Mountbatten, on 9 January 1942, less than two months before Dalton's removal:
'CCO calls and stays for an hour. He asks many questions about the origin of my
show and its relations with others.'[18]

Dalton evidently considered the meeting highly important. It was one of
the few entries in his diary for this period that merited an additional and more
detailed record of their meeting. From the outset it appeared there were 'good
contacts between his Show and SOE; I wished for full co-operation with him.
He said that he had already had valuable help from us in his Norwegian raids.'
For his part, Mountbatten used the meeting to pump Dalton about SOE's relationship with both the Foreign Office ('adept at passing the buck and hindering
action') and SIS with whom 'he had the impression there was rivalry and some
difficulty as regards signals'. It was hardly something he could have missed. SOE's
reliance upon SIS for wireless communications then came in for discussion, as
did Mountbatten's puzzlement at the many different organisations charged with
the collection of intelligence. Perhaps of most significance, Mountbatten and
Dalton agreed to exchange Chiefs of Staff directives through their immediate

subordinates, Brigadier Haydon, the Vice Chief of Combined Operations Staff, and Brigadier Colin Gubbins, SOE's then Director of Operations and Training. Despite effusive mutual enthusiasm for reliance upon the French industrial working class for the provision of recruits for clandestine operations, Dalton remained wary: 'All this is good as far as it goes and quite amusing, but he may become, or be presented by others as, an uncomfortable acquisitive force.'[19]

Acquisitive Mountbatten most certainly was. By early 1942 Combined Operations was in the ascendant and marked down for rapid expansion. Like SOE, the role of Combined Operations was clarified in that same directive of 12 May 1942 by the Chiefs of Staff which stated *inter alia* that:

> The War Cabinet has approved that plans and preparations should proceed without delay for Anglo-US operations in Western Europe in 1942 and 1943, the intention being to develop an offensive in stages as follows:

> A series of raiding operations to be carried out during the summer of 1942 on a front extending from the North of Norway to the Bay of Biscay, coupled with –

> - An active air offensive over NW Europe.
> - A large scale raid to bring about an air battle and/or the capture of a bridgehead in France within the area in which adequate naval and air cover can be given during the summer of 1942.
> - A large scale descent on Western Europe in the spring of 1943.[20]

Evidently, the head of Combined Operations had his own directive from the Chiefs of Staff, but the essentials did not change. His role, like that of SOE, was now defined with pressing clarity: there was to be a series of raids of increasing size and complexity on the enemy coast, culminating in a full-scale invasion from the sea in spring 1943. To which end Mountbatten, initially working simply as RN commodore 'adviser' to the Chiefs of Staff on all aspects of the planning and training for Combined Operations, now oversaw this period of explosive growth. The Joint Planners had already predicted, in the month of Mountbatten's appointment, that Combined Operations would require 2,250 landing craft (tank), plus the trained crews to man them. Lord Mountbatten inherited from Keyes a staff of just twenty-three, including typists and messengers;[21] a month after his appointment the Second Sea Lord estimated that Combined Operations, as ultimately envisaged, would require 1,500 officers and at least 20,000 ratings. By May 1943 that figure had swollen to well over 50,000 all ranks. Unsurprisingly perhaps, the expansion of Combined Operations was hardly welcomed by other services:

Combined Operations began in an atmosphere of controversy and acrimony. They were hated by all three established services, and came in for loathing from the Admiralty, an attitude that stemmed from two sources. First, the Admiralty were traditionally jealous of what they imagined might become a rival concern. Secondly, they associated Combined Operations very closely with Admiral Sir Roger Keyes.[22]

The youthful enthusiasm brought to his new task by the dashing ex-captain of destroyers with royal connections was not regarded necessarily as an asset in all quarters:

The staid and the stripe-trousered might or might not admire his eagerness, but some of them tended not to take his enthusiasm seriously. After all, Whitehall was neither a polo field to be scarred by galloping hooves, nor a stretch of water to be churned up by the propellers of a destroyer flotilla proceeding somewhere at 35 knots. And there was in some quarters a disposition to assess at longish odds the chances against a minor royalty turning out to be a major military personality.[23]

One of those officers appointed to join Lord Mountbatten's staff later became an MP. He commented after the war: 'while politics are reckoned to be a dirty game, they are holy-stone clean as compared with the dirty work which went on in the Service Ministries to undermine COHQ [Combined Operations Headquarters] during the first six months of Mountbatten's tenure.'[24]

As adviser to the Chiefs of Staff, Mountbatten initially attended their meetings as a junior officer, not as an equal but one whose presence was initially resented by his seniors. 'Up until then they had thought of themselves as a three-pronged fork,' recalled General Hollis: 'They did not want a fourth prong.'[25] Wanted or not, a fourth prong was what they got. To ensure parity around the table Dalton had once coveted, in March 1942, as he told the American president in confidence, Churchill promoted Mountbatten to Chief of Combined Operations (CCO) with the triple ranks of lieutenant general, air marshal and vice admiral. Somewhat surprisingly, relations with the Chiefs of Staff improved thereafter although General Sir Leslie Hollis observed that, even post-war, senior officers still resented Mountbatten's swift and unorthodox promotion:

It was typical of the attitude of the other three services to Combined Operations during the war. The three service members of the Chiefs of Staff Committee did not like to admit that an outside organisation such as Combined Operations, responsible only to the prime minister and not to them, could have such an important part to play.[26]

One of Mountbatten's earliest moves was to 'gather in' the loose reins of a ponderous, overly complicated, Keyes-inherited, ad hoc system of raiding command and control. Until his arrival – Operations *Claymore* (Lofoten) and *Colossus* (Italy) notwithstanding – raiding had been 'a rather unfruitful field'.[27] Now, with an overall awareness that successful raiding would pave the way to a successful invasion, raiding stepped up apace. In the first six months of 1942, ten raids, both large and small, were carried out. SOE had provided the Italian interpreter for *Colossos* and *Kompani Linge* Norwegian exiles for *Claymore*. SOE had also been involved in the abortive Combined Operations raid Operation *Kitbag*, which was to land members of No. 6 Commando at Floro, south of Stadlandet, Norway, in October 1941. The raid began badly after a grenade accident aboard one of the landing ships killed seven,[28] with two of the casualties SOE men from *Kompani Linge*, and the raid was later abandoned after the naval commander failed to locate their target. SOE then had a failure of its own when the leader of Operation *Arquebus* drowned along with forty-two others aboard the Norwegian fishing boat *Blia*, lost in a hurricane between 11 and 14 November 1941 somewhere in the North Sea as she attempted to bring refugees back to Britain from Norway as part of SOE's *Shetland Bus* operations. Agents had been inserted by sea into Norway with a faulty radio earlier that same month. With the death of *Arquebus'* team leader it would be a whole year before that W/T link was restored. In December 1941, Operation *Anklet* had been a second CO raid to the Lofoten Islands in support of Operation *Archery*, which had raided tiny Vaagso Island 450 miles further south.[29] SOE's role in operations such as these was one of informal and 'second fiddle' technical support,[30] a reflection of that 'rather vague'[31] blurring of lines of demarcation for jurisdiction over small raids and *coup de main* operations that had been permitted to endure since the early days of Admiral Keyes. It was a situation that appears not to have changed. One SOE file records: 'In 1942 Combined Operations were, it was felt, inclined to usurp SOE's function of *coup de main* actions against industrial targets.'[32] The responsibility for target allocation was divided between Combined Operations and SOE, but 'it was not easy to say where the frontier lay'.[33] Both Combined Operations and SOE were in 'close sympathy', claims Mackenzie, adding that whilst there was healthy rivalry there was 'no serious confusion'.[34] As will be seen, that rather cosy assumption of operational compatibility does not withstand close scrutiny.

Just one week before Dalton and Mountbatten had that extended, amicable meeting in Dalton's office and agreed that it was time to put their relations on a stronger footing,[35] a senior SOE officer was reporting: 'I am profoundly dissatisfied with the situation CCO. Either he and his headquarters know nothing, or else he deliberately keeps his staff officers in complete ignorance of what is going on.'[36]

The report goes on to state that SOE was still awaiting a report on the deaths of two of its men on Operation *Kitbag I* and a decision was awaited on whether there was to be a formal inquiry into the abortion of the same mission; the fate of two SOE men on Operation *Archery* was still unknown and a report was still wanting on Operation *Anklet*. The report concluded: 'It hardly seems worthwhile to us to maintain a special liaison officer with CCO's office if he is never given any information about such matters as I have set forth above.' A first attempt to establish regular liaison between SOE and CCO had withered by neglect. That 'SO Board' created to establish a measure of formal liaison between SOE and Combined Operations had simply disappeared without explanation in February 1941. No one had bothered to ensure its replacement. There is a record of an exchange of projects in March of that year and then nothing is recorded until after Mountbatten's appointment in October 1941. Thus one is tempted to hazard the view that, despite a theoretical perception of the need for co-operation, liaison and a mutual sharing of information, simple tribal organisational loyalty and inter-service rivalry often intervened. SOE was quite prepared to share knowledge. What it was not always prepared to share, it appears, were plans and intentions: 'SOE staff willingly shared such knowledge as they had with people from COHQ who had good reason for inquiring, and SOE was kept informed of CCO's main intentions and achievements. No one expected that such information should be reciprocated.'[37]

In February 1942 Combined Operations mounted Operation *Biting*, a paratroop assault upon a new German *Würzburg* radar unit on the very edge of the coast of France at Bruneval, opposite Portsmouth. The intention was to attack the installation, remove secret components and withdraw for evacuation by sea. SOE's role was to equip the raiders,[38] all members of 2nd Battalion, the Parachute Regiment under the command of Major John Frost, with 'a number of special stores and tools which were essential for the unusual type of operation'.[39] SOE also provided a Sudeten German whose role was to shout conflicting orders in the dark and so confuse the German garrison. The plan was the first truly 'combined' operation. It worked to perfection with just six killed, five wounded and six missing. General Kurt Student, the German paratroop commander, wrote after the war: 'I was particularly impressed by the suggestion ... to take the Bruneval Station in a *coup de main* from the air. This was a grand plan, just to my liking ... The successful execution by Major Frost sent a great shock through Hitler's headquarters.'[40] SOE/CCO liaison, too, had worked well:

SOE provided, in addition to the Sudeten German, a number of special stores and tools which were essential for the unusual type of operation. The CRE Airborne Division reported that all this equipment had proved first class during training. I have asked him for a detailed report of its use in the operation, but, in the meantime, may this 'bouquet' be passed on to the departments concerned?[41]

Despite Dalton's meeting with Lord Mountbatten, whatever feelings of kinship Operation *Biting* may have generated between SOE and Combined Operations appear, however, to have been short-lived. Three months later, in May 1942, the SOE/CCO liaison officer was reporting: 'A paper on the unsatisfactory nature of the present liaison between SOE and CCO in the matter of Technical Intelligence, Planning and Training was forwarded to MG, LDFSR on 23 May.'[42]

That report was submitted two months after Operation *Chariot*, a large-scale Combined Operations raid mounted from Falmouth upon the dock caisson of St Nazaire, France, on 28 March 1942. The aim was to deny *Tirpitz*, Germany's most powerful battleship, docking and repair facilities and so keep her out of the North Atlantic. SOE's role for this tactical raid with a strategic purpose, once again, was intelligence briefing and technical support: the 1.5 tons of explosive used against the docks was prepared by SOE's Station XII at Stevenage, Hertfordshire, where the raid's demolition parties received specialist training from SOE. Four months earlier, in November 1941, Mountbatten had asked SOE if their 'cloak and dagger' agents in France could carry out the dock demolition on their own. SOE studied the project in detail and turned it down. Notwithstanding the paucity of SOE agents then on the ground, it was far too big a task.[43] SOE's contribution to the raid was to make up a number of special charges and equipment, including underwater charges, tubular ladders and other specialised equipment. Despite the success of Operation *Chariot* – at terrible cost – liaison between SOE and Combined Operations appears to have still been unresolved three months later. That same SOE liaison officer recorded on 3 June 1942: 'The question of liaison CCO/SOE and the provision of a technical Officer at CCO now actively being taken up at COHQ.'[44] A month later SOE was reporting that there was now 'no difficulty in keeping in touch with COHQ'.[45] Whether COHQ were finding it as easy to keep in touch with SOE is not recorded.

The success of Operation *Chariot* was followed in August 1942 by the disaster of Operation *Jubilee*: the mismanaged, ill-conceived raid on Dieppe that was to cost almost 3,500 Canadian dead, wounded or captured. The purpose of the raid baffled British and Germans alike: 'Too big for a raid, too small for an invasion: what *were* you trying to do?' demanded a German interrogator of a Canadian prisoner.[46] The failure at Dieppe damaged Mountbatten's reputation; in the eyes of many, irreparably. Nigel Hamilton, Montgomery's respected biographer, claimed Mountbatten was 'a master of intrigue, jealousy and ineptitude, like a spoilt child, he toyed with men's lives with an indifference to casualties that can only be explained by his insatiable, even psychopathic ambition'.[47] To others, the raid's failure simply confirmed the inadvisability of placing what was essentially an army/land operation in the hands of a youthful former captain of destroyers. SOE's role, once again, had been to provide explosives. Their use, however, was thwarted by the failure of troops to clear the steep shingle beaches.

Amongst those lost at Dieppe amidst the folly of Combined Operations' planning was Sapper Major David Wyatt, killed ashore whilst attempting to establish contact with local resisters:

> I believe my father went [on the raid] on his own initiative to gain first hand knowledge of the German coastal defences and the various methods devised to overcome them. He was on Mountbatten's planning staff and as such would not normally have gone along.[48]

An explosives expert, Major Wyatt's job at COHQ appears to have been to act as liaison officer between SOE and Mountbatten's growing organisation. Thus, in theory at least, Combined Operations seems to have been keen to avoid treading on the toes of SOE. Once again, however, there is no indication of reciprocity. And even that supposition of structural clarity appears shrouded in its own small mystery: after Major Wyatt's death at Dieppe, Lord Louis Mountbatten wrote to his widow claiming her husband had been 'engaged in particularly important and secret work on my staff'. Yet we now know that Wyatt was actually appointed, from 24 February 1941, for 'special duties' with the Inter-services Research Bureau at 64 Baker Street. The ISRB was the early cover name for the Special Operations Executive. However unlikely, is it remotely possible that even Mountbatten did not realise that the popular and highly efficient liaison officer in their midst owed his primary loyalty not to COHQ but to Mountbatten's rival organisation? In any event, such comments and suggestions that could be made by Combined Operations both before and after the death of Major Wyatt were only as helpful as the timely accuracy of the information shared with them by SOE – information which would appear, at times, to have been discreetly 'laundered' to suit SOE's more private purpose. Frank Nelson, CD, wrote to Gladwyn Jebb, his CEO, after the latter had presented a paper outlining a proposed level of disclosure to Combined Operations: 'The revised copy of our Plans and Projects attached however is, to my mind, a very proper version to give to Commander Fletcher.'[49]

Both Professor Foot and William Mackenzie claim that, by the time of Major Wyatt's death, SOE and Combined Operations were 'so close' that, even though it would be some months before he was replaced, his role had become almost superfluous.[50] That assertion, however, is at curious odds with extant files at The National Archives in Kew. Through to the end of 1943, those records that do survive – and it has been estimated that some 87 per cent of SOE files have been deliberately, inadvertently or accidentally destroyed since the end of the Second World War – show a persistent plea for better liaison between SOE and Combined Operations together with an awareness of the dangers of trespass and duplication. In August 1942, General Hollis' Defence Committee remarked upon the need for better liaison with SOE.[51] On 15 December 1942, COHQ wrote to Brigadier Colin Gubbins about small-scale raids and the 'obvious and inevitable clash of interests between such raids and the activities of your organisation'. That letter continued: 'Although, thanks to your most helpful attitude, matters have been settled so far, it was thought that the implications on the future of your organisation should be known so that the Chiefs of Staff should realise that these raids do constitute a real threat to your organisation.'[52]

That paper and its date are not without irony. Just eight days previously, Operation *Frankton* had been launched amidst a level of duplication, high-level ignorance and lack of liaison that was to be to the detriment of both organisations. Operation *Frankton* apart, it appears that the problems of effective liaison persisted: almost a year later, in October 1943, the Chiefs of Staff once again called for better liaison between SOE and Combined Operations whilst making a firm recommendation that SOE should circulate weekly reports and work more closely with the COS Joint Planners.[53]

The implication of such directives is clear: a full year after the Dieppe raid and the death of a specially tasked liaison officer, and despite the eventual creation of 'a new liaison system in London by which a dozen GSOIs and IIs made contact direct with their opposite numbers on CCO's staff',[54] the level of SOE/CCO co-operation was still falling short of expectations. Such reports of co-operation as do exist indicate a flow of information from Combined Operations to SOE, yet nowhere is there evidence of reciprocity. That lack of openness, of liaison between SOE and Combined Operations, whether deliberate or unintentional, whether nurtured by a commendable sense of security or as a direct result of that climate of rivalry and encirclement that dogged SOE since its inception, was to have fatal consequences.

In the grand scheme of events that coloured Allied wartime fortunes in 1942, those particular consequences do not appear to have been of great or significant moment: they did not affect the course of history, nor did they influence grand strategy. Yet, as a direct result of a particular inadequacy of planning, co-operation and trust, the lives of young men – 'Cockleshell Heroes' all – were squandered. Lack of strategic impact notwithstanding, to the homes and families of those who would receive those long-dreaded, cold and impersonal telegrams of notification and condolence, their deaths represented devastating and precious loss. In that spirit, they are thus worthy of close and particular examination. But before the immediate events leading up to those deaths can be explored, it is necessary to step away from Combined Operations and its HQ in

Richmond Terrace, where SOE 'maintained an active agency'[55] and where SOE and CCO officers were supposed to share plans and intentions, and examine events further afield.

Notes

1 In File CHAR 20/54A/38 at Churchill Archives Centre, Churchill College, Cambridge. Private letter from Churchill to Lord Selborne dated 25 July 1942.

2 Lord Selborne to Prime Minister Winston Churchill: Quarterly Report of SOE Activities March–June 1942, p.2. Sent to Churchill in July 1942. In File HS 8/899 at The National Archives, Kew.

3 Operation *Anthropoid* was launched on 28 December 1941 with the parachuting of SOE agents and would-be assassins into Czechoslovakia who 'Know that they cannot come out of the attempt alive'. A bomb – which did not contain lethal toxins – was thrown at Heydrich's open car by one of the agents on 27 May 1942. Heydrich died from wound infection on 4 June 1942. Six days later the village of Lidice was razed to the ground and 192 men killed, and all women and children deported to concentration camps as a reprisal. The two SOE-trained assassins committed suicide after being cornered in a Prague church and betrayed by one of their own, Karl Curda. Source: Macdonald, Callum, *The Assassination of Reinhard Heydrich* (Birlinn, Edinburgh, 2007).

4 File HS 8/899 at The National Archives, Kew. Report: SOE Activities – Summary for the Prime Minister: Quarter Report July–September 1942.

5 Professor Michael Foot claims that, in fact, after the final collapse of the AUTOGYRO circuit in August 1942, F Section was left with no organised circuits at all and 'hardly a single useful agent'. Source: Foot, *SOE in France*, p.175.

6 File HS 7/121 at The National Archives, Kew. File entitled 'F Section History', p.4. Written by Colonel Maurice Buckmaster, Head of F Section.

7 Mackenzie, *The Secret History of SOE*, p.280.

8 Travers, T. and Archer, C. (eds), *Men at War: Politics, Technology and Innovation in the Twentieth Century* (Precedent, Chicago, 1982), p.123.

9 Travers and Archer, *Men at War: Politics, Technology and Innovation in the Twentieth Century*, p.123 and sourced to FO 898/9.

10 In File HS 8/358 at The National Archives, Kew. Internal SOE report on communication and signals liaison with SIS dated August 1941.

11 Jeffery, *MI6: The History of the Secret Intelligence Service 1909–1949*, p.355.

12 In File HS 8/321 at The National Archives, Kew. CD to Gladwyn Jebb, January 1942.

13 In File HS 8/321 at The National Archives, Kew. Undated Dalton notation on SOE/SIS Signals' annex.

14 Mackenzie, *The Secret History of SOE*, p.384.

15 Hinsley, *British Intelligence in the Second World War*, p.14.

16 Sweet-Escott, *Baker Street Irregular*, p.105.

17 Wilkinson and Astley, *Gubbins and SOE*, p.98.

18 Pimlott (ed.), *The Second World War Diary of Hugh Dalton: 1940–1945*, p.345. Diary entry for 9 January 1942.

19 Pimlott (ed.), *The Second World War Diary of Hugh Dalton: 1940–1945*, p.346. Additional note: diary entry for 9 January 1942.

20 Reproduced in Mackenzie, *The Secret History of SOE*, pp.766–9. Appendix G.

21 Fergusson, *The Watery Maze*, p.90.

22 Leasor and Hollis, *War at the Top*, p.119.

23 Fergusson, *The Watery Maze*, p.119.

24 Fergusson, *The Watery Maze*, p.120.

25 Leasor and Hollis, *War at the Top*, p.127.

26 Leasor and Hollis, *War at the Top*, p.139.

27 Fergusson, *The Watery Maze*, p.130.

28 Lovat, *March Past*, p.228.

29 SOE provided tools, bombs and food parcels for the local inhabitants. SOE also provided detailed lists of Quislings and targets, pilots, guides and interpreters. Source: File HS 8/818 at The National Archives, Kew.

30 Hinsley, *British Intelligence in the Second World War*, p.12.

31 Mackenzie, *The Secret History of SOE*, p.94.

32 In File HS 7/174 at The National Archives, Kew, p.264.

33 Mackenzie, *The Secret History of SOE*, p.652.

34 Mackenzie, *The Secret History of SOE*, p.652.

35 Stafford, *Britain and European Resistance 1940–1945*, p.76.

36 File HS 8/818 at The National Archives, Kew. Internal SOE liaison file dated 2 January 1942.

37 Foot, *SOE in France*, p.167.

38 Stores provided or developed by SOE included cameras, surgeon's head torches, overhead telephone wire-cutters, special clams, jemmies, electrical tools and equipment. Source: File HS 8/818 at The National Archives, Kew.

39 Foot, *SOE in France*, p.166.

40 George Millar, *The Bruneval Raid* (Bodley Head, London, 1974), p.13. In foreword by Admiral of the Fleet, the Earl Mountbatten of Burma.

41 CCO/SOE liaison officer's report No. 58 dated 1 March 1942 42 in File HS 8/81 at The National Archives, Kew.

42 CCO/SOE liaison officer's report No. 84 dated 1 June 1942 in File HS 8/819 at The National Archives, Kew.

43 Lucas Phillips, C.E., *The Greatest Raid of All* (Atlantic Monthly Press, Boston, 1960), p.19.

44 Liaison officer report of 1 June 1942 in File HS 8/819 at The National Archives, Kew.

45 Liaison officer report of 14 July 1942 in File HS 8/81 at The National Archives, Kew.

46 Neillands, Robin, *The Dieppe Raid* (Aurum, London, 2006), p.1.

47 Ziegler, *Mountbatten: The Official Biography*, p.293.

48 Note from Jonathan Wyatt, son of Major David Wyatt, to the author dated 25 January 2011. It has since emerged that Major Wyatt was posted to Combined Operations 'for special duties under the Inter-Services Research Bureau'. This was the early cover name for SOE. His appointment took effect from 26 February 1941 and was kept secret even from his wife. It emerged only with the release of Major Wyatt's army records to his son in February 2011.

49 In File HS 8/818 at The National Archives, Kew. Undated internal SOE memo from Gubbins to Gladwyn Jebb.

50 Mackenzie, *The Secret History of SOE*, p.362.

51 In Paper DEFE 2/415 in The National Archives, Kew.

52 File HS 8/818 at The National Archives, Kew. Paper marked 'Small Scale Raiding' and tagged 'Most Secret' dated 15 December 1942.

53 File COS (43) 505 (O) & COS (43) 240th Meeting. At The National Archives, Kew.

54 Foot, *SOE in France*, p.167.

55 Phillips, *Cockleshell Heroes*, p.10.

CHAPTER NINETEEN

LEFT HAND

Lord 'Top' Selborne inherited more than just the Special Operations Executive when he succeeded Dr Hugh Dalton in February 1942. He also inherited Dalton's Ministry of Economic Warfare and with it that ministry's obsession with the business of sea blockade and Axis shipping that was running often unhindered between Japan and German-occupied Europe. On 9 May 1942, Selborne wrote to the prime minister stating:

> I attach a note, based on the evidence available, showing that:
> (a) Blockade running, both ways, between German Europe and the Far East is beginning and is likely to increase;
> (b) Even a few cargoes will appreciably strengthen both Germany and Japan;
> (c) The first cargoes are likely to be much the most important.
>
> I submit, therefore, that everything practicable should be done quickly to ensure that blockade runners in either direction shall be located and intercepted.[1]

Since 1 July 1941, twelve vessels were known to have completed voyages from the Far East to Bordeaux. Their cargo capacity was estimated at between 70,000 to 80,000 tons and 'very substantial quantities of rubber would certainly have been included in these cargoes'.[2] At least six other vessels had left Bordeaux for the Far East. In a note remarkable for the wealth of detailed intelligence it contained,[3] Lord Selborne stated that Germany planned to import 250,000 tons of commodities from Japan during the year ending July 1943, of which 35,000 tons were to be loaded during July and August 1942. Twenty-four or twenty-five ships would be required to meet this schedule whose cargo manifest would include the delivery of 60,000 tons of rubber. Germany was to reciprocate by sending Japan specialised equipment for manufacturing, prototypes for various weapons and special component parts.

On 22 June 1942 and with Churchill absent from London in Washington, Lord Selborne was writing to Deputy Prime Minister Clement Attlee about a deterio-rating situation. Pointing out that now seven Axis blockade runners had arrived in Bordeaux since 1 April 1942 and that Germany had received approximately 50,000 tons of goods, including rubber from the Far East, in the last two months, Lord Selborne continued: 'As the highest priority goods will be shipped first in each direction, the need for immediate action is urgent. Suitable ships for this long distance blockade-running are limited in number and their destruction would in itself slow up the rate of deliveries. If a succession of sinkings could be achieved it might well stop the traffic altogether.'[4] Evidently at this stage at least, Lord Selborne's mind was running towards attack from the air only. He continued:

> The lack of suitable aircraft both for spotting and for attacking these blockade runners remains the obstacle to successful counter-action. The matter seems of so great importance that if it is impossible to provide sufficient planes for the purpose without an increased supply from America, the prime minister might perhaps be asked to take the matter up in Washington.

Lord Selborne's detailed letter of 22 June 1942 to the deputy prime minister represented merely the point of end-user delivery of a steady supply of detailed intelligence provided to SOE by one man, Robert Leroy.[5] Born in 1911 in Brest, Leroy joined the French Navy at 17 and served for five years, leaving with the rank of *Quartier Maître* (quartermaster). He then joined the French Merchant Marine and served for eight years, leaving as petty officer artificer. He ran arms into Spain during the Civil War and found himself in a banana boat in the Cameroons when war broke out. Returning home to Brest, he fled to England when the Germans arrived in June 1940. He joined the Free French Navy under General de Gaulle and was recruited by SOE after nine months stationed at Portsmouth. One report claims he 'deserted' from the Free French Navy to join SOE. Described as 'very tough and intelligent of the sailor type, a man of great resource and native wit', he was someone who would, as his SOE Special School instructors delicately put it, 'be out of place in an Officers' Mess'.[6] He could neither speak nor understand English, but Leroy began SOE training in April 1941 at Special Training Schools 5 (Wanborough Manor), 25 (Garramor), 51 (Ringway) and 31 (Beaulieu). He refused his second parachute jump and was removed from the course. Moved back to London, he was inserted into France with other agents by sea in September 1941. Leroy was landed ashore on the beach at Barcares, north-east of Perpignan in the ZNO (*Zone Non-Occupée*) after a seventeen-day voyage aboard the SOE 'Q' ship HMS *Fidelity*.[7] Nicholas Bodington, Buckmaster's second-in-command of F Section who joined the party at Gibraltar to watch their departure to France, reported: 'they were all *gonflé à bloc* ["on top of their form"].[8] Leroy slipped ashore as *Alain* on the night of 19 September 1941 along with SOE agents Basin (*Olive*), R.B. Roche and A.J.R. Duboudin of the AUTOGYRO and URCHIN circuits[9] after HMS *Fidelity* had closed the enemy coast disguised first as a Norwegian and then as a Spanish merchant ship.[10] Working alone, Leroy's orders were to make for Bordeaux and recce the dock area. Once there he found work first as a dock labourer and then as a tractor driver with the TODT labour organisation (OT)[11] before working on ship repairs in the docks themselves. Leroy – code name *Louis* – even managed to persuade a Bordeaux docks' director and German collaborator to stamp his dock permit papers *'indispensable pour port de Bordeaux'*[12] which gave him unrestricted access to all areas within the dock complex whilst wearing the blue worker's blouse of the authorised permit holder.

Bordeaux was a vital sea port offering access to the Atlantic and had long been the subject of SOE interest. On 10/11 September 1941, eight days before Leroy landed at Barcares, SOE mounted the *Barter* mission in which two RF Section agents, Roger Donnadieu (*Barter I*) and Pierre Laurent (*Barter 2*), a leader/sabotage instructor and his W/T operator, were dropped south and west of Bordeaux to make contact with potential resistants, identify future targets – particularly around the German aerodrome at Merignac – and recce possible air-landing grounds for both men and equipment.[13] *Barter I* rapidly found that 'contrary to what he had been told, no organisation existed and everything would have to be created from the start'.[14] The attack on the aerodrome at Merignac near Bordeaux could not be carried out. *Barter I* managed to create groups in Bayonne and Bordeaux where he selected landing grounds and set up reception committees. The *Barter* mission then went rapidly downhill with W/T failure, an abortive trip to Paris and organisational chaos that led to a significant falling out between both agents. In January 1942 Leroy returned to London via Spain, taking with him valuable information from inside the docks together with the contacts that would soon form the effective SOE SCIENTIST circuit. Robert Leroy returned to France in June 1942 and made his way once more to Bordeaux where he was given the Bassens area as his target. In the absence of the pertinent files it is reasonable to surmise that it was Leroy's initial intelligence reports,[15] enhanced by SCIENTIST's agents and contacts in the heart of the docks, which gave Lord Selborne's reports to the prime minister their extraordinary and detailed reliability. It is a view supported by Vera Atkins, F Section intelligence officer, assistant to Colonel Maurice Buckmaster and the woman many believe was the driving force and intelligence behind the work of F Section:[16]

> Bordeaux docks were very well organised and one got information on the blockade runners and U-boat movements and all that sort of thing which was slightly outside the normal SOE run. But of course we had very good chaps

there and very good connections with the docks; very useful information was passed and very much appreciated by the Chiefs of Staff.[17]

Delivering his 136-page review[18] entitled 'The British Circuits in France' on 30 June 1946 (the day SOE was wound up[19]) Colonel R.A. Bourne-Paterson, F Section's former planning officer and later Buckmaster's deputy, stated that Leroy 'established certain contacts which were later to prove useful and brought back information concerning the river and docks'.[20] His report went on to include this 1943 assessment of the work of the SCIENTIST *réseaux* in Bordeaux:

> … one result of very great value was achieved. A mass of information began to come out of Bordeaux concerning the movements of shipping in and out of the estuary of the Garonne. This was of such volume and of such accuracy that the Admiralty wrote in September 1943 (the following are extracts):

> 1. The information brought by SCIENTIST on his last visit, was the most important he had had and enabled successful measures to be taken by the Admiralty.
> 2. Although air photography has contributed a little to the results, it is the ground intelligence from Bordeaux which has virtually put an end to blockade-running between Europe and the Far East this year. The stoppage of this traffic is of the highest importance as the supplies ordered are vital to the Japanese.
> 3. Source has given a better intelligence service than has been available from any other enemy port.[21]

Central to events as they unfolded in Bordeaux that summer and autumn of 1942 was SOE agent and Chief Circuit Organiser Claude de Baissac. Colonel Maurice Buckmaster, the head of F Section, described Claude de Baissac as 'the most difficult of all my officers, without any exception'.[22] Professor Michael Foot remembers him as 'a thirty-five-year-old Mauritian agent of exceptional character'[23] and to this author as: 'Amongst SOE's organisers, he was personally probably the most forceful and one of the most efficient. I wouldn't put him right at the top, but pretty close to it.'[24]

Claude de Baissac passed through the SOE Special Training School at Arisaig in western Scotland. Initially, he struck his 'Preliminary' course instructors as over-confident, inexperienced and unfit: 'May have been a fair athlete earlier in life but has put on flesh and at present lacks energy.'[25] That was in April 1942. De Baissac, however, persevered. An excellent pistol shot, his physical training steadily improved. 'Very good indeed,' conceded his physical training instructor on the second stage or 'Paramilitary' course a month later: 'Is surprisingly athletic for a man of his age and build. He does not spare himself, and has set a good example.' The instructor's remarks at the end of his course concluded:

> The first week I couldn't quite make him out, but he has opened up and showed himself to be a first rate man. He has a very firm intention of causing a lot of damage operationally, with the ability to do it and look after himself. A great love of his country and keenness to do his part should prove him to be of great value. His training here has been most satisfactory, and his ability in all subjects is unquestionable.[26]

All de Baissac needed now was a mission. That final report on his abilities was written on 15 May 1942, five and a half weeks before Lord Selborne wrote to the deputy prime minister emphasising the scale of Axis traffic running the Allied blockade in and out of Bordeaux. Lord Selborne's letter was passed to both the Admiralty and the Royal Air Force, although both declined to become involved: for the Royal Navy, Bordeaux was simply too far from the sea and too deep inside enemy-occupied territory; for the Royal Air Force, the art of bomb-dropping was still in its relative infancy and a bombing raid on blockade shipping would cause unacceptable civilian casualties in the town around the docks. The problem was passed to Combined Operations whose Examination Committee considered what became known as the 'Bordeaux problem'. They estimated that a Combined Operations raid against the port would need three divisions or about 50,000 men.[27] In early July 1942 the idea was dropped. On 27 July Combined Operations' five-man Search Committee[28] revisited the problem that was to become Operation *Frankton*, raked over the same cold ashes and concluded without evident enthusiasm:

> It was thought that any or a combination of the following measures were the best available.
>
> 1. Bombing. But it was pointed out that the target area is large, and a large number of bombers would be required to have any marked effect.
>
> 2. Mining the mouth of the Gironde.
>
> 3. Submarine patrol off the mouth of the Gironde. This might be able to be intermittent if our intelligence were very good, but if continuous would require a large number of submarines to be used for this patrol alone.
>
> 4. SOE or Commando Saboteurs. These would probably be landed on the coast by submarine and Folboat. Their activities would be easier if done in an air raid.[29]

C.E. Lucas Phillips, the author of *Cockleshell Heroes*, concludes his account of this period with the remark: 'But no action ensued.'[30] In fact, it already had. Seven days earlier, on 20 July 1942, SOE had 'arranged to obtain from MEW details of the actual berths being occupied by potential blockade runners at Bordeaux in case a project could be arranged'.[31]

Now, unknown to Combined Operations, that 'project' was well on its way. Four days after that note, on 24 July 1942, Claude de Baissac received his mission briefing. He was to be dropped into France to organise the attack on Axis blockade runners in Bordeaux. His mission brief was quite specific. In order of priority his target objectives were set out as:

Rubber & other cargoes from Far East entering the port of Bordeaux.

Attack:
1. The ships
2. Cargo in ship
3. Cargo on wharf or in Warehouse
4. Cargo on rail
5. Dredgers
6. Lock Gate (on supply side mainly unless Louis fails)
7. Other railway targets in and around Bordeaux[32]

Items 1, 2 and 3 were marked with an 'x' indicating 'for immediate action'. Item 4, the railway targets, were 'to be reserved'. For perhaps the first time in SOE's brief and anguished history, its agents had been tasked to attack a target of strategic significance.[33] The destruction by SOE of blockade runners in Bordeaux, supposedly beyond the reach of any other agency, would immeasurably enhance SOE's beleaguered reputation amid the labyrinthine corridors of Whitehall.

Six days later Claude de Baissac, alias *David*, was parachuted into France. He was dropped 'blind' at night near Caissarghes, Gard, in the ZNO, far to the south and east of Bordeaux. With him dropped his radio operator, Harry Peulevé (*Jean/Hilaire*), another of those who had gone through the Arisaig SOE training process at the same time. Both agents were dropped too low and in a strong crosswind. Landing heavily with a poorly deployed parachute, de Baissac sprained an ankle, while Peulevé suffered a broken leg and facial bruising.[34] Ordering Peulevé to stay hidden until 1030hrs to give him time to get away, de Baissac limped to the railway station, Peulevé's vital radio link with London left behind, hidden in a ditch.[35] Supposed to link up with Robert Leroy, confusion over contact addresses kept them apart for months. Mindful of his briefing instructions 'remember that above all your primary task is to RECONNOITRE and to REPORT. To prepare for concerted action when you receive the order and to receive in as large quantities as possible the material which will make that action effective',[36] de Baissac did precisely that. He decided he needed reinforcements, although getting them without radio contact was a slow process with hidden letters travelling slowly to England through Lyons. It would be late September before his sister Lise (*Odile*) parachuted in to act as liaison officer between SCIENTIST and the PROSPER and BRICKLAYER circuits nearby. And it would be the very last day of October 1942 before the radio operator so badly needed by de Baissac arrived in Bordeaux. Whether or not the Operation *Barter* W/T operator was still in the Bordeaux area at this time remains unclear.

The W/T operator who did now arrive – and who would later take over the SCIENTIST circuit from Claude de Baissac – was Roger Landes (*Aristide*), another graduate from the same courses at Wanborough and Arisaig, who would immediately set about organising the airdrop of explosives and supplies needed for the attack on the ships in Bordeaux.[37] Linking into a growing band of potential resistants in the Bordeaux area, the SCIENTIST circuit was now growing apace. On 28 November, 34-year-old Captain Victor Charles Hayes (*Yves*), code name *Printer*, was dropped to help de Baissac in his planning for the Bordeaux attack. Given separate targets, his main briefing emphasised that he was to 'act as specialist in electrical demolitions and arms to SCIENTIST, to advise, reconnoitre and prepare targets and, if necessary, to lead the attacking party'.[38]

Six days after Claude de Baissac was parachuted into France, Lord Selborne took up his pen once more to Clement Attlee, the deputy prime minister. Reminding him tartly of his previous letters of 9 May and 22 June 1942, he wrote:

> Hardly a day passes without my seeing convincing proof of the determination of both countries [Germany and Japan] to execute their programme. The importance of this traffic is no less today than when I wrote my previous minutes. If immediate action could be taken it would not be too late.[39]

Selborne's letter was placed before the Chiefs of Staff two days later. Beyond endorsing the conclusions of the Combined Operations Search Committee taken on 27 July, once again, no further action ensued.[40]

Notes

1 File HS 8/897 (microfilm) at The National Archives, Kew. Lord Selborne to the prime minister, 9 May 1942. Minute entitled 'Blockade Runners'.
2 File HS 8/897 (microfilm) at The National Archives, Kew. Lord Selborne to the prime minister, 9 May 1942. Minute entitled 'Blockade Runners'.
3 The note goes on to list the name and give precise tonnage of all twenty-five potential blockade runners from both France and Japan.

4 File HS 8/897 at The National Archives, Kew. Lord Selborne to Clement Attlee, the Deputy Prime Minister, 22 June 1942. Letter from the Ministry of Economic Warfare headed 'Most Secret'.

5 File HS 9/916/2 at The National Archives, Kew. Ensuing details from Robert Leroy personal file.

6 Robert Leroy's personal file HS 9/916/2 at The National Archives, Kew. Early and repeated requests for access to this file were refused. I am greatly indebted to Lord Paddy Ashdown whose personal intervention and tenacity ensured the release of this file into the public domain.

7 Formerly the French cargo vessel Le-Rhin refitted at Barry docks.

8 Foot, SOE in France, p.157.

9 Richards, Secret Flotillas, p.670.

10 File HS 8/831 at The National Archives, Kew. HMS Fidelity file.

11 Organisation TODT: A German civil and military engineering group that became notorious for its use of forced labour. Named after German Minister for Armaments and Munitions, Fritz Todt. File HS 6/469 (microfilm) at The National Archives, Kew. Bourne-Paterson post-war report on French circuits. Also on paper in HS 7/122.

12 File HS 9/75 at The National Archives, Kew. Information in Leroy debrief document dated 6 September 1943.

13 File HS 6/418 at The National Archives, Kew. Details of Operator Barter and the deployment of SOE RF Section agents Donnadieu and Laurent.

14 File HS 6/418 at The National Archives, Kew. Barter agents' operational report.

15 Leroy was recalled to England in July 1943 after he become 'brule' (Lit: burnt; i.e. known to the Germans) and transferred to the Free French Merchant Navy. Source: File HS 9/916/2 at The National Archives, Kew.

16 Fuller, Jean Overton, Double Agent? (Pan Books, London, 1961), p.25.

17 SOE Sound tape interview with Vera Atkins No. 12302 held at the Imperial War Museum, London. Recording date unspecified. Vera Atkins died in 2000.

18 Compiled to assist British diplomats abroad who might be asked to adjudicate over post-war claims by French men and women of SOE/Resistance involvement.

19 West, Secret War, p.5.

20 File HS 6/469 at The National Archives, Kew. Bourne-Paterson post-war report on French circuits. On microfilm and on paper in HS 7/122.

21 File HS 6/469 at The National Archives, Kew. Bourne-Paterson post-war report on French circuits. On microfilm and on paper in HS 7/122.

22 Foot, SOE in France, p.179.

23 Foot, SOE in France, p.179.

24 Interview with Professor Michael Foot by the author at his home in Royston, Herts, on 26 January 2004.

25 File HS 9/75 at The National Archives, Kew. Claude de Baissac's personal fitness and training report.

26 File HS 9/75 at The National Archives, Kew. Claude de Baissac's personal fitness and training report.

27 Phillips, Cockleshell Heroes, p.12.

28 Commander Unwin, Wing Commander Homer, Major Powells, Major Collins and Captain Hann.

29 File DEFE 2/217 at The National Archives, Kew. Minutes by Commander J.H. Unwin RN (NRP 3) to COHQ Search Committee dated 27 July 1942. The minutes' distribution list included the COHQ Examination Committee and something called 'The Special Registry' – an oblique and shielded reference perhaps to SOE.

30 Phillips, *Cockleshell Heroes*, p.13.

31 File HS 8/203 at The National Archives, Kew. SOE Council Minutes.

32 File HS 9/75 at The National Archives, Kew. SCIENTIST Mission Brief and Final Instructions (General).

33 It would not be their last. Operation *Grouse/Gunnerside*, a saboteur attack against the German heavy-water plant at Vemork, Norway, in February 1943, from which every man returned would remain arguably SOE's greatest strategic contribution to the war.

34 De Baissac's personal account of his landing and ensuing ordeal in HS 9/75 differs from that cited by both Professor Foot and E.H. Cookridge. Harry Peulevé was smuggled into hospital, treated and escaped back to England. He returned to France on his second mission almost exactly a year later. Source: File HS 6/469 at The National Archives, Kew.

35 De Baissac received the OBE for helping Peulevé. The official citation for that award states that 'in spite of his own injury [he] succeeded in getting his brother officer to safety without being detected, saved their kit and the [wireless] set, made all the arrangements for medical care for Peulevé, finally installing him in a clinic, where he made a good recovery'. De Baissac's own 'After Action' report admits to nothing of the kind, stating with disarming honesty: 'As we were only 300 metres from a large farmhouse, I told *Hilaire* [Peulevé] not to give any sign of life before 1030 so that I should have enough time to get right away. I left him his money and all the provisions, and limped off with a sprained ankle toward Nimes.' Source: File HS 9/75 at The National Archives, Kew. Endorsed in Peulevé's autobiography. Source: Perrin, Nigel, *Spirit of Resistance* (Pen & Sword, Barnsley, 2008), p.43.

36 File HS 9/75 at The National Archives, Kew. Capital letters as in original.

37 File HS 6/469 (microfilm) at The National Archives, Kew. In the next few months, *Aristide* was to be highly successful. Between November 1942 and August 1943, 121 dropping operations were made to the SCIENTIST circuit. In these, 1,600 containers and 350 packages were delivered. These included 18,400lb of HE, 7,500 Stens, 300 Brens, 1,500 rifles and 17,200 grenades.

38 File HS 9/916 at The National Archives, Kew. Hayes' personal file. Captain Charles Hayes MC was posted 'Missing', believed killed, in January 1944. Last seen in cell 18 in the military prison in Rue de Pessac, Bordeaux. He had been captured after a gun battle in which 'he fought a great battle for his life and conducted himself in accordance with the best traditions of the service'. From file citation.

39 File DEFE 2/217 at The National Archives, Kew. Lord Selborne to Deputy Prime Minister Clement Attlee 5 August 1942. As a point of historic irony only peripherally related to Operation *Frankton*, it is nevertheless worth noting that, on the very same day that the Chiefs of Staff passed Lord Selborne's letter to Combined Operations for action, the Objectives Board of SOE at their headquarters in Baker Street were considering trading copper or nitrate for rubber with the Japanese. Their minutes of 7 August 1942 reveal: '1. EXCHANGE WITH JAPAN OF COPPER OR NITRATE FOR RUBBER. SOE mentioned a proposal to effect such an exchange. MEW (Ministry of Economic Warfare) agreed that the suggestion was interesting and they would investigate it. In the meantime, SOE would find out the circumstances in which it was made. MEW were rather against the idea of relieving our own deficiencies by trading with the enemy as Japan's deficiencies were on the whole more acute than those of the Allies and such deals would tend to lessen our relative advantage.'

40 Southby-Tailyour, Ewen, *Blondie* (Leo Cooper, London, 1998), p.71.

CHAPTER TWENTY

LISTENING EARS AND SILENT MOUTHS

The 'Bordeaux problem' may have languished unresolved in a file in COHQ in Richmond Terrace, but 80 miles to the south-west, events and personalities were already beginning to come together that would lead, in five months' time, to its explosive resolution. The event was the creation, in early 1942, of the Combined Operations Development Centre (CODC), formerly known as the Inter-services Training and Development Centre, commanded by Captain Tom Hussey RN. One of its newest officers in January 1942 was Major H.G. 'Blondie' Hasler, then aged 28, a career Royal Marines officer and one of the few – Brigadier Colin Gubbins of SOE was another – whose reputation had been enhanced by his actions during the débâcle of the British campaign in Norway. For these he had been awarded the OBE, a Mention in Despatches and the French *Croix de Guerre*. Called 'Blondie' throughout the family of the Marine Corps because of his once-fair head of hair (Hasler was now bald), he had a passion for small boats. Hasler was brought in to CODC specifically to concern himself with attacking enemy shipping in harbour by stealth. A year earlier he had submitted a paper detailing how ships in dock might be attacked by canoe and underwater swimmers. His proposals were rejected as fanciful, then remembered after the Italians started attacking Allied shipping in Alexandria harbour using explosive motor torpedo boats. Hasler's work was new and experimental and, officially at least, he was working for Combined Operations. One of his officers, however, remembers things differently, claiming that, in its earliest evolution, the unit Hasler was working for answered to SOE. Asked 'Were you ever under SOE?', William Pritchard-Gordon, the Officer Commanding No. 2 Section of Hasler's soon-to-be-formed Royal Marines Boom Patrol Detachment (RMBPD) replied, 'Yes, we were in the early days. That is so. Because the research unit in which Sir Donald Campbell worked with Captain Hussey, that was definitely all part and parcel of SOE.'[1] Until now, that possibility had slipped by without notice. It appears, however, that from the very outset Hasler and SOE, at a personal level, were already exchanging dangerous ideas.

The day after Hasler joined CODC he went to COHQ in Richmond Terrace and met Lord Louis Mountbatten, who approved the terms of reference Hasler had written for himself. These were to study, co-ordinate and develop all methods of stealthy seaborne attack by very small parties: 'In particular you will be responsible for the development of a British version of the explosive motor-boat, and pay particular attention to methods of attacking ships in harbour.'[2] Within a fortnight Hasler was picking the brains of a Commando captain who was also developing ideas of attack on ships in harbour by canoe. Yet even that idea was not his. A Lieutenant Courtney of No. 8 Commando had conducted mock canoe sabotage attacks upon ships moored in Loch Fyne, Argyll, under the eyes of Admiral Sir Roger Keyes when he had been in charge of Combined Operations.[3] Impressed by the canoe's potential as a stealth raider, Keyes sent Courtney and his men to Arran to develop their ideas.[4] It was this unit that developed into 101 Troop of 1st Special Service Brigade under Captain Gerald Montanaro. Major Hasler visited him on 13 January 1942 and failed to impress. Captain Montanaro wrote in his private diary later that night: 'Visit by Major Hasler RM. No authy behind him. Dam' nonsense of a scheme, Crackers! Lead him along quite happily.'[5] The scheme that was 'crackers' one may presume was that relating to attack by explosive motorboat, not attack by canoe. In that sphere, Montanaro's own plans were already far in advance of Hasler's.

On the night of 12/13 November 1941 Montanaro's unit had lost an officer, Lieutenant Keith Smith (later reported captured), during a night recce by canoe on a beach near Calais. In April 1942, three months before the formation of Hasler's own unit, the RMBPD, Captain Montanaro would be awarded the DSO and Sergeant Preece, his No. 2, a Distinguished Conduct Medal (DCM) for a successful limpet attack by canoe upon a tanker in Boulogne harbour. Both raiders were splashed by a beer bottle thrown into the sea by drunken Germans above and then hid from sentries by paddling inside a large hole already blown by torpedo in one of the tanks of their target ship. On 9 February 1942 Major 'Blondie' Hasler was rubbing shoulders once more with SOE. The CCO/SOE liaison officer, Major David Wyatt, wrote: 'I have obtained permission from DSR [Colonel D.M. Newitt] and D/CE [Major General J.H.F. Lakin] to arrange a meeting between an officer from Station XII and Major Hasler of CODC to discuss attacks on warships in harbour.'[6] Station XII was the secret SOE production base at Aston House near Stevenage that concerned itself with the production, packaging and despatch of clams (mines), time-pencils and explosives.[7] Two days later, on 11 February 1942, that same CCO/SOE liaison officer was reporting: 'I have arranged a meeting in CCO's office on 18 February between Major Hasler CODC DDSR and officers from CCO to discuss the possible methods of achieving the above desirable object.'[8] The 'above desirable object' was headlined: 'Destruction of Enemy Shipping in Port'. Thus, as early as 11 February

1942, an officer (Major Wyatt) of the 'Inter-Services Research Bureau' – SOE – was sharing ideas with Combined Operations about how best to attack enemy ships in harbour.

Hasler's primary work with CODC was to develop a British counter-craft to the Italian explosive motorboat.[9] Despite this, it was not long before Hasler turned his mind and attention to the possibilities of the unobtrusive and silent canoe. In March 1942 he attended a meeting at COHQ in Richmond Terrace where he, Roger Courtney and Gerald Montanaro discussed and then formalised their joint requirements for the wartime canoe.

On 18 February Lord Louis Mountbatten was promoted from commodore RN to Chief of Combined Operations with the equivalent tri-service ranks of vice admiral, lieutenant general and air marshal with – more useful than gold braid – a permanent place on the Chiefs of Staff Committee. Three days later, two members of Montanaro's 101 Troop were attached to CODC for training whilst at the end of the month Montanaro's unit put on a demonstration day-time limpet attack for Hasler in Dover harbour. Hasler recorded: '1200–1300. Discussion with Montanaro. 1415 Examined equipment; saw demonstration with Cockles Mk 1 and I* [sic] including placing "R"-type mine.'[10] Hasler then spent two hours in a fresh south-westerly wind trying their craft and raiding techniques for himself.[11]

The exercise crystallised his thoughts on the kind of canoe he wanted and the role such a craft might play: not a frail, wood and canvas-decked and bottomed, thinly disguised civilian Folboat, but something more rigid that could be laden with stores, paddled by two men, passed through the forward torpedo hatch of a submarine and dragged, fully laden, across a shingle beach. Such a craft, he believed, might support and then extract the crew of the Boom Patrol Boat (BPB) once they had been delivered, over boom and harbour obstacle, to their target in an enemy harbour. Hasler's prototype Cockle Mk II would evolve slowly, with many modifications and some setbacks, over the ensuing months. Such thoughts, however, gave swift rise to another, as Hasler recorded in his diary: 'April 21st 1942. Birth of embryo idea (in the bath) for more active service role for yours truly.'[12]

If canoes, underwater swimmers and BPBs were to operate together then they needed to train together, reasoned Hasler. There thus needed to be a new unit, the operational wing of CODC, to enable this to happen. This, in turn, would need a Royal Marines commander. Hasler took his thinking to his immediate superior at CODC, Captain Tom Hussey RN, who formalised the idea and passed it forward to Mountbatten's Chief of Staff, Colonel G.E. Wildman-Lushington. On 12 May Major Hasler's plans were sanctioned to develop Cockles in conjunction with the BPB.

Eight days later, on 20 May 1942, Hasler's plans received formal approval from Lord Mountbatten, who changed the unit's cover name from Royal Marine

Harbour Patrol to the more obtuse Royal Marine Boom Patrol Detachment. The call then went out through the corps for 'volunteers for hazardous service ... men eager to engage the enemy ... indifferent to personal safety'.[13] Meanwhile, it appears that attempts to formalise regular liaison between SOE and Combined Operations were still evolving: 'CCO/SOE Liaison Officer's Report No. 85', dated 3 June 1942 records, '3. Organisation. The question of liaison CCO/SOE and the provision of a Technical Officer at CCO are now being actively taken up at COHQ'.[14]

Whilst Hasler threw himself into a rigorous self-devised training programme of canoeing, personal fitness, fieldcraft and live firing of platoon-scale weapons to ready himself for his new command, the Royal Marines recruiting and selection machine swung into action. Hasler recruited his own administrative second-in-command, Lieutenant J.S. (Jock) Stewart, after dinner over a glass of port in the officers' mess. In mid-June, Hasler made his pitch for volunteer junior officers to the Royal Marines Small Arms School at Browndown on the north Solent coast, west of Gosport. Amongst those who listened to his pitch – and promptly decided it was not for them – were two second lieutenants: William Pritchard-Gordon and Jack MacKinnon:

> I was not selected as one of Hasler's two lieutenants. In fact, MacKinnon and I were congratulating ourselves on not being selected when our names were called on the CO's tannoy. The CO had over-ruled Hasler and suggested that Mackinnon and I were the two people he was looking for. We joined Hasler in Southsea seven days later.[15]

William Pritchard-Gordon, the tall, good-looking public schoolboy, would later describe Jack MacKinnon, the Glasgow groundsman's son commissioned from the ranks, as 'my closest friend ever'. As will be seen, that tannoy summons from the school commandant who thought he knew best was to be Lieutenant Jack MacKinnon's death sentence.

As Major Hasler scoured nearby bases for his marines – he would travel to Plymouth the following week and select one sergeant, one corporal and four Royal Marines – SOE and Combined Operations were still trying to move towards some kind of agreement on technical demarcation between their two organisations. Under 'Item 8. Developments' the CCO/SOE liaison officer (Major Wyatt) reported: 'D/SR now in direct touch with Capt. Hussey and Professor Bernal at COHQ and with CODC. Developments of common interest in these departments include underwater suits, limpets and fuses.' To which an unknown hand has added neatly in ink: 'This will I hope prevent some of the duplication and crossing of lines that has been going on.'[16]

The record shows that, a fortnight later, Combined Operations was still trying to agree some kind of formal liaison between SOE and COHQ in a minute which listed a number of fundamental proposals.[17] Under 'Intelligence and provision of special personnel for operations, etc.' it was suggested that the Combined Operations' senior intelligence officer would deal direct with the department concerned; in regard to operations and policy: 'Royal Marine Adviser to deal direct with DCD (O) [Deputy CD (Operations)]' whilst 'General Liaison' between CCO and SOE was to be through SOE(L). Behind the dense tangle of jargon and inter-service hieroglyphics this meant it was proposed (but not yet confirmed) that the Royal Marine adviser, Colonel Robert Neville, was to deal direct with SOE's D/CD(O) – Brigadier Colin Gubbins. And that general liaison between Combined Operations and SOE should be through the SOE liaison officer – Major David Wyatt. There was more – and all this in the middle of July 1942, when the war was in its fourth year and both SOE and Combined Operations were already 2 years old. Why, one is tempted to ask, had the critical issues of liaison and demarcation, the dangers of which had been flagged up by General Bourne back in 1940, not been resolved months ago?

Hasler's officers arrived at Eastney barracks on 4 July 1942, and the advance party of senior NCOs two days after that. His men were billeted not in barracks but in private houses in town, with the officers staying in a furnished house in Spencer Road and the men living in St Ronan's Road and Worthing Road nearby. The unit paraded together for the first time on 24 July 1942. There was a unit address by Hasler at 0815hrs, after which they took their canoes to sea, where, according to Hasler's diary: 'New troops almost drowned themselves. PM: Salvaging boats.'[18] Hasler had selected his men with care, but they were not supermen. Some could not swim and none, certainly, had any experience of the canoe. On 10 August Hasler was 'rescuing six of No. 1 Section from watery deaths'.[19] These new men of his were 'just a good cross section of average young fellows and we had to do the best with what was offered to us'.[20] In fact, and as events were to prove, they were a good deal better than that.

Hasler's men floundered around in the shallows shortly after Robert Leroy had slipped ashore dry-shod at Antibes four nights earlier. Under the code name *Buckthorn* he was part of SOE Operation *Peppertree* which disembarked a total of six agents from the Felucca *Sea Wolf*.[21] Attempts at liaison between CCO and SOE continued up to mid-August 1942 when Major David Wyatt reported on Operation *Knotgrass/Unicorn*:[22] 'This is now fully prepared, training has started and all stores have been delivered. The objective lies near to the area of an SOE operation projected for approximately the same date. The matter is therefore to be discussed in the near future by a representative from COHQ, MG and the head of the "Country" section concerned.'[23] Later that same day the same officer reported:

> No difficulties are being experienced in keeping in touch with plans and operations at COHQ. D/CCO is a member of the Search and Examination Committee

by which practically all plans are considered. D/CCO keeps the Country Sections concerned in touch with any developments which may affect them.[24]

Every indication suggests, however, that this was a one-way street with SOE and its 'Country' sections only feeding selected information back to Combined Operations. Professor Michael Foot had eighteen months' wartime experience as intelligence officer with Combined Operations before moving on to SAS in February 1944. He dealt directly with SOE:

> I'll give you my personal experience. When I had information on a particular raid I would ring up and get onto somebody in F Section who would answer to three different names over the telephone with the same voice and was inclined to say: 'I'm sorry, old boy, we can't help you at all'. This was their general line. SOE was a secret service and made a great to-do of being a secret service which meant they didn't talk to anyone about anything. On the operational front, I found them strictly cellular. SOE in principle didn't trust anybody, not even themselves, much.[25]

For the next few weeks Hasler and his men flung themselves into a programme of arduous training.[26] In addition to canoeing by night, there was seaman-ship and navigation, capsize drills, fitness training and assault courses by day. There was also swimming and speed marching, Tommy gun, Bren and pistol shooting, field sketching and note taking; unarmed combat, camouflage and concealment, escape and evasion exercises and the use of limpet mines; and they visited nearby harbours to learn about dock layout and ships' mooring procedures.[27] Much of this was new, not just to the men but to Hasler himself, who planned, devised and perfected most of their training drills and proce-dures. His painstaking attention to detail, to the design and fit not just of the canoes but of every last piece of specialised equipment for his soon-to-be-raiders, remains the enduring memory of those who served with him: 'Among all his idiosyncrasies and demands, petty and great, it was his thoroughness based on personal experience that remains the longest lasting memory of those who served in the RMBPD', wrote his biographer.[28] There was a scare for Major Hasler in mid-August when he attended a meeting at COHQ where, not for the first time, there was talk of amalgamation between Major Courtney's army Commando canoe unit, Major March-Phillipps' SSRF in Dorset and his own RMBPD. 'Managed to stave it off for the present,' wrote Hasler gloomily, 'but I fear CCO will overrule it.'[29]

Two days after that diary entry, Combined Operations mounted Operation *Jubilee*, the disastrous and ill-planned raid on Dieppe from which Major David Wyatt did not return and whose last liaison report has been quoted above. He would not be replaced and there would be no further 'Liaison Officer's Reports' until 29 December 1942. Until now, however, these had been frequent: between Report No. 51 of 11 February 1942 and Report No. 85 of 3 June 1942 there were, evidently, thirty-four reports – eight per month – which do not appear to have survived but which one may cautiously assume recorded the decisions taken by Combined Operations in some measure of consultation with SOE.

That SOE was consulted is self-evident: SOE was an integral part of the liaison process where, within COHQ we are told, SOE 'maintained an active agency'.[30] At some level, Major Wyatt worked for them; it is reasonable to assume Major Wyatt was tasked to learn as much as he could about all CCO/ SOE operational intentions for only then could he flag up possible areas of conflict and cross-interest as illustrated by the reference to Operation *Knotgrass/Unicorn*. Yet Professor Foot recalls there were no formal liaison meetings between the two rival organisations and that Major Wyatt was left to 'wander the corridors [of COHQ] picking up what he could'.[31] The fact that official historian William Mackenzie states Major Wyatt was not replaced for four months enforces the suggestion of a laxity or oversight of convenience that appears to owe something to inter-organisational rivalry, despite his assurance that both organisations had become so close as to make formal liaison unnecessary.[32] The lack of that necessary and effective liaison was to have significant consequences.

In early September the impatient Lord Selborne once more returned to the subject of blockade runners. A ship had been spotted by the Royal Navy but not engaged, far less intercepted. In a stinging rebuke to the senior service, he wrote: 'It seems to me important that a blockade runner should be attacked whenever it is sighted. Does the Admiralty consider it impossible to take such further action as will ensure this?'[33]

Meanwhile, with Courtney's unit active, Captain Montanaro already decorated for a raid by canoe and with revived talk of amalgamation, Hasler was a man in a hurry. On 18 September 1942, less than two months after his unit's formation, Hasler saw Colonel Robert Neville, the chief planning co-ordinator at Combined Operations HQ. There he lobbied for a chance to commit his newly formed unit to active operations:[34] so long as this first mission did not require very good navigation or seamanship, Hasler believed his men were ready to face the enemy. He was shown some files; nothing seemed suitable and Hasler returned to Southsea.

The next day, de Baissac reported back from Bordeaux: he had eventually linked up with *Louis* (Robert Leroy) in Tarbes and both had crossed back into the *Zone Occupée* (ZO). Reported de Baissac:

His one aim is to attack the targets.

His chief collaborateur is Bourrière with whom he works for the moment. Bourrière found a reception ground near Cadillac and has already organised a reception committee. Louis is only waiting for the necessary material in order to get on with the job. He can then work on the painting of the boats down in the hold, he has already informed you how he needs the goods (small packages which could easily go into a workman's haversack).[35]

De Baissac submitted two reports to SOE that day – 'David Report No. 1 and David Report No. 2'. The first related to his disastrous entry into France by parachute on 30 July 1942, the second, to Leroy's readiness to attack shipping in Bordeaux docks. Both reports were seen, notated and circulated amongst senior SOE officers. These appear to have included, amongst several other lesser appointments:

D/R: David Keswick, Regional Controller NW Europe and Colonel Buck-master's immediate superior;
D/F: Leslie Humphries, i/c DF or Escape Section;
FL/1: Flight Liaison Officers either André Simon or Major Vaillant De Guelis;
FL4: Lt. G. Barabier;
FM: Gerry Morel ['F.Ops'];
FP: Colonel Robert Bourne-Paterson, F Section's Planning Officer and Buck-master's 2 i/c ['F Plans'];
FV: Vera Atkins, F Section Intelligence Officer.[36]

Implicit in the ticks and scored lines through their assumed *noms de guerre* at the head of those two reports is that those officers had both seen and read de Baissac's two intelligence reports. They therefore knew, from 19 September onwards, that de Baissac had entered France and that Leroy was poised to attack Axis shipping in Bordeaux. As from that date, or very soon thereafter, several – although probably not all – of those officers were in a position, either personally or through the established chain of command upwards through their superiors, to alert Combined Operations, if they so chose, to SOE's imminent intentions in Bordeaux. There is no evidence that they did so.

Notes

1 Taped interview conducted by unknown interviewer with William Pritchard-Gordon on 14 August 1984. Source: Imperial War Museum Sound Archives, No. 8266, Reel 4.
2 Phillips, *Cockleshell Heroes*, p.19.
3 Allan, Stuart, *Commando Country* (National Museums Scotland, Edinburgh, 2007), p.99
4 Even he was not the first. In the Mediterranean, in 1941, the British Army used canoes on fifteen submarine-launched operations. Source: Southby-Tailyour, *Blondie*, p.46.

5 Ref GB 0099 KCLMA Montanaro. The papers of Brigadier Gerald Montanaro held at the Liddell Hart Centre for Military Archives, King's College, London. Private diary entry for 13 January 1942. Source: Small red Collins Diary in Box 2 [of 4] amongst those papers.

6 File HS 8/819 at The National Archives, Kew. CCO/SOE liaison officer's report No. 49.

7 Boyce and Everett, SOE: The Scientific Secrets, p.289.

8 File HS 8/819 at The National Archives, Kew. CCO/SOE liaison officer's report No. 49. Hasler would have at least one further meeting with Major Wyatt, on 18 June. It is possible Wyatt was also among an 'SOE party' Hasler showed around Lumps Fort on 25 June. Source: Hasler's personal diary for those two dates.

9 Having attacked his target, the Italian saboteur's only hope of survival was to abandon his craft and surrender to the enemy. Although Major Hasler's professional ethos recoiled at the suggestion of such pre-determined surrender for British raiders, he and his superiors would do remarkably little to prepare his Operation Frankton marines for evasion in heavily defended enemy territory, or for resistance to interrogation in the likely event of subsequent capture. This despite the early realisation that extraction by submarine would not be an option. Hasler's plans did, however, include the paragraph 'Training for escape' in his 'Outline Plan' of 29 October 1942. Source: File DEFE 2/218 at The National Archives, Kew.

10 Extract from Hasler's diary for 31 March 1942. This obtained from Hasler's widow, Mrs Bridget Hasler, by Lord Paddy Ashdown.

11 Southby-Tailyour, Blondie, p.56.

12 Hasler's personal wartime diary marked Code 28-96 No. 3. Diary entry for 21 April 1942.

13 Southby-Tailyour, Blondie, p.64.

14 File HS 8/819 at The National Archives, Kew. liaison officer's report No. 85 dated 3 June 1942.

15 Sound only interview with William Pritchard-Gordon, recorded August 1984 on behalf of the Imperial War Museum. Interview No. 8266, Reel 4. Interviewer unknown.

16 File HS 8/819 at The National Archives, Kew. CCO/SOE liaison officer's report No. 89 compiled by Major David Wyatt and dated 27 June 1942.

17 File HS 8/818 at The National Archives, Kew. File dated 14 July 1942 and entitled 'Liaison With SOE'.

18 Hasler's personal diary marked Code 28-96 No. 3. Diary entry for 24 July 1942.

19 Hasler's personal diary marked Code 28-96 No. 3. Diary entry for 10 August 1942.

20 Southby-Tailyour, Blondie, p.68.

21 Richards, Secret Flotillas, p.674.

22 Operation Knotgrass/Unicorn: the first planned joint CCO/SOE coup de main operation. In September 1942 ten men from Combined Operations and two from SOE were transported by submarine to Bjerangfjord on the Norwegian west coast to attack the Glomfjord power station. The attack was successful but only four survived the raid. One was fatally wounded, the others were captured and subsequently shot. Source: Cruickshank, Charles, SOE in Scandanavia (Oxford University Press, Oxford, 1986), p.204.

23 File HS 8/819 at The National Archives, Kew. CCO/SOE liaison officer's report No. 93 dated 14 August 1942.

24 File HS 8/819 at The National Archives, Kew. This report, dated 14 August 1942, was filed just five days before the raid on Dieppe from which Major David Wyatt did not return.

25 Interview with Professor Foot by this author on 26 January 2004.

26 A copy of Hasler's personal 'Training Notes [S 575f D 195]' passed to this author by Lord Paddy Ashdown.

27 Hasler's personal diary and 'Training Notes'.
28 Southby-Tailyour, *Blondie*, p.72.
29 Hasler's personal diary. Entry for 17 August 1942.
30 Phillips, *Cockleshell Heroes*, p.10.
31 Professor Michael Foot in conversation with Lord Paddy Ashdown, 12 October 2010.
32 Mackenzie, *The Secret History of SOE*, p.362.
33 Letter from Lord Selborne to First Lord of the Admiralty A.V. Alexander dated 7 September 1942. Located by Royal Marines historian Major Mark Bentinck at the Royal Marines Museum, Eastney, Portsmouth. Now in file ADM 199/549.
34 Phillips, *Cockleshell Heroes*, p.64.
35 File HS 9/75 at The National Archives, Kew. 'David Report No. 2' dated 19 September 1942.
36 Names compiled from Yellow Binder entitled 'SOE – Key to Symbols' in the Open Reading Room at The National Archives, Kew, and with the assistance of Professor Michael Foot.

CHAPTER TWENTY–ONE

FRANKTON PRELUDE

Two days later, on 21 September 1942 whilst training at Southsea, Major Hasler received a note from Lieutenant Colonel Cyril Horton, the senior Royal Marines planner with Combined Operations in Richmond Terrace. Horton had been about to respond to Lord Selborne's third letter of entreaty of 5 August 1942 urging action against the German blockade runners in Bordeaux. He fully intended to reply that, after consideration, an attack was simply 'not on' – that most final and unanswerable of military dismissals. Then Colonel Neville mentioned Hasler's fishing trip to COHQ on Friday, 18 September and Horton sent Hasler a note: 'I think we have got something that might interest you; it might be worth your while to come up.'[1]

Hasler went to Richmond Terrace the following Monday and was shown the *Frankton* Bordeaux docket. He was immediately attracted: '21st September '42: 1024 train to London. AM, examining dockets on *Frankton*. PM, following up various other lines. Evening – seeing Neville re *Frankton*. Slept at RORC.'[2] He studied the *Frankton* papers, worked out rough timings and distance and examined the known enemy dispositions and local topography. He then withdrew overnight to the Royal Ocean Racing Club in St James' Place, a short walk away. By dawn he believed he had a viable solution to Lord Selborne's 'Bordeaux problem': a 100-mile clandestine paddle over four nights through enemy territory followed by a limpet attack on enemy shipping by canoe.[3] Six Royal Marines would paddle three canoes, each carrying eight limpets. Given all canoes reached their target area, the intention was to sink between ten and twenty of the blockade runners lying alongside the docks at Bordeaux. The party would then withdraw. They would either sink or destroy all their remaining equipment and escape overland or paddle back down the river on successive nights to RV with the carrying ship lying no more than 8 miles from the mouth of the estuary.[4]

That next morning Hasler submitted his one-and-a-half-page 'Outline Plan' to Colonel Neville.[5] It was, said Neville afterwards, 'the quickest outline plan of its kind on record'.[6] It would also be a plan, however, whose haste in compilation would ensure it contained at least one significant oversight. Hasler returned to Southsea to continue a stepped-up training regime for his Royal Marines that now had both goal and defined purpose.

Seven days' leave followed, some of which Hasler spent 'digging holes in garden',[7] after which, after taking only Jock Stewart, his second-in-command, into his confidence, preparations intensified. The plan was revised: stores, weapons, food and loading schedules devised, amended and revised again; the canoes were further improved and modified. Hasler obtained permission for a submarine to be used to drop them off and discovered, in so doing, that they would have to sail from the Clyde. He discovered also that there would be no possibility of a pick-up; no chance of making an RV with the same submarine afterwards. There had been many small raids before at this stage of the war; what set *Frankton* apart was their level of exposure, the depth of penetration into enemy territory and the small number of canoes he proposed to use.

Meanwhile, events took a sinister development which was to have direct consequences for Hasler and his party. On 4 October 1942, Major March-Phillipps' SSRF launched Operation *Basalt*. Commanded by Major Geoffrey Appleyard, *Basalt* was a 'butcher and bolt' raid on the tiny island of Sark in the Channel Islands. Prisoners were taken and their hands tied behind their backs,[8] but on the withdrawal one or several of the prisoners made a bid for freedom. They were chased and shot. The party withdrew, leaving the bodies, hands tied, to be discovered next dawn by the German garrison.[9] It was a gift duly exploited by German propaganda. Two weeks later, on 18 October, Hitler issued his infamous 'Commando Order' or *Kommandobefehl.* This stated, *inter alia:*

> From now on all men operating against German troops in so-called Commando raids in Europe or in Africa, are to be annihilated to the last man. This is to be carried out whether they be soldiers in uniform, or saboteurs, with or without arms; and whether fighting or seeking to escape; and it is equally immaterial whether they come into action from Ships and Aircraft, or whether they land by parachute. Even if these individuals on discovery make obvious their intention of giving themselves up as prisoners, no pardon is on any account to be given. On this matter a report is to be made on each case to Headquarters for the information of Higher Command.[10]

However, Operation *Basalt* was not the only raid cited as responsible for this infamous order.[11] Operation *Jubilee*, the raid on Dieppe in August, was cited too when, against every instruction, a Canadian brigadier took plans ashore. These were captured and showed, allegedly, that prisoners were to be bound. The Commando Order was issued the same day that Hasler and a staff officer at COHQ, Lieutenant Commander G.P. L'Estrange, compiled the first revised

'Outline Plan' for submission to Mountbatten. Three days later, Hasler received another shock: though the raid would have his full support, Mountbatten had decreed that Hasler himself could not take part. As their only canoe specialist, he was simply too valuable to risk on an operation from which, Mountbatten believed, few were likely to return. Hasler was appalled. He told Colonel Neville, the Royal Marines officer responsible for the co-ordination of planning at COHQ: 'If they go without me, Sir, and don't return, I shall never be able to face the others again.'[12] Neville agreed to press Hasler's case with Mountbatten. Hasler himself followed up with a formal written memorandum to COHQ outlining five reasons why he should go. He stated that the operation had 'a good chance of success', but that those chances would be 'materially reduced if the most experienced officer available were not sent'.[13] On 29 October 1942 COHQ held a meeting, presided over by Mountbatten, at which Operation *Frankton* was discussed in detail. Hasler was invited to attend. He did so and persuaded Mountbatten to let him lead the raid. Hasler wrote in his diary: '1700 – conference with CCO, Haydon, Selly, Neville to decide if I should be allowed to go. Won after a ding-dong battle.'[14]

That same day Hasler submitted a revised 'Summary of Outline Plan'. Operation *Frankton* would be an attack on blockade runners in the Bassens-Bordeaux area by six Royal Marines paddling three canoes under his command. The intention – now downgraded – was to sink between six and twelve cargo vessels.[15] The next day, 30 October 1942, Lord Louis Mountbatten formally commended Operation *Frankton* to the Chiefs of Staff:

> Operation *Frankton* has been planned to meet Lord Selborne's requirement, referred to in COS (42) 223 (O) and subsequent papers, that steps should be taken to attack Axis ships which are known to be running the blockade between France and the Far East. Both seaborne and airborne methods of attacking the ships have been carefully examined and the plan now proposed is the only one which offers a good chance of success.[16]

The phrase 'a good chance of success' was perhaps placing the odds a little high. In the opinion of Hasler's biographer, Operation *Frankton* stood 'at the pinnacle of risk-taking. Out of a risk factor of ten, I should think it was nine-and-a-half. It was clearly the most horrendously risky business, paddling canoes that distance up that river and I know that river well. It was as risky as you can get in wartime.'[17] Professor Foot agreed: 'The *Frankton* raid was, I would have thought, extraordinarily risky. Indeed, I think I said so at the time.'[18] The Chiefs of Staff authorised Operation *Frankton* at their 306th meeting on 3 November 1942.[19]

Operation *Frankton* was submitted to the Chiefs of Staff by Lord Mountbatten because he believed that Hasler's plan was the 'only one' that offered a chance of success. It fact, it was not. Claude de Baissac's SCIENTIST SOE mission to

Bordeaux had been active for three months. Yet, with SCIENTIST committed by parachute on 30 July with a priority mission to attack the blockade runners in Bordeaux, no evidence has come to light that shows SOE shared with Combined Operations any suggestion that the Bordeaux blockade-runner plan of attack devised by Major Hasler of Combined Operations and those of SOE's SCIENTIST circuit might be on a collision course. This, despite that flurry of liaison meetings and that earlier meeting in February 1942 when SOE discussed with Hasler the 'desirable object'[20] of attacking enemy ships in port. At any stage between SCIENTIST's deployment on 30 July and the launch of Operation *Frankton* on 7 December 1942, SOE could have alerted Combined Operations to their own conflicting intentions. They did not choose to do so.

Nor, it appears, did SOE confide in the Chiefs of Staff. Their 'Review of Activities' for the month ending 15 August 1942 – the period that would cover SCIENTIST's deployment on 30 July, a time during which SOE admitted to having 'the greatest difficulty'[21] in re-establishing their organisation in occupied France after the capture of their chief organiser, merely states: 'Further personnel and a considerable amount of stores safely landed.' Meanwhile the 'Review of Activities' for the period 15 November to 15 December 1942 records: 'Progress has been made in the development of the sabotage groups at TOURS, POITIERS and BORDEAUX. Reports have been received that personnel sent out in October to join these groups have made successful contact with them. The BORDEAUX area has now been successfully organised.'[22]

Did Lord Selborne himself know of the SCIENTIST mission launched against 'his' Bordeaux blockade runners by those who worked for SOE, the agency he controlled? The author has found no evidence that he did. In fact, to the contrary: in an earlier context Major Morton was requested to refer all queries direct to either CD (by then Sir Charles Hambro) or his CEO (replaced in both name and title by Harry Sporborg as Selborne's principal private secretary) 'owing to the fact that only "CD" and myself are in a position to see the whole picture'.[23] Selborne, one surmises, would be briefed on the results that might please the prime minister's ear, not the myriad of plans, projects and missions that might turn to ashes. Further down the chain of command, however, Professor Foot claims there was close contact between David Keswick, the head of SOE Operations in North-western Europe, and Colonel Robert Neville, chief planning co-ordinator at COHQ. Unless Neville deliberately and cynically invested in duplication (in that he was told by Keswick but said nothing to comrades in Combined Operations), it appears that nothing was said by Keswick at this senior level either. Why not? Because of distrust and professional rivalry? Because of SOE's endemic obsession with secrecy, its sense of beleaguered encirclement within a Whitehall-focused intelligence community? Or because SOE saw their opportunity to gain plaudits for their own attack upon this 'jewel in the crown',[24] this first target of major strategic significance for an organisation that badly needed to impress? We do not know. All we can say for certain is that, sometime within an ample and generous time frame,[25] it lay within SOE's gift to tell Combined Operations about SCIENTIST. And that they did not choose to do so. 'Of course, better co-operation between SOE and Combined Operations would have been a good thing. But it did not fit in with SOE's mystique of itself as a secret service that must never reveal anything to anybody.'[26] What would Lord Mountbatten have done about Operation *Frankton* if he had known of SOE's simultaneous plans to attack Axis shipping in Bordeaux?

> I think he would have cancelled the raid. I don't think there is any doubt about that. He would have had no alternative but to cancel the raid. And if he hadn't and it had gone ahead and it became known that he knew, then I think Mountbatten's position would have been an extremely difficult one to support.[27]

Professor Foot is more guarded, saying only that, faced with that same informa-tion, Lord Mountbatten 'might' have called off the raid.[28] What is known for certain is that Lord Mountbatten was not told. And Operation *Frankton* was not cancelled. Lord Mountbatten had put *Frankton* forward to the Chiefs of Staff for their approval on 30 October. The following night, 31 October 1942, and at his fifth attempt,[29] Roger Landes, alias *Aristide*, was dropped into France to assist de Baissac. With a radio link to London, *Aristide* could now start to arrange the airdrop of stores and explosives for which Claude de Baissac and Robert Leroy had been waiting so impatiently.

In the week that followed *Aristide*'s arrival, Hasler's Royal Marines practised hoisting-out techniques with their fully laden 480lb canoes using the quarter davits[30] aboard HMS *Forth* in the Clyde. By this time – and at Lord Mountbatten's personal insistence – the *Frankton* team, in what had become known as 'Hasler's Party', had doubled in size. There would now be six canoes and twelve raiders. It was to prove a wise decision.[31]

On the night of 3/4 November 1942, the same day the Chiefs of Staff in London gave their formal approval to Operation *Frankton*, SOE courier Mary Herbert (*Claudine*), code-named *Jeweller*, landed by SOE Felucca *Seadog* at Port-Miou on the south coast of France, near Cassis, as part of Operation *Watchman III* from Gibraltar. From there *Claudine* travelled by bicycle and train to Bordeaux where she was to work closely with Claude de Baissac running messages between SCIENTIST and other *réseaux*, recruiting new members and arranging landing grounds for future parachute drops.

In Scotland, meanwhile, Hasler and his Royal Marines were busy practising hoisting out their laden canoes using the quarter davits aboard HMS *Forth* and the Dutch vessel *Jan Van Gelder*. They conducted dummy attacks on the latter both by day and by night with the *Jan Van Gelder* underway to simulate tidal flow.[32] By this time the new Cockle Mk II canoes had been shipped to Scotland. All agreed they were a great improvement. On 7 November, after launch sea trials using submarine *P339* in the lee of the western coast of Arran before they became weather-bound, Hasler and his Royal Marines travelled south once more, this time for Exercise *Blanket*. But not before Hasler had fended off yet another proposed take-over, recording in his diary: 'Put in mild protest at proposal to put unit under army command.'[33]

On 8 November 1942, Allied forces landed in French North Africa. As a direct result, Hitler ordered German troops to push south and east to occupy that part of France known as the ZNO – the *Zone Non-occupée*. Operation *Attila* was completed by 12 November. As a direct result of that invasion, reaching freedom for Hasler and his men in just a month's time had suddenly become immeasurably harder.

Just before Exercise *Blanket* commenced, de Baissac signalled London that, in the next moon period, he could receive explosives, ammunition, Sten guns, food and motor-bicycle tyres on 'Landing Ground 45B' at Sauveterre.[34]

Exercise *Blanket*, the final dress rehearsal for Operation *Frankton*, began on 10 November. It was not an unqualified success. None of the canoes managed to paddle the entire distance in the time allocated – from Margate to Deptford, a total of 70 miles – in three and a half days: 'The whole formation became dispersed in rough weather on the third night. One canoe got within two miles of Deptford. The remainder failed to complete the approach, due largely to poor navigation and lack of stamina.'[35] Each canoe was spotted and challenged at least twice and after three nights' paddling everyone was exhausted, with Hasler himself 'very weary'.[36] Hasler later described the exercise as a 'complete failure'[37] but vital lessons were learned, whilst Lord Mountbatten himself affected a cheerful optimism when he met Hasler in the COHQ canteen afterwards. Operation *Frankton* was on. It would not be postponed.

The following night SOE London told *Aristide*, SCIENTIST's W/T operator, that they accepted the ground offered for airdrop – Landing Ground 45B – and would send the stores he had asked for from 16 November onwards.[38] The next night the aircraft flew to the DZ but failed to see the ground recognition signal and returned. The night after that the aircraft returned home to base with engine trouble. On the third occasion, on the night of 20 November, the mission, *Scientist II*, was successful.[39] An undated SOE 'Delivery Report' marked 'Bordeaux' reported thereafter: 'Repeated efforts have been made to get stores to this group, but only one has been successful – on 20.11.42. This was a mixed consignment of arms and explosives, the explosives consisting of 60lbs of PE and 15 clams.'[40]

Hasler had spent a day at Welwyn with SOE just three days earlier: '0819. Train to London. To King's Cross, but failed to catch a train to Welwyn. Got a lift from Baker Street [SOE] at 1300. PM: Discussion on limpets, time delays and chain and wire cutters.'[41] Although he would never know it, Hasler had been as close as he would ever come to discovering that the mission from which his own commander-in-chief thought he was unlikely to return was being duplicated by SOE, who would airdrop explosives and clams to SCIENTIST for exactly the same purpose. But at Welwyn, as with everywhere else that came within SOE's ambit, secrecy was paramount.

Whilst members of the SCIENTIST circuit unpacked their parachuted stores and dispersed them to safe houses, Hasler and No. 1 Section of RMBPD were busy practising fitting holsters and fighting knives to their camouflaged 'Cockle suits' and fusing 'live' practice limpet mines.[42] On 22 November they practised dropping real bombs on the seabed in Holy Loch from a ship's lifeboat. Three out of four detonated. There were more practice limpet attacks the following day whilst on 24 November they practised 'speed build and unbuild exercises'[43] with their canoes before being granted overnight leave in Glasgow. For many, it would be the last pint, the last woman bedded, of their lives. The final ship-tied, loch-based days slipped by; the cargo bags carried by each canoe – five in each stowed fore and aft and between the legs of the No. 2[44] – were packed, emptied, stowed and restowed 'with the cycle being repeated in the dark until every weapon, item of clothing or piece of equipment could be reached and instantly identified by touch'.[45] Hasler's crews practised setting and fusing their limpets until that too could be done safely and deftly in the dark. In the last few days leading up to their departure, Hasler took his men on long cross-country forced marches during which they fired their personal weapons – the .45 Colt automatic and the silent Sten gun. They also trained with the Fairbairn-Sykes fighting knife before returning to over-paint their named canoes[46] in disruptive camouflage colours and sew badges of rank and the Combined Operations formation symbol – eagle, Thompson sub-machine gun and fluke anchor – on their waterproof hooded Cockle jackets beneath the Royal Marines shoulder flash. To Hasler and COHQ, members of RMBPD were engaged upon a legitimate operation of war and, as such, entitled to protection on capture by the Geneva Convention. It was a belief that would shortly be disabused.

Eight days later another saboteur was dropped to assist Claude de Baissac in Bordeaux. This was 35-year-old Captain Victor Charles Hayes (*Yves*), code-named *Printer*. His targets were primarily the power station, gas works and electricity pylons spanning the Garonne River. He had also been sent to help expedite de Baissac's attack on Bordeaux shipping and, if necessary, to lead the attack.[47] Meanwhile, back in Scotland, to the members of No. 1 Section the signs of imminent operational deployment were unmistakable. Sensing something was in the wind but told only to prepare for a long exercise, they wrote their last letters home[48] believing they were about to attack German warships holed up in Norwegian fjords. It was a rumour Hasler did nothing to dispel. On 28 November Hasler stepped aboard HMS *Tuna* and met its commander, Lieutenant Dick Raikes DSO. He made an immediate impression: 'In the end I thought he was a very great man indeed. He was a born leader. Very quiet, never raised his voice, almost casual.'[49] At 1030hrs on 30 November 1942, and with Hasler's marines lining the forward casing at rigid attention in 'big ship' tradition, HMS *Tuna* slipped her moorings under a bright sky and proceeded quietly downriver to the open sea and the enemy shore that waited beyond.[50]

Notes

1 Phillips, *Cockleshell Heroes*, p.65.

2 Hasler's diary. Entry for 21 September 1942.

3 File DEFE 2/217 at The National Archives, Kew. Hasler's original 'Outline Plan' of 22 September 1942.

4 File DEFE 2/217 at The National Archives, Kew. Hasler's original 'Outline Plan' of 22 September 1942.

5 File DEFE 2/218 at The National Archives, Kew. The operation was to be under the command of 'Major H.G. Hasler RM'.

6 Phillips, *Cockleshell Heroes*, p.66.

7 Hasler diary. Entry for 25 September 1942.

8 The initial Operation *Basalt* 'After Action' report by the raid commander makes no mention of prisoners' hands being tied. Major Geoffrey Appleyard confirms, however, that four Germans were killed. Source: File HS 6/306 (microfilm) at The National Archives, Kew.

9 Document MB1/B58 from the Mountbatten Collection, Hartley Library, Southampton, offers another version of these disputed events.

10 Combined Operations web page. Hitler order quoted in full.

11 Its first victims were seven members of Operation *Musketoon*. Ten Commandos from No. 2 Commando and two Norwegian members of SOE raided the hydro-electric plant at Glomford between 11–21 September 1942. The raid was a success, though only four of the raiders escaped capture. Those caught were executed by pistol at Sachsenhausen concentration camp on 23 October 1942. Captured before the Hitler order was issued, their later deaths were the first attributed to the *Kommandobefehl*.

12 Southby-Tailyour, *Blondie*, p.82.

13 In File DEFE 2/217 at The National Archives, Kew. Hasler's five-paragraph letter dated 21 October 1942.

14 Hasler diary. Entry for 29 October 1942.

15 File DEFE 2/218 at The National Archives, Kew. Hasler's 'Revised Summary of Outline Plan' for Operation *Frankton*.

16 File DEFE 2/218 at The National Archives, Kew. Letter from Louis Mountbatten, Chief of Combined Operations, to the Secretary of the Chiefs of Staff Committee dated 30 October 1942.

17 Interview with Ewen Southby-Tailyour conducted by the author at his home in Ermington, Devon, on 11 February 2004.

18 Interview with Professor Foot by the author on 26 January 2004.
19 File DEFE 2/218 at The National Archives, Kew. Chiefs of Staff meeting 3 November
   1942. COS (42) 306th meeting on 3 November 1942.
20 File HS 8/819 at The National Archives, Kew. CCO/SOE liaison officer's report No. 49.
21 File HS 8/244 at The National Archives, Kew. HQ File Reports to Chiefs of Staff
   Committee March–December 1942.
22 File HS 8/244 at The National Archives, Kew. HQ File Reports to Chiefs of Staff
   Committee March–December 1942.
23 File HS 6/309 (microfilm) at The National Archives, Kew. Letter from Gladwyn Jebb,
   then SOE CEO, to Major Desmond Morton at 10 Downing Street regarding liaison.
   Letter dated 15 February 1941.
24 Lord Paddy Ashdown in conversation with the author, 22 July 2010.
25 SCIENTIST committed by air 30 July 1942. *Frankton* team deployed from HMS *Tuna*
   7 December 1942.
26 Interview with Professor Michael Foot by the author on 26 January 2004.
27 Interview with Ewen Southby-Tailyour by the author on 11 February 2004.
28 Interview with Professor Michael Foot by the author on 26 January 2004.
29 SOE attempted to drop 'Landes' to de Baissac on 21 September, 23 September,
   24 October, 27 October and 31 October. The long gap between attempts two and three
   are accounted for by the absence of moonlight.
30 Hasler's diary. Entries for week commencing 1 November 1942.
31 File DEFE 2/218 at The National Archives, Kew. Paper stating:'In view of the possibility
   of some canoes not reaching their destination, it was decided that the force should be
   the largest the submarine could carry.'
32 Hasler diary. Entry for 4 November 1942.
33 Hasler diary. Entry for 8 November 1942.
34 File HS 7/245 at The National Archives, Kew. SOE War Diary (F Section: October–
   December 1942), p.163.
35 File DEFE 2/218 at The National Archives, Kew. Debrief on Exercise *Blanket*.
36 Hasler diary. Entry for 14 November 1942.
37 Southby-Tailyour, *Blondie*, p.87.
38 There had been three previous unsuccessful attempts to drop arms and explosives to
   SCIENTIST: on 21, 24 and 27 October 1942. Source: File HS 6/418 at The National
   Archives, Kew.
39 File HS 7/245 at The National Archives, Kew. SOE War Diary: F Section, October–
   December 1942.
40 File HS 9/75 in The National Archives, Kew. Clams: small explosive charges less powerful
   than limpets but capable of causing significant damage.
41 Hasler diary. Entry for 17 November 1942.
42 Limpet mines – devised by SOE – were small canisters of explosives mounted on a steel
   frame on to which were fixed six magnets that would cling to the steel side of a ship.
   The bombs would detonate once acid had eaten through a thin acetate shield to trigger
   detonation. The acid came in carefully cushioned coloured glass ampoules, each colour
   indicating a differing strength of acid and thus a longer or shorter time delay before
   detonation. The mines were activated by turning down a metal screw until it crushed the
   glass ampoule. Each canoe carried eight such limpets which would be lowered against
   the ship's side under water on the end of a long placing rod. Source: Royal Marines
   Museum, Southsea, Portsmouth.
43 Hasler diary. Entry 24 November 1942.
44 File DEFE 2/218 at The National Archives, Kew. Diagram in file drawn by Major Hasler.

45 Southby-Tailyour, *Blondie*, p.88.

46 *Catfish* (Major Hasler and Marine Sparks), *Crayfish* (Corporal Laver and Marine Mills), *Conger* (Corporal Sheard and Marine Moffatt), *Cuttlefish* (Lieutenant MacKinnon and Marine Conway), *Coalfish* (Sergeant Wallace and Marine Ewart) and *Cachalot* (Marine Ellery and Marine Fisher). Marine Norman Colley would be embarked as 13th, or spare men. Most were Royal Marines from the Plymouth Division.

47 File HS 9/916 at The National Archives, Kew. Captain Hayes personal file.

48 This author uncovered a love letter from Marine Robert Ewart to his girlfriend, Heather Powell, with whose parents he was billeted at 'White Heather' in Worthing Road. The letter remained unknown to his family for sixty years. It began: 'I trust it won't be necessary to have this sent to you but since I don't know the outcome of this little adventure, I thought I would leave this note behind in the care of someone who will forward it to you if anything unexpected happened.' Heartbroken by loss, Heather Powell died of tuberculosis in 1943 on the eve of her seventeenth birthday. Letter passed to next of kin. Hasler had written his own 'next of Kin' letter on 4 October. Source: Hasler diary. Entry for 4 October 1942.

49 Lieutenant Commander Dick Raikes DSO interview with the author on 1 April 2004 at his home in Shaftesbury, Dorset. Lieutenant Commander Raikes died in June 2005, aged 93.

50 Interview with former Royal Marine Norman Colley at his home in Pontefract, Yorkshire, conducted by the author on 12 December 2010.

CHAPTER TWENTY—TWO

OPERATION FRANKTON

On 31 October SOE Captain Roger Landes, code name *Aristide*, was dropped into France by parachute. He was to work as W/T operator for the SCIENTIST circuit in Bordeaux under Claude de Baissac and establish radio communications with London for the supply of arms, explosives and ammunition. The explosives were to be used to blow up German blockade runners in Bordeaux docks.

As soon as HMS *Tuna* had sailed and the men were confined below decks in the forward torpedo space that had been cleared for their use, Hasler broke the news: they were now on a real operation against the enemy. Over the hours that followed he outlined the plan piece by piece, drew the route on a small blackboard, showed how far they would paddle each night with a flooding tide behind them and where they planned to lie-up in concealment during daylight.[1] He told them too about the plans for evasion afterwards across country to Spain. Marine Bill Sparks remembered:

> Well, you could have knocked me down with a feather. Yes, I was keen to have a crack at the enemy, but I hadn't bargained for this challenge. Looking about me I exchanged a few nervous grins with the others. We were not in any way prepared for this one; no-one had even mentioned the likelihood of it.[2]

HMS *Tuna* made passage on the surface down the Irish Sea and Bristol Channel. The weather was rough, the men were seasick and Marine Colley was one of those who 'brought his heart up'.[3] On the afternoon of the third day HMS *Tuna* dived and from then on, as she made her way towards the Bay of Biscay, she dived during the day, only surfacing at night to recharge her batteries. Below decks, Hasler refined his orders, allocated targets and planned the winch-out and launch procedure with Dick Raikes. Planning to launch that night, 6 December, Raikes brought HMS *Tuna* in towards the coast for a visual fix but, although land was sighted, visibility was bad and the land too low-lying for Raikes to establish his position with certainty. They postponed the launch for another twenty-four hours. The weather then cleared during the night, allowing a good star fix at dawn on 7 December. HMS *Tuna* then spent the rest of that day 'tip-toeing along the coast'[4] and obtained another good fix at 1345hrs as she worked her way perilously close to a recently laid minefield: 'The minefield was the thing that worried us most. The RAF had sown hundreds of magnetic mines. We'd been degaussed not once but twice because the water's quite shallow off the entrance to the Gironde and the nearer you get to a mine the easier it explodes', recalled Dick Raikes more than sixty years later. Presently they picked up their position to Raikes' final satisfaction: 'We caught sight of Cordouan Light which I recognised because I'd been there before in 1940 when I was in HMS *Talisman* and we landed a couple of spies.' They were in position, off the mouth of the Gironde. At 1917hrs Dick Raikes ordered the submarine to surface. She did so at 45 21 08 N; 01 14 01 W and within sight of a patrolling enemy trawler about 4 miles distant and within the electronic sweep of a local radar station. Lying stern-on against the shadow of the land, however, HMS *Tuna* remained unseen. Raikes asked Hasler if he wanted to go. Hasler replied simply: 'Yes.'[5] Raikes ordered the canoes to be brought on deck, then he and Hasler parted. Raikes remembers:

> By then of course I knew they were going on a risky mission. I couldn't think how they were going to do it. They were very brave men. My last conversation with Blondie was when he said: 'I'll be back in April. Book a table at the Savoy for the first of April and we'll have lunch together'. I said, not bloody likely, not the first of April but the second, yes. Not April Fool's Day![6]

Below decks the men made their final preparations and assembled their canoes for the delicate business of extracting them up to the deck through the narrow forward torpedo hatch. One by one the canoes were handled up on deck. But not all made it. *Cachalot*, crewed by Marines Fisher and Ellery, was damaged. Hasler had brought a spare man (Colley) but not a spare canoe. It was one of few omissions, accounted for, perhaps, by the space restrictions on board a cramped submarine. Hasler ordered the boat struck down and the two men to stay behind. Eric Fisher, her No. 2, broke down and cried:[7]

> They were very upset. There were tears. But I think my chaps soon got a bit of rum inside them and they were alright. It saved their lives, absolutely. I met their mothers some years later and they thanked me profusely for not letting them go but there was no alternative. I wasn't going to let them go off in a damaged canoe. The fact that they didn't go saved their lives.[8]

The remaining five canoes were lowered into the long Atlantic swell without further incident. The last boat was afloat just after 2000hrs. Raikes watched them paddle away into the darkness:

They were young, they were great, full of fun but very serious with it all. My crew was very impressed with them. In fact they behaved rather badly because when they went off they all went with chocolate and stuff like that which was strictly against Blondie's wishes because they had to carry the minimum of weight. By then of course I knew they were going off on a risky mission. I couldn't think how on earth they were going to do it. They were very brave chaps.[9]

The five remaining canoes paddled away north-east across a flat oily-calm sea with a long, rolling Atlantic swell beneath a clear, moonless sky. The land to their right was covered by a slight haze. It was very cold. *Catfish*, Hasler's canoe, led the way with the other boats behind in arrowhead formation. Hasler steered a course of 035 degrees Magnetic[10] to pass 2 miles to the west of Pointe de la Negade. HMS *Tuna* submerged. Dick Raikes wrote in his log: '2003. Operation completed. Waved *"au revoir"* to a magnificent bunch of black-faced villains with whom it had been a real pleasure to work.'[11] Submerged, HMS *Tuna* withdrew to the south and west.

The canoes paddled about 20 yards apart, before pausing after an hour's paddling to regroup. During that hour, Sergeant Wallace in *Coalfish* was heard being sick. Shortly before midnight, as the flood tide swept them forward at 4 knots, Hasler heard an ominous roaring ahead. It was the first of three tide-races for which they were neither briefed nor prepared. It was, said biographer Ewen Southby-Tailyour, 'a hideous surprise. And indeed a deathly, deadly surprise.'[12] Hasler closed up with the other four canoes, told them what was ahead and then led the way through. Sparks, his No. 2, recalled:

We proceeded in the direction of the roar. As we got nearer I could see the white foaming surf; against a black sky it looked awesome. The tide was carrying us along at a fair old pace, so before I had time to worry any more we were in swirling waters and being thrown around like a cork. I dug deep, using every ounce of strength, conscious of the need to keep the canoe balanced, and struck ahead. Suddenly, we were in calm waters once more.[13]

Hasler's professional, objective and understated report after the raid states simply:

There appears to be no specific mention of tide-races or overfalls, either on the chart or in the Bay of Biscay Pilot. In practice, the following were experienced whilst negotiating the South Pass in flat calm weather, Spring Tides: Heavy overfalls with waves about 4ft high and breaking crests.[14]

Ewen Southby-Tailyour would write later:

Although delighted with the intelligence support he had received throughout the planning he would, in later years, express concern verging on anger that this fundamental obstacle had been unknown to the hydrographers.[15]

Yet the information about the overfalls was available in the relevant guides at the time Hasler made his initial assessment. Less haste in initial planning and overnight commitment back at COHQ in September might well have revealed these lethal obstructions. Now four canoes came through unscathed to join up on the far side. But one was missing: *Coalfish*, paddled by regular Royal Marine Sergeant Samuel Wallace and Marine Robert Ewart, a 6ft Scot and former textile worker, was never seen again. Post-war records suggest *Coalfish* capsized close inshore and that both men were washed, exhausted and hypothermic, on to the beach at Pointe de Grave. Hasler and the remaining canoes waited as long as they dared, then turned and paddled on, the spring tide sweeping them north towards Pointe de Grave guarding the mouth of the Gironde estuary.

Another hour of paddling for the four remaining canoes – and then that sound again 'nearer, clearer, deadlier than before'.[16] Hasler recorded simply: 'Similar overfalls to the above but waves estimated about 5ft high.'[17] Again Hasler and Sparks punched through. The crew of *Conger*, however, Corporal George Sheard from Plymouth and Marine David Moffatt from Halifax, did not. Now *Conger* capsized in the confused steep cross-seas. Both men came through this second tide-race clinging to their upturned canoe, gasping with cold. It proved impossible to empty the canoe and right her. On Hasler's orders Sparks slashed at the canvas sides of the canoe with his clasp knife to scuttle her as Hasler ordered both men to hang on to the stern of two other canoes. They would try to tow them towards the beach. After that both men would have to take their chances, swim to shore and then try to escape overland to Spain. 'At this point,' remembered Sparks, 'to say our hearts were heavy would be the understatement of the century. We paddled on.'[18] Now they heard a third tide-race ahead. This time, mercifully, it was less violent than the other two: 'Small overfalls, waves about 3ft high and breaking.'[19] This time, all three boats came through unscathed. Once through, Hasler ordered the remaining canoes to raft up. Lucas Phillips claims: 'Hasler leaned over the side and said to Cpl Sheard: "I am sorry, but we have got to leave you here. You must swim for it. It is no distance. I am terribly sorry".[20] Cpl Sheard, grey and trembling violently from the cold, gasped out: "That's all right, Sir. I understand. Thanks for bringing us so far." They all shook hands, their sodden gloves meeting in an awkward clasp … As the two unfortunate men dropped off he said: "God bless you both."'[21]

The two men had already been in the December water more than an hour: 'I cannot describe how I felt at leaving my two mates in the water to fend for themselves. It was devastating.'[22] Marine David Moffatt never reached the shore.

His body was washed up on Gros Joncs beach, Ile de Ré, on 14 December 1942, 50 miles to the north. *Conger* was washed up nearby.[23] The body of Corporal George Sheard was never found. Post-war records show that Sergeant Wallace and Marine Ewart, the exhausted crew of *Coalfish*, came ashore near Soulac, stumbled to a cottage and knocked on the door. They hoped to be helped by French patriots. Instead, they found the door opened by a German soldier, one of a number from Section 595 of the 2nd Mobile Battery of Flak *Abteilung 999*[24] billeted in the house. Both Royal Marines were captured without a struggle. Interrogated, Marine Ewart said nothing. Fast-thinking Irishman Sam Wallace claimed they were ship-wrecked survivors from a torpedoed warship. It was a story that, thanks to German administrative incompetence, would buy time for the surviving members of Operation *Frankton*.

The three remaining canoes – *Catfish* with Hasler and Marine Sparks, *Cuttlefish* with Lieutenant MacKinnon and Marine Conway, and *Crayfish* with Corporal Laver and Marine Mills – now had to pass between the jetty at Le Verdon and a line of four German *Chasseur* warships anchored in line ahead just offshore. Each passed through without detection to the mouth of the estuary beyond. But when they regrouped in the safety of the darkness, *Cuttlefish* was missing. They would never see her again. In fact, separated from the others, MacKinnon and Conway would press on alone towards their target. But dawn was now approaching. Swinging round to a new bearing of 196 degrees and hugging the south-west bank of the Gironde, the remaining two canoes searched for their first lying-up place.[25] At 0630hrs they crept ashore at Pointe aux Oiseaux. They had been paddling for eleven hours and covered 26 miles, and had lost a total of eight companions – two-thirds of the raiding force – on the first night of operations.

Ashore, custody of Sergeant Wallace and Marine Ewart was transferred to the German *Kriegsmarine*. A few hours later they were moved across the estuary to Royan. There they became the prisoners of the German Security Service, the *Sicherheitsdienst* (SD). Early that morning, 8 December, local area commander Admiral Bachmann was told a strange canvas boat had been seen marooned on a sandbank but had floated off and disappeared before it could be recovered. The head of counter-intelligence in Bordeaux, a Lieutenant Harstick, was ordered to interrogate both captured marines in Verdon. At 1600hrs the tide began washing up debris and equipment from one of the canoes: tins of rations and water, a magnetic mine and placing rod, a silenced Sten gun and ammunition and, perhaps most compromising of all, aerial photographs of Bordeaux with maps of the river showing German defensive positions. Admiral Bachmann ordered Lieutenant Harstick to interrogate both men about their mission. He is alleged to have added that, after interrogation – and in accordance with the Führer's order – both were to be shot.[26] At some time during this evening, coastal defences around Bordeaux were placed on a heightened state of alert and told by teleprinter to guard against possible sabotage attempts against ships and harbour installations. Neither man at this stage was threatened or subjected to brutal treatment. Faced with this damning evidence of their real mission, Wallace admitted they were Royal Marines and told the Germans about their methods of recruitment and training. He told them two canoes had been sent to attack shipping in Bordeaux docks, that the only other boat had been damaged on extraction from the submarine and that her crew were probably now back in England. With hindsight, it was a ploy that strayed dangerously close to the truth: within a few short hours of the start of Operation *Frankton*, the Germans had heard an enemy raider admit that Bordeaux shipping had been the target of canoe-borne raiders. A guarded and patrolled temporary boom flung across the river anywhere upstream close to the docks and a couple of searchlights could have put an end to *Frankton*'s chances. The results of the Wallace/Ewart interrogation were passed to Admiral Bachmann. Admiral Bachmann phoned the information through to Naval High Command in Paris who ordered the executions postponed for three days so interrogation could continue. The family of Sergeant Wallace claim to this day that he acted with heroism and courage in the face of almost certain execution and that his fabricated story, thin though it was, bought his comrades vital time; that, indeed, faced with the damning evidence of his true intentions washed up on the beach the morning after capture, further denial would have been futile. Others claim that 'Name, Rank and Number' is all that a prisoner is permitted to divulge, regardless of circumstance. To the author, writing as a civilian from the security and safety of peacetime, that seems a harsh judgement. It is perhaps one that is best left to those who have personally confronted the same awful dilemma faced by Sergeant Sam Wallace that cold, bleak winter morning with thoughts of a firing squad never far away.

Soon after daybreak that first morning, 8 December, Hasler and his three companions in their camouflaged hide at Pointe aux Oiseaux heard the sound of motors. Presently about thirty small boats came down the creek to their right and made out into deeper water. At the same time, women appeared from a faint track nearby and began to make fires as the men beached their boats on the mud and came ashore for breakfast. It was soon evident to Hasler that they had been seen. Hasler identified himself to the fishermen as an English soldier and asked them not to tell anyone they had seen them. After they had gone, the Royal Marines remained hiding in cover, eating, resting, cleaning their weapons and planning their night's passage.

They were tide-tied until 2230hrs when the flood tide began to flow upstream in their favour. Hauling their flat-bottomed canoes by painter, negotiating more than half a mile of the thick, glutinous mud that was exposed at low water, Hasler and Marine Sparks in *Catfish* led Corporal Laver and Marine Mills in *Crayfish* north into mid-channel before striking south upstream towards distant

Bordeaux. The weather was flat calm with no clouds, and was bitterly cold. Apart from being passed by a convoy of six or seven merchantmen heading upstream, this second night's passage passed without incident. They covered 25 miles before reaching their second hide between a double hedge on the east bank of the Gironde, opposite the little village of St Estèphe. Here they ate, rested and lightened their canoes by burying some weapons and stores Hasler considered no longer essential.[27] Somewhere nearby, Lieutenant Jack MacKinnon and Marine James Conway were also in hiding. They too were preparing to move closer to their objective.[28]

That same day, 9 December, as Hasler and his surviving Royal Marines lay shivering concealed in a ditch between two hedges opposite St Estèphe on the banks of the river Gironde, SOE held a meeting in London. At this it was reported 'that CCO was contemplating various guerilla [sic] warfare schemes … It was agreed that such proposals would probably involve serious crossing of lines with SOE and "CD" agreed to talk to the CCO'.[29] But not, presumably, about SOE's own well-advanced plans to attack Combined Operations' targets in Bordeaux docks.

The third night's paddle was complicated by the set of the tide. Consequently, Hasler planned a broken voyage that involved an early launch before full darkness, a short paddle, then a six-hour lie-up followed by another three-hour paddle on the next flood tide before dawn forced them into hiding once more. Again, however, they were seen, this time by a friendly farmer in the gloaming as they prepared to launch. He invited them up to his farmhouse for a drink. They declined and paddled away. Three hours later, at 2045hrs, they made a difficult landing among the vertical mud banks and high reeds on the north end of a small island opposite St Julien. They stayed there almost six hours.

At 0245hrs on 10 December, after a difficult launch down the steep muddy bank, they were afloat once more and paddling strongly on the flood using 'single paddles'[30] to lessen their profile as they moved silently down the dangerously narrowing western bank of the Gironde towards that night's objective, the southern end of Îsle de Cazeau. They reached it at 0630hrs when they landed and went ashore only to find a German anti-aircraft battery 50 yards inland.[31] They re-embarked and paddled south, desperate now for a landing place before the onset of dawn. Eventually they found it on the extreme southern tip of the island. They hauled their boats ashore, set up their camouflage netting and sat in silence, wet and cold in the boats, conscious of the noise of traffic and movement already audible on the mainland. It was their most dangerous and uncomfortable hide of the mission, yet in three nights they had paddled 60 nautical miles[32] and were now in the Garonne, with Bordeaux only 12 miles away.

That same evening, British listening stations intercepted a German communiqué which stated that:

On the 8th December a small British sabotage squad was engaged at the mouth of the Gironde and was finished off in combat.

Combined Operations noted: 'As a "squad" can hardly consist of less than four men, it is thought that the communiqué refers to at least two crews.' In fact, it referred to only one, that of Sergeant Wallace and Marine Ewart. We now know that Lieutenant MacKinnon and Marine Conway in *Cuttlefish* spent the same day on the same island about 3 miles north and on the eastern bank.

At 1845hrs on 10 December, Hasler and Corporal Laver launched their two boats down that difficult, slippery mud wall once more.[33] Hasler had decided to delay the attack originally scheduled for the night of 10/11 December for twenty-four hours and thus add one more lying-up place to their approach; a hide that would place them within sight of their quarry at Bassens South. This night the weather was in their favour: low cloud, the occasional shower and a moderate sound-muffling southerly breeze. They set off paddling in the centre of the channel.

At 2100hrs that same night, Lieutenant MacKinnon and Marine Conway left their hide on the north-eastern side of the same island and launched *Cuttlefish* upstream. Almost immediately, disaster struck. *Cuttlefish* was holed on a submerged stake opposite Bec d'Ambes and sank.[34] Snagged in the cockpit, Marine Conway was almost taken down with her. Separated, the two Royal Marines managed to clamber ashore on to the east bank, their roles changing instantly from hunters to evaders deep inside enemy territory.

At almost exactly the same moment that Lieutenant MacKinnon and Marine Conway scrambled ashore, Sergeant Samuel Wallace and Marine Robert Ewart were being led to their place of execution. For years it has been believed that both were placed up against the wall of a wartime bunker and shot. Indeed, bullet strike marks against the concrete were thought to support such a theory and helped turn the eighteenth-century Chateau Magnol on the outskirts of Bordeaux into a place of pilgrimage. New evidence, however, suggests this is unlikely to have been their place of execution. In detailed testimony, a Lieutenant Theodor Prahm states he was in charge of a sixteen-man detail of the *Kriegsmarine* HQ defence platoon that carried out the executions.[35] At some time after 2200hrs on 10 December the two prisoners – who, he claimed, had spent the afternoon with a priest before being read their death sentences – were driven by car to a wood 5–10km north-east of the city. Here they were led to a sandpit and tied to two posts. The scene lit by the car's headlights, they were then executed by rifle fire. Two SD security men then delivered the *coup de grâce* with pistol shots to the back of the head. The bodies were loaded into coffins which were then driven away by truck. Their graves have never been found.

Notes

1 Information provided by Norman Colley during interview conducted by the author on 12 December 2010.

2 Bill Sparks, *Cockleshell Commando* (Pen & Sword, Barnsley, 2002), p.3.

3 Interview with Norman Colley by the author on 12 December 2010.

4 Southby-Tailyour, *Blondie*, p.100.

5 Phillips, *Cockleshell Heroes*, p.118.

6 Commander Dick Raikes DSO interview with the author on April Fools' Day 2004. He and Hasler kept that luncheon date.

7 Later to do good work in Leros, Greece, in June 1944: Source: James Ladd, *SBS: The Invisible Raiders* (Book Club Associates, London, 1983), p.87.

8 Lieutenant Commander Dick Raikes DSO interview with the author on 1 April 2004.

9 Lieutenant Commander Dick Raikes DSO interview with the author on 1 April 2004.

10 File DEFE 2/218 at The National Archives, Kew. Operation *Frankton*: Detailed Report by Military Force Commander (Major Hasler). Dated 8 April 1943.

11 Phillips, *Cockleshell Heroes*, p.119.

12 Interview with Ewen Southby-Tailyour with the author on 11 February 2004.

13 Sparks, *Cockleshell Commando*, p.7.

14 File DEFE 2/217 at The National Archives, Kew. Report entitled 'Operation *Frankton*: Intelligence Report by Military Force Commander – Gironde Area: Approaches, Night 7/8 December 1942'. Dated 12 April 1943.

15 Southby-Tailyour, *Blondie*, p.104, Footnote 12.

16 Phillips, *Cockleshell Heroes*, p.123.

17 File DEFE 2/217 at The National Archives, Kew. Report entitled 'Operation *Frankton*: Intelligence Report by Military Force Commander – Gironde Area: Approaches, Night 7/8 December 1942'. Dated 12 April 1943.

18 Sparks, *Cockleshell Commando*, p.8.

19 File DEFE 2/217 at The National Archives, Kew. Report entitled 'Operation *Frankton*: Intelligence Report by Military Force Commander – Gironde Area: Approaches, Night 7/8 December 1942'. Dated 12 April 1943.

20 Phillips, *Cockleshell Heroes*, p.127. Verbatim quotes. The book was written thirteen years after the event 'with the co-operation of Lieutenant Colonel H.G. Hasler'. Presumably this passage is as accurate as memory permitted.

21 Phillips, *Cockleshell Heroes*, p.127. Verbatim quotes. The book was written thirteen years after the event 'with the co-operation of Lieutenant Colonel H.G. Hasler' so presumably this passage is accurate.

22 Sparks, *Cockleshell Commando*, p.8.

23 Letter from Corporal George Sheard's nephew Peter Siddall to the author after attending the unveiling of a plaque at Boise-Plage on 7 December 2005.

24 Manuscript of 'Operation*Frankton*' written by Francois Boisnier and Raymonde Muelle. Published in France *as Le Commando de L'Impossible* (Tresor, Paris, 2003), footnote p.111.

25 File DEFE 2/217 at The National Archives, Kew. Operation *Frankton*: Intelligence Report by Military Force Commander. Gironde Area. Pointe Aux Oiseaux. Dated 12 April 1943.

26 Boisnier and Muelle, *Le Commando de L'Impossible*, p.115. This account based upon captured German interrogation reports.

27 File DEFE 2/218 at The National Archives, Kew. Operation *Frankton*: Detailed Report by Military Force Commander, p.3. Dated 8 April 1943.

28 Southby-Tailyour, *Blondie*, p.108, Footnote 22.

29 File HS 8/204 at The National Archives, Kew. HQ Files CD's Weekly Meetings November 1942–March 1944. Meeting of 9 December 1942. Item 34: 'CCO Guerilla Warfare'.

30 Paddles 'broken' at the centre joint to halve their length and reduce their profile. Used on different sides by each paddler.

31 File DEFE 2/218 at The National Archives, Kew. Operation *Frankton*: Detailed Report by Military Force Commander, p.4. Dated 8 April 1943.

32 File DEFE 2/218 at The National Archives, Kew. Operation *Frankton*: Detailed Report by Military Force Commander, p.5. Dated 8 April 1943.

33 Phillips, *Cockleshell Heroes*, p.146.

34 Southby-Tailyour, *Blondie*, p.108.

35 File WO 309/1604 at The National Archives, Kew. Detailed testimony by Lieutenant Theodor Prahm sworn before Major E.A. Barkworth of the British Army of the Rhine at Wuppertal, Germany, on 29 April 1948.

CHAPTER TWENTY-THREE

BRAVE MEN AND DARK WATERS

Hasler and Sparks were paddling close inshore upstream on single paddles, hugging the western bank of the Garonne which was lined with thick reeds. At 2300hrs Hasler and Sparks in *Catfish* and Laver and Mills in *Crayfish* slipped beneath the pontoon pier opposite Bassens South, found a gap and forced their canoes deep into the reeds. As the tide receded the boats settled on the mud leaving them hidden from sight with high overhead reed cover. It was an ideal final 'hide'. Surrounded by the noise of dock traffic, the four Royal Marines spent the rest of that night and all the next day hidden in the reeds. They were able to smoke and even stand up within sight of the ships they would attack the following evening. Hasler spent most of that day planning his sequence of attacks. They needed to place their limpets on the last of the flooding tide which would carry them down on to their targets. Then, when that tide began to ebb, those same waters would assist them in their paddle away downstream; both canoes would travel north independently for as long as the new ebbing tide and the onset of daylight permitted. Then they were to scuttle their canoes and escape overland. With high water at midnight, Hasler estimated the ideal time for departure was 2040hrs, but the sky was clear and the young moon would not set until 2130hrs, meaning they ran the risk of being seen in moonlight. Accordingly, Hasler delayed departure until 2110hrs on the night of 11/12 December 1942.[1]

Catfish (Hasler and Sparks) was to attack enemy ships along the western bank of the main docks, some 3 miles distant and upstream from where they now lay hidden; *Crayfish* (Laver and Mills) was to work the east side. If *Crayfish* found no targets there, Corporal Laver was to return and place his limpet mines on the two ships they had been watching all day opposite at Bassens South. At 2100hrs the limpets were fused, armed and set for a nine-hour delay, with Hasler, says Sparks, 'watching over us like a hawk'.[2] Lucas Phillips records from Hasler's recollection that, for his part, Sparks was 'trembling with excitement'.[3] The sixteen limpets, eight in each canoe, were timed to detonate at 0600hrs on 12 December at Low Water. The two crews shook hands, wished one another good luck and eased their canoes out of the reeds and back on to the river. It was 2115hrs. They separated: two silent, dark shapes on a dark, swiftly flowing river. The attack was under way.

It was flat calm and there was a clear sky. An hour of paddling brought *Catfish* in sight of their targets, seven ships moored alongside, their deck and flood-lights blazing along Bordeaux's western quay on their right as they stalked forward. Approaching outside the ring of bright deck-lights thrown by his tar-gets, Hasler's after-action report[4] shows he paddled *Catfish* along the outboard flank side of the first two vessels – a tanker and a cargo liner – before placing his first three limpet mines on the side of cargo vessel *Tannenfels* and the next two on *Speerbrecher*, a German naval patrol vessel. As they slid along the side of this vessel on the first of the ebbing tide they were caught in the torchlight of a German sentry high above on deck. They froze, moved close in to the side of the ship and then drifted slowly downstream towards the bows listening to the clang of the sentry's boots on the steel deck above as he followed them down the length of the ship. Under the flaring bows Sparks anchored them silently against the ship's side with their magnetic holdfast. They clung there: 'We waited with baited breath hoping to hear the sound of the sentry's receding steps. None came.'[5] They waited no longer than an age. The torch finally wandered away and, presently, *Catfish* drifted away on the tide, log-like and undetected. It was a fine, mute tribute to their courage, their professionalism and the thorough-ness of Hasler's meticulous training and preparation. *Catfish* now moved past the *Tannenfels* and placed their last three limpets on the sterns of two vessels – a tanker and another cargo ship – moored side by side just beyond the cargo liner they had ignored. In doing so *Catfish* was almost crushed as both sterns swung together on the ebbing tide. Arms spread, Hasler and Sparks eased *Catfish* back-wards. 'I felt,' reported Hasler afterwards, 'like Atlas holding up the world.'[6] Their mission was accomplished.

Hasler took *Catfish* out into mid-channel and they began paddling strongly downstream on single paddles, the newly ebbing tide pushing behind them. Presently they changed to double paddles and made rapid progress downstream. Just past Îsle de Cazeau where they had spent the last night but one, they heard the sound of approaching paddles: 'It sounded like a Mississippi stern-wheeler at full speed',[7] recounted Hasler later as they linked up again with Corporal Laver and Marine Mills in *Crayfish*. It was a buoyant reunion. *Crayfish* too had been successful. Laver reported that, finding no ships on the east bank, they had divided their eight limpet bombs five and three between the two ships they had seen opposite their last hide at Bassens South. Both canoes now paddled on briefly together before separating shortly afterwards to land a quarter of a mile apart near the village of Blaye.

Coming ashore with difficulty up a steep, muddy bank after scuttling their canoe,[8] Hasler and Sparks moved through the darkness clutching their cargo bags containing a little food, water and their escape kits. Presently they found a remote wood between St Genes de Blaye and Fours. Here they hid, ate, washed and rested. In the days that followed they buried their weapons, scrounged food and threadbare civilian clothes from frightened villagers and moved slowly north-east towards the town of Ruffec where they had been told the Resistance was expecting them.[9]

The limpet mines began to go off at 0700hrs local time on 12 December 1942 and continued, according to captured enemy documents,[10] until 0955hrs. Five bombs went off on the *Alabama*, two on the *Tannenfels*, two on the *Dresden* and one on the *Portland*. Another limpet detonated on the seabed beneath the *Speerbrecher* that had received limpets four and five from Hasler's canoe. But five of the limpets evidently failed to cause any damage at all. In April 1944, SOE's F Section received a copy of a captured German document, signed by Keitel, dated 15 December 1942. Part of the first paragraph reads:

On 12 December 1942 four valuable merchant vessels were slightly injured [sic] in the port of Bordeaux by underwater magnetic devices. This action is attributable to an English sabotage *Truppe* of which two members had previously been caught several days before and had given information of their intention to carry out this exploit. The case is the more incomprehensible in that the intention of this sabotage group was revealed in advance and increased security measures taken.[11]

Captured documents further revealed that all damage was similar: a hole about a metre and a half wide blown in the hulls of each ship below the water line. Members of the SCIENTIST circuit could be even more specific. Their men had been in the docks and witnessed the limpets going off: 'SOE were actually on the quay making their final recce before they attacked the following night when they heard some quiet pops below the water and their targets started to settle into the water under their noses.' 'They were furious,' claims Professor Foot.[12] SCIENTIST reported on 22 March 1943:

In spite of the comparative lack of material SCIENTIST was well on the way to organising an attack on his shipping targets by the introduction of a reasonably large quantity of explosives through the dockers and the paint sealers working on the vessels … At the critical moment, however, the unfortunate (from SCIENTIST's point of view) Commando attack took place.

SCIENTIST's information on this is that charges were laid on seven ships but that the only result was that the ships settled one metre into the water and were immediately raised. Only one had to go to dry dock. SCIENTIST, rather indignantly, asks why he was not informed of this attack on one of his targets.

As a result of this attack, which must be considered abortive, the Bordeaux docks are now in a state of continuous alert. The guards operate both on the ships and on the quay and fire at sight. There are sounds of shots every night and any floating piece of wood is immediately fired at. Searchlights are ready and mine-sweepers and corvettes are available with steam up. As a result, SCIENTIST has had to give up these targets.[13]

De Baissac returned to this theme in a further and later report to F Section which shows that Leroy, after finding that his initial target at Bassens was too heavily guarded, 'concentrated himself on the big ships which left from time to time for Japan and the Middle East'. De Baissac continued:

I was with Louis this afternoon and he gave me the following information.

His idea was to organise proper teams to see that these ships were blown up when they were fully laden just before, or as they were leaving the port. Unfortunately, however, some unorganised saboteur caused premature and very ineffective action, in which a few one metre holes were blown in the sides of some ships which were only partly laden. This incident gave rise to very heavy restrictions on the dockers and in the dockyard area and made it impossible for Louis to continue with his plan.[14]

Hasler's declared objective on *Frankton* had been to sink the twelve largest ships lying in the Bassens-Bordeaux area. But now it appeared that Hasler's 'very ineffective' attack had caused only temporary damage to four Axis ships. More significantly, perhaps, it had resulted in a heightened state of German awareness that had effectively closed down many of SCIENTIST's sabotage and intelligence–gathering options for the immediate future.

Blockade running was to continue. By April 1943 there were, according to 'a report of an interview between an officer in NID and a well-informed French officer' (almost certainly Claude de Baissac, who was in Bordeaux up until the middle of March 1943): 'Six in port and ready to sail. The blockade runners are good ships in excellent condition. The morale of all the naval crew is excellent. They are quite sure they are winning the war.' That same source reported on the results of Operation *Frankton*:

As far as source could ascertain three ships had been sunk. Of these, two sank on an even keel in very shallow water and were repaired quickly. The third heeled over on to her side but the Germans managed, presumably by flooding tanks, to right her so that she fell over on the other side, leaving the damage exposed; temporary repairs were made but the ship has been in dock since. Vigilance has been very greatly increased.[15]

Whatever damage might have been done, it appears not to have dented German intentions. In June 1943 SOE HQ reported that their instructions from the Chiefs of Staff were for 'a continuation of sabotage against military and industrial objectives. In this connection, it is particularly important to hamper U-boat and blockade running operations and to sabotage communications and military and industrial targets by every means possible.'[16] The next month, in July 1943, Lord Selborne wrote once more to the First Sea Lord: 'In spite of the great successes which your department and the Air Ministry had in the spring [sic] against the Far Eastern blockade runners, the enemy is planning to resume the traffic. The importance of holding up Japanese development and increasing Germany's weakness is as great as ever.'[17]

By August 1943 Combined Operations had received a second request to attack blockade runners in Bordeaux. This time one ship was ready to leave and more would soon follow with U-boat spare parts for the Far East. The favoured option – for a short while at least – was a re-run of Operation *Frankton*. Major Hasler was consulted. He observed that, in anything other than flat, calm conditions, the set of tide-races that had cost Wallace, Ewart, Sheard and Moffatt their lives would be likely to prove an insurmountable obstacle. Hasler was forbidden to take part in the second raid although it was conceded that there was no other officer available with his skill in that type of boat work close inshore. The sober contemplation of *Frankton 2* by careful men resulted in a thorough review of the original attack and the techniques it had used. But it was the use of limpets themselves that was now open to challenging scrutiny:

> It is pointed out that limpet attacks on vessels in harbour are unlikely to make the vessel a total loss except in the case of very deep harbours such as the Norwegian fjords. In the case of a normal harbour, such as Bordeaux, where the vessels lie alongside quays in a depth of water that has been dredged out just sufficiently to take them, a successful limpet attack results in the vessel resting on the bottom so that they are well out of the water at low tide and can be salvaged fairly easily. It is for consideration whether a device on the same lines as a limpet can be evolved which does not take action until the ship is at sea.[18]

Which was precisely what Robert Leroy had intended. After careful consideration COHQ staff decided that: 'Weighing up the above considerations, it is considered that the chances of bringing off successfully another operation on the same lines as *Frankton* are about four to one against.'[19] Perhaps mercifully, *Frankton 2* was abandoned.

At 0600hrs on the morning of 12 December 1942, Laver and Mills slipped ashore with their cargo bags and found refuge in a small shed. There they were discovered the next morning by a farmer out with a catapult hunting for rabbits.

They asked him the way to Angoulême. The farmer told a teacher friend, Pierre Gacis, what he had found and the teacher took his wife's rabbit stew to the two muddy strangers in uniform.[20] Laver and Mills then moved on. They were spotted again five hours later and, again, were not betrayed as they hid beside a road; Madame Michelle Ringeade, then aged 9, still remembers the fear as her parents whispered about the two men.[21] Later still, Laver and Mills stumbled upon a barn on the outskirts of Montlieu le Garde. Here a young farm worker, Raymond Furet,[22] had left his lunch while he worked in the fields. The two Englishmen took it – and left a note of thanks, in English. They moved on and were seen again. This time their luck ran out. Told to wait hidden in another barn at farm *Chez David* while help was found, the man went instead to the local *Gendarmerie* and reported what he had found to the police. If they were not arrested soon, said the traitor, he would call the Germans. The police dawdled, hoping the men had moved on. They had not. Laver and Mills were arrested and handed over to the Germans for interrogation.

What is perhaps surprising is not that Laver and Mills were captured but that they remained at liberty for so long. Cast adrift, hunted, in the depths of winter and in a foreign country teeming with enemies, they had little chance of either escape or evasion. Neither had been abroad before, neither spoke a word of French. Those chances, slim though they were, would have been increased if they had been given proper escape rations and civilian clothing, the possession of which would have obviated the need to approach strangers within the target area in those critical early days after coming ashore. Indeed, once the 'Hitler Order' began to be suspected in Combined Operations, one officer minuted several months after *Frankton*: 'It is for consideration whether the men undertaking such duties should not wear plain clothes. This would improve their chances of escape and they would be no worse off if captured.'[23]

Co-operation between SOE and Combined Operations would also, of course, have made an immeasurable difference. Setting aside the mission conflict between SOE's SCIENTIST and the men of Combined Operations, if there had been proper liaison, W/T contact between SOE Bordeaux and London could have given Hasler's canoeists a riverbank RV that same night with members of de Baissac's SCIENTIST circuit. SCIENTIST could then have spirited all survivors of *Frankton* into an established 'Escape Line' that would have moved them swiftly towards safety long before the first limpets went off. Such an RV would have been no more dangerous to SCIENTIST than any other secret agent RV in a land teeming with *Gestapo* and informers. Hasler had been told to make for Ruffec, 70 miles to the north-east, where he was told the French escape organisation had been warned to expect them.[24] But they had not been so warned. In Ruffec, Hasler trusted the luck that had eluded Laver and Mills and found himself eating in a bistro staffed by those with underground connections. He and Sparks were spirited away to Spain via the *Marie-Claire* escape line. Hasler returned to England in April 1943, Sparks a month later.

It has emerged that, not only was SCIENTIST highly organised by the time Hasler and his marines planted their limpets on Bordeaux shipping, but that SOE may not have been the only British intelligence circuit active in that town. It now appears at least possible that SIS had another team of agents in Bordeaux at the same time. And that members of the SIS PHALLANX-PHYDIAS circuit – perhaps even others – may also have been poised to attack the Bordeaux blockade runners within the same *Frankton*/SOE time frame. Substance is given to this possibility when one considers the frequency with which NID and DDOD(I) intelligence reports are cited both before and after Operation *Frankton*.[25] As shown in an earlier chapter, NID and Slocum's DDOD(I) always revealed a preference for working with SIS rather than SOE. The wartime files of the SIS, however, remain closed.

However, what of Lieutenant MacKinnon and Marine Conway? They moved away south-east of Bordeaux and were befriended by a Monsieur Jaubert of Cessac who gave the two Royal Marines food and shelter. With both in civilian clothes and with Lieutenant MacKinnon limping from a painful boil on his knee, they then made their way to the village of La Reole to entrain for Toulouse. There they entered the local hospital[26] where they were betrayed to the Germans and interrogated. According to one source, a German Security Services document dated 29 December states: 'The two prisoners belong to the Commando unit which carried out acts of sabotage in Bordeaux harbour during the night of 7/ and 8/12/42. The marine made a full confession, the officer is still refusing to answer questions.'[27] Corporal Laver and Marine Mills are also alleged to have made significant admissions[28] during interrogation by members of the SD: 'From statements made by some of the prisoners, the German authorities considered that they had gained complete information about, and training for, the actual carrying out of the operation.'[29] It was to avail the captured Royal Marines little. It is claimed that Lieutenant Jack MacKinnon, Marine James Conway, Corporal Albert Laver and Marine Bill Mills were taken to Paris and executed on 23 March 1943.[30] They have no known graves:

> Although it is now almost sixty years on, reading these secret documents for the first time sent a shiver down my spine … I can't believe that our lads disclosed so much … Had I known, during our escape through occupied territory, that the Germans not only had our names, but also exact descriptions of Major Hasler and myself, it would have added an even heavier burden to the one we were already carrying …[31]

Setting aside admiration for the undaunted courage of brave men, with no ships sunk or significantly damaged and with the German garrison in Bordeaux now thoroughly alerted, it is germane to ask what was actually achieved by Operation

Frankton in return for the death and capture of almost all who took part. Certainly, any German sense of complacent invulnerability far from the sea had been dissolved and much had been learned about clandestine attack by canoe. But was that all? In the years since the war and the release of the *Cockleshell Heroes* film and book that ensued, one of the justifications for the raid has been that it lifted British morale at a critical time. This is fallacious. The public was not told about *Frankton* until long after the war. In January 1943 the Admiralty was ordered to record as 'Missing' those who had not returned from *Frankton* but to omit any mention of the operation itself.[32] On 29 April 1943 Mountbatten forwarded Hasler's report on Operation *Frankton* to the Admiralty and stated that, in his opinion, 'this brilliant little operation carried through with great determination and courage is a good example of the successful use of "limpeteers".'[33] Four months earlier the prime minister had wished to record his own appreciation of what seemed to have been 'an extremely gallant and enterprising operation'.[34]

Shortly after *Frankton* was concluded, a new 'clearing office' was set up under ACNS(H) (Assistant Chief of the Naval Staff (Home))[35] in the Admiralty to get notice of all operations, however secret, that were being planned in England to prevent precisely that 'notorious'[36] confusion of role and intention that had shadowed an operation described by the enemy as 'the outstanding Commando raid of the war'.[37] The new system seemed to work. COHQ minutes for February 1943 recorded under the heading Small Scale Raids (Item 6): 'ACCO [Assistant Chief of Combined Operations] undertook to discuss with ACNS(H) the list of special targets which had been selected by COHQ with a view to obtaining their exemption from the ban on small-scale raiding in certain areas.'[38] When it became apparent that there had been that earlier confusion between SOE and Combined Operations, the feeling at COHQ was:

What an awful nuisance. Why didn't we know beforehand? Of course, we didn't know beforehand because SOE was working so secretly. We cast stern looks at our Romilly [Major H.M. Romilly, Quartermaster General in charge of raiding supplies at COHQ and Major David Wyatt's replacement in December 1942]: 'Well? Nobody told me. Why should they?'

Romilly was there to establish liaison between SOE and Combined Ops. But if SOE didn't tell him what they were up to, he was in no position to demand that they should. After it became clear in London that there *had* been this major mix-up between two services, a controlling officer was appointed whose name I never knew. One was given his name, one was given the telephone number of the Admiralty switchboard and anybody planning a raid would be given that number and they would ring up and say: 'Good morning, my name is so-and-so and I work for such-and-such a service. I'm talking about Operation *Shovel*, latitude so and so, longitude so and so, dates so and so.' He would say: 'Very good" and put the receiver down. Five minutes later one's telephone would ring and a voice would say: '*Shovel*, no' and the receiver would go down again. You didn't waste any more time planning *Shovel*. That was a direct result of *Frankton* and was useful.

The appointment of a Controlling Officer was a statement by the Chiefs of Staff that there should be better coordination between the various secret services. And, from there forward, there was. It [the *Frankton*/SOE confusion] was cited in the inner circle as an example of how badly people could co-ordinate.[39]

Although SOE Council minutes exist which cover the period 1 January 1941 to 31 December 1942 and 1 January 1943 to 31 December 1943,[40] the author has been unable to trace any reference to the Operation *Frankton* duplication of intention between SOE and Combined Operations, nor to any post-Operation *Frankton* meeting of explanation or apology other than that cited in the CCO Executive minutes of Combined Operations on 2 February 1943 referred to above. Four months later, however, SOE minutes recorded:

> CD reported that he had seen the CCO yesterday. The latter had asked whether he thought there was any overlapping in our operations and suggested that an agreement might be reached as to each organisation's spheres.[41]

So, despite Professor Foot's optimism, six months after the conclusion of Operation *Frankton* and the creation of the new Admiralty 'clearing house' ACNS(H) notwithstanding, operational demarcation between SOE and Combined Operations still appears to have been unresolved.

Mountbatten put Hasler's name forward for the 'highest recommendation permissible for a feat of this nature', stating that, in his view, Hasler should receive 'at least' a DSO and Brevet Majority for his action.'[42] On 25 June 1943 Major 'Blondie' Hasler's 'courage and enterprise' was recognised by the award of the DSO. Marine Bill Sparks received the Distinguished Service Medal (DSM):

> Dad went back to Portsmouth and he was obviously the new boy having worked with such a close-knit team and having built up such camaraderie with the members of *Frankton*. He told me he actually felt quite lonely and quite out of it. He would walk up and down Southsea seafront, on his own, wondering about what happened to his mates and he would look out at sea and just *hope* that they would come paddling back over the horizon and then he would be with his mates once again. But, of course, that was never ever going to happen and I think, deep inside, Dad knew that.[43]

Had they survived, both Corporal Albert Laver and Marine William Mills would also have received the DSM. In death, both received a posthumous Mention in

Despatches.[44] In a final letter to his parents, 21-year-old Bill Mills wrote: 'Please don't make too much fuss. I only died doing the job for which I volunteered.'[45]

In December 1942 Lord Selborne told Prime Minister Winston Churchill that recent attacks on five merchant ships in Bordeaux had been carried out by SOE agents.[46] To the last full stop of our story, the Special Operations Executive, it appears, practised to deceive its friends as well as its enemies.

Notes

1 File DEFE 2/218 at The National Archives, Kew. Operation *Frankton*: Detailed Report by Military Force Commander, p.4. Dated 8 April 1943.

2 Sparks, *Cockleshell Commando*, p.13.

3 Phillips, *Cockleshell Heroes*, p.150.

4 File DEFE 2/218 at The National Archives, Kew. Operation *Frankton*: Detailed Report by Military Force Commander, pp.4–5. Dated 8 April 1943.

5 Sparks, *Cockleshell Commando*, p.14

6 Phillips, *Cockleshell Heroes*, p.58.

7 Phillips, *Cockleshell Heroes*, p.159. This description omitted from Hasler's Detailed Report by Military Force Commander in DEFE 2/218.

8 It was soon salvaged by the Germans. So ineffectual had been Hasler's attempt to scuttle *Catfish* ('the cutting of the boat hull occurred on one side and to a rather small extent') that German intelligence in Bordeaux wondered if its discovery had actually been intended. Source: Interrogation Section Dulug Nord Wilhelmshaven quoted in Sparks, *Cockleshell Commando*, p.139.

9 File WO 208/3312 at The National Archives, Kew, contains Hasler's detailed MI9 Escape and Evasion Report. Sparks' sparse E & E Report is in WO 208/3313.

10 File DEFE 2/218 entitled: 'Enquiry regarding Results of Operation *Frankton*'. Docket No. NID 4036/46 dated 12 July 1946 at The National Archives, Kew.

11 File DDMO/300 in DEFE 2/217 at The National Archives, Kew. Translation of German document detailing damage to Bordeaux shipping on 12 December 1942.

12 Interview with Professor Michael Foot conducted by the author on 26 January 2004.

13 File HS 9/75 at The National Archives, Kew. Document dated 22 March 1943 entitled 'SCIENTIST'S Target Report' evidently dictated by de Baissac and typed by his London interrogation officer. This states specifically that the first target allocated to SCIENTIST was: 'Blockade Runners and their cargoes in the port of Bordeaux.'

14 File HS 9/75 at The National Archives, Kew. Report from Claude de Baissac dated 6 September 1943.

15 File DEFE 2/217 at The National Archives, Kew. NID intelligence analysis report post-Operation *Frankton* dated 3 April 1943.

16 File HS 8/199 at The National Archives, Kew. Review of Operations from PLANS dated 25 June 1943. File covers period May–December 1943.

17 File HS 8/907 at The National Archives, Kew. Letter dated 30 July 1943 from Lord Selborne to First Lord of the Admiralty A.V. Alexander.

18 File DEFE 2/217 at The National Archives, Kew. Post-Operation *Frankton* intelligence assessment by COHQ. Report dated 22 August 1943.

19 File DEFE 2/217 at The National Archives, Kew. Post-Operation *Frankton* intelligence assessment by COHQ. Report dated 22 August 1943.

20 Interview with the author with French historian Francois Boisnier during research in
   Blaye on 11 March 2004.
21 Madame Michelle Ringeade was interviewed by the author near Blaye on 11 March 2004.
22 Interview with Monsieur Raymond Furet by the author outside his barn at Montlieu le
   Garde on 11 March 2004.
23 File DEFE 2/218 at The National Archives, Kew. Memo to CCO from A.H. Head S.R.
   46/43. Undated, but probably 23 February 1943.
24 Phillips, *Cockleshell Heroes*, p.173.
25 File DEFE 2/217 at The National Archives, Kew. 'I understand that S10 will require DNI to
   assess the damage believed to have been done to the ships attacked, from reports from his
   special sources.' Handwritten note on the end of *Frankton* docket CR 2991/43. Undated.
26 Phillips, *Cockleshell Heroes*, p.321.
27 Sparks, *Cockleshell Commando*, p.132.
28 Boisnier and Muelle, *Le Comando De L'Impossible*, p.150 (original MS).
29 File DEFE 2/218 at The National Archives, Kew. NID Intelligence assessment NID
   24/X 92/46 Docket No. NID 4036/46 entitled 'Enquiry Regarding Results of Operation
   Frankton', p.3. Dated 12 July 1946.
30 Despite war crimes trials in Hamburg in 1948 at which Marine Bill Sparks gave
   evidence to confirm that all raiders had worn Royal Marines shoulder titles, Combined
   Operations formation badge and badges of rank, no German officer was ever punished
   for the six executions that took place in relation to Operation *Frankton*. Admiral
   Bachmann is believed to have been killed by Allied shellfire on 2 April 1945. Source: File
   WO 309/1604 at The National Archives, Kew.
31 Sparks, *Cockleshell Commando*, p.141.
32 In File DEFE 2/217 at The National Archives, Kew. Note from Lord Louis Mountbatten
   dated January 1943.
33 File DEFE 2/218 at The National Archives, Kew. Letter from Lord Mountbatten, Chief
   of Combined Operations, to the Secretary of the Admiralty dated 29 April 1943 and
   copied, a little tartly perhaps, to (then) Major General Colin Gubbins of SOE.
34 In File DEFE 2/218 at The National Archives, Kew. Minutes of the 198th meeting of the
   Chiefs of Staff on 19 December 1942.
35 ACNS(H): Acting Chief Naval Staff (H). Foot, *SOE in France*, p.27.
36 Foot, *SOE in France*, p.26.
37 Phillips, *Cockleshell Heroes*, p.4.
38 File DEFE 2/1017 at The National Archives, Kew. Minutes of the meeting of the Chief of
   Combined Operations and Executive dated 2 February 1943.
39 Professor Michael Foot to the author in interview on 26 January 2004.
40 Files HS 8/198 and HS 8/199 at The National Archives, Kew.
41 File HS 8/204 at The National Archives, Kew. Meeting of SOE Directors and Regional
   Heads, 23 June 1943. File entitled CD's 'Weekly Meetings November 1942–March 1944'.
42 File DEFE 2/217 at The National Archives, Kew. Letter of Recommendation from Lord
   Mountbatten dated 13 May 1943.
43 Terry Sparks, son of Bill Sparks DSM, in interview with this researcher at *La Citadelle*,
   Blaye, Bordeaux, on 11 March 2004.
44 File DEFE 2/217 at The National Archives, Kew. Hasler's recommendations for awards to
   those involved with Operation *Frankton* dated 19 May 1943.
45 Excerpt from that letter quoted in the *Kettering Leader*, 11 January 1946, p.16. In a further
   cruel irony, Bill Mills' fiancée, laundress Kitty Faulkner – like the girlfriend of fellow Royal
   Marine Robert Ewart – was also to die from illness shortly after he was posted 'Missing'.
46 File HS 8/899. Lord Selborne Quarterly Summary of SOE activities to the Prime
   Minister October–December 1942, p.3.

CONCLUSION

These last few chapters have shown how three disparate and un-associated pressures – political, military and personal – conspired together in 1942; how a new Minister of Economic Warfare impatient for measures to be taken against blockade runners goaded SOE, the Admiralty and Combined Operations into action and how a professional Royal Marines officer, Major 'Blondie' Hasler, rose magnificently to that challenge. He did so on the assumption that those who stood in safety behind him would not place him or his men needlessly in harm's way. That faith was misplaced.

Those same chapters have identified, for the first time, the poignant moments of option and choice at which SOE could have told Combined Operations of their own plans to attack the same targets in Bordeaux. The apparatus for such disclosure existed. This was a chance that came not once, fleeting, to be slipped, fumbled or lost at a single missed opportunity, but over a total potential disclosure period of almost three months. Yet, instead of co-operation and a sharing of trust and intention, the raid that has entered legend as the 'Cockleshell Heroes' was sanctioned because it was perceived erroneously at the highest military level that it was the 'only one' likely to achieve Lord Selborne's strategic objective. The lack of tactical clarity that enshrouded Operation *Frankton*, of unresolved operational duplication and administrative overlap, would not be tolerated in the future. Yet it was permitted, even indulged, on Operation *Frankton*. If courage brings with it an expectation, it is that Major Hasler's Royal Marines deserved better.

This book has attempted to assemble, analyse and interpret events surrounding the early evolution of the Special Operations Executive. It has done so from the safety of seventy years' distance and from an age of vastly different asymmetric threat and perception from those which were common coin in 1940. It has examined an organisation, moreover, whose major participants are deceased and whose records – whether through fire, carelessness or deliberate act – are mostly destroyed. Those that remain are filed in an arcane system of cross-referencing most worthy of the clandestine, secretive organisation that spawned them.

It seems apposite to make two particular observations as this book winds to its close. The first is that the informed, measured and altogether comfortable considerations today's historians are at liberty to apply to this subject simply were not available to a Britain fighting for survival in 1940. Those who cast around then for means of national deliverance, for ways in which victory might yet be plucked from the jaws of imminent invasion and looming conquest, could never have predicted when they considered Dalton's 'Fourth Arm' concept and a Europe rising against the German invader, that both America and the Soviet Union would enter the war on Britain's side. SOE was a novel concept; the exploitation of subversion and clandestine warfare was, indeed, a desperate solution to desperate times. But it was conceived and developed, above all, because there was nothing else. The surprise must surely be not that so much went wrong, but that so much did not.

Second, the closing chapters of this book have focused upon Operation *Frankton*, the raid that has entered legend as the epitome of British courage as brave men in small boats penetrated deep into the dark heart of occupied Europe. Thanks to an inaccurate film, an honourable book and a stirring march, the 'Cockleshell Heroes' have assumed a post-war stature that would probably have amused and perhaps even discomforted those who took part. For, at the time, *Frankton* was a raid of important but limited strategic value. Those who planned the attack – and those, within SOE, who listened to those plans but said nothing of their own – were dealing simply with a six-man (later twelve-man) mission by canoe that might well not have succeeded. To a harassed staff in Richmond Terrace, there would have been many such raids, many such dockets, many such plans and folders. We should be cautious lest the glow of post-war prominence imbues Operation *Frankton* with a contemporary hue and significance it never enjoyed. That said, nothing the author has discovered has in any way diminished his respect for the courage and fixity of purpose displayed by 'Blondie' Hasler and the nine men who gathered with him on the wet casing of HMS *Tuna* that night in December 1942.

If 'Hasler's Party' were let down in any way it was by the silence of SOE, the manner in which that organisation was created and the atmosphere of beleaguered encirclement endemic to Dalton's watch that ensured SOE always felt under threat. That threat came from many directions, not least because of what Dalton and SOE represented. This was not just 'ungentlemanly conduct' of the kind disparaged by Lord Portal when asked to supply RAF aircraft for Operation *Savanna*. The creation of SOE uncorked the bottle; it brought with it the threat, real or imagined, of left-wing Socialist change and revolution at home; of domestic and political subversion that many feared would undermine the very foundations of parliamentary democracy in post-war Britain. It was a fear that blinded politicians and soldiers alike to SOE's true potential. An SOE document that dared peer into the future recorded:

There is a great need that officers ... should be made aware of the possibilities and potentialities of clandestine intelligence and warfare. It was
painfully evident that commanders in chief in the early years of the war
without exception regarded the clandestine effort as not only a nuisance but
also as a serious handicap.[1]

As has been shown, however, not all SOE's enemies wore German uniform.
Principal amongst these was SIS, controlled from above by the Foreign Office.
Despite the fact that Britain was *in extremis* and fighting for survival, time and
again this author has been surprised by the extent of the 'turf war' that existed
and indeed flourished between various powerful organisations in the British
military and intelligence establishments. From the very outset, it lay within the
prime minister's gift to identify the threat of inter-departmental conflict and
take the necessary steps to ensure that lines of demarcation between SIS, SOE,
the Admiralty and Combined Operations were clearly defined. He did not. And,
consequently, they were not. That was, perhaps, one of the casualties of Churchill
taking on the twin roles of prime minister and Minister of Defence: there was an
obvious limit to his capacity for detailed involvement. Yet, he was warned. And not
once, but twice. First by General Bourne, the Royal Marines general he dismissed
who warned on departure of the dangers of overlapping confusion between 'several service and government departments' stressing that overall control should
be asserted by a single minister of Cabinet rank, a view already publicly espoused
by the then Viscount Wolmer (later Lord Selborne) in his prescient letter to *The
Times* of 5 December 1939. There was a second warning by Sir Stewart Menzies,
the head of SIS, who 'predicted sadly the difficulties that would follow when two
sets of secret agents worked independently into the same territory'.[2] The 'Playfair
Report' concluded that, without doubt, the soured relationship between SOE and
SIS was putting lives at risk; Mountbatten, in conversation with Dalton, raised an
aristocratic eyebrow at the proliferation of separate intelligence organisations at a
time when the delineation of intelligence-gathering was also confused. Churchill,
the man who played favourites and permitted the Bracken/Dalton row to run
its disgraceful course, merely commented that such 'lamentable' conflict as that
between SOE and SIS was an 'inevitable feature of our affairs'. It did not have to
be. Clarity of early thinking – about SOE's role regarding propaganda, about *coup
de main* operations, intelligence-gathering and the unresolved clash of interests
between SOE, SIS and Combined Operations, might well have created a more
productive climate of mutual support. As matters stood, however, and as William
Mackenzie has observed, it was 'intolerable that lives should be endangered by
competition and confusion between British secret services'.[3]

War is often the birthplace of myth and legend. Operation *Frankton* became,
in its reincarnation as the 'Cockleshell Heroes', the iconic small unit Commando

raid of the Second World War, a raid in which men armed with little more than courage paddled frail canoes into the heart of danger. For many years that raid has been perceived as a shining and uncomplicated example of all that was best in British wartime spirit; a raid unblemished by darker shadows. This book has attempted to show the darker face of rivalry, of duplication and deception that surrounded that heroic endeavour; a duplication whose roots lay in the haste and manner in which SOE was created. On Operation *Frankton* lives were not simply endangered, they were squandered and lost. Had those earlier warnings been heeded, had those responsible for the creation of SOE been able to put more time, thought and clarity into its construction and remit, then SOE might have felt less beleaguered, been more generous with its knowledge. And if that had happened, then it is at least possible that young men who died then might have lived to be old men today.

Notes

1 SOE File HS 7/1 at The National Archives, Kew. History of SOE 1938–45.
2 Mackenzie, *The Secret History of SOE*, p.70
3 Mackenzie, *The Secret History of SOE*, p.750

BIBLIOGRAPHY

NATIONAL ARCHIVES, KEW

Admiralty Papers

ADM 1/12297	Operation *Kitbag*
ADM 1/12659	SOE Helford
ADM 1/14353	Operation *Frankton* – awards
ADM 1/16951	SOE Helford
ADM 1/18344	Bordeaux war crimes
ADM 12/1757	Ships' Index
ADM 173/16583	HM submarine *Talisman* Operational Log
ADM 199/549	Selborne re: Japanese blockade running
ADM 202/310	RMBPD War Diary
ADM 202/399	Hasler after-action report re: Operation *Frankton*
ADM 223/480	SOE Naval Section; Operation *Rubble*
ADM 223/481	SOE Naval Records
ADM 223/500	SOE Naval Records
ADM 223/851	Naval Intelligence Division (NID)
ADM 334/19	Cmdr Lourd Diary 1943
ADM 324/21	Commander Lourd Correspondence with Captain Slocum
ADM 334/23	Commander Lourd personal papers
ADM 324/24	Commander Lourd papers
ADM 324/28	Commander Lourd personal papers 1942/44

Air Ministry Papers

AIR 2/7689	Operation *Biting*
Air 14/835	Operation *Josephine*
AIR 20/2759	Harris memo re: Dalton dinner
AIR 20/2901	SOE air facilities – 1941
AIR 32/8	Operation *Biting*

Cabinet Papers

CAB 63/113	C0S meeting 19 May 1940
CAB 66/10	MI R) Paper 4 July 1940
CAB 79/12	JP (41) 444 (microfilm)
CAB 79/17/4	Operation *Kitbag*
CAB 79/24/6	Chief of Staff minutes
CAB 79/24/27	Operation *Frankton* – 25 November 1942
CAB 79/24/63	Operation *Frankton*
CAB 79/58	Mountbatten report back to CoS
CAB 79/58/45	Chief of Staff minutes
CAB 79/58/48	Operation *Frankton*
CAB 79/58/50	Operation *Frankton* – 18 Dec 1942
CAB 80/56	Selborne re: underground warfare. COS Directive to SOE
CAB 80/62	COS (42) 133 (O)
CAB 80/69	SOE report on spirit of Resistance. CoS (43) 212 (0)
CAB 84/85	JIC Report (42) 156 (O) (Final)

Combined Operations Papers

DEFE 2/6	SSRF
DEFE 2/217	Operation *Frankton*
DEFE 2/218	Operation *Frankton;* Operation *Chariot* Air Recon PRU
DEFE 2/415	Better liaison needed between SOE/CCO
DEFE 2/1017	Small Scale Raids: minutes of CCO

Special Operations Executive Files

HS 2/136	Norwegian arms drops
HS 2/139	Operation *Arquebus*
HS 2/166	Operation *Penguin*
HS 2/199	Operation *Anklet*
HS 2/200	Operation *Bittern*
HS 2/203	Operation *Title*
HS 2/208	SOE *Vestige* raids
HS 2/209	SOE *Vestige* raids
HS 2/210	SOE *Vestige* raids
HS 2/226	Liaison and Combined Operations: general survey
HS 2/243	Operation *Ratweek*
HS 2/266	Televaag reprisals
HS 3/147	SOE Middle East
HS 3/193	Middle East 'Anti-SOE' dossier
HS 4/39	Operation *Anthropoid*
HS 6/206	SOE liaison
HS 6/236	Policy, Planning and Organisation
HS 6/268	Liaison SOE/PWE
HS 6/272	Operation *Ratweek*: liquidation of traitors
HS 6/277	Collaboration

HS 6/304	NID (microfilm)
HS 6/309	Operation *Savanna* and de Gaulle politics
HS 6/416	Use of Limpets (N/g)
HS 6/418	Operation *Barter*
HS 6/469	Bourne-Paterson report on British circuits (microfilm)
HS 6/589	SOE Sabotage in France
HS 6/592	Liaison and FO; Action against Vichy shipping
HS 6/721	Chiefs of Staff papers re: Operation *Braddock*
HS 6/906	SOE *Coup de Main*
HS 7/1	History of SOE 1938–1945
HS 7/123	RF/BCRA
HS 7/3	Section D Early History – September 1940
HS 7/4	Section D Holdsworth Cruising Club, Norway
HS 7/5	Section D
HS 7/14	SOE AL/Q Sub Section
HS 7/22	MV *Maid Honor* and SSRF
HS 7/23	Naval Operations
HS 7/121	F Section History by Colonel Buckmaster
HS 7/122	British Resistance Circuits in France (Bourne-Paterson)
HS 7/123	RF Section/BCRA
HS 7/124	RF Section (1943)
HS 7/174	Oslo/Himmler assassination plot
HS 7/182	SOE *Shetland Bus*
HS 7/211	SOE File reviewing creation of SOE
HS 7/212	SOE/SIS relationship; Spears/de Gaulle re: Operation *Savanna*
HS 7/215	Jebb report: 'Prospects of Subversion'
HS 7/220	'Open warfare' between SO1 and SO2, Cairo
HS 7/222	Operation *Chariot*
HS 7/244	F Section: July–September 1942
HS 7/245	SOE War Diary October–December 1942; F Section October–December 1942
HS 8/81	SOE/CCO liaison re: Operation *Biting*
HS 8/130	SOE Liaison and Air Ministry
HS 8/131	SOE Liaison and Bomber Command
HS 8/193	SOE Projects Board
HS 8/195	SOE Liaison and FO
HS 8/198	SOE Council minutes January–December 1942
HS 8/199	SOE Council minutes January–December 1943
HS 8/200	SOE Council minutes 1 Jan 1943–31 Dec 1944
HS 8/203	Minutes of SOE objectives meeting 20 July 1942
HS 8/204	Gubbins Weekly Reports 1942 onwards
HS 8/205	AD/E Weekly Meetings January 1943–December 1944
HS 8/214	Section D Europe
HS 8/216	SOE Executive Committee Weekly Reports 1940/41
HS 8/219	SOE Weekly Progress Reports
HS 8/220	SOE Executive Committee Weekly Reports January–December 1942
HS 8/244	SOE Progress Reports to Chiefs of Staff
HS 8/251	SOE aircraft shortage in February 1941
HS 8/252	SOE Lord Selborne 'Playfair Report'
HS 8/263	MI(R) War Diary

HS 8/268	SOE Origins; SOE minutes
HS 8/275	SOE HQ Policy and Planning July–December 1942
HS 8/319	Liaison Joint Planning Staff January 1942–December 1943
HS 8/321	SOE SIS memo
HS 8/358	SOE W/T and SIS memo
HS 8/388	W/T and SI
HS 8/770	Commander Slocum memo re: Helford Flotilla
HS 8/771	Helford Flotilla
HS 8/777	Helford Flotilla
HS 8/778	Helford Flotilla
HS 8/779	SOE Base and vessels
HS 8/783	MV *Mutin* development and fitting out
HS 8/806	Small Scale Raiding Force
HS 8/818	SOE/CCO early co-operation
HS 8/819	SOE file relating to SOE/SIS demarcation
HS 8/823	SOE Memo to Gubbins re: ineffectual *Carpenter* Ops
HS 8/828	SOE Sea Operations. Summaries
HS 8/830	Helford River base logbook
HS 8/831	HMS *Fidelity*
HS 8/897	Lord Selborne Blockade Runner minute
HS 8/898	Sir Charles Hambro Papers
HS 8/899	Quarterly Report: Selborne to Churchill
HS 8/900	Selborne to Attlee
HS 8/907	Selborne to/from Admiralty
HS 8/909	Selborne correspondence and Brendan Bracken
HS 8/919	Selborne to Chiefs of Staff
HS 8/924	Selborne reaction to 'Playfair Report'; Selborne to Morton
HS 8/964	Liaison with SOE
HS 8/965	SOE Organisational chart and Council
HS 8/1018	Criticisms of SOE January–December 1942
HS 9/75	Claude de Baissac DSO Personal 'P' file
HS 9/118	Major Gus March-Phillipps DSO 'P' file
HS 9/171/1	Major Nicholas Bodington 'P' file
HS 9/232	Colonel Maurice Buckmaster 'P' file
HS 9/421	Henri Derricourt 'P' file
HS 9/729	Gerald Holdsworth 'P' file
HS 9/916	Captain Charles Hayes MC 'P' file
HS 9/916/2	Robert Leroy 'P' file
HS 9/173/2	Jean Bohec 'P' file
HS 9/1283	Gus March-Phillipps' file (additional)
HSW 9/1661	Jean Bloch 'P' file
WO 165/39	MI9 Files
WO 208/3242	MI9 Code III
WO 208/3298	MI9 – 1940
WO 208/3312	Hasler E&E Report (1) to MI9
WO 208/3313	Sparks E&E report to MI9

WO 208/3342   MI9 Code III
WO 252/93   ISTD Gironde Report 1942
WO 252/118   ISTD Gironde Report 1942
WO 309/1604   War Crimes. Lieutenant PRAHM original testimony re: executions
                   of Sergeant Wallace & Marine Ewart

Prime Minister's Papers

PREM 3 185/1   WSC re: 'lamentable' rows with SOE/SIS

INTERVIEWS

Norman Colley   Interview December 2010
Judy Birkin   Interview August 2001
Professor M.R.D Foot   Interview January 2004 and January 2008
Raymond Furet   Interview March 2004
Paul O'Brien   Interview August 2001
Lieutenant Commander Richard Raikes DSO   Interview April 2004
Sir Brooks Richards DSC   Interview August 2001
Michelle Ringeade   Interview March 2004
Ewen Southby-Tailyour   Interview February 2004
Peter Siddall   Interview March 2004
Terry Sparks   Interview January 2004
Ursula Townsend   Interview July 2001
Jonathan Wyatt   Interview September 2010

PERSONAL CORRESPONDENCE AND PAPERS PRIVATELY HELD

Richard Townsend MS
The Guy Liddell Diaries – MS loaned by editor Nigel West
Private Helford Flotilla papers of Paul O'Brien
Personal papers of Judy Birkin
Personal papers of David Birkin DSC
Papers of Colonel Gilbert Renault DSO alias 'Remy' (Copies)
Papers of Richard Townsend DSC
Papers of Stephen Mackenzie DSC
Papers of Major David Wyatt (courtesy of his son Jonathan)

PRIVATE PAPERS, RECORDS AND OTHER SOURCES BY INSTITUTION

Imperial War Museum Sound Archives

9970   Sir Brooks Richards DSC
27462   Robin Richards
12304   Gerry Holdsworth DSO
11721   Freddie Bourne

12302   Vera Atkins
8266   William Pritchard-Gordon

The Bodleian Library, Oxford

Letter from Viscount Wolmer to *The Times*, 5 December 1939. Amongst the Selborne Papers in File C. 1015.

Selborne Papers:
2 Special Correspondence. Shelfmark: MS. Eng. Lit. Hist. D.450
3 Correspondence. Shelfmark: MS. Eng. Lit. Hist. C. 985

Attlee Papers:
MSS. Attlee. Dep. 1–4; 131; 142.

The Churchill Archives Centre, Churchill College, Cambridge

CHAR 20/73   Churchill to Roosevelt re: Mountbatten
CHAR 20/96B   Churchill to Roger Keyes
CHAR 20/97B/206   Letter stating Mountbatten recovering from chronic fatigue
CHAR 20/54A/38   Churchill to Selborne re: SOE
CHAR 20/34/12–15   Bracken to Churchill re: Viscount Wolmer
                              (Lord Selborne) not wanting office

The London School of Economics and Political Science

DP 7/3   Dalton Papers
DP 18/2   Dalton Papers

The Liddell Hart Centre for Military Archives, King's College, London

GB 0099   Personal papers of Brigadier Gerald Montanaro DSO

The Broadlands (Mountbatten) Archive, Hartley Library, University of Southampton

MB1/B58   Mountbatten Papers
MB1/1202   Mountbatten/Hasler file
MB1/B53C   Operation *Frankton*
MB1/B55   Combined Operations
MB1/B56   Combined Operations
MB1/B57   Combined Operations
MB1/B58   Combined Operations
MB1/B59   Combined Operations

PRIMARY PUBLISHED SOURCES

Bailey, Roderick, *Forgotten Voices of the Secret War* (Ebury Press, London, 2008)

Dilks, D. (ed.), *Diaries of Sir Alexander Cadogan* (Cassell, London, 1971)

Halpern, Paul (ed.), *The Keyes Papers*, Volume III (George Allen & Unwin, London, 1981)

James, Robert Rhodes (ed.) *Chips – The Diary of Sir Henry Channon* (Weidenfeld & Nicolson, London, 1967)

James, Admiral Sir William, *The Portsmouth Letters* (Macmillan & Co., London, 1946)

Lyttelton, Oliver, *The Memoirs of Lord* Chandos (Bodley Head, London, 1962)

Millar, George, *Maquis* (Heinemann, London, 1945)

Nicolson, Harold, *Diaries and Letters 1939–45* (Collins, London, 1968)

Nicolson, Harold, *Diaries & Letters: The War Years 1939–1945*, Volume 2 (Athenaeum, London, 1967)

Pimlott, Ben (ed.), *The Second World War Diary of Hugh Dalton: 1940–1945* (Cape, London, 1986)

Renault, Colonel Gilbert, *Memoires d'un Agent Secret de la France Libre* (Editions de Crémille, Geneva, 1991)

Steinbeck, John, *The Moon is Down* (English Theatre Guild, London, 1943)

Young, Kenneth (ed.), *Diaries of Sir Robert Bruce Lockhart*, Volume 2 (Macmillan, London, 1980)

SECONDARY PUBLISHED SOURCES

Addison, Paul, *The Road to 1945* (Quartet Books, London, 1987)

Allan, Stuart, *Commando Country* (National Museums Scotland, Edinburgh, 2007)

Amphibious Warfare Headquarters, *Official History of the Combined Operations Organisation 1940–1945* (London, 1956)

Andrew, Chris, *The Defence of the Realm: The Authorised History of MI5* (Allen Lane, London, 2009)

Aspinall-Oglander, Cecil, *Roger Keyes* (The Hogarth Press, London, 1951)

Beevor, J., *SOE Recollections & Reflections 1940–1945* (Bodley Head, London, 1981)

Bennett, Gill, *Churchill's Man of Mystery* (Routledge, London, 2007)

Binney, Marcus, *Secret War Heroes* (Hodder & Stoughton, London, 2005)

Binney, Marcus, *The Women Who Lived For Danger* (Coronet, London, 2002)

Bishop, Patrick, *Bomber Boys* (Harper, London, 2008)

Birkenhead, Lord, *Walter Monckton* (Collins, London, 1969)

Boisnier, François and Muelle, Raymond, *Commando De L'Impossible* (Tresor, Paris, 2003)

Braddon, Russell, *Nancy Wake* (The History Press, Stroud, 2009)

Booth, Nicholas, *ZigZag* (Portrait, London, 2007)

Boyce, Frederic and Everett, Douglas, *SOE: The Scientific Secrets* (Sutton Publishing, Stroud, 2003)

Boyle, Andrew, *Poor, Dear Brendan* (Hutchinson, London, 1974)

Broadhurst, Robin, *Churchill's Anchor* (Leo Cooper, London, 2001)

Buckmaster, Maurice, *They Fought Alone* (Panther, London, 1960)

Buckmaster, Maurice, *Specially Employed* (Batchworth Press, London, 1952)

Butler, J.M.R., *History of the Second World War. Grand Strategy*, Volume 2 (HMSO, London, 1957)

Churchill, Winston, *The Second World War*, Volume 2: 'Their Finest Hour' (Cassell, London, 1949)

Cobb, Matthew, *The Resistance* (Simon & Schuster, London, 2009)

Cookridge, E.H., *They Came from he Sky* (Heinemann, London, 1965)

Cookridge, E.H., *Inside SOE* (Barker, London, 1966)

Cooper, Duff, *Old Men Forget* (Hart-Davis, London, 1957)

Costello, John and Hughes, Terry, *Battle of the Atlantic* (Collins, London, 1977)

Cowburn, Benjamin, *No Cloak, No Dagger* (Frontline Books, London, 2009)

Cowdry, Terry, *SOE Agent* (Osprey, Oxford, 2008)

Cowdry, Terry, *French Resistance Fighter* (Osprey, Oxford, 2007)

Cowling, Maurice, *The Impact of Hitler* (London, Cambridge University Press, 1975)

Cunningham, Cyril, *Beaulieu: The Finishing School for Secret Agents* (Barnsley, Pen & Sword, 2005)

Dalton, Hugh, *The Fateful Years* (Frederick Muller, London, 1957)

Deacon, Richard, *A History of the British Secret Service* (Granada, London, 1969)

De Vomecourt, Philippe, *Who Lived to See the Day* (Hutchinson, London, 1961)

Fuller, Overton, Jean, *Double Agent?* (Pan Books, London, 1961)

Fuller, Overton, Jean, *The German Penetration of SOE* (Mann, Maidstone, 1996)

Fergusson, Bernard, *The Watery Maze* (Collins, London, 1961)

Foot, M.R.D., *SOE in France* (Frank Cass Publishers, London, 2004)

Foot, M.R.D., *SOE: The Special Operations Executive 1940–1946* (Pimlico, London, 1999)

Foot, M.R.D., *Memories of an SOE Historian* (Pen & Sword, Barnsley, 2008)

Ford, Ken, *The Cockleshell Raid* (Osprey, Oxford, 2010)

Gardner, Brian, *Churchill in His Time: A Study in a Reputation* (Methuen, London, 1968)

Garnett, David, *The Secret History of PWE* (St Ermin's Press, London, 2002)

Gilchrist, Donald, *Castle Commando* (West Highland Musuem, Fort William, 2005)

Gilbert, Martin, *Winston Churchill, The Wilderness Years* (Macmillan, London, 1981)

Gilbert, Martin, *Winston S. Churchill*, Volume V (Heinemann, London, 1976)

Gilbert, Martin, *Winston S. Churchill*, Volume VI (Heinemann, London, 1983)

Gilbert, Martin, *Winston S Churchill*, Volume VIII (Heinemann, London, 1986)

Gladwyn, Lord, *The Memoirs of Lord Gladwyn* (Weidenfeld & Nicolson, London, 1972)

Greenwood, Sean, *Titan at the Foreign Office* (Nijhoff, Boston, 2008)

Gwyer, J.M.A., *Grand Strategy*, Volume 2 (HMSO, London, 1964)

Hampshire, Cecil, *The Secret Navies* (Sphere, London, 1980)

Harvey, John (ed.), *The War Diaries of Oliver Harvey* (London, Collins, 1978)

Hastings, Max, *Bomber Command* (Pan, London, 1981)

Hastings, Max, *Finest Years* (Harper Press, London, 2009)

Hastings, Max, *Overlord* (Michael Joseph, London, 1984)

Hauklid, Knut, *Skis Against the Atom* (Fontana, London, 1973)

Helm, Sarah, *A Life in Secrets* (Little Brown, London, 2005)

Hinsley, F.H., *British Intelligence in the Second World War*, Volume 1 (HMSO, London, 1979)

Hinsley, F.H. and Strip, Alan., *Code Breakers* (Oxford University Press, Oxford, 2001)

Holmes, Richard, *Tommy* (Harper Collins, London, 2004)

Howarth, David, *The Shetland Bus* (*The Shetland Times*, Lerwick, 1998)

Jackson, Julian, *France: The Dark Years* (Oxford University Press, Oxford, 2001)

James, Robert Rhodes, *Bob Boothby* (Hodder & Stoughton, London, 1991)

Jeffery, Keith, *MI6: The History of the Secret Intelligence Service 1909–1949* (Bloomsbury, London, 2010)

Jefferys, Kevin, *May 1940: The Downfall of Neville Chamberlain* (Parliamentary History, 1991)

Jones, R.V., *Most Secret War* (Hamish Hamilton, London, 1978)

Kahn, David, *Seizing the Enigma* (Arrow, London, 1996)

Kelso, Nicholas, *Errors of Judgement* (Robert Haler, London, 1988)

Koestler, Arthur, *Scum of the Earth* (Collins, London, 1955)
Kramer, Rita, *Flames in the Field* (London, Penguin, 1995)
Ladd, James, *SBS: The Invisible Raiders* (Book Club Associates, London, 1983)
Langalaan, George, *Knights of the Floating Silk* (Hutchinson, London, 1959)
Leasor, James and Hollis, General Sir Leslie, *War at the Top* (Michael Joseph, London, 1959)
Lockhart, Sir Robert Bruce, *Comes the Reckoning* (Putnam, London, 1947)
Lovat, Lord, *March Past* (Weidenfeld & Nicolson, London, 1978)
Lukacs, John, *Five Days in London, May 1940* (New Haven, Yale University, 2001)
Lyttleton, Oliver, *The Memoirs of Lord Chandos* (Bodley Head, London, 1962)
Macdonald, Callum, *The Assassination of Reinhard Heydrich* (Birlinn, Edinburgh, 2007)
McCall, Gibb, *Flight Most Secret* (Kimber, London, 1981)
Mackenzie, William, *The Secret History of SOE: The Special Operations Executive 1940–1945* (St Ermin's Press, London, 2000)
Manchester, William, *The Caged Lion* (Michael Joseph, London, 1988)
McLaine, Ian, *Ministry of Morale* (George Allen & Unwin, London, 1979)
Manus, Max, *Underwater Saboteur* (Kimber, London, 1953)
Marcot, François, et al., *Dictionnaire Historique de la Resistance* (Paris, Bouquins, 2006)
Marks, Leo, *Between Silk and Cyanide* (HarperCollins, London, 1998)
Marshall, Bruce, *The White Rabbit* (Pan, London, 1952)
Marshall, Robert, *All the King's Men* (London, Fontana, 1988)
Medlicott, W.N., *The Economic Blockade*, Volume 1 (HMSO, London, 1952)
Merrick, Ken, *Flight of the Forgotten* (Arms & Armour Press, London, 1989)
Middlebrook, M. and Mahoney, P., *Battleship* (Penguin, London, 1979)
Millar, George, *Horned Pigeon* (Heinemann, London, 1946)
Millar, George, *The Bruneval Raid* (Bodley Head, London, 2004)
Miller, Russell, *Behind the Lines* (Secker & Warburg, London, 2002)
Minney, R.J., *Carve Her Name With Pride* (Pen & Sword, Barnsley, 2006)
Minshall, Merlin, *Guilt Edged* (Bachman & Turner, London, 1976)
Moss, Stanley W., *Ill Met By Moonlight* (Efstathiadis Group, Athens, 1999)
Neillands, Robin, *The Dieppe Raid* (Aurum, London, 2006)
Neave, Airey, *Saturday At MI9* (Coronet, London, 1969)
Nicholson, David, *Aristide: Warlord of the Resistance* (Leo Cooper, London, 1994)
Olson, Lynne, *Troublesome Young Men* (Farra, Straus & Giroux, New York, 2007)
Perrin, Nigel, *Spirit of Resistance* (Pen & Sword, Barnsley, 2008)
Philby, Kim, *My Silent War* (Macgibbon & Kee, London, 1968)
Phillips, Lucas C.E., *Cockleshell Heroes* (Heinemann, London, 1956)
Phillips, Lucas C.E., *The Greatest Raid of All* (Little Brown, Boston, 1960)
Piekalkiewicz, Janiz, *Secret Agents, Spies & Saboteurs* (David & Charles, Newton Abbot, 1974)
Pimlott, Ben, *Hugh Dalton* (Macmillan, London, 1985)
Piquet-Wicks, Eric, *Four in the Shadows* (Jarrolds, London, 1957)
Probert, Henry, *Bomber Harris* (Greenhill Books, London, 2001)
Ramsey, Winston (ed.), *After the Battle* (No. 118 Battle of Britain International, London, 2002)
Ranfurly, Hermione, *To War with Whitaker* (Mandarin, London, 1995)
Read, A. and Fisher D., *Colonel Z* (Hodder & Stoughton, London, 1984)
Richards, Brooks, *Secret Flotillas* (HMSO, London, 1996)
Rigden, Dennis (Intro.), *SOE Syllabus* (The National Archives, London, 2004)
Roberts, Andrew, *Eminent Churchillians* (Weidenfeld & Nicolson, London, 1994)
Roberts, Andrew, *The Holy Fox* (London, Phoenix, 1991)

Robertson, Terence, *Channel Dash* (Pan, London, 1958)

Schoenbrun, David, *Soldiers of the Night* (Robert Hale, London, 1981)

Seaman, Mark, *Special Operations Executive: A New Instrument of War* (Routledge, London, 2006)

Sebag-Montefiore, Hugh, *Enigma: The Battle for the Code* (London, 2001)

Shennan, Andrew, *De Gaulle* (Longman, London, 1993)

Shute, Nevil, *Most Secret* (Pan, London, 1968)

Soames, Mary (ed.), *Winston & Clementine* (Doubleday, London, 1998)

Southby-Tailyour, Ewen, *Blondie* (Leo Cooper, London, 1998)

Southby-Tailyour, Ewen and Hue, André, *The Next Moon* (Penguin, London, 2005)

Sparks, Bill, *Cockleshell Commando* (Pen & Sword, Barnsley, 2002)

Sparks, Bill, *The Last of the Cockleshell Heroes* (Leo Cooper, London, 1992)

Spears, E., *Assignment to Catastrophe* (Heinemann, London, 1954)

Stafford, David, *Britain and European Resistance 1940–1945* (Macmillan Press, London, 1980)

Stafford, David, *Secret Agent: The True Story of the SOE* (BBC, London, 2000)

Stafford, David, 'The Detonator Concept', *Journal of Modern History*, Volume 10, Part 2, 1975

Russell, Douglas, *Winston Churchill Soldier* (Brassey's, London, 2005)

Stewart, Graham, *Burying Caesar* (Weidenfeld & Nicolson, London, 1999)

Sweet-Escott, Bickham, *Baker Street Irregular* (Methuen, London, 1965)

Travers, T. and Archer, C. (eds), *Men at War: Politics, Technology and Innovation in the Twentieth Century* (Precedent, Chicago, 1982)

West, Nigel, *Secret War* (Hodder & Stoughton, London, 1992)

Wilkinson, Peter and Astley, Joan, *Gubbins and SOE* (Leo Cooper, London, 1993)

Wilkinson, Peter, *Foreign Fields* (Tauris Publishers, London, 1997)

Ziegler, Philip, *Mountbatten: The Official Biography* (Book Club Associates, London, 1985)

INDEX

If you enjoyed this book, you may also be interested in...

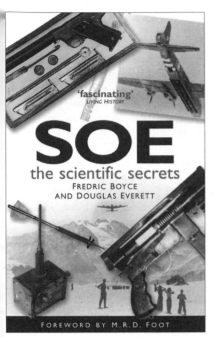

SOE: The Scientific Secrets
FREDRIC BOYCE & DOUGLAS EVERETT

The history of Special Operations Executive (SOE) seems to spring a never-ending run of surprises, and here are some more. This book explores the mysterious world of the tools SOE used for their missions of subversion and sabotage. An often grim reality is confronted that is more akin with the world of James Bond and Q's workshop than previously believed. Written by two scientists, one of whom served in the SOE and one who was tasked with clearing up after it was disbanded; their insider knowledge presents a clear account of the way in which SOE's inventors worked. From high-explosive technology to chemical and biological devices; from the techniques of air supply to incendiarism; from camouflage to underwater warfare; and from radio communications to weaponry. *SOE: The Scientific Secrets* is a revelation about the tools that allowed the murky world of spying and spies to operate during wartime.

978-0-7524-5329-3

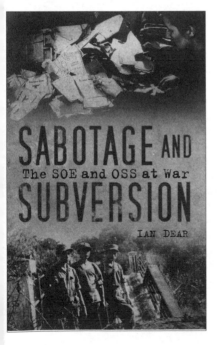

Sabotage and Subversion
IAN DEAR

During the Second World War daring and highly unusual missions were mounted by the Special Operations Executive (SOE) - formed on Churchill's orders 'to set Europe ablaze' - and its American counterpart, the Office of Strategic Services (OSS). In sixteen separate chapters the author describes how the fearless individuals in these clandestine organisations were recruited, trained and armed, and examines some of their guerrilla operations in Europe, Africa and the Far East, such as the raid on Fernando Po, the destruction of Gorgopotamos Bridge in Greece and the strike against Japanese shipping in Singapore harbour. Also covered are the means SOE and OSS used to subvert the enemy, by employing black propaganda, forgery, pornography and black market currency manipulation. It may well read like fiction but the stories are fact, and shows to what lengths the Allies were prepared to go to crush the Axis powers.

978-0-7524-5738-3

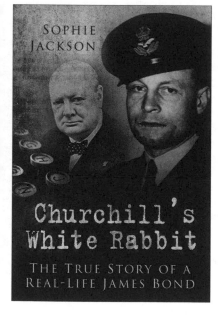

Heroines of SOE
SQUADRON LEADER BERYL E. ESCOTT

The history of SOE has been told many times and much is known about the men who fought underground. However, less is known about the women who also risked their lives in their duties.

By 1942 SOE (Britain's Special Operations Executive) was in desperate need of new recruits for their dangerous missions in France and they turned to a previously unexplored group – women. These female recruits came from all levels of society and were often motivated by an idealistic love of France and a desire to play a part in its liberation. Many displayed unexpected qualities, some proved good leaders and others showed astonishing courage through terrible privations, and many of them died bravely and painfully.

Here, for the first time is the extraordinary account of all forty SOE F women agents. It is a story that deserves to be read by everyone.

978-0-7524-8729-8

Churchill's White Rabbit
SOPHIE JACKSON

Edward Yeo-Thomas GC was one of the bravest of the brave. A fluent French-speaker, he joined SOE and was parachuted into occupied France three times to work with the Resistance. Appalled by the lack of help the British were providing, he managed to arrange a five-minute meeting with Winston Churchill, during which he persuaded him to do more. On his third mission he was betrayed and captured by the Gestapo; he suffered horrendous torture before being sent to Buchenwald concentration camp, from where he eventually managed to escape, making it back to Allied lines before the end of the war.

Sophie Jackson's biography reveals new information about how the torture affected Yeo-Thomas, the state of SOE-Resistance co-operation, Gestapo typhus experiments at Buchenwald and how 'White Rabbit', Yeo-Thomas, provided the inspiration for Ian Fleming's famous secret agent, James Bond.

978-0-7524-6748-1

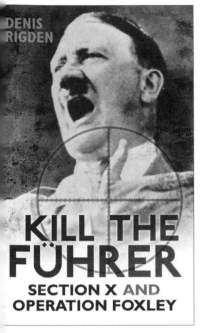

Kill the Führer

DENIS RIGDEN

During the Second World War, Britain's top-secret Special Operations Executive plotted to assassinate Hitler. A small department of SOE known as Section X had the tantalisingly complex task of investigating how, when and where the deed might be done. The section also envisaged killing Goebbels, Himmler and other selected members of Hitler's inner circle. Only Section X and a handful of other SOE staff knew of these projects, respectively codenamed Operation Foxley and Operation Little Foxleys. As history has shown, these schemes turned out to be pipedreams. Even so, Section X, renamed the German Directorate in 1944, made a huge contribution to the Allied war effort through the organisation of sabotage and the clandestine distribution of black propaganda. This is the full and fascinating story, based on top secret documents and private sources.

978-0-7524-5473-3

SOE's Secret Weapons Centre

DES TURNER

The full story of Aston House in the Second World War has never been told before. Its activities were top secret and as important to the Allied war effort as those of Bletchley Park. Situated near Stevenage, Aston House was one of many British country houses requisitioned during the Second World War by the SOE. Born out of Bletchley Park, where it began life as SIS Section 'D' (for Destruction), Station 12's scientific and military personnel invented, made and supplied 'toys' for the Commandos, Special Boat Service, SAS, and resistance groups. Included in their deadly arsenal of weapons were plastic explosives, limpet mines, incendiary bombs and more. They worked on the tools for famous operations, such as the St Nazaire and Dieppe Raids, and the assassination of Himmler's deputy in Prague. Also revealed are the human stories of personnel stationed in this extremely remote village.

978-0-7524-5944-8